ARNHEM
THE BATTLE
REMEMBERED

ARNHEM
THE BATTLE
REMEMBERED

Robert Jackson

Airlife

Picture Credits
All photographs, except where indicated below, are from the
author's archives. United States Army: pages 14, 138. Ministry
of Defence: pages 19, 31, 53, 58 (top), 61, 76, (right) 91. Air
Marshal Sir Frederick Sowrey: page 25. Wing Commander Jack
Rose: page 35. Bundesarchiv: pages 37, 39, 40, 41, 64, 71, 79, 86,
99, 104 (bottom), 116, 121, 129, 139, 140, 158, 161. Bill Ison: pages
43, 151. United States Air Force: pages 47 (top), 50. Jack
Brennan: pages 47 (bottom), 82. *St Louis Globe-Democrat:* page
52. Imperial War Museum: pages 72, 132. Walter Langham:
pages 104, 111, 153, 162, 163. Marian Roguski: page 159
(bottom).

Map Credits
The maps were drawn for this book by Robert McManners

First published in the UK in 1994
by Airlife Publishing Ltd

This edition published 2003

British Library Cataloguing-in-Publication Data
A catalogue record for this book
is available from the British Library

ISBN 1 84037 437 3

Printed in India.

Contact us for a free catalogue that describes the complete range of Airlife Books

Airlife Publishing Ltd

101 Longden Road, Shrewsbury SY3 9EB, England
Email: airlife@airlifebooks.com
Website: www.airlifebooks.com

CONTENTS

	Acknowledgements	vii
Chapter 1	The Thousand-Year Reich had entered its Final Year	1
Chapter 2	Airborne Army	9
Chapter 3	The Airborne Plan	24
Chapter 4	The Germans Regroup	37
Chapter 5	Final Preparations, 16–17 September 1944	45
Chapter 6	D-Day, 17 September 1944	50
Chapter 7	D Plus One, 18 September 1944	76
Chapter 8	D Plus Two, 19 September 1944	98
Chapter 9	D Plus Three, 20 September 1944	115
Chapter 10	D Plus Four, 21 September 1944	126
Chapter 11	D Plus Five, 22 September 1944	137
Chapter 12	D Plus Six, 23 September 1944	145
Chapter 13	D Plus Seven to D Plus Nine, 24–26 September 1944	150
	Epilogue	160
	Notes and Sources	164
	Bibliography	169
	Maps	170
	Index	177

ACKNOWLEDGEMENTS

Millions of words have been written about Operation *Market Garden*. It was therefore with some trepidation that I set about writing this volume, and my hope was that this would not be 'just another book' on the subject. I have tried throughout to strike a balance between hard fact and personal experience, without drawing too heavily on material already published. I hope that I have succeeded, and that I have produced an accurate account.

Luckily, the path was smoothed by many earnest and willing people – some veterans of Arnhem, others not – who showed a great desire to help.

Foremost among them was that most gallant, sensitive and literate soldier, General Sir John Hackett, who was kind enough to read my manuscript chapter by chapter and steer me away from many less obvious pitfalls. My discussions with him provided a rare insight not only into the problems of command that had to be faced during those nine desperate days in Holland, but also into certain omissions of planning and execution of which I was not aware.

One vital point he made, which I have singled out for isolated mention here rather than have it included and perhaps overlooked in the main text, because it is absolutely crucial to the entire operation, was this. *In pre-war Netherlands Army manoeuvres, any commander who attempted to push armour and infantry forward along the exposed main artery that led to the Rhine was adjudged to have had his force destroyed and was sent back to barracks.* Yet no-one consulted with the Dutch on this matter before the operation. I will let that point stand without further comment.

I owe a great debt to Sir John Hackett, and I am also indebted to the following.

Ray Anderson; F. Anthony; H.A. Backinsell; Major Y.F. Barnett; John D. Bellamy; Mrs Betty Bode; Roger F. de Boer; P. Booth; Lawrence Bovey; Mrs M.C. Bradley; Wallace Brereton; Mrs A. Brophy; David Brown; Bill Carr; Hugh Carling; Dennis Clapham; D.P. Conley; T.W. Cotterill; Sebastian Cox; T.E. Davies MBE; F.E. Dear; Alan Dracup; H. Eckersley; Des Evans; Mrs Marjorie Fordham; Trevor Foster; Edward Hales; Leo Hall; Ron Hall, MM; Bert Harget; Mrs Susan Hartley; Frederick Heath; Quentin Hill; Ken Hope; Lt-Col John Humphreys, OBE, DL; Mrs J.M. Innocent; Lilian Kearn; James Kendall; Charles King; Oliver Kingdon; J. Lacey; Walter Langham; Stan Mann; H. Martin; Syd Martin; Ted Mason; Roland Mayer; Royston Mitchell; R.D. Mitten; Mrs M. Moon; R.P. Moon; James Moore; R.H. Moore; Kevin Murphy; Tony Parkinson; H. Pearsall; F.C. Ponsford; Eric Price; D.C. Puckett; D. Rankin; Stanley Roberts; Marian J. Roguski; Leo Rumley; W.D. Salt; A.C. Sanders; H.H. Schueler; Sqn Ldr Peter Singleton; Del Stokes; James Swanston; A.V. Swanick; Alan A.B. Todd; John Thompson; R. Thompson; H. Towers; P.R. Upton; Norman Walker; T.B. Whitehouse; C. Woolgar.

I also wish to thank those anonymous members of the various Market Garden Veterans Associations which I visited for their valued comments and I owe special thanks to Dr Robert McManners for his work on the maps.

Robert Jackson

CHAPTER 1

The Thousand-Year Reich had entered its Final Year

The unfolding tale of its eventual doom was written in blood and fire across the face of Europe. This was August, 1944. On the Russian steppes, Army Group Centre, ordered to stand firm and fight to the last man to the east of Minsk, had been virtually annihilated, opening the way for a massive Soviet drive across Poland to the frontiers of Germany, while on the Western Front the Allied armies, free at last from the murderous fighting in the *bocage* of Normandy, were pursuing the broken German armies across the Seine. By 19 August, the French 2nd Armoured Division's tanks were in Paris, and on the following day Anglo-Canadian and American forces linked up to the east of Falaise, trapping 50,000 Germans and all the heavy equipment of the Fifth and Seventh Panzer Armies in a narrow corridor from which there was no escape from the relentless onslaught delivered by the Allied tactical air forces.

The collapse of the German armies in the west was so rapid that it overtook the situation reports that were reaching the *Führer's* Headquarters. By the third week in August, the battle maps were still showing Army Group B, which controlled all the armies in north-west Europe apart from First Army on the Biscay coast, as a coherent fighting force; the facts were otherwise. Of the 56 infantry divisions which the *Oberbefehlshaber* (Supreme Commander) West had committed to the battle for Normandy, fewer than 20 were still fit for action, and of the twelve Panzer divisions, only one. Some 210,000 German soldiers had been killed or wounded, and another 240,000 taken prisoner; 1,800 tanks and assault guns out of a total of 2,200 had been destroyed. The catastrophe was complete.

On 17 August, *Feldmarschall* Walther Model, who, as officer commanding Army Group Centre on the Eastern Front, had succeeded in halting the Soviet offensive before Warsaw, took up appointment as *Oberbefehlshaber* West and commander of Army Group B in place of *Feldmarschall* Günther von Kluge, who had been relieved of his command on suspicion of implication in the 20 July bomb plot against Hitler. Von Kluge committed suicide the next day.

Model arrived just in time to salvage something from a situation that was becoming ever more desperate by the hour. His first task was to supervise the rescue of what was left of the German army from Normandy, and in this he was aided by the fact that even Hitler now realised the futility of ordering any form of last stand on the west bank of the Seine. Materially, Model was also helped by the presence, on the banks of the Seine, of the many carefully-camouflaged ferries and floating bridges that had been used to transport men and material into Normandy in the aftermath of the Allied invasion of 6 June. Organizing the divisions that were still in fighting shape into a covering force, Model directed his exhausted armies either north-eastward towards the so-called Kitzinger Line, a temporary defensive barrier that had been established along the lines of the Somme and the Aisne, or eastward towards the more formidable natural obstacles of the Meuse and Moselle.

While the Germans retreated, the Allied armies (Canadian First with six divisions, British Second with nine and US Third with six) lay temporarily at rest on a long arc from the Bay of the Seine to the upper reaches of the river at Troyes while a heated debate took place among their commanders over what form the pursuit of the fleeing enemy should take.

Well before the D-Day landings, the planning staff at Supreme Headquarters Allied Expeditionary Force (SHAEF) had worked out an overall strategy for the drive towards Germany. The first priority, once the lodgement area had been secured, was to accumulate reinforcements and supplies within it while work progressed in repairing damage to road and rail communications caused by ground fighting and air interdiction. It was anticipated that these tasks would have been completed by the end of September, whereupon the Allied armies would launch a major offensive across the Seine roughly in line abreast. On the left, the British 21st Army Group under General Bernard Montgomery, comprising the British Second Army (Lieutenant-General M.C. Dempsey) and the Canadian First Army (Lieutenant-General H.D.G. Crerar), supported by the Second Tactical Air Force under Air Marshal Sir Arthur Coningham, was to advance through Belgium to debouch into Holland north of the Ardennes; on the right, the US 12th Army Group, commanded by General Omar Bradley and comprising the US Third Army (General George S. Patton) and the US First Army (General Courtney H. Hodges), supported by the USAAF Ninth Air Force under Major-General Hoyt S. Vandenberg, would drive across France and, on the upper Rhone, would make contact with the US Seventh Army (General Alexander M. Patch), which – having landed on the French Riviera with General de Lattre de Tassigny's French First Army – would have advanced northwards through Provence. It was expected that the Germans would relinquish Normandy and Brittany fairly quickly once the Allies were firmly established ashore and consolidate behind the Seine after withdrawing more or less in good order, then fight a series of delaying actions along the lines of major rivers before making a final stand at the Siegfried Line. By this time (the spring of 1945), the SHAEF planners believed that the enemy would be exhausted by mobile warfare, and that the Allies would be able to cross the Rhine with comparative ease.

What the SHAEF planners had not envisaged seriously was that the Germans, on Hitler's orders, would fight for a decision in Normandy. They could therefore not have foreseen how rapid the collapse of the German armies in the west would be once that decision had gone in the Allies' favour. Once this was established as a fact, the logical strategy was to pursue the retreating German army as rapidly as possible and hound it to destruction.

On 17 August, with the signs of German collapse in Normandy apparent, General Montgomery outlined a plan of future operations to General Bradley. It contained three principal points.

1 After crossing the Seine, the 12th and 21st Army Groups would form a 'solid mass of some forty divisions' which would move north of the Ardennes and throw a pincer around the Ruhr, the 12th to the south and the 21st to the north.
2 South of the Ardennes a 'strong American force' would be 'positioned in the general area Orleans-Troyes-Chalons-Rheims-Laon with its right flank thrown back along the River Loire to Nantes'.
3 The American 7th Army Group would be directed from Lyon to Nancy and the Saar. But, Montgomery stipulated, 'We ourselves must not reach out with our right to join it and thus unbalance our strategy . . . The basic object of the movement would be to establish a powerful air force in Belgium to secure bridgeheads over the Rhine before the winter began and to seize the Ruhr quickly'.

According to Montgomery, Bradley agreed with this plan, although in his memoirs the American general makes no mention of it.[1] But the plan itself took little account of logistical problems, which were later summed up by General Dwight D. Eisenhower, the Supreme Commander Allied Forces in Europe.

Against a defeated and demoralized enemy almost any reasonable risk is justified and the success attained by the victor will ordinarily be measured in the boldness, almost foolhardiness, of his movements. The whole purpose of the costly break-through and the whirlwind attacks of the succeeding three weeks was to produce just such a situation as now confronted us; we had been preparing our plans so as to reap the richest harvest from the initial success. But the difficulties of supply, once our columns began their forward race, was a problem that required effective solution if we were to gain our full battle profit.

Our logistic formations had been confined in a very restricted area during the entire Battle of the Beach-head. The only operating ports were Cherbourg and the artificial port on the British beaches near Arromanches. The repair of Cherbourg had presented many difficulties. The harbour and approaches had to be cleared of hundreds of mines, many of them new and particularly efficient types. We began using the port in July, but it did not reach volume production until the middle of August. The artificial port on the American beaches had been completely demolished in the June storm. From Arromanches and Cherbourg we had not been able to project forward the roads, railways and dumps as we would have done had our breakout line actually been as far to the southward as the base of the Cotentin Peninsula, where we originally expected it to be. All our marching columns, therefore, had to be supplied from stocks located near the beaches and over roads and railways that had to be repaired as we advanced.

These meagre facilities could not support us indefinitely and there was bound to be a line somewhere in the direction of Germany where we would be halted, if not by the action of the enemy, then because our supply lines had been strained to their elastic limit.[2]

During the last week of August, the supply difficulties were already becoming apparent. There were now 36 Allied divisions in France, together with 450,000 trucks, but fewer than 15,000 of these were long-distance load carriers, and much of the available motor transport was being used in support of General Bradley's 12th Army Group in its drive to the Seine east of Paris. As Eisenhower pointed out:

With thirty-six divisions in action we were faced with the problem of delivering from beaches and ports to the front lines some 20,000 tons of supplies every day. Our spearheads, moreover, were moving swiftly, frequently seventy-five miles per day. The supply service had to catch these with loaded trucks. Every mile of advance doubled the difficulty because the supply truck had always to make a two-way run to the beaches and back, in order to deliver another load to the marching troops. Other thousands of tons had to go in advanced airfields for construction and subsequent maintenance. Still additional amounts were required for repair of bridges and roads, for which heavy equipment was necessary.[3]

By this time, General Bradley, after consulting with his senior commanders – in particular General Patton, whose rampaging armoured divisions were a full 100 miles ahead of anyone else's by 22 August – came up with his own plan for delivering the fatal blow against Germany. He suggested that the main Allied thrust be made by his own 12th Army Group. If he were given priority in fuel and ammunition supplies, he would drive due east from 12th Army Group's present positions, cross the Rhine south of Frankfurt and thrust deep into Germany.

If Bradley's scheme were adopted, it would mean reducing Montgomery's 21st Army Group to a secondary role. Montgomery's plan for a rapid northward thrust to the Ruhr, on the other hand, meant that the lion's share of logistical support would need to be assigned to the forces under his command, which would include the bulk of the US First Army; this in turn would mean that 12th Army Group, reduced to some ten divisions in order to provide reserves for the northern thrust, would play little more than a static part on the edge of the Argonne.

Both cases were placed before General Eisenhower on 23 August. The arguments that raged between the respective commanders over the issue are well known; in the end, Eisenhower – who was to assume direct control of all land operations on the continent from 1 September – decided on a compromise. On 26 August, he issued orders dictating a dual thrust. Montgomery's 21st Army Group would advance as rapidly as possible on the left through northern France and Belgium, clearing the area from which German V-1 sites had been launching a steady stream of missiles at southern England; the principal objective was the early capture of the vital port of Antwerp. General Hodges' US First Army would advance abreast of the British formations, roughly in the general direction of Aachen, to secure Montgomery's flank, while the remainder of 12th Army Group would thrust forward on the right to effect a junction with US forces advancing from the south. The main axis of this thrust would be towards the Saar.

Eisenhower decreed that Montgomery's northward drive into Belgium was to have first priority in combat supplies. Once Antwerp had been taken, the Allied land armies would revert to the pre-invasion plan of all forces having an equal share of supplies and advancing towards the Rhine on a broad front north and south of the Ardennes. The news that Montgomery was to have logistical priority sent General Patton into a rage, for he knew that it was bound to result in a halt to his armoured dash towards the Rhine. He was later to refer to the decision as 'the most momentous error of the war'. This may have been an overstatement, but there is some validity in Patton's comment; had he been halted on the Troyes-Chalons-Reims front, the Germans would not have lost the forces he subsequently trapped and decimated between the Marne and the Moselle, with a loss to the enemy of 22,600 prisoners, 474 tanks, and 482 guns. Also if the inner flanks of Patton's Third Army and Patch's Seventh Army had not joined up, it would not have been possible to trap and capture 19,600 German troops west of the Loire, a victory reported on 12 September.

The decision, however, had been made. While the

Canadian First Army cleared the Channel coast, the British Second Army would break through the remaining German resistance in northern France and plunge on into Belgium, advancing through Amiens and Arras to Brussels; Montgomery's exhortation to his commanders was 'to drive ahead with the utmost energy; any tendency to be sticky or cautious must be stamped on ruthlessly'.

By 28 August, engineers had succeeded in bridging the Seine – often under fire – at the selected British and Canadian crossing points. Early the next day the armoured columns had crossed, and the pursuit across northern France and Belgium – to become known as the 'great swan' to the Anglo-Canadians – was on.

For the three British spearhead divisions – 7th, 11th, and Guards Armoured Divisions – the ground that lay ahead was far different from the nightmarish Normandy *bocage*, with its tangled hedgerows surmounting high earthen banks. As far as central Belgium, the terrain was flat, open and unwooded, crossed by reasonable roads and almost uninterrupted by water obstacles. It was, in short, excellent country for armoured penetration – as the Germans had found during the *Blitzkrieg* offensive of May 1940.

From the beginning, the armoured brigades were able to adopt an open order of advance. An attached armoured car regiment, reconnoitring the terrain ahead, was followed by the tanks on a two-regiment front, with the mechanized infantry brigade and the motor transport battalion bringing up the rear. The advance met with a good deal of resistance on the first day, as German forces had been deployed in villages along the route to fight delaying actions; XXX Corps found the going particularly tough, and its tanks advanced no more than twenty miles by nightfall on 29 August. The next morning the tanks pushed on to Beauvais, and later in the day XXX Corps received orders to drive on during the night a further 35 miles to seize crossings over the Somme east and west of Amiens.

By first light on 31 August the leading vehicles of 11th Armoured Division were in the outskirts of Amiens, and by noon both the town's main bridges had fallen intact into British hands. Three more, east of the town, were captured by the Corps armoured car regiment, 2nd Household Cavalry. The following day, 1 September, the Guards and 11th Armoured Divisions made another 35-mile dash to Arras and Aubigny on the River Scarpe, meeting with no organized resistance.

As darkness fell on 1 September, the orders were for XXX Corps to proceed rapidly to the Belgian frontier, but – for reasons which will be apparent later – these were countermanded and the advance slowed down, the Corps advancing fifteen miles to Lens and Douai on 2 September. In fact, the break in tempo was welcome, because the logistics problems foreseen by Eisenhower and others were beginning to make themselves felt, with supply vehicles operating over a distance of 100 miles. Corps personnel took the opportunity to service their fighting vehicles and there was an added advantage in that XII Corps, whose divisions had crossed the Seine on the left flank two days behind XXX Corps, was now able to catch up a little.

Meanwhile, the advance of the US First Army, supporting Montgomery's drive, was going well. On the right, US VII Corps, with 3rd Armoured Division in the lead, had broken out of its bridge-head at Melun, passed through Laon on 30 August, and crossed the Franco-Belgian frontier from Avesnes and Meubeuge, reaching Mons at dusk on 2 September. On the left of the US First Army, XIX Corps advanced at the same speed along the axis Nantes - Montdidier - Cambrai - Tournai. Between Mons and Cambrai, 20,000 Germans – the remnants of twenty different divisions – were trapped between the two advancing American columns and surrendered to VII Corps.

The removal of this potential threat to its right flank left XXX Corps free to resume its high-speed dash, and in the evening of 2 September the orders arrived: 11th Armoured Division was to make for Antwerp and the Guards for Brussels, respectively 90 and 75 miles away from the start line.

After some fighting en route, the 5th and 32nd Brigades of the Guards Armoured Division reached Brussels in the afternoon of 3 September to what must surely have been the most tumultuous welcome ever accorded to liberating troops. Meanwhile, 11th Armoured Division, leaving 50th Infantry Division to clear Lille, which was still in enemy hands, advanced 65 miles on 3 September and took part in a series of running fights with the enemy before halting in Alost at nightfall. The Division covered the last 25 miles to Antwerp the next day and, with considerable help from the Belgian Resistance, secured the port area intact. In

one sense it was a hollow victory, for the Germans succeeded in blowing all the bridges across the Albert Canal north of the city and in establishing strong garrisons along both banks of the Scheldt estuary, which afforded the port access to the sea. In his memoirs written fifteen years after the war, XXX Corps commander, General Sir Brian Horrocks, was of the opinion with hindsight that the order given to 11th Armoured Division was a 'serious error'.

My excuse is that my eyes were fixed entirely on the Rhine, and that everywhere else seemed of subsidiary importance. It never entered my head that the Scheldt would be mined, and that we should not be able to use Antwerp port until the channel had been swept and the Germans cleared from the coastline on either side. Nor did I realise that the Germans would be able to evacuate a large number of the troops trapped in the coastal areas across the mouth of the Scheldt estuary from Breskens to Flushing.[4]

A wiser move – again with the benefit of hindsight – would have been to by-pass Antwerp and push the whole of 11th Armoured Division across the Albert Canal before the Germans had time to blow the bridges, then make for the Woensdrecht isthmus, fifteen miles north-east of Antwerp, which had the only metalled road linking the Zeeland archipelago to the mainland. This would have cut

Walcheren Island. The capture of this objective, and the Scheldt estuary, in the autumn of 1944 would have thrown the German forces in Holland into complete confusion.

off the Germans left behind in the Scheldt estuary and freed the port to sea traffic within a few days. As it was, the port was not opened to merchant vessels until 26 November 1944, and then only after much costly fighting to secure the banks of the Scheldt and Walcheren Island.

Antwerp was a key factor in dictating the course of Allied strategy during the weeks that followed, and its importance was summed up admirably by the official historian of the Royal Navy 1939–45, Captain S.W. Roskill RN.

It is, of course, impossible to prove that if we had concentrated on opening the river Scheldt early in September, 1944, we could have restored the Army's mobility in time for it to strike into Germany while the enemy was still off-balance and regrouping his forces; but what seens undeniable is, firstly, that without the use of Antwerp the Allied land forces could not undertake a large scale new offensive and, secondly, that the river banks could have been cleared very much sooner. Had we merely 'masked' the German garrisons in the Channel ports (which were being dealt with by the British I Corps, the Canadian II Corps and French forces – author), which in any case were so badly wrecked that they could not handle any appreciable quantity of supplies for many weeks, and driven ahead for Breskens early in September, we could surely have gained control of the south bank more quickly – for all that the country was intersected by many easily defended canals, and large areas were under water; and the capture of Breskens, besides getting half-way towards opening the river, would have trapped large numbers of the German Fifteenth Army which, retreating from the Seine valley, actually managed to cross the Scheldt and reform to the north of the river. But the Supreme Commander gave no strategic directions to accomplish such a purpose. One may also feel that our forces around Antwerp were fully adequate to clearing the north bank of the river soon after the port itself was captured; but the Army Group commander's eyes were at the time turned to the north-east – in the direction in which he desired to thrust into Germany . . . It may be . . . that it was to the Naval Staff and the Admiralty that we should have looked for a full appreciation of its importance in 1944. Yet no joint plans had been prepared in advance to take immediate advantage of the capture of the historic port; and the rapid preparation of such plans was probably handicapped by the wide separation of the Supreme Commander's headquarters from those of the 21st Army Group and the Naval C-in-C in September-October 1944. Lastly, it does seem difficult to understand why the pressure exerted by the Combined Chiefs of Staff, by the Supreme Commander, and by Admiral Ramsay to get the Scheldt opened was so long in producing the desired action by Field-Marshal Montgomery.[5]

But Montgomery was convinced that the free use of the port of Antwerp was not the only way of bringing a speedy end to the war. He was more than ever convinced that the Allies must profit from the enemy's disorganization to punch their way quickly across the Rhine north of the Ardennes, even if it meant halting the US 12th Army Group's offensive in order to lend weight to his own.

What Montgomery failed to appreciate – although, in fairness, neither did any of the other Allied commanders – was the speed at which the Germans were recovering from the débâcle in Normandy. Much later, it became clear that XXX Corps had been fortunate in finding a gap in the Germans' order of retreat during the headlong dash across Belgium, pushing between the German Fifteenth Army, which was hugging the coast, and Fifth Panzer and Seventh Armies which were being pursued by the US 21st Army Group into Luxembourg and the Saar.

Pushing up the coast on XXX Corps' left flank, XII Corps had met with much stronger resistance, encountering six intact divisions of the Fifteenth Army which had been joined by the remnants of five more retreating from Normandy. This force, amounting to some 100,000 men, retreated into Holland and 65,000 troops, together with a substantial amount of equipment, were successfully evacuated across the Scheldt. Had 11th Armoured Division pushed on beyond Antwerp to cut the Woensdrecht isthmus, these forces would have been trapped.

The Supreme Commander, General Eisenhower, was now faced with a choice. Either he could delay the north-eastward drive of 21st Army Group until the all-important facility at Antwerp became available, or he could allow it to continue in the hope of securing a possible bridgehead across the Rhine in proximity to the Ruhr. Montgomery had already decided on 4 September to continue the drive into Holland, leaving the Canadians to clear the approaches to Antwerp; now, fuelled with enthusiasm, he suddenly proposed to Eisenhower that, if 21st Army Group were supported with all available supply facilities – which would mean halting Patton's Third Army offensive in Lorraine – it could drive right through to Berlin.

On 6 September, with fuel and supplies now drawn from a newly-established base at Brussels, 11th and Guards Armoured Divisions resumed their advance from Antwerp and Brussels. Both were now confronted by the defended line of the Albert Canal, which proved a formidable obstacle. The 11th Armoured Division could make little headway against the canal defences at Antwerp, so it handed the sector over to 50th Division and switched to the Guards' right. The Guards, although they had taken Louvain without trouble, had to fight hard to force and hold a crossing over the canal at Beerlingen on 7 September; the next day 50th Division also seized a crossing at Gheel, east of Antwerp.

The next two days witnessed heavy fighting as the Guards Armoured Division pushed on towards the Meuse-Escaut Canal, particularly around Bourg Leopold and Hechtel, where the Germans held the main roads. The breakthrough came on 10 September, when units of the Household Cavalry came upon an unmapped road and the 2nd Armoured and 1st Battalions of the Irish Guards pushed on past a German strongpoint at Hechtel to seize the bridge at De Groote Barrier. With this objective in Allied hands, German resistance in north-east Belgium collapsed rapidly.

The capture of De Groote Barrier, on the Belgian-Dutch border, placed the spearhead of Second Army within striking distance of Eindhoven. Thirty miles beyond that lay Nijmegen, and the Rhine. It was powerful ammunition for Montgomery when, meeting with Eisenhower in Brussels on 10 September, he once again argued forcefully for maintaining the thrust towards Germany, and even for driving on to Berlin. But Eisenhower justifiably remained fearful of the supply situation; after all, the Second Army's impetus so far had been maintained only at the expense of immobilising the US VIIIth Corps, which had been engaged in operations to clear Brest and the surrounding coastal area and whose fuel allocation had been diverted to Dempsey's forces.

Eisenhower . . .

. . . explained to Montgomery the condition of our supply system and our need for the early use of Antwerp. I pointed out that, without railway bridges over the Rhine and ample stockage of supplies on hand, there was no possibility of maintaining a force in Germany capable of penetrating to its capital. There was still a considerable reserve in the middle of the enemy country and I knew that any pencil-like thrust into the heart of Germany such as he proposed would meet nothing but certain destruction. This was true, no matter on what part of the front it might be attempted. I would not consider it.[6]

In any case, the military situation at this juncture no longer lent itself to a fast, *Blitzkrieg*-type armoured thrust deep into enemy territory. Broadly, the position was as follows. The First United States Army had advanced as far as the Siegfried Line; the Third United States Army, under General Patton, had established bridgeheads over the Moselle river; and the British Second Army, having advanced through Belgium against stiffening enemy resistance, was being organized on the defensive lines of the Albert and Escaut Canals from Antwerp to Maastricht. In the rear of the enemy, three waterways – the Maas, the Waal and the Maas–Waal Canal – formed natural lines of defence against any northern thrust by 21st Army Group. Montgomery's strategy was to advance across the three waterways, secure crossings of the Rhine in the area Grave–Nijmegen–Arnhem, outflank the Siegfried Line and attack towards northern Germany.

Although Eisenhower was firmly set against any swordthrust deep into Germany, the idea of seizing and holding a bridgehead over the Rhine in the

By the autumn of 1944, few bridges were left intact over the Rhine, as this view of the river at Cologne shows.

Arnhem region was attractive. Not only would it turn the defences of the Siegfried Line; it would also establish the Allies firmly on the lower Rhine, securing the northern flank and forming an extension of the defensive line Eisenhower wanted to establish while the port of Antwerp was cleared. To stop short of the lower Rhine would have left the Allied forces in the Low Countries in a very exposed position, particularly when Montgomery would have to concentrate a large part of those forces in clearing Walcheren Island. This was to be the priority task, once the bridgehead over the lower Rhine had been established.

The seizure of the Rhine bridgehead would mean the use of airborne forces on a hitherto unparalleled scale; a massive airborne carpet laid across Holland ahead of Second Army's advance. Even General Omar Bradley conceded that it was a bold stroke, as he later wrote:

Had the pious teetotaling Montgomery wobbled into SHAEF with a hangover, I could not have been more astonished than I was by the daring adventure he proposed. For in contrast to the conservative tactics Montgomery ordinarily chose, the Arnhem attack was to be made over a 60-mile carpet of airborne troops. Although I never reconciled myself to this venture, I nevertheless freely concede that Monty's plan for Arnhem was one of the most imaginative of the war.{7}

The airborne forces needed to implement Montgomery's imaginative plan were already in place in England. They were ready to go. In fact, they had been ready to go for some time.

CHAPTER 2

Airborne Army

Although the Germans pioneered the effective use of airborne forces during the Second World War, first of all during the campaigns in Norway and the Low Countries in 1940 and then during the invasion of Crete in the following year, the severe losses sustained during the latter operation made them wary of mounting similar large-scale efforts later on. Had it not been for their experience in Crete, the Germans – with Italian support – would almost certainly have launched a massive airborne assault on Malta.[8] If that island had been captured, the Mediterranean would probably have been lost to the Allies, with incalculable consequences. But apart from limited operations by special forces, Crete marked the end of the use of German airborne forces in their intended role; they were henceforth used as elite infantry.

It was therefore left to the Allies to develop the concept of airborne operations, and by the summer of 1944 they had amassed considerable experience in the field. The first operation by British paratroops took place on 10 February 1941, when 38 volunteers of No 2 Commando – the first British unit formed for airborne operations – were dropped to attack the Tragino Aqueduct in southern Italy. Although the damage they caused was negligible and the members of the attacking force were taken prisoner, the raid (Operation *Colossus*) proved that parachute troops could be used to strike at objectives deep inside enemy territory.

The expansion of the British Army's airborne forces continued during 1941, and by September sufficient numbers of personnel had completed the parachute training course at the Central Landing Establishment, Ringway, Manchester, to permit the formation of the 1st Parachute Brigade under Lt-Col R.N. Gale. Also in September, the 11th Special Air Service Battalion, which had been formed in November 1940 from the Parachute and Glider

Squadrons of No 2 Commando, was redesignated the 1st Parachute Battalion. In October 1941, the 31st Independent Brigade Group, which had already received specialised training in mountain warfare, became the 1st Air Landing Brigade, assuming the role of Britain's first glider-borne infantry, and in December the Glider Pilot Regiment was formed. This was followed, in February 1942, by the formation of No 38 Wing RAF, with the specific task of providing aircraft for use by the airborne forces. Its headquarters were at Netheravon, Wiltshire, and its initial establishments were No 296 (Glider Exercise) Squadron, with a mixture of Hawker Hector and Armstrong Whitworth Whitley aircraft for light and heavy towing duty, and General Aircraft Horsa and Airspeed Hotspur gliders, and No 297 (Parachute Exercise) Squadron, with Whitleys.

On the night of 27/28 February 1942 there was a further demonstration of the viability of airborne forces when 120 men (including one RAF specialist) of C Company, 2nd Parachute Battalion under Major J.D. Frost, were dropped at Bruneval, near Le Havre, to bring back scientific intelligence on a new German radar installation. As No 297 Squadron was still without its complement of aircraft, the Whitleys of No 51 Squadron – which had also taken part in Operation *Colossus* – were brought in to make the drop. The mission (Operation *Biting*) was entirely successful, the attacking force being evacuated by sea together with parts of the radar equipment and two prisoners at a cost of two men killed, six missing and six wounded.

When the airborne forces became a reality late in 1941, it was still undecided whether or not the force would ever operate at more than Brigade strength. However, General Sir Alan Brooke, Commander-in-Chief, Home Forces, advocated the formation of an Airborne Divisional HQ from the outset, partly for reasons of morale and convenience, and partly because the knowledge that the airborne forces were expanding to divisional status was likely to impress the enemy. Brigadier F.A.H. Browning, DSO, formerly commanding the 24th Guards Brigade Group, was appointed General Officer Commanding the Airborne Division and, together with a nucleus of staff officers, reported to GHQ Home Forces for his new duties on 3 November 1941. His primary task was to co-ordinate the whole development and training of the Airborne Force, and one of his first acts as GOC was to visit Air Marshal Sir Arthur Barrett, who as C-in-C Army Co-operation Command, was the senior RAF officer most concerned with the airborne forces. It was as a direct result of the discussions between Browning and Barrett that No 38 Wing came into being.

In the spring and summer of 1942, to help meet the growing manpower needs of the airborne forces, infantry battalions from selected line regiments were sent through the paratroop selection course as units. The first two such battalions, the 7th Battalion, Queen's Own Cameron Highlanders and the 10th Battalion, Royal Welch Fusiliers, were trained and reformed as the 5th (Scottish) and 6th (Welch) Parachute Battalions. Along with the 4th (Wessex) Parachute Battalion, these units were formed into the 2nd Parachute Brigade under the command of Brigadier Eric Down in July 1942. The usual complement of a parachute battalion was between 600 and 800 men, while glider battalions comprised 976 men. With its three battalions, a Brigade had a strength of between 1,800 and 2,400 men. In August 1942 the Parachute Regiment was formed and officially listed as an infantry regiment of the line. Its insignia depicted the Greek hero Bellerophon, astride the winged horse Pegasus – a monster-slaying combination from Greek mythology. The distinctive maroon beret that was to become the proudest symbol of the British airborne forces was also adopted at this time.

In June 1942, the 1st Parachute Brigade stood ready to take part in the planned large-scale combined operation at Dieppe, its mission to destroy coastal batteries east and west of the town, but when the operation was postponed until August the mission was assigned to the Commandos and, in the following month, the 1st Parachute Brigade was ordered to prepare for combat operations in North Africa.

Meanwhile, in June, the first American paratroops – the 2nd Battalion of the 503rd US Parachute Regiment – had arrived in Britain on the direct invitation of Prime Minister Winston Churchill, who was in consultation with President Roosevelt on the question of stepping up deliveries of US transport aircraft for use by the British airborne forces,[9] and towards the end of September Major-General Browning was informed by General Mark Clark of the US Army that these troops would be required to take part in the North African campaign planned for November. Browning suggested that the proposed campaign, which would be conducted over great distances in suitable country and with probably comparatively light opposition, offered tremendous possibilities for the use of airborne troops on much more than battalion scale. He sought and obtained the approval of the C-in-C Home Forces and of the War Office; and the British 1st Parachute Brigade was assigned to the North African operation.

As no RAF aircraft were available for the forthcoming operation, C-47 transports of the 60th Group, 51st Wing – based at Greenham Common, Berkshire – were assigned, and on 9 October 1942 a practice drop from these aircraft was made by 250 British paratroops. Three men were fatally injured during the exercise, having made faulty exits; the British paratroops had no experience in jumping from a side door and were used to dropping from an aircraft in level flight, whereas the Americans released in a pull-up from a shallow dive. British equipment was not suited to this technique, and while the matter was being investigated further practice drops were suspended. The result was that the bulk of the 1st Parachute Brigade – which included personnel drawn from other Brigades – left for North Africa without having jumped from a C-47.

The Allied landings in North Africa, Operation *Torch*, began on 8 November 1942, and the first airborne operation of the campaign took place on that day when 39 C-47s dropped troops of the 503rd Parachute Infantry Battalion in an attempt to capture Tafaraoni airfield near Oran. It was the longest operational flight involving airborne troops during the war, the aircraft taking off from St Eval and Predannack, Cornwall, and flying non-stop to North Africa. Unfortunately the mission was abortive, the paratroops being scattered over a wide area. It has to be said that 25 of the aircraft carried

RAF navigators, most of whom had just completed their training.[10]

The first British drop took place on 12 November, when 60th Group C-47s put down the 3rd Battalion, 1st Parachute Brigade (Lt-Col R.J. Pine-Coffin) on Bone airfield, midway between Algiers and Tunis. Although somewhat scattered, the Battalion took its objective without opposition and, with No 6 Commando, held the airfield for a week until relieved by advancing Allied forces. One man was killed during the drop and there were three more fatalities when two aircraft crash-landed in the sea.

Meanwhile, the remainder of the 1st Parachute Brigade had arrived by sea and moved up to Maison Blanche airfield to await orders; the 2nd Battalion, 503rd US Parachute Infantry, was placed under its command. On 15 November this battalion made a successful drop to seize the airfields of Tebessa and Youks les Bains, and on the following day the British 1st Battalion (Lt-Col S.J.L. Hill) dropped near Souk el Arba with orders to capture the crossroads there, make contact with French forces at Beja and patrol eastwards to harass the enemy. On 6 December, the 1st Battalion was joined by the 3rd Battalion, both fighting as conventional light infantry under the tactical control of V Corps.

The 2nd Parachute Battalion (Lt-Col John Frost) had been held in reserve for a drop on three enemy airfields at Pont de Faha, Depienne and Oudna. This was scheduled to take place on 29 November, but at the last minute it was learned that the Germans had abandoned the first two objectives and the Battalion was diverted to Oudna, where it occupied the airfield and local railway station. Early the next morning the Germans counter-attacked in strength, supported by armour and aircraft, and Lt-Col Frost – having found nothing worthwhile in the way of aircraft or stores to destroy at the airfield, which had been his primary mission – decided to withdraw westwards to join up with troops of the British First Army who were about to drive on Tunis. The drive, however, was postponed, and for the next three days 2nd Battalion withdrew over difficult hilly country under continual attack by tanks, infantry and aircraft. During this fighting the Battalion suffered 260 personnel killed, missing or wounded, so that by the time the leading elements reached the Allied lines at Medjaz on 3 December its fighting strength was down to about 150. During the week that followed, some 100 of the missing men rejoined,

having fought their way individually or in small groups to the Allied lines. It was a splendid tribute to the 2nd Battalion's fighting prowess, but there was no escaping the fact that the heavy casualty rate had been attributable to faulty information and inadequate arrangements for co-ordination with the advance of the main ground forces. There was a clear lesson for the future to be assimilated here.

The whole of the 1st Parachute Brigade regrouped at Bone in January 1943, and for the next three months was used as a mobile infantry reserve, committed to action wherever the fighting was heaviest. During this time the Brigade established a formidable reputation as a fighting force, and some of its officers also established personal traditions; John Frost, for example, used a hunting horn to help his men rally to him when assembling after a drop. It became his trademark.

The use of the 1st Parachute Brigade in the North African campaign was rather in the nature of a last-minute experiment. The justification for it was to prove the value of large numbers of parachute troops in action. But the British airborne operations – which could not have taken place without USAAF support, using valuable aircraft diverted from their primary air transport role – could easily have ended in disaster, at least on two occasions, if there had been enemy opposition. So the effect was twofold; the pro-airborne were more firmly convinced than ever that an adequate and efficient air component was all that was needed to turn the Airborne Force into a potent weapon, while the anti-airborne were more convinced than ever that airborne operations were, if not a failure, at least not worth the colossal effort and expenditure of the air forces which they involved, since equally satisfactory results could be obtained by more usual methods of warfare.

In May 1943, the availability of sufficient numbers of trained personnel permitted the 1st Airborne Division to become fully operational under the command of Major-General G.F. Hopkinson. The major components of the division were the 1st and 2nd Parachute Brigades, the 1st Air Landing Brigade and the 1st Airborne Light Regiment, Royal Artillery. The 6th Airborne Division also began forming in May 1943 under the command of Major-General Richard Gale; its initial component was the 3rd Parachute Brigade, comprising the 7th, 8th and 9th Parachute Battalions (drawn mainly from the

Somerset Light Infantry, Royal Warwickshire Regiment, and the Essex Regiment). The 1st Canadian Parachute Battalion was also assigned to the Division at a later date. The 6th Air Landing Brigade formed the glider-borne element, while the 53rd (Worcestershire Yeomanry) Airborne Light Regiment RA formed the artillery component.

In June 1943 the 4th Parachute Brigade under Brigadier J.W. Hackett was assigned to the 1st Airborne Division. Raised in the Middle East, this Brigade comprised the 10th, 11th and 156th Parachute Battalions. It was to be retained in reserve while the 1st and 2nd Parachute Brigades, together with the 1st Air Landing Brigade, took part in the next major Allied airborne operation: the invasion of Sicily (Operation *Husky*).

The overall planning for the airborne forces' part in this operation was undertaken by Major-General Browning, who had handed over command of the 1st Airborne Division to become Airborne Advisor to the Supreme Commander, General Eisenhower, and General Alexander, the Land Forces Commander. The plans were formulated by 10 May 1943 and provided for three successive brigade assaults against objectives ahead of the advance of XIII Corps. The objectives allotted to the 1st Airborne Divison were the Ponte Grande bridge south of Syracuse and the western outskirts of the town; the bridge and high ground west of Augusta; and the Ponte di Primosole bridge over the river Simeto. In addition to these British operations, the 82nd Airborne Division under the command of the US Seventh Army would also carry out attacks on D night and D+1 night, to cover the landings of the US Fifth Army in south-west Sicily. The 82nd Airborne Division had been activated alongside the 101st Airborne Division in August 1942 at Camp Claibourne, Louisiana; comprising the 504th and 505th Parachute Infantry Regiments and the 325th Glider Infantry Regiment, it arrived in North Africa from the United States on 10 May under the command of Major-General Matthew B. Ridgeway.

The 1st Airborne Division arrived in North Africa in two main convoys – 2nd Parachute Brigade on 26 April 1943, and 1st Air Landing Brigade on 26 May – and began intensive training, establishing a main operational base at Kairouan near Sousse, Tunisia. By 8 July there were 140 Waco CG-4A and nineteen Airspeed Horsa gliders at Kairouan, where six airstrips were also shared by the 51st Troop Carrier Wing USAAF and by 28 Armstrong Whitworth Albemarle and seven Handley Page Halifax aircraft of Nos 296 and 297 Squadrons RAF. Most of the British glider pilots had to be converted to the CG-4A; only three weeks were available for night training, but despite a number of problems – one of which was a complete lack of communication between tug and glider – 1,800 night lifts were made without serious casualty.

The first phase of the airborne landings in Sicily, Operation *Ladbroke*, took place on the night of 9/10 July 1943, when the 1st Air Landing Brigade set out for Syracuse in 137 Waco and ten Horsa gliders towed by 109 C-47s of USAAF Troop Carrier Command and No 38 Wing's Albemarles and Halifaxes.

The operation began to go wrong from the beginning, when six Wacos, for various technical reasons, either cast off or crashed between Kairouan and the coast. The remaining tug/glider combinations, flying individually and not in formation, encountered unexpectedly high winds of up to 45 mph, throwing the timing of the operation into disarray. But other factors contributed to the inaccuracy of the drop. First, it was necessary to judge the distance from the Sicilian shore by moonlight, and even experienced pilots tend to underestimate distance. Second, map-reading proved difficult because the run-in to the target was made down-moon and the flight was at low altitude; and third, the low altitude of the approach allowed little or no margin to correct any errors in release or to allow for increased wind speed. Consequently, there were serious miscalculations in judging the times of release, so much so that 69 gliders landed in the sea and 56 were scattered along the south-east coast of Sicily.

There was also considerable flak, and, according to the official Air Ministry narrative on airborne operations, produced in 1951,

The probable cause of so many gliders landing in the sea was the fact that the Americans were unaccustomed to flak, that the C-47 aircraft were not armoured and had no self-sealing tanks and that their navigation was not up to the standard required. Major-General Browning . . . stated that No 38 Wing had aircraft armed and designed to face it. This was not entirely so as the two aircraft used by No 38 Wing, the Albemarle and Halifax, were not armoured against flak but only against lateral fire.[11]

Only twelve gliders landed near the bridge, the closest – a Horsa – being 300 yards away from it. The eight officers and 65 other ranks that reached the objective managed to hold and remove the demolition charges which had been placed by the Italians. The glider troops hung on until 1530 hours on 10 July, when the survivors were overrun, but the enemy in turn were driven away by Eighth Army infantry, advancing from the beaches, before they were able to demolish the bridge. Some of the other glider-borne troops who had been scattered along the coast, operating in small groups, neutralized a coastal gun battery and knocked out a couple of pill boxes, causing some confusion along the Italian defences.

All the glider tugs that had taken part in this operation returned safely to their African bases. Casualties were 605 officers and men, of whom 326 were presumed to have drowned.

Two hours after the British operation, Colonel James M. Gavin's reinforced 505th Regimental Combat Team, scheduled to drop at Gela on the south coast with the task of securing all roads leading inland from the beaches and of occupying key points within the drop zone (DZ) so that it could be used again by the other parachute regiment of the 82nd Airborne Division, had set off in 226 C-47s. The aircraft became widely scattered and the drop was a disaster, the paratroops coming down all over the southeast corner of Sicily. Eight aircraft were shot down by flak. Nevertheless, the wide dispersal of the paratroops gave the enemy the impression that more massive airborne assaults were taking place, creating more confusion and contributing in some measure to the success of the landward drive from the beaches.

The second planned British airborne operation, by the 2nd Parachute Brigade against the bridge and high ground west of Augusta – scheduled for the night of 10/11 July – was cancelled, having been rendered unnecessary by the speed of the 5th Division's advance. However, an operation by the 504th Regimental Combat Team of the US 82nd Airborne Division was mounted that night from North Africa, the paratroops having been requested by General Patton to help strengthen the large American beachhead. The mission should have been little more than a routine night training jump, as the selected DZ – Farello airstrip near Gela – lay within an area that had already been secured by

Gavin's force, and the route that was to be followed by the 144 transport aircraft had been carefully planned so that the whole of it passed over friendly territory. Also, every conceivable precaution was taken to ensure that friendly naval and land forces would hold their fire as the transports crossed the invasion area; the precise timing of the air drop was given to all units, and General Ridgeway flew to Sicily in person to ensure that Seventh Army Headquarters had disseminated the warning order to all anti-aircraft units.

The first drop, at 2240 hours, was made without incident, even though it took place just after enemy aircraft had made bombing runs over the invasion area and the anti-aircraft gunners had been heavily engaged. The trouble began when the second wave of C-47s made their approach; an unidentified machine-gunner opened fire on the low-flying aircraft, and within seconds ships and shore batteries had joined in. Twenty-three transports were shot down, all by friendly fire, and over half of the aircraft that regained Africa were so badly damaged that they were out of the line for months. Thirty-seven had to be scrapped. Of the 2,000 paratroopers on the mission, 318 had been killed, including Brigadier-General Charles L. Keerans Jr, deputy commanding general of the 82nd Airborne Division.

The last airborne operation over Sicily, Operation *Fustian*, took place on the night of 13/14 July 1943, its object being to capture and hold the Primosole bridge over the river Simeto on the road to Catania. The force earmarked for the operation comprised 1,836 paratroops and 77 glider-borne troops of the 1st Airborne Division. In addition to two and a half battalions of the 1st Parachute Brigade, the 1st Parachute Squadron of the Royal Engineers, the 16th Parachute Field Ambulance and an Airborne Anti-Tank unit of the Royal Artillery were also committed.

The plan was for two platoons of the 1st Parachute Battalion and the squadron of the Royal Engineers to seize the objective, while two platoons of the 3rd Parachute Battalion, dropping five minutes later, were to overrun an adjacent anti-aircraft battery. The remainder of the 1st Parachute Battalion would then organize the defence of the bridge, while the remainder of the 3rd would establish a bridgehead in a loop of the Simeto 1,000 yards to the north of Primosole. Meanwhile, the 2nd Parachute Battalion would hold the high ground south of the bridge.

British and US paratroops co-operated for the first time in the Mediterranean Theatre. This group is seen after taking part in the invasion of southern France, August 1944.

The force, under the command of Brigadier G.M. Lathbury, was transported to Sicily by 124 C-47s of the 51st Troop Carrier Wing USAAF and eleven Albemarles of No 38 Wing RAF. As the columns flew past Cape Passero, the tragedy of two nights previously was repeated: Allied anti-aircraft gunners opened fire and ten C-47s, laden with paratroops, were shot down. Fifty other aircraft were hit but pressed on towards the DZ, but 27 more at the end of the column turned back for Africa.

Meanwhile, thirty minutes in advance of the main force, several teams of the 21st Independent Parachute Company had jumped over the target area to mark the LZs and DZs with lights and radio beacons. This company had been formed within the 1st Airborne Division specifically for the pathfinder role, and *Fustian* marked its first operational use. The beacons enabled several transport crews to make accurate drops, but in general the force was widely scattered. Nevertheless, by dawn on 14 July the bridge had been secured, the demolition charges removed by the Royal Engineers, and defensive positions set up. The difficulties of landing, forming up and collecting the equipment dropped in the containers were compounded by the fact that German paratroops landed on the DZs literally minutes before the British arrived, leading to numerous skirmishes between the two sides. This resulted in a considerable delay before the bridge was captured, so that when the glider-borne troops arrived they had to postpone the unloading of their heavy weapons and lend a hand in the assault on the objective. The gliders themselves had experienced problems; of the eleven Horsas and six CG4As involved, only four Horsas made accurate landings on their intended LZs; one Horsa was lost at sea, and four were shot down by enemy gunners after release. Three of the Wacos made disastrous crash-landings, and the other three landed among enemy positions.

The British paratroops held on to the bridge throughout 14 July, fighting off strong counter-attacks by their German counterparts. By the end of the afternoon the attacks had heavy artillery support, and after dark the defenders – who were running out of ammunition – were compelled to withdraw to where the 2nd Battalion was holding its positions to the south of the bridge. Early on the morning of 15 July the delayed advance units of the Eighth Army arrived, and early the next morning the bridge was captured and held by the Durham Light Infantry. By this time the 1st Parachute Brigade had suffered 295 casualties, of whom more than one-third were killed or wounded.

Apart from a few small demonstration drops there were no further airborne operations by the British in the Mediterranean area. However, the 1st Airborne Division played an important part as ground troops during the invasion of Italy, capturing Taranto on 9 September 1943 and moving on to Foggia where they were halted while other divisions continued their advance. Meanwhile, the US 82nd Airborne Division remained in Sicily and carried out ordinary ground divisional duties, at readiness to carry out future airborne operations in Italy as required. On 1 October 1943 the 1st Airborne Division was notified of its impending return to England and in November it sailed, less the 1st Airlanding Light Regiment which rejoined the Division three months later. No 38 Wing's units also returned to England with the exception of No 296 Squadron, which remained in North Africa and Sicily for a further three months and was used for training the 51st Troop Carrier Wing.[12]

The Allied airborne operations in Sicily produced a series of conclusions that were to have a far-reaching effect on subsequent, larger-scale operations in Europe. General Eisenhower – although expressing a belief that airborne forces should be organized in self-contained units about the size of a regimental combat team, rather than of divisional strength – stated in his report on Sicily that the outstanding tactical lesson of the whole campaign was the potential value of air operations. The main lessons learned were summarized at the time as follows:[13]

1 All airborne operations are air operations and must therefore be the responsibility of the Air Commander-in-Chief. This factor was stressed repeatedly but never met with full Army approval. (In fact, there were sharp differences of opinion over various procedures between the Airborne Forces and the RAF, particularly concerning night glider operations, which the RAF considered unsound even for highly trained crews – Author).

2 There must be better planning and greater co-ordination between the three Services. A high percentage of losses caused by 'friendly' AA fire was due to faulty co-ordination. Technical experts must be available and adequate time allowed for preparation.

3 Very thorough and intensive training is absolutely vital. The assumption that parachute operations can be carried out by crews lacking in operational experience is fallacious. Apart from preliminary operational experience the crews need particular training in low flying, navigation over sea and judging distances by moonlight. Inability in the latter caused many pilots to fly too near the coast during the last Sicilian operation with costly results. The general standard of navigation by both British and American crews was poor throughout; approximately 60 per cent of the pilots lost their way and only 30 per cent found their destinations. (In fact, this was rather unfair on the RAF. An examination of the results achieved in the two operations involving No 38 Wing showed that they had achieved very creditable results. Out of 134 aircraft taking part in the first operation only 32 belonged to No 38 Wing, and 26 of these released their gliders over the correct zone. In the second operation No 38

Wing towed all seventeen of the gliders and, apart from those shot down or otherwise lost en route, released the rest over the zone –Author).

4 Suitable means of aircraft identification must be provided (IFF and Very Lights). The onus of identification is always with the aircraft.

5 Corridors for the airborne force to follow should be made at least five miles wide and marked if possible by naval craft.

6 It was considered important to provide pathfinder aircraft to lead in the force, which would considerably facilitate finding the Dropping or Landing Zone.

7 Routeing was of extreme importance. Wherever possible convoys should be avoided.

8 The glider force should be preceded by a parachute party to provide flares, beacons or flare path; and to provide homing devices, lights or other signals to indicate the release point and landing zones.

It was clear from these recommendations that the Allied airborne forces had indeed learned much from their sorry experiences in Sicily; yet the emphasis remained very much on night operations, the conclusion being that airborne forces were vulnerable by day.

While the 1st Airborne Division had been involved in the Sicilian operations, the formation of the 6th Airborne Division (the number 6 was chosen to mislead the enemy) had been proceeding on a phased basis in the United Kingdom. The Division was ordered to mobilize on 23 December 1943, and three days later Headquarters Airborne Troops, responsible for all matters pertaining to airborne forces, was formed under the command of 21st Army Group. At its head, Major-General Browning was promoted to the rank of Lieutenant-General.

Another important step, in the winter of 1943–44, was the expansion of the RAF's air transport facilities to support the airborne forces. Firstly, No 38 Wing was expanded to the status of a Group,[14] its strength being augmented by the transfer of squadrons from other RAF Commands, so that by 16 March 1944 it had ten squadrons, four equipped with Albemarles, four with Short Stirlings and two with Halifaxes. Meanwhile, a second Group – No 46 – had also been formed within Transport Command on 17 January 1944 in order to ensure an adequate supply of aircraft for the airborne operations that would form a key element in the forthcoming Allied invasion of Europe. By March 1944 this Group had an establishment of five squadrons, all equipped with the Douglas Dakota, as the C-47 was known in RAF service. The original role of the five Dakota squadrons was re-supply, operating under the control of No 38 Group.

When Operation *Overlord*, the Allied invasion of Europe, was launched on 6 June 1944, the British task in the airborne plan (Operation *Neptune*) was allocated to the 6th Airborne Division, the 1st Airborne Division remaining in England as reserve. The American tasks were assigned to the 82nd and 101st Airborne Divisions.

The story of the Allied airborne operations in Normandy is well known and does not need repetition here, especially as the formation central to this narrative – the 1st Airborne Division – was not actively involved. One point, however, is worth emphasizing. On the evening of D-Day, the British mounted Operation *Mallard*, the transporting of the remainder of the 6th Airborne Division to France. This was the first daylight glider operation of any magnitude, and it was a success. Of 256 gliders despatched, 246 landed on their correct zones. Timing was precise, and air superiority complete. The opinion of those who favoured daylight airborne operations appeared to be vindicated.

On 2 June 1944, four days before *Overlord* was launched, Supreme Headquarters Allied Expeditionary Force, in a letter to the British and American Chiefs of Staff, had proposed the formation of an organization that would bring all airborne troops under SHAEF control. The idea was not new; the British had already recommended the establishment of a headquarters to command all Allied airborne formations in the European Theatre, and although this had not proved necessary in Normandy because British and American airborne operations there were separate, it was clear that future operations involving several airborne divisions might need central control. The SHAEF proposal recommended that a Commanding General be selected by the Supreme Commander and that the Headquarters be formed around the British Headquarters Airborne Forces, which was already in existence.

On 20 June 1944 General Eisenhower approved the plan for a unified airborne forces command, but indicated that troop carrier units ought to be included as well. General George Marshall, the US Army Chief of Staff, and General Carl Spaatz, commanding the US Strategic Forces in Europe, were in agreement; in fact, in December 1943 Marshall had already written to Spaatz urging that both airborne and troop carrier forces in Britain be placed under one headquarters for training and operations. He also advocated placing such a command under the US Ninth Air Force.

The Air Commander-in-Chief at SHAEF, Air Marshal Trafford Leigh-Mallory, did not agree. Although lending his approval to a unified airborne forces command, his opinion was that the inclusion of troop carrier units would involve more complex planning, preparation and execution. Apart from this, Eisenhower's proposals met with little opposition, and the plan went ahead.

There remained the question of who was to command the new organization. The British felt strongly that it should be headed by Lieutenant-General Browning; the Americans thought that the job should go to an American, since they would be contributing the majority of the forces involved. In the end, Eisenhower selected an American, 54-year-old Lieutenant-General Lewis H. Brereton, who was junior in rank to Browning by about four months.

Brereton had an interesting career behind him. Commissioned first into the US Navy, he had transferred to the Army in 1911 and had seen active service as a fighter pilot in the 1914–18 War, winning a DSC. Between the wars he had served on the staff of Colonel William 'Billy' Mitchell, where he had played a prominent part in developing dive-bombing techniques. During the Second World War, he had so far served with distinction in every major theatre of war. As a major-general commanding the Far Eastern Air Force in the Philippines when the Japanese attacked, he had organized a small force of B-17 bombers to strike back at the enemy; in 1942 he had been sent to India to organize the Tenth Air Force and establish an air supply route across the Himalayas to China; later, he had commanded the Ninth Air Force in North Africa and then England.

It was not until 8 August 1944 that SHAEF officially announced the establishment of Combined Airborne Headquarters with General Brereton in command. On 16 August this organization was redesignated First Allied Airborne Army. It was placed directly under SHAEF control and was given command of all Allied airborne troops, as well as operational control of RAF and USAAF troop carriers.[15]

In the meantime, Brereton had been gathering his staff around him. On 2 August, the day on which he received notification of his appointment from SHAEF (along with a personal note from General Eisenhower, asking him to pay particular attention to improving troop carrier navigation) Brigadier-General Floyd L. Parks reported for duty as his Chief of Staff. The next day Brereton named Brigadier-General Ralph S. Stearly as G-3, Operations, and Brigadier-General Stuart L. Cutler, formerly on the staff of First US Army Group, as Chief of Staff, Plans. Finally, on 4 August, he accepted the appointment of Lieutenant-General Frederick Browning as his deputy commander. The Headquarters of the new organization was at Sunninghill Park, near Ascot, close to the rear HQ of the US Ninth Air Force. Later, an advanced HQ was set up at Maison Laffitte, Paris, where the planning section was able to maintain close contact with SHAEF HQ at Versailles.

The principal functions of the Airborne Army were to supervise training, prepare plans for airborne operations – including resupply – and exercise control over these operations until a junction was effected between the airborne and ground forces. It was also to prepare outline plans for airborne operations in conjunction with SHAEF, consult with naval and air commanders-in-chief on matters concerning them, and conduct detailed planning in conjunction with the ground force and air force commanders.

The Airborne Army exercised command of the British airborne troops through Headquarters, Airborne Troops (subsequently redesignated I Airborne Corps) under Lieutenant-General Browning, and command of American airborne troops through XVIII Airborne Corps, a new headquarters under General Ridgeway, who had handed over command of the 82nd Airborne Division to General Gavin.

Despite spirited protests by Air Marshal Leigh-Mallory, the Airborne Army also took over operational control of USAAF IX Troop Carrier Command from the Allied Expeditionary Air Forces. The Airborne Army also exercised operational control of Nos 38 and 46 Groups RAF except where aircraft were needed for tasks in

connection with Special Air Service or Special Operations Executive (SOE) operations with resistance movements on the Continent. Because of this rather ambiguous position, the RAF was not at first represented in Brereton's Headquarters, a matter of some concern to Air Vice-Marshal L.N. Hollinghurst, commanding No 38 Group. On 31 August, he requested the inclusion of an RAF element in Headquarters Airborne Army. Hollinghurst had his way, and on 6 September an establishment was drafted which included fifteen RAF officers.

In the weeks following Operation *Overlord*, while the Allied Airborne Army was in the process of formation, no fewer than sixteen airborne operations were planned and subsequently cancelled. Most of these – at least up to the end of July –involved the British 1st Airborne Division, as none of the three airborne divisions committed to the fighting in Normandy would be ready for further operations until they had undergone at least 75 days of training and refitting. The 101st Airborne Division had been kept in action until 27 June, the 82nd until 8 July, and the British 6th Airborne Division was not relieved until 26 August. There was a further reduction in airborne capabilities when about one-third of the US troop-carrying aircraft were sent to the Mediterranean to take part in Operation *Anvil*, the Allied invasion of southern France.

The first of the projected airborne operations for the employment of the 1st Airborne Division was that the Division be dropped on 13 June in an area south-west of Caen, behind the German lines, to assist in encircling the enemy. The operation, code-named *Wildoats*, was discussed on 11 June 1944 at a conference held at Headquarters, AEAF, and presided over by Air Marshal Leigh-Mallory. The delegates felt that the operation was not feasible because:

a the area was too heavily defended for paratroops to be dropped in daylight;
b the night of 12–13 June was not in a favourable moon period;
c the operation would involve flying over the Fleet for three hours and no guarantee could be given by the Allied Naval Commander, 'X' Force, or by the commanding officers on the beaches that the aircraft would not be fired upon;

d an approach over the Cotentin Peninsula would involve crossing hostile territory without radio aids.

The second of the planned operations that never took place was *Beneficiary*, which was intended to capture the port of St Malo. Planning for this operation continued throughout June, but HQ Airborne Forces advised against the final plan for reasons stated in a report by General Browning, dated 7 July. The landings would have to be made too close to enemy flak positions; the Navy would not be able to use St Malo harbour until seven days after its capture, and so resupply would have to be done by air. It would also involve using the only available airborne reserves, and in any case the US First Army considered that the area could be captured without

Lieutenant-General Frederick Browning, commander of I Airborne Corps. The siting of his Corps HQ at Nijmegen was a tactical error and a waste of valuable resources.

difficulty by approaching from the south and south-east.

The third operation, *Hands Up*, was a proposed joint airborne and Naval operation to capture Quiberon Bay for use as a port. The operation was unsound from the Naval point of view, because the route lay too near convoys and U-boat bases. It was also unlikely that sufficient forces would be available. In addition, it was estimated that three weeks' planning would be necessary, and operational conditions could not be forecast that far ahead. At a meeting of the Chiefs of Staff on 15 July it was therefore decided to cancel the operation, but to file the plan for reference.

The fourth planned operation, *Swordhilt*, seemed more promising. This was planned to assist in the capture of Brest during July, and from the air point of view the plan was sound from all aspects. However, the successful breakout by American forces from the St Lo area during the last days of July rendered the airborne operation superfluous and it was cancelled on 29 July.

The American breakthrough at St Lo transformed a stable situation into an extremely fluid one. By 30 July a gaping hole had been torn in the German lines through which armoured units drove to Avranches at the base of the Normandy Peninsula. From Avranches, General Patton's Third Army swept southeast around the left flank of the German Seventh Army, covered 100 miles in a week, and reached Le Mans on 8 August. Two days earlier, SHAEF and Combined Airborne Headquarters, anticipating that this threat would soon force the Germans to retreat, agreed on an airborne operation called *Transfigure*.

The purpose of *Transfigure* was to land a large airborne force in the north of the Paris–Orleans Gap. As Patton approached Orleans, the airborne troops would cut off the main escape routes for the Germans west of the Seine. In its final form, the plan envisaged parachute and glider operations by the US 101st Airborne Division near St Arnoult-en-Yvelines and by the British 1st Airborne Division and the Polish Parachute Brigade in the vicinity of Rambouillet. By 13 August the plan had been worked out in detail and the troops moved to their respective airfields, and by the 16th every available troop-carrying aircraft was standing by. In the event, the progress of Patton's Third Army was fast enough to make the operation unnecessary and it was cancelled on 18 August, although 40 jeeps and men of 2 SAS were landed by glider and moved through the enemy lines to Auxerre for operations with the French Forces of the Interior (FFI). This was known as Operation *Wallace*.

On 24 August, a further airborne operation – *Boxer* – was approved by SHAEF in support of Montgomery's northward drive from the Seine. It envisaged an air drop and glider landing some 30 miles inland from Boulogne, the object being to take that port and harass the German retreat. On the following day, however, the plan was rejected by 21st Army Group on the grounds that it was an indecisive operation off the main line of advance, but at the same meeting a further airborne operation was agreed between General Brereton and Montgomery's Chief of Staff, Major-General Sir Francis de Guingand.

The objective of this operation, *Linnet* was to place a large airborne force in the Lille–Arras–Douai area, ahead of the British drive into Belgium, in order to cut off the German retreat. By 26 August, HQ Airborne Army had picked Tournai and the vicinity as the objective, and on the 27th preliminary orders were given to airborne and troop-carrier commanders. Outline planning was completed by 29 September, and 21st Army Group approved 3 September as the target date – which was the reason why Montgomery's northward push into Belgium was temporarily slowed down, as we have seen in chapter one. On the last day of August the airborne troops once again began arriving at their departure airfields, and by 2 September the assembly process was complete. Late that evening, however, Montgomery's Headquarters sent word that *Linnet* was no longer necessary. British and American forces had joined up in Tournai.

General Brereton had foreseen that this would almost certainly happen, and that bad weather predicted for 3 September would probably force the cancellation of *Linnet* in any case. In the afternoon of 2 September, he had therefore asked SHAEF to approve a second operation, *Linnet II*, whose objective was to secure crossings over the Meuse north of Liège on 4 September. Eisenhower left the decision to Montgomery, who ruled against it; again, it was away from the main line of advance. Apart from that, there was a serious lack of target intelligence on that area, and an airborne operation on the scale envisaged – three divisions plus one brigade group – might easily have ended in disarray, if not disaster.

A further operation, requested by Montgomery on 3 September, seemed more feasible. This would involve landing the 1st Airborne Division and the Polish Parachute Brigade to secure a crossing of the

The capture of the road bridge at Arnhem, seen here in an oblique shot taken just before *Market Garden*, seemed an attractive proposition.

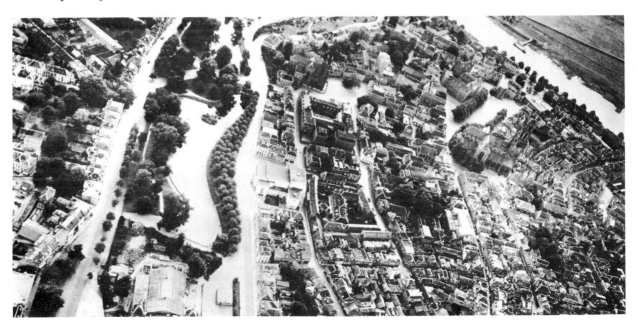

Rhine in the Arnhem/Wesel area in the afternoon of the 6th or the morning of the 7th. On 4 September, intelligence reports indicated that the concentration of flak in the Wesel area would make an airborne landing there extremely dangerous, and so Montgomery's staff selected Arnhem as the crossing point.

On the same day the First Airborne Army began to prepare detailed plans for the operation, which was given the name *Comet*. The target date was set for 8 September, and the operation would begin at 0430 hours with the seizure of the Arnhem bridge by a *coup de main* party in eighteen gliders. Pathfinder troops would begin dropping at 0645 hours from twelve Stirlings, and at 0715 hours the main force would arrive, beginning with 340 gliders towed by aircraft of Nos 38 and 46 Groups. Thes would be followed by paratroops transported in aircraft of the 52nd Troop Carrier Wing. In the afternoon, further missions would be flown by 320 British aircraft towing gliders, 114 aircraft of the 52nd Troop Carrier Wing with paratroops, and 114 carrying supplies. The next day, if conditions permitted, 157 gliders towed by the 61st and 442nd Groups would bring in the US 878th Aviation Engineer Battalion to prepare an airfield for the landing of the airportable British 52nd (Lowland) Division, as reinforcements.

The troops tasked with the capture of the Arnhem bridge were to be flown via a northerly route to a DZ and LZ some five miles north-west of the town; the remainder would be inserted via a more southerly route to zones south of Nijmegen to seize the bridges over the Waal at Nijmegen and over the Maas at Grave.

By 7 September the planning for *Comet* was complete and the appropriate orders issued, but then storm warnings led to a 24-hour postponement. A further postponement was requested by 21st Army Group the next day, after Field-Marshal Montgomery received news of stiffening enemy resistance and even of German counter-attacks led to yet another postponement on the 9th. The whole situation was weighed in the balance. The Nijmegen-Arnhem area was still more than 50 miles behind the German front line, and in between lay seven canals and rivers which the enemy would most likely contest bitterly. If they succeeded in holding any of these natural defensive lines, the predicament of the airborne forces in the rear would be very dangerous. With this realization, *Comet* was

cancelled on 10 September, and all forces involved were ordered to stand by for further operations.

Montgomery remained convinced that an airborne operation to secure the Rhine crossings was the key to the rapid success of his northward thrust, although the Second Army commander, General Dempsey – whose Intelligence staff was constantly reporting mounting German activity in central Holland – thought that it would be better to strike out in an easterly direction towards the Rhine at Wesel, alongside the Americans, rather than to 'go off at a tangent into Holland' alone. On 10 September Dempsey made his viewpoint known to Montgomery; he was unaware that another, crucial factor had come into play.

On 8 September, the first German V-2 rocket had exploded in Chiswick, London. The British public, as yet, were unaware of this new threat; the first sign of the missile's arrival was when a large crater appeared in the ground. But the Chiefs of Staff were well aware of the dangers, and a signal was urgently despatched to Montgomery asking what could be

Allied commanders were seriously alarmed by the V-2 rocket threat. Photograph shows the trail of a V-2 after launch from a site in Holland.

done to capture or cut off the sites near the Hague from which the V-2s were being launched.

The rocket menace – on which the Chiefs of Staff had not yet formally reported to the Cabinet – provided a new lever for Montgomery's plan, which he continued to press when he met General Eisenhower in Brussels on 10 September to discuss the strategy they would employ in the weeks to come. The meeting was stormy; Eisenhower was at first reluctant to agree to the plan. It involved the withdrawal of large numbers of transport aircraft from routine supply duties, and this had already happened on three occasions when the air transport forces stood by to support airborne operations that were ultimately cancelled.

The operation that Montgomery now proposed – in effect, an expanded version of *Comet* – would involve all available airborne forces and would also require the use of all available British and American troop-carrying aircraft for a period of at least two days.

The axis of advance chosen by Field-Marshal Montgomery was not entirely satisfactory. One disadvantage was that the Second Army would arrive too far north of its first objective, the Ruhr. Another was that the ground which Second Army had to cover did not led itself to a swift advance. But, given the element of surprise, the operation presented a golden opportunity to outflank the defences of the Siegfried Line.

Montgomery emerged from the meeting of 10 September having obtained Eisenhower's approval for the airborne operation. Montgomery also wanted all ground operations outside Belgium brought to a standstill so that his plan could have absolute priority, but Eisenhower would not agree to this. Neither would he agree to anything more than limited priority in the provision of additional supplies and transport from American sources. This was a crucial factor, because all the logistical reserves of 21st Army Group were in full use; even tank transporters were being used to ferry essential supplies, and new transport companies promised from England had not yet arrived.

Lieutenant-General Brian Horrock's XXX Corps, which would form the spearhead of Second Army's attack once the airborne forces had captured the bridges, could not rely on the US First Army for support as long as Patton's advance continued in the south, and would therefore have to be supported by the British VIIIth Corps, brought up on its right. The problem here was that most of VIIIth Corps' transport was in use by other units of Second Army, and the extra transport promised by the Americans would not be enough to make good the shortfall. Accordingly, on 11 September Montgomery informed Eisenhower that the operation, tentatively planned for 17 September, would have to be postponed until at least the 21st.

This was an alarming prospect, as German resistance was stiffening daily. On 12 September, Eisenhower therefore authorized the provision of enough trucks to make a daily delivery of 1,000 tons of supplies to Brussels; he also undertook to halt the American offensive towards the Saar and to divert supplies from the US 12th Army Group to First Army, which would then be in a position to support XXX Corps on the right when the advance began.

Having obtained these conditions, Montgomery was able to confirm that the operation would go ahead on 17 September. It was given the name *Market Garden*. *Market* referred to the airborne part of the operation, and *Garden* to the operations of the relieving columns of the Second Army.

So the plan was agreed in broad outline. What remained now was to determine its precise objectives.

CHAIN OF COMMAND AND ORDER OF BATTLE: *MARKET*

First Allied Airborne Army:	Lt-Gen Lewis H. Brereton (Commanding)
	Lt-Gen Frederick A.M. Browning (Deputy)
1st British Airborne Corps:	Lt-Gen Frederick A.M. Browning (Commanding)
	Brig Gordon Walch
1st British Airborne Division:	Maj-Gen Robert E. Urquhart (Commanding)
	Capt G.C. Roberts (Aide)
Divisional HQ:	Lt-Col Charles MacKenzie (G-1 COS)
	Maj C.F. Newton-Dunn (Ops)
	Maj D.J. Madden (Ops Air)
	Maj Hugh Maguire (G-2 Int)
	Lt-Col Robert Loder-Symonds (Arty)
	Lt-Col E.C.W. Myers (Eng)
	Lt-Col Michael St John Packe (Supply)
	Col Graeme Warrack (Medical)
	Lt-Col G.A. Mobbs (Seaborne Tail)
1st Parachute Brigade:	Brig Gerald W. Lathbury
1st Battalion:	Lt-Col David Dobie
2nd Battalion:	Lt-Col John Frost
3rd Battalion:	Lt-Col John Fitch
4th Parachute Brigade:	Brig John W. Hackett
156th Battalion:	Lt-Col Sir Richard des Voeux
11th Battalion:	Lt-Col George H. Lea
10th Battalion:	Lt-Col Kenneth B.L. Smyth
1st Polish Parachute Brigade:	Maj-Gen Stanislaw Sosabowski
1st Battalion:	Col Rawicz Szczerbo
2nd Battalion:	Capt Sobocinski Waclaw
3rd Battalion:	Maj Ploszewski Waclaw
1st Airlanding Brigade:	Brig Philip H. Hicks
1st Bn The Border Regt:	Lt-Col Thomas Haddon
7th Bn the King's Own Scottish Borderers:	Lt-Col Robert Payton-Reid
2nd Bn South Staffords:	Lt-Col W.D.H. McCardie
1st Airlanding Light Regt, Royal Artillery:	Lt-Col W.F.K. Thompson
21st Independent Parachute Company (Pathfinders):	Maj B.A. Wilson
1st Airborne Reconnaissance Squadron:	Maj C.F.H. Gough
1st Airborne Divison Signals:	Lt-Col T.C.V. Stephenson
	Maj A.J. Deane-Drummond (Deputy)
XVIII US Airborne Corps:	Lt-Gen Matthew B. Ridgeway (Commanding)
82nd US Airborne Division:	Maj-Gen James Gavin (Commanding)
504th Parachute Infantry Regt:	Lt-Col Reuben Tucker
505th Parachute Infantry Regt:	Lt-Col Vandervoort
508th Parachute Infantry Regt:	Lt-Col Lindquist
319th, 320th, 376th and 456th Field Artillery Battalions	
80th Anti-Tank Battalion	
325th Glider Infantry Regiment:	Col Charles Billingslea
101st US Airborne Division:	Maj-Gen Maxwell Taylor (Commanding)
501st Parachute Infantry Regt:	Lt-Col Harry W. Kinnaird
502nd Parachute Infantry Regt:	Lt-Col John H. Michaelis
506th Parachute Infantry Regt:	Col Robert F. Sink
321st, 327th, 377th and 907th Field Artillery Battalions	
81st Anti-Tank Battalion	
327th Glider Infantry Regiment:	Col Joseph P. Harper
326th Airborne Engineer Battalion	
Air Transport Forces	
USAAF IX Troop Carrier Command:	Maj-Gen Paul L. Williams
RAF No 38 Group:	AV-M Leslie Hollinghurst
RAF No 46 Group:	Air Cdre L. Darvall

Base	Units	Aircraft
No 38 Group RAF		
Brize Norton	No 296 Sqn	Albemarle
Manston	No 297 Sqn	Albemarle (Det from Brize Norton)
Harwell	No 295 Sqn	Stirling
	No 570 Sqn	Stirling
Keevil	No 196 Sqn	Stirling
	No 299 Sqn	Stirling
Fairford	No 190 Sqn	Stirling
	No 620 Sqn	Stirling
Tarrant Rushton	No 298 Sqn	Halifax
	No 644 Sqn	Halifax
No 46 Group RAF		
Broadwell	No 512 Sqn	Dakota
	No 575 Sqn	Dakota
Down Ampney	No 48 Sqn	Dakota
	No 272 Sqn	Dakota
Blakehill Farm	No 233 Sqn	Dakota
	No 437 Sqn (RCAF)	Dakota
USAAF IX Troop Carrier Cd		
Barkston Heath	61st TCG	C-47
Folkingham	313th TCG	C-47
Saltby	314th TCG	C-47
Spanhoe	315th TCG	C-47
Cottesmore	316th TCG	C-47
Aldermaston	434th TCG	C-47
Welford	435th TCG	C-47
Membury	436th TCG	C-47
Chilbolton	437th TCG	C-47
Greenham Common	438th TCG	C-47
Balderton	439th TCG	C-47
Bottesford	440th TCG	C-47
Langar	441st TCG	C-47
Ramsbury	442nd TCG	C-47
North Witham	IX TCC Pathfinder School	C-47

Notes: Each USAAF Group comprised three squadrons; Major-Gen Williams therefore had 42 troop-carrier squadrons at his disposal. The two RAF transport Groups had sixteen squadrons between them.

The Douglas C-47, although the same aircraft as the Dakota, was only known by the latter name in RAF service.

Glider equipment of IX TCC consisted entirely of the Waco CG-4A Hadrian. No 38 Group RAF had Horsas and Hamilcars, No 46 Group only Horsas.

CHAPTER 3
The Airborne Plan

In the afternoon of 10 September, General Browning flew back to England from Brussels and notified HQ Airborne Army of the decision on *Market*, and at 1800 hours General Brereton held a conference of his troop carrier and airborne commanders and their staffs at Sunninghill Park. One notable absentee was General Ridgeway, who was in France.

The commanders agreed that the 1st British Airborne Division, together with the Polish Parachute Brigade, should be concentrated for the assault on Arnhem, the principal objective being to capture the bridges there and establish a bridgehead around them. The US 82nd Airborne Division was to capture crossings at Nijmegen and Grave and hold the high ground between Nijmegen and Groesbeek; the advance headquarters of the Airborne Corps were to fly in with the first glider lift of this division. The 101st Airborne Division was to seize the bridges and defiles between Eindhoven and Grave. The decision on the deployment of the two American airborne divisions was made for two main reasons: first, it would ensure that aircraft carrying the 82nd Airborne, which was concentrated in Lincolnshire, would not cross the path of those carrying the 101st Airborne from southern England; and second, it ensured that the 101st Airborne, which had less combat experience than the 82nd, would be the first to make contact with the relieving ground forces.

Field-Marshal Montgomery's proposal for the deployment of the 101st Airborne Division called for it to be landed over a 30-mile strip extending from the primary objectives to within artillery range of the Second Army front. The idea of such extreme dispersion was greeted with dismay by the divisional commander, General Maxwell Taylor, and he had the support of General Brereton. The question still had not been resolved when the conference ended at about 2300 hours.

One decision made on 10 September was that the allocation of aircraft and airfields for *Market* would be essentially the same as the allocation for *Linnet*. In fact, with the exception of a change of assignments between the 437th and 442nd Troop Carrier Groups, there was very little difference in the paratroop serials. As far as the glider serials were concerned, the plan for *Linnet* had envisaged that two gliders would be towed by each tug, whereas in *Market* the tug aircraft were restricted to one glider each. This made it necessary to add two glider serials to the original sequence, and to schedule additional missions on D plus 2 and D plus 3 to bring in the displaced gliders. Another requirement which had not been necessary for *Linnet*, was to schedule a series of resupply missions on D plus 2 and succeeding days.

Another ruling, made by General Brereton on 10 September, was that *Market* would be a daylight operation. This was not without precedent; *Transfigure*, *Linnet* and *Comet* had all been planned as daylight operations. In the case of *Comet*, however, the decision had been made on the assumption that the troop-carrying aircraft and gliders would not meet with serious opposition from German fighters or flak; the position was now rapidly changing for the worse. It was expected that the German night fighter force would provide more effective resistance than the day fighters, but, on the other hand, the flak would be much more accurate by day than by night. General Brereton's decision was influenced by the belief that the supporting air forces could knock out flak positions in advance and also destroy them during the airborne operations; a further reason for preferring to operate in daylight was the fact that the Americans, as yet inexperienced in night navigation to the high standard required, and used as they were to the 'follow-my-leader' principle that had proved so ineffective in Sicily

and Normandy, naturally preferred to operate by day.

The risks involved were that the flak was known to have increased by 35 per cent in the *Market* area, the troop-carrying aircraft were unarmoured, were not equipped with self-sealing tanks, and flew at slow speeds. The decision to operate in daylight when *Comet* was being planned had prompted the AOCs of Nos 38 and 46 Groups to express the opinion that the casualties involved might reach 40 per cent; this opinion was founded on the fear of a leak in security measures, for which the Americans were responsible. In fact, security remained tight until the launching of *Market*.

One reason for drawing heavily on the cancelled airborne operational plans was that, on 10 September, Brereton and his commanders – as yet unaware of Montgomery's supply problems – expected that *Market* might have to be launched as early as the 14th, and it was therefore essential to make the maximum use of existing arrangements. Brereton, however, was concerned about the need to obtain and secure adequate photographic intelligence; in his opinion, H-hour should not be less than 72 hours after the receipt of photographic coverage.

Air reconnaissance was a problem that was never satisfactorily solved during the planning of *Market*. During the week 10–17 September a limited number of tactical air reconnaissance sorties were flown over the proposed landing zones, but they yielded little, if any, useful information about the movements of the enemy. Two RAF reconnaissance wings were involved in this task; No 35 (Recce) Wing of No 84 Group, and No 39 (Recce) Wing of No 83 Group. The latter, which had an

Mustangs of 2nd TAF carried out much of the air reconnaissance task, but were heavily committed elsewhere.

---

establishment of four squadrons (No 400 RCAF with a mixture of Spitfire XIs and Mosquitoes, Nos 414 and 430 RCAF and No 168 RAF with Mustangs) was somewhat hampered during this period by being unable to fly from advanced landing grounds; only the TacR Spitfires of No 400 Sqn were located in the forward area at Brussels/Evere, the rest of the Wing remaining south of the Seine at Avrilly, about 60 miles from Paris. On the other hand, No 35 Wing – Nos 2 and 268 Sqns (Mustangs) and No 4 Sqn (Spitfire XI) – was based near St Omer and was well within range of the Lower Rhine.

Another factor which prevented good reconnaissance was the weather, which during the week before the airborne landings was often misty, causing a number of reconnaissance missions to be abandoned. Also, the enemy exploited to the utmost his ability to camouflage himself and to conceal his movements in the wooded countryside around Arnhem.

Since the two reconnaissance wings had to perform multiple tasks on behalf of the Second Tactical Air Force – keeping a constant watch on enemy movements at the mouth of the Scheldt and searching for V-2 launching sites in Holland accounted for much of the sortie time – only two squadrons were detailed to provide information for the Second Army. Number 400 RCAF Squadron, operating from Brussels, carried out tactical reconnaissances of the roads north of Antwerp and reported on the state of the bridges over the numerous canals and rivers from Turnhout to the banks of the river Maas. Tactical reconnaissances were also made over the Eindhoven region. From Avrilly, No 2 Squadron's Mustangs were despatched to cover the Arnhem sector on 12, 15 and 16 September; the second of these missions had to be abandoned because of poor visibility, but on the other two occasions pilots reported that they had observed no movement in the area. No more than eight Mustangs were employed for the missions over Arnhem – a lamentably weak effort, in view of the importance of securing information on enemy dispositions around the proposed dropping/landing zones.

Other sources of intelligence, from inside Holland itself, were fragmentary and unreliable. A principal problem was that the activities of the Special Operations Executive, which played a vital role in liaising with the various resistance movements in occupied Europe, gathering intelligence and arranging sabotage, had been severely disrupted in Holland during 1943, when the organization had been infiltrated by the Gestapo. There had subsequently been no real co-ordination, and although information did continue to trickle through from the Dutch resistance movement it usually arrived too late to be acted upon and was often based on surmise. This was certainly true in the case of enemy movements in the Arnhem area subsequent to June 1944; there were plenty of estimates, but direct evidence in support was seriously lacking.

There were two main external intelligence-gathering sources. The first was the 'Y' Service, which held the Germans under permanent radio surveillance. Operated by the RAF, it was responsible for the monitoring of all German signals, whether in low-grade or high-grade cypher, radio telephony, or non-Morse transmissions. Then there was Station 'X' at Bletchley Park, the war station of the Government Code and Cypher School, whose highly skilled staff had broken the German *Enigma* codes and endowed the western Allies with the priceless gift of *Ultra*, through which the resulting information was disseminated. By 16 September, *Ultra* was already giving warnings that German resistance in the Arnhem area was likely to be much stiffer than anticipated. Unfortunately, those warnings did not reach key personnel

involved in the planning of *Market* for the simple reason that they were not on the approved list of those cleared to receive the highly sensitive and top secret *Ultra* information. So planning for *Market* proceeded on the assumption that the whole operational area might contain some 15,000 troops and that 8,000 of them would be in the Ede and Arnhem area, which information received prior to June had shown to be an important training centre for the armoured and motorized troops of the SS *Hermann Göring* Division.

It must be stressed, at this point, that at no time during the pre-*Market* preparations and briefings was any real emphasis laid on the fighting qualities and capabilities of the German troops that the airborne forces were likely to encounter, nor on their ability to organize themselves and react quickly to a threat situation. This lack of attention to detail caused concern among some of the Allied airborne commanders; General Sosabowski, in particular, knew very well what the Germans were capable of achieving, and his views were supported by Brigadier J.W. Hackett.[16]

At the Sunninghill Park meeting, General Brereton named Major-General Paul L. Williams as air commander for *Market*, exercising operational control of IX Troop Carrier Command, Nos 38 and 46 Groups, and any bomber aircraft that might be used for resupply. The next morning, Williams came to Brereton with a problem. There were not enough aircraft and gliders to deliver all three airborne divisions and the Polish Brigade to Holland on D-Day. Using every available aircraft, the best Williams could do would be to deliver half the required troop strength on the first day. Vital glider-borne equipment, such as anti-tank guns, artillery and jeeps could only be delivered to units expecting to face strong and immediate counter-attacks.

This was a blow to Brereton, who had anticipated delivering over one-third of the Airborne Army to Holland by glider on D-Day, the remainder going in by parachute. Williams's news now meant that the Airborne Army would have to be delivered piece-meal over a three-day period. The risks attending a commitment of this kind were clear. After the first lift, the enemy would be fully alerted and anti-aircraft fire would intensify with each passing day. Enemy counter-attacks might succeed in surrounding and destroying isolated airborne units before a ground link-up could be made. And there was the danger that prevailing weather conditions, always unpredictable in a European September, might deteriorate to such an extent that the operation would be halted at any time during the three-day period. As an alternative to the three-day plan, it was suggested that the US and British transport forces fly two shuttle missions on the first day; Williams, however, was concerned that any attempt to fly two missions in the hours of daylight available would leave insufficient time for proper maintenance, and this would lead to casualties. The RAF suggested flying the first lift in before dawn, allowing time for a second mission in daylight, but the standard of night flying and navigational training amongst the US aircrews was inadequate for such a task.

A further planning conference was held at 0900 hours on 11 September, this time at Eastcote, the Troop Carrier Command Post where the principal items on the agenda were selection of routes, selection of dropping/landing zones, and early decisions on the loading plan. The troop-carrier and airborne staffs had been working well into the night, a troop-carrier planning committee working out route plans for approval by the Airborne, and Airborne divisional staffs selecting drop and landing zones for acceptance by the conference.

The base airfields for the complete operation formed two distinct groups – a southern group of eight British and six US airfields and an eastern group of eight US airfields. Aircraft from the southern group would form up over Hatfield, Hertfordshire, and those from the eastern group over March, Cambridgeshire. From these initial rendezvous points on D-Day, serials of aircraft for the Arnhem and Grave–Nijmegen sectors would form up over Aldeburgh, on the coast of east Suffolk, before taking the northern route, and those destined for the Eindhoven sector over the North Foreland for the southern route.

The sea crossing on the northern route was from the rendezvous at Aldeburgh direct to the western end of Schouwen Island, a distance of 94 miles, and from there straight on for a further eighteen miles to the island's eastern tip. The route then continued for another 52 miles to the initial point, which was code-named *Ellis*; this was about three miles south of 's Hertogenbosch and was readily identifiable because of several road intersections in the area.

From here, the Arnhem zones lay 30 miles to the north-east and the Nijmegen zones 25 miles east-north-east.

On the southern route, aircraft skirted the London metropolitan area, avoiding the capital's AA and barrage balloon defences, and crossed the coast at Bradwell Bay in Essex before turning south-east to the North Foreland, a 34-mile flight over the Thames estuary. From the North Foreland the route ran for 159 miles to the initial point, named *Delos*, at the position where the route intersected the Albert Canal. At *Delos*, aircraft turned north-eastwards to the landing zones at Eindhoven, cutting between known flak concentrations at Eindhoven and Tilburg. On 16 September, General Williams decided to bend the route slightly southwards to avoid a pocket of German troops who were holding out to the south of the Scheldt. The revised route ran from *Catalina*, a landfall point four miles north-east of Ostend, to the outskirts of Ghent airfield and from there to *Delos*.

On the northern route, from the initial rendezvous at Hatfield, the aircraft were to fly in three parallel streams one and a half miles apart; this system had first been devised for Operation *Linnet*. The total time length of the column on D-Day would be about 65 minutes.

Further concentration was achieved by spacing the American parachute serials at four-minute intervals and glider serials at seven-minute intervals, a procedure made possible by the fact that the operation was mounted in daylight. During the night operations in Normandy, the spacing had been six and ten minutes respectively. The closer spacing of serials in *Market* and the use of two routes, each with three lanes of traffic, meant that if all went well 1,055 loads of paratroops and 478 gliders could be delivered within 65 minutes.

On completion of their mission, all transport aircraft were to turn immediately through 180° on a reciprocal course to clear the target areas. On the southern route, American troop-carrying aircraft were to maintain 1,500 ft on the outward trip, descending to 500 ft to make their drop or release, then return at 3,000 ft to avoid incoming traffic. The American troop-carriers were to fly in serials of between 27 and 45 aircraft, each serial being composed of Vs of nine aircraft in line astern. Tug and glider combinations would be in serials of between 30 and 50, flying in pairs in echelon to

Pathfinders of the 21st Independent Parachute Company being briefed before the Arnhem operation. They carried out their task with success.

starboard of the troop carriers. On the northern route, the tug and glider combinations of Nos 38 and 46 Groups would proceed in a loose column of pairs at ten-second intervals, flying at 2,500 ft (1,000 ft above the troop-carriers) en route to the landing zones. After release, they would climb to 5,000–7,000 ft for the flight home.

D-Day for *Market* had already been tentatively agreed at the initial conference on 10 September; the operation was to begin on Sunday the 17th. On 12 September, H-Hour – the moment when the first troop carrier serials, exclusive of pathfinders, would arrive over their zones – was set for 1300 hours, Zone A Time, which was one hour ahead of Greenwich Mean Time.

While the routes to the objectives were being settled, the airborne division commanders and their staffs were at work selecting the dropping and landing zones in their respective areas. All were agreed on one matter; the terrain, especially in the north at Arnhem, was more favourable for airborne operations than Normandy's.

The town of Arnhem, which in 1944 had a population of some 100,000, lay on the rising ground which formed the northern bank of the Lower Rhine. The terrain north of the town rose to over 100 feet above sea level and consisted mainly of open heath and arable land interspersed with thick belts of pine forest. The southern bank of the Rhine opposite the town was mostly meadowland and polder (fenland), so low-lying that it was prone to flooding if the river rose by more than a few feet. Consequently, this area was sparsely settled, contrasting with the thriving urban community on the northern bank. The flooding factor dissuaded the planners from choosing landing and dropping zones in that area, because extricating airborne forces from sodden ground invariably resulted in a considerable loss of effort. This had happened in Normandy, where one of the dropping zones selected for the 6th Airborne Division's pathfinder teams had proved to be extremely wet and treacherous. In addition to the risks attending an air-drop on boggy ground, the area on the southern bank of the Rhine was very exposed and could easily be covered by fire from the opposite bank. Another factor was a network of irrigation ditches which, it was thought, might jeopardize the safe landing of gliders and paratroops as well as hindering the concentration of men and vehicles.

The main landing and dropping zones were therefore selected on the high ground west-north-west of the town at distances varying from five to eight miles from 1st Airborne Division's principal objective, the single-span steel bridge by which the highway running north from Hasselt crossed the Lower Rhine into Arnhem. The terrain in this area was excellent for landing both paratroops and gliders; it consisted of open clearings and heath country mostly covered with heather, which would provide a cushioning effect for landings.

The fact that all the zones were screened on two and often three sides by thick belts of pine woods constituted a mixed blessing. From the airborne forces' point of view the surrounding woods provided an effective screen for unloading and rendezvous activities, and because of the clear demarcation between thick wood and open country the zones were easily discernible from the air. However, once the element of surprise had been lost the woods would provide good cover for counter-attacking enemy forces.

A major contributory factor in the selection of the zones was the fear expressed by the AOCs of the two RAF transport groups that flak concentrations known to exist close to Arnhem might lead to unacceptable casualties. There is no doubt that the RAF commanders were badly shaken when the plan for *Market* was first revealed and the decision was made to fly at low level in daylight to an area considered to have heavy flak defences. On 11 September, Air Vice-Marshal Hollinghurst, AOC No 38 Group, wrote to General Williams:

McIntyre (AEAF's representative at the initial planning conference held on the previous day) points out that the heavy flak around the three towns in which we are interested has approximately doubled during the last two days. This information has been obtained from a comparison of air photographs. He also mentioned that a force of Lightnings lost 12 out of 35 near Aachen yesterday – most of these were from flak.

It looks therefore that the ground situation as regards

Market is worsening daily. I feel that the whole area should now be re-examined from the point of view of flak . . . we should then be able to give a fresh estimate of the probable losses so that those responsible can consider whether it affects their decision that the game is worth the candle . . . we should, I think, be blameworthy if we left the Army under any delusion (sic) as to what proportion of the force we thought would be safely delivered.[17]

Intelligence continued to predict that flak defences were increasing around Arnhem, and the formidable total thought to be available on 14 September was assessed as follows:

Arnhem: Light flak – 73 occupied and 31 unoccupied
                              emplacements.
              Heavy flak – 17 occupied and 6 unoccupied
                              emplacements.
Deelen: Light flak – 57 occupied and 17 unoccupied
                              emplacements.
              Heavy flak – 17 occupied and 12 unoccupied
                              emplacements.

Faced with this sort of appreciation, it is little wonder that the RAF commanders shuddered at the thought of the losses likely to be incurred by slow-flying transport aircraft, without armour or self-sealing tanks, flying in formation at a height where every type of weapon from heavy flak to small arms fire was effective. Their predictions of 40 per cent casualties do not seem so unreasonable without the benefit of hindsight. They were therefore very reluctant to agree to the landing zones being placed too near to such formidable defences, and the existence of excellent areas of ground away from most of the anti-aircraft fire must have seemed purpose-made to the aerial planners.

Criticism has also been laid at the feet of the 1st Airborne Division's commander, Major-General Robert 'Roy' Urquhart. In the words of one historian,

Unlike the other two airborne division commanders going into Holland, Urquhart had never made a parachute jump and had never been inside a glider. He had, quite unexpectedly, been chosen for his airborne assignment when the previous division commander, General Eric Down, was transferred to India in January 1944 to organize new airborne units there. But although he was short on airborne service, Urquhart was long on combat experience. In many vicious battles across North Africa, on Sicily, and in Italy, he had proven himself an exceptionally competent combat leader with the 51st Highland Division. . . .

As General Urquhart correctly saw it, the formidable highway bridge in Arnhem was his primary D-Day objective. But with no airborne combat experience to guide his thinking, and the RAF's complaining about the very real danger of numerous German flak batteries around Arnhem, Urquhart made the fatal error of plotting his DZs and LZs six to eight miles west of the highway bridge. In so doing, he sacrificed surprise – an absolute necessity for success in any initial airborne strike – and consigned his troops to marching for more than two hours across territory full of alerted enemy soldiers. During those two hours, even the worst German tactician in Arnhem would be able to guess the objective of the British airborne troops and would order the bridge either to be destroyed or to be strongly reinforced.[18]

In fairness to both the RAF transport commanders and General Urquhart, only hindsight has revealed the full impact that the final selection of zones was to have on the course of the Arnhem battle. Jumping ahead a little, the zone selection was surely at least partly justified by the results of the first drop. The drop, near Heelsum, was almost entirely untroubled by the flak defences of Arnhem, but, instead of receiving credit for selecting zones which reduced both the number of guns able to fire and the effectiveness of those that could, the very success of the plan on the first day has been turned around and used to justify a point of view which belittles the effectiveness of the flak and states that drop zones could safely have been located near the bridge on the south bank of the Rhine. Apart from the problem of unsuitable terrain, if the drop had been undertaken on the open areas to the south of the bridge the transports would have faced the full weight of the Arnhem and Deelen defences. After dropping, the aircraft would have been forced to turn away from the zones in a northerly direction, because the proximity of the Nijmegen drop zones and the risk of collision with American aircraft turning north after their drop precluded a turn to the south. A turn to the north would not only have taken the transports across the town of Arnhem; it would also have meant overflying the defences at Deelen, effectively requiring that the returning aircraft fly over two belts of anti-aircraft guns. Furthermore, an important command bunker for the *Luftwaffe* fighter defences in the west was situated to the north of Arnhem, between the town and Deelen airfield, and this bunker was also protected by flak positions.

The danger that might have attended such a

course is well illustrated by the losses suffered by a force of Mosquitoes from No 2 Group which bombed barracks in Arnhem shortly before the first lift arrived: of 32 aircraft which attacked, two were shot down and several more were damaged, and the fast and manoeuvrable Mosquito presented a much more difficult target to a flak gunner than the Stirlings, Halifaxes and Dakotas of Nos 38 and 46 Groups. It should also be remembered that anti-flak operations were not permitted inside the bomb line established before the operation began.

Many critics also point to the fact that the Americans landed as close to their objectives as possible, and quote General Gavin's comments on the subject with approval: 'It is in general better to take losses and land on the objective than to have to fight after landing in order to reach the objective.' In general this is true, and few of the RAF officers involved in planning *Market* would have disagreed, but in particular cases it may not be an immutable law, and there is one significant exception to the placing of US landing zones close to their objectives during *Market*. At Nijmegen, Gavin himself chose not to land troops of the 82nd Airborne Division close to the bridge primarily because the town was thought to contain 86 light and 22 heavy anti-aircraft guns. This was the only objective in the US sector which was heavily defended by adjacent flak positions (other than Eindhoven which was also ignored, partly because of flak and partly for other reasons) and it is significant that Gavin chose to leave its capture until he had secured his other objectives. In the event, it was not captured until D plus 3, a delay which had serious consequences for the troops fighting in and around Arnhem.

The 1st Airborne Division's initial paratroop drop was to be made essentially on the same spot selected for the first drop of Operation *Comet*. This zone, DZ X, lay about six miles north-west of the centre of Arnhem, north of the village of Heelsum, and just south of the Amsterdam–Arnhem railway. It was an irregular area of about one square mile. Also as envisaged in *Comet*, the first British gliders were to land on LZ 'S', a narrow strip over a mile long and about half a mile wide, a little way north-east of DZ 'X' and on the other side of the railway. The next serial of gliders, which in the *Comet* plan had been assigned to the Nijmegen area, was now assigned a new zone, LZ 'Z', which adjoined DZ 'X' and extended for about half a mile to the east of it.

On D Plus 1 a second instalment of paratroops, originally assigned to the Nijmegen sector in *Comet*, was to drop on DZ 'Y', a quadrangle of open ground north of the Amsterdam railway and about a mile west of LZ 'S'. Its big advantage was that it was a good eight miles away from the highway bridge. Gliders on D plus 1 would use DZ 'X' as a landing zone, and supplies were to be dropped on DZ 'L', a piece of ground one-quarter of a square mile in area located about half a mile east of LZ 'S'.

The success of this plan depended on establishing and maintaining control over a strip of land eight miles long and up to three miles wide extending from DZ 'Y' to the Arnhem road bridge, a major task for half an airborne division. And although the road bridge was the primary objective, it was not the only one. A second highway bridge into the town had been destroyed, but a railway bridge two and a half miles east of the highway was still intact, and at Heveadorp, a mile below the railway bridge, there was a ferry. The Germans were also known to have built a pontoon bridge near the highway. All these objectives were to be seized if possible.

The Germans constructed a pontoon bridge over the Rhine near Arnhem, but quickly destroyed it.

The seizure of the main bridge was to be carried out by the 1st Parachute Brigade, which would then form a small semi-circle running through the town of Arnhem, its ends firmly anchored on the Lower Rhine to east and west. It was hoped that the 1st Brigade would be able to accomplish its main tasks by nightfall on D-Day. As soon as the remainder of the Division landed on D plus 1, they were to advance on Arnhem and construct a large perimeter running around the town itself, along the high ground to the west and north-west and across the flat land to the east and south-east. As soon as this second perimeter was formed, the 1st Parachute Brigade would come into reserve and be reinforced by the Polish Parachute Brigade, which would drop on DZ 'K' just south of the river near the main bridge. Part of the Brigade was to land in gliders on the second day just north-east of the village of Wolfheze. So, by the end of the second day, when it was expected that the 1st Airborne Division would be relieved by spearheads of XXX Corps, there would be an outer defence around Arnhem and a solid reserve around the bridge itself. Also on D plus 2, during which the outlying areas would be abandoned to shorten the line of defence, troops and equipment of the US 878th Aviation Engineer Battalion would land by glider on DZ/LZ 'L'; the function of this battalion was to prepare landing strips north of Arnhem to enable Dakotas to fly in the 52nd Lowland Division provided the military situation permitted. The airstrips were to be defended by the 2nd Airlanding Light AA Battery, which was also to be landed by glider. Supply drops on D plus 2 were to be made at Supply Drop Point (SDP) 'V', at a road junction less than a mile west of the outskirts of Arnhem.

Fourteen miles south of Arnhem, the task of Brigadier-General Gavin's US 82nd Airborne Division was to capture and hold a bridge over the Maas outside the village of Grave five miles south-west of Nijmegen, at least one of four bridges over the Maas-Waal Canal between Grave and Nijmegen, and the bridge over the Waal at Nijmegen itself. Success in holding these objectives depended on capturing the Groesbeek Heights, a ridge two miles south-east of Nijmegen. About 300 feet high, it was the only high ground in the vicinity and dominated the whole area.

After assessing the tactical situation, Gavin decided that his best plan would be to leave Nijmegen to be taken by ground forces after his other objectives had been secured. It was not only the threat from known or suspected enemy flak positions that influenced this decision; Gavin realized that without possession of the ridge and the other crossings, the Nijmegen bridge would be of little immediate value. He therefore planned that on D-Day he would drop the 505th and 508th Parachute Infantry Regiments and the 376th Parachute Field Artillery Battalion into two DZs, both located between the Groesbeek Heights and the Reichswald Forest. These lay between three and four miles south-east of Nijmegen and would put his forces in a good position for a speedy attack on the ridge with maximum force prior to setting up a defensive perimeter that would include both ridge and zones. This action, Gavin hoped, would prevent the zones from being overrun by strong enemy counter-attacks, as had happened in Normandy.

The northernmost zone, DZ 'T', was in the form of an oval 3,000 yards long from east to west and three-quarters of a mile wide. It lay in a triangle formed by a railway running along its southern edge and by two roads which intersected at the village of Wyler, several hundred yards to the north-east. Serials approaching this zone would pass close to the bridge at Grave, seven miles to the west, and then cross the Maas-Waal Canal about three miles away.

About 3,000 yards south-west of DZ 'T' was a slightly smaller oval, DZ 'N', flanked on its northern and western sides by the woods of the Groesbeek ridge. Transport crews approaching this zone would have an excellent landmark on the line of flight: the junction of the canal and the Maas river, a mile and a half to the west.

The landing zones selected by General Gavin lay between the two DZs and overlapped them both. Together, the LZs formed an area three and a half miles from north to south and a mile and a half from east to west. It was calculated that the two zones, LZ 'T' and LZ 'N', would be able to receive between 700 and 900 gliders, sufficient for the Division's needs. The southerly zone, LZ 'N', was also designated for parachute resupply missions.

Having made certain that he had forces in sufficient strength to capture the Groesbeek Heights, Gavin selected a third jump area, DZ 'O', within his airhead. This lay on flat, open land astride the Eindhoven–Nijmegen highway midway between the big iron road bridge over the Maas north of Grave. The troops of Colonel Reuben Tucker's 504th Parachute Infantry Regiment, assigned to this DZ, were to attack both the Grave bridge a mile to the west of the zone and also three bridges over the canal between one and two miles to the east.

Tucker, certain that the bridge at Grave would be defended and prepared for demolition, pressed for a company of paratroops to be drooped on a special DZ on the south side of the river half a mile from the end of the bridge so that a rapid attack could be made. The ground was low, marshy and criss-crossed by ditches, but the poor nature of the terrain was judged to be an acceptable risk and the plan was adopted 36 hours before *Market* began. It is perhaps worth noting that a similar plan for the rapid seizure of the road bridge at Arnhem by a *coup de main* force had been adopted when Operation

Comet was planned, but it was dropped during the *Market* planning and nothing was put in its place.

The final mission into the 82nd Airborne Division's airhead on D-Day would be carried out by No 38 Group RAF, which would deliver General Browning and the entire staff of I Airborne Corps to LZ 'N' in 32 Horsa and six CG-4A gliders; it would be the first time that any Corps HQ was brought into combat in this way. Browning and his staff were scheduled to land at 1400 hrs and set up their HQ alongside General Gavin's command post just south of Groesbeek, a couple of miles from the edge of the Reichswald.

In planning his D plus 1 operations, General Gavin decided on a large-scale landing by 454 CG-4As, carrying the bulk of his divisional artillery into LZ 'N'. The airborne mission in this sector would end on D plus 2 with a landing by 406 Wacos on LZ 'T', bringing in the 325th Glider Infantry Regiment, the 80th Anti-Aircraft Battalion and various engineer, reconnaissance and military police glider units.

The selection of the 101st Airborne Division's dropping zones, as mentioned earlier, had been surrounded by some controversy, General Maxwell Taylor objecting strongly to Montgomery's proposal that the Division be strung out along a 30-mile strip. General Brereton personally took up the matter with Montgomery after the original planning conference at Sunninghill, and it was agreed to let the matter be settled by direct discussion between General Taylor and the Second Army Commander, General Miles Dempsey. They met at Montgomery's headquarters on 12 September and worked out a solution. Since Dempsey was confident of Second Army's ability to break through to Eindhoven quickly, the 101st Airborne Division's tasks were redefined. It would now be responsible for taking a series of crossings in a sixteen-mile area between Veghel and Eindhoven, postponing the assault on the town until later on D-Day. A parachute drop close to Eindhoven was therefore unnecessary, leaving Taylor free to select dropping and landing zones further north.

The initial tasks allotted to the 101st Airborne Division were to take a bridge over the Wilhelmina Canal at Zon, five miles north of Eindhoven; a bridge over the Dommel river at St Oedenrode four miles north of Zon, and four bridges over the Aa river and the Willems Canal at Veghel, which was five miles north-east of St Oedenrode and thirteen

miles south-west of Grave. Of these objectives the two canal bridges were the most important, since the canals were twenty yards across and too deep for tanks. None of the rivers, on the other hand, was more than 25 feet wide. When these objectives were secured the paratroops were to advance on Eindhoven, and if possible take four bridges there over the upper Dommel.

Taylor's plan envisaged landing the bulk of his Division in a single large area halfway between Zon and St Oedenrode, from which his forces could strike quickly at both objectives and then move against Eindhoven. The chosen area was on the western side of the Zon–St Oedenrode highway, bounded to the south by the Zonsche Forest. The Wilhelmina Canal lay on the other side of this belt of woods, running east–west to intersect a road and railway running north–west from Eindhoven.

In this open area, a large oblong measuring 4,000 by 2,800 yards was marked out. This was split into two equally-sized drop zones, DZs 'B' and 'C'. A landing zone, LZ 'W', was superimposed on the DZs, being slightly narrower from north to south and extending 1,000 yards further west.

Taylor planned to drop all three of his parachute infantry regiments – the 501st, 502nd and 506th – into this area on D-Day, so that his forces could be rapidly assembled, but this was modified to allow for the dropping of one regiment, the 501st, farther north for the attack on Veghel. For this purpose a third drop zone, DZ 'A', was selected about a mile south-west of the town. This zone, also an oval, was about two miles long from east to west and some 2,000 yards wide; it was bounded to the north by a railway line running east to Veghel, and to the south-east by the Eindhoven–Arnhem highway. The bridges over the Willems Canal were only a few hundred yards to the north-east, but the Aa river was a mile further on. To reach it, the paratroops would have to secure a crossing over the canal and then advance through a populated area before they would be in a position to attack the road and railway bridges over the river. This led to a further modification in the plan, a smaller zone known as DZ 'A-1' being picked about a mile to the north of DZ A on the opposite side of the canal. From DZ 'A-1', a single battalion of the 501st could quickly assemble and move on the river bridges.

Before nightfall on D-Day, General Taylor planned to bring in 70 Waco gliders with supporting artillery and other essential equipment; on D plus 1 450 more Wacos would land in the same area, LZ 'W', carrying two battalions of the 327th Glider Infantry Regiment, the 326th Airborne Engineer Battalion, and the 326th Airborne Medical Company. Finally, on D plus 2, another 385 Wacos would deliver the third battalion of the 327th Glider Infantry, three battalions of artillery, and the 81st Anti-Tank Battalion.

The possibility that poor navigation might upset the smooth running of *Market* was a matter of great concern to the planners, who were at pains to ensure that adequate radio and radar navigational devices were available to the troop-carrier formations. The first of these was *Gee*, a fixing system that relayed electronic pulses from three ground stations to receiver equipment in the aircraft. The latter measured the difference in time of receipt of signals from the ground stations and converted the resulting information into terms of distance. Two sets of readings were plotted on a special chart, the point of intersection being the aircraft's position. *Gee* had been fitted to aircraft of No 38 Group RAF since the autumn of 1943, and at a later date No 46 Group's Dakotas were also equipped with the device. After the Normandy operations, Gee was also installed in aircraft of IX Troop Carrier Command, although only the lead crew of each serial was authorized to use it. The Americans also had a limited number of SCR-717 sets; the SCR-717 was a height-finding device developed for use in aircraft operating at low altitude.

The other principal aid was a homing device called *Rebecca/Eureka*. Developed by the Tele-communications Research Establishment at Great Malvern, *Eureka* was a beacon, set up on the ground and set to receive and transmit on fixed frequencies; *Rebecca* was the transceiver equipment carried in the aircraft. On receiving an impulse from the aircraft's *Rebecca* set, *Eureka* on the ground automatically replied, giving the aircraft captain his bearing to and distance from the beacon. *Eureka* beacons were set up at the troop-carrier assembly points and also – together with non-directional beacons called *Occults* – at departure points on the English coast. In addition, marker boats with *Eureka* beacons and green holophane lights were positioned on the northern and southern routes; these craft were code-named *Tampa* and *Miami*. On the southern route, which was mostly over friendly territory, the initial

point *Delos* was to have a *Eureka* beacon and a holophane light and was to be marked by green smoke. As a further aid to route identification, a large white panel T was to be laid out by the ground forces near Gheel, with smoke markers beyond its tip pointing the way to the front line. The front itself was also to be marked as clearly as possible with smoke generators and panels. A combination of *Eureka* beacons, smoke and panels was also to be used by the pathfinder teams, which were to go in to their respective zones fifteen to twenty minutes before the main force arrived.

With en route communications assured as adequately as possible, the planners turned their attention to the question of air support for *Market*. This was to be co-ordinated from the AEAF Rear HQ at Stanmore, Middlesex, where a conference was convened by Air Marshal Leigh-Mallory in the late afternoon of 12 September. Since many of the air support requirements had already been worked out in connection with the two earlier planned airborne operations, *Linnet* and *Comet*, it did not take long to determine the roles that would be played by the various air forces. In summary, the air support plan was as follows:

a On D-Day, all flak positions along the route were to be attacked by the Eighth US Army Air Force and by squadrons of the Air Defence of Great Britain (ADGB).

b Throughout the whole operation, the Eighth US Army Air Force was to provide heavy escort over the route, both to and from the dropping zones.

c After the air landings, cover was to be maintained over the landing areas by the Ninth US Army Air Force in the daytime and by ADGB at night.

d Bomber Command aircraft were to attack enemy day fighter airfields and fixed flak positions on D minus 1.

e Forty aircraft of Bomber Command were to drop dummy parachutes west of Utrecht, east of Arnhem and at Emmerich on the night of D/D plus 1.

f Aircraft of No 2 Group RAF were to attack parks in the dropping and landing zone area, their attacks to finish by H minus 25.

g Aircraft of 2nd Tactical Air Force, RAF, were to carry out armed reconnaissance in the dropping and landing zone areas.

h Aircraft of RAF Coastal Command were to carry out diversionary missions outside the area of airborne operations.

In addition, tentative plans were made for a resupply mission by about 250 bombers of the Eighth Air Force on D plus 1; this would free the transport aircraft from resupply duties, enabling them to bring in more airborne troops.

The original air support plan was somewhat revised and refined on 15 September, when Leigh-Mallory called a second conference at Stanmore. It was attended by representatives of ADGB, Bomber and Coastal Commands and the Eighth and Ninth US Air Forces. There was, however, no representative from 2nd TAF, although one had been requested in a signal sent by AEAF Rear. It is not recorded which 2nd TAF representative had been selected by its commander, Air Marshal Sir Arthur Coningham, to attend the meeting, but bad weather curtailing flights from Brussels was apparently the reason for his absence. The meeting went ahead without the viewpoint of 2nd TAF being aired, and as historian John Terraine points out:

It is extraordinary that Coningham was prepared to accept this situation – especially in view of what the Airborne Army plan contained. It is equally astonishing, of course, that General Brereton, that Army's commander, and an ex-Tactical Air Force commander himself, should also have accepted it. It is astonishing that Montgomery and his 21st Army Group Staff accepted it. For what was laid down was this:
    In the final plan the local tactical air group (83 Group) was ordered to be grounded during the time of airlifts and resupply. When these were postponed for several hours because of bad weather in England, 83 Group's aircraft remained grounded until released from England. During those hours the whole Arnhem operation had no close air support from Second Tactical Air Force.[19]
    At the 15 September meeting, Airborne Army also asked that four groups of US fighter-bombers be provided to neutralize flak and ground fire on the southern route between the IP and DZ during the operation. Ninth AF operations section was informed of this request by telephone some hours after the meeting; as the official US history comments rather wryly, 'A great deal of preliminary notification on assignments in *Market* appears to have been done by telephone from Eastcote or Stanmore.'[20]

The telephone call, nevertheless, appears to have reached the right ears, because in the event the four Ninth Air Force fighter groups were despatched on

The Hawker Typhoon was the most effective Allied fighter-bomber, but at Arnhem its operations were severely restricted.

schedule to deal with the enemy flak, as we shall see later. But it was a different story with the RAF 2nd Tactical Air Force's contribution. Here, there is evidence that the tactical air plan never got as far as the group commanders who were supposed to put it into action. The AOC No 83 Group, Air Vice-Marshal Harry Broadhurst, commented later:

Here I had all these rocket-firing Typhoons but I didn't even know there was going to be an airborne drop about fifteen miles ahead of me. I was told not to interfere, to look after XXX Corps; the Eighth Air Force would look after the airborne drop, but of course they had no communications with the people on the ground. I got an *Ultra* which Hitler had sent, moving another armoured division up to the drop area, but I couldn't do anything about it except to warn General Dempsey to get his Y people working hard on it to ascertain the movements of this armoured division. Eventually we got information from Y and I rang up headquarters to be told to mind my own business. So that armoured division was not attacked in any way. I had friends in our airborne army whom I talked to long after the war and they didn't even know what army co-operation was. They had been separated from the run-of-the-mill day-to-day stuff; they were a magnificent bunch of chaps but the thought of dropping down and communicating immediately with the aircraft overhead hadn't dawned on them. . . It had been very disheartening to see what happened at Arnhem, when an enormous amount of courage was expended by people who hadn't a clue how to ask the Air Force to come and help.[21]

This was not really the case; two air support parties with SCR-193 radios for contacting Second Army with requests for air support, and VHF SCR-522 sets for direct communication with tactical aircraft, were allotted to each of the airborne divisions and to Browning's headquarters. The fact that they failed to play their intended part was due entirely to misfortune.

Yet Broadhurst's comment is interesting, because it does reveal a serious communications failure somewhere down the line. It would not be the last.

CHAPTER 4

The Germans Regroup

On 4 September, 1944 – the day that General Horrocks' tanks entered Antwerp – troops of the German 719th Infantry Division under the command of *Generalleutnant* Karl Sievers began to form a defensive line on the north bank of the Albert Canal. The 719th Infantry was a fortress division which had been on garrison duty on the Dutch coast since 1940; it was composed mainly of elderly 'B' troops, considered unfit for active service at the front. Some had seen active service in the previous world war, but few had heard a shot fired in anger in the present one. Their ranks were bolstered by some *Luftwaffe* ground personnel and a Dutch SS battalion. In general, morale was low, equipment poor and desertions frequent, particularly from the ranks of the Dutch SS.

Yet this division, occupying a front from Antwerp to Hasselt, was the only coherent German force partially blocking a previously undefended gap nearly 60 miles across between Antwerp and Maastricht. The bulk of Sievers' forces lay on the western sector of the tenuous front. Had there been a strong Allied thrust against the western sector at this point, the whole defensive line would have crumbled. But it would be 48 hours before Horrocks' armoured divisions, starved of fuel and supplies, were in a position to resume the northward drive.

The German High Command was unaware of 21st Army Group's supply difficulties, and the capture of Antwerp, coming hard on the heels of the disintegration of Army Group B in the west and of Army Group Centre in the east, was a profound shock to the General Staff. In the early afternoon of 4 September, *Generaloberst* Alfred Jodl, head of the *Wehrmacht* Operations Staff, made a telephone call from Hitler's headquarters at Rastenburg in East Prussia. Its recipient was *Generaloberst* Kurt Student, commanding the German airborne forces. Jodl instructed him to collect all available units and build a new front on the Albert Canal. The 'available units' were to come under the orders of a new formation to be known as the First *Fallschirmjäger* (Paratroop) Army. Its core was to be formed from 30,000 *Luftwaffe* personnel released from other duties by *Reichsmarschall* Hermann Göring.

Generaloberst Kurt Student, the resourceful and experienced commander of the 1st *Fallschirmjäger* Army. His powers of organisation were astonishing.

Amidst all the frantic improvisation, the Albert Canal defences were reinforced from an unexpected quarter. On 4 September, the battered remnants of the German 85th Infantry Division, commanded by *Generalleutnant* Kurt Chill, reached Turnhout in northern Belgium, having collected scattered units of the 84th and 89th Divisions en route. At Turnhout, Chill received orders from Seventh Army to take his troops to the Rhineland for rest and reinforcement. He also learned that Brussels had fallen to the Allies.

Chill, an energetic and determined commander, at once decided to ignore Seventh Army's orders. On his own initiative, he moved his troops to the northern bank of the Albert Canal between Massenhoven and Kwaadmechelen. He also set up reception centres at the bridges to the east and west of Herentals, where groups of German soldiers fleeing northwards were collected and assigned to his command. On 5 September, Chill contacted Sievers and the two agreed that Chill would defend the eastern part of the canal while Sievers would be responsible for the sector between Herentals and Antwerp. This arrangement was confirmed the next day by *General der Infanterie* Hans Reinhardt, commanding LXXXVIII Corps, who detached a regiment of the 719th Division to strengthen Chill's line. Chill's formation now became known as *Kampfgruppe* (Battle Group) Chill, a somewhat grandiose title for what was essentially a collection of exhausted, demoralized men; yet they were to prove capable of fending off the first British attacks across the canal.

More German reinforcements arrived to plug the gap. *General der Flieger* Friedrich Christiansen, the *Wehrmacht* Supreme Commander in the Netherlands, diverted *Luftwaffe* personnel to the field forces; many of these were very effective, being experienced in handling the dual-purpose 88-mm anti-aircraft/anti-tank gun. Then, on 7 September, the 176th Infantry Division began arriving from Aachen; a so-called *Kranken* Division, it comprised personnel who had been classed as medically unfit for front-line service. Commanded by *Oberst* Christian Landau the 176th had previously been assigned to the defences of the Siegfried Line. Now, placed under the orders of Kurt Student, it went into position along the Albert Canal between Hasselt and Maastricht.

There was now an unbroken line, if not a particularly strong one, stretching along the Albert Canal from Antwerp to Maastricht. Whether that line could be held for any length of time depended on the speed with which the First *Fallschirmjäger* Army could be formed and brought into action.

On 5 September, when Student flew to Berlin for a meeting with *Feldmarschall* Model, commanding what was left of Army Group B, his First *Fallschirmjäger* Army was already becoming something more than an organization on paper. The forces available to it at this point included *Fallschirmjäger* Regiment 6, the 1st Battalion of *Fallschirmjäger* Regiment 2, and five newly-raised parachute regiments. Three of the latter, all untrained, were in the process of being formed into 7 *Fallschirmjäger* Division. By far the most effective formation was *Fallschirmjäger* Regiment 6 under *Oberstleutnant* Friedrich-August Baron von der Heydte, veteran of the airborne assault on Crete. The regiment had taken a terrible mauling in Normandy, losing 3,000 men killed or missing in a series of bitter actions against US forces. Just over 1,000 had escaped from France, and now the regiment was reforming in Güstrow-Mecklenberg in Germany; as befitted a veteran, battle-hardened formation, its morale remained high.

At the end of his discussions with Student, Model assigned the First *Fallschirmjäger* Army to a 75-mile front running from the North Sea to Maastricht and placed Reinhardt's LXXXVIII Corps under Student's command, so that there was now a front of 32 battalions supported by a limited amount of artillery and armoured fighting vehicles. Student had succeeded in obtaining 20 heavy, medium and light anti-aircraft batteries, together with 25 self-propelled assault guns and tank destroyers; the 88-mm batteries, each with six to eight guns, would at least enable him to form an effective anti-tank defence at key points.

The assignment of the First *Fallschirmjäger* Army to the front in Holland was a masterpiece of logistical organization. From assembly areas all over northern Germany, the first units were on their way 48 hours after mobilization, collecting weapons and other equipment deposited at designated railway stations, much of it salvaged from other units decimated during the fighting in France. As yet the Paratroop Army numbered only about 20,000 men, but more were to come.

In western Holland, General von Zangen's

A soldier of Student's Paratroop Army digs in at the Neerpelt bridgehead. German resistance to the advance of XXX Corps stiffened with amazing speed.

established a bridgehead across the canal at Beeringen, and then pushed slowly forward to gain two more bridgeheads over the Meuse–Escaut Canal. The most important of these, at De Groote Barrier on the Hechtel–Eindhoven road, was established on 10 September. This, the so-called Neerpelt bridgehead, gave XXX Corps a foothold over the Meuse–Escaut Canal while the territory north of the Albert Canal was progressively cleared of Germans from a second bridgehead at Gheel. The Germans had been unable to stem the relentless drive of the British armour, but they had won time. Whereas XXX Corps had covered a distance of 250 miles in the six days up to 4 September, the fifteen miles from the Albert Canal to the Meuse–Escaut Canal had cost four days of bitter fighting.

The Meuse–Escaut (or Maas–Scheldt) Canal was the last water barrier separating Belgium from Holland, and the capture of the bridge just to the west of Neerpelt was a serious setback for the Germans, who at once set about strengthening their defences immediately opposite. One of the newly-formed German parachute regiments, under *Oberst* von Hoffmann, which had just arrived at the front, was immediately moved up to this sector and Hoffman charged with containing any further British advance along the Hechtel–Valkenswaard road. The Regiment *Hoffmann* had three battalions and an anti-tank company with eight 75 mm guns. It was only partly trained and many of its personnel had no combat experience. Its task was to eliminate the Neerpelt bridgehead; the attack was to be made on 13 September in conjunction with an assault from the north-west by von der Heydte's 6th *Fallschirmjäger* Regiment.

Fortunately for Hoffmann's inexperienced troops, a staff officer sent by Student to assess the situation at the Neerpelt bridgehead reported back with the tidings that the newly-arrived paratroop regiment was far from ready for such an undertaking, so the planned attack was cancelled. Student decided to wait until more combat-effective troops became available, and also decided that one man be given command of all units to be used against the bridgehead. The man he chose was an *Oberst* Walther, who had commanded *Fallschirmjäger* Regiment 4 for several years. Arriving at Valkenswaard early on 13 September, he set about forming what was to become known as *Kampfgruppe* Walther.

Fifteenth Army, its six original divisions joined by the remnants of five more retreating from Normandy – the whole amounting to nearly 100,000 men – was attempting to withdraw to the north-east. Nine of these divisions were evacuated across the Scheldt; two, the 245th Infantry Regiment under *Oberst* Gerhard Kegler and the 59th under *Generalleutnant* Walter Poppe, withdrew into North Brabant on 16 September and were assigned to the First *Fallschirmjäger* Army. They were battered and poorly armed, but they had both anti-tank guns and howitzers and they formed a valuable addition to Student's command.

During the fortnight following the formation of Student's Paratroop Army, renewed British probes against the Albert Canal met stiffening resistance. On 7 September the Guards Armoured Division

More German reinforcements arrived on 13 and

German infantry waiting to go into action beside a Mk IV tank, camouflaged among the trees.

14 September, increasing the strength of von der Heydte's *Fallschirmjäger* Regiment 6 to four infantry battalions, each with between 150 and 200 men. Its assets included an 81 mm mortar company, a motorized anti-tank company with 125 mm guns, an air defence machine-gun company and five 20 mm *Flakvierling* quadruple cannon, as well as reconnaissance and engineering companies. From II SS *Panzer* Corps came two *Panzergrenadier* battalions, and also elements of *Panzerjäger Abteilung* 10, a tank destroyer battalion which sent fifteen Mk IV tanks armed with long-barrelled 75 mm guns. There were also six 105 mm field howitzers forming a motorized battery, and four rifle companies of *Luftwaffe* Penal Battalion 6. The final addition to Walther's force came in the form of two 88 mm and three 20 mm guns, which were used to strengthen the air defences.

With these forces in place, Student felt confident enough to authorize the attack on the Neerpelt bridgehead to proceed on 15 September. It developed at 0800 hrs, with von der Heydte's regiment attacking from the north-west, but

although some ground was gained initially the assault was soon broken up by British artillery fire and it became bogged down. On the following day, with British reinforcements continuing to arrive in the bridgehead, Walther's battle group dug in to the north astride the Hechtel–Valkenswaard road, with the Erdmann *Fallschirmjäger* Division on the left and the 85th Infantry Division on the right. *Fallschirmjäger* Regiment 6, which had suffered substantial casualties during the attack, lay to the north-west, with von Hoffmann's regiment to the north.

At 2000 hrs on 16 September, Model, who had set up his headquarters at Oosterbeek near Arnhem, informed his army commanders of the demarcation lines between their operational areas. *General der Flieger* Christiansen, C-in-C of the *Wehrmacht* in Holland, retained command north of a line running from the Brielsche Gat on the Dutch coast via Dordrecht along the Waal and the Maas to Nijmegen and from there to the Dutch-German border, forming a rear combat zone. The front line in Holland was formed by the Fifteenth Army and the First *Fallschirmjäger* Army, both subordinate to Army Group B. The two were divided by a line running from a point east of Antwerp via Tilburg to the village of Rossum on the Waal above 's Hertogenbosch; Fifteenth Army's sector, which comprised West Brabant and Zeeland, was to the east of this line, while Student's First *Fallschirmjäger* Army, with its HQ in Vught, was to the east.

It was in the eastern sector, Model was convinced, that the renewed British offensive would develop. There was no longer any doubt that Montgomery's forces were making for the Ruhr, and the road leading to that objective ran diagonally across the territory occupied by Student's scattered units. What the Germans could not forecast with any certainty was the precise axis the British advance would follow, although the Army Group B Intelligence Staff were certain that airborne troops would be used in conjunction with it.

As early as 6 September, German Intelligence had been predicting that large Allied airborne landings would take place in the area of the Siegfried Line, either north of Aachen – where the line's defence in depth was relatively weak – or in the Saar, opposite the advance of General Patton's US Third Army. By 14 September, the German Intelligence assessment was that

The Second British Army . . . will assemble its units at the Maas–Scheldt and Albert Canals. On its right wing it will concentrate an attack force mainly composed of armoured units, which, after forcing a Maas crossing, will launch operations to break through to the Rhenish–Westphalian Industrial Area (Ruhr) with the main effort via Roermond. To cover the northern flank, the left wing of the (Second British) Army will close to the Waal at Nijmegen, and thus create the basic conditions necessary to cut off the German forces committed in the Dutch coastal areas. In conjunction with these operations a large-scale airborne landing by the First Allied Airborne Army north of the Lippe river in the area south of Münster is planned for an as yet indefinite date.[22]

The German Intelligence assessment of Montgomery's intentions, therefore, was almost completely wrong. It envisaged no large-scale Allied combat operations north of the Waal, which was precisely the area in which the bulk of the airborne forces assigned to *Market* would be dropped. Yet in mid-September, Allied Intelligence was equally unaware of the growing strength of the German forces in this area, especially in the vicinity of Arnhem.

At the time of the collapse of Army Group B in France, there were already some potentially

Sturmbannführer Sepp Krafft, the SS officer whose blocking action did so much to thwart the advance of the 1st Airborne Division on Arnhem Bridge.

effective fighting units in the area north of the Waal. One was the SS NCO School under SS *Obersturmbannführer* Hans-Michael Lippert, where SS troopers came from all fronts (mainly the Russian) for NCO training. Almost all of them had at least one year's combat experience. The School had two infantry companies and a heavy weapons platoon, equipped with a variety of mortars, machine-guns and some 20 mm cannon. Lippert, who had set up his HQ in some deserted *Luftwaffe* buildings at Schoonrewoerd near Leerdam, west of Arnhem, was responsible for the western sector of a reception screen set up along the Waal to deal with the broken and heavily demoralized German Army units retreating into northern Holland. The eastern sector was under the command of SS *Sturmbannführer* Sepp Krafft, who also commanded the SS *Panzergrenadier* Depot and the 16th Reserve

Battalion. Taken from positions on the Dutch coast, this command was now installed as a divisional reserve in the Oosterbeek area, and was therefore virtually on the outskirts of Arnhem itself. It had twelve officers and 294 other ranks, divided between one heavy weapons and two infantry companies; these were supplemented by trench mortar, anti-tank, flak, flame-thrower and heavy mortar sections. Krafft, like Lippert, was subordinate to *Generalleutnant* Hans von Tettau, who was in overall command of the Waal river reception screen.

In addition to these fairly effective commands, there were other units of more dubious reliability based in the Arnhem area. One of them was *Wachbattalion* 3, a Dutch SS surveillance battalion which had originally been formed to guard a concentration camp at Amersfoort, north of Arnhem. It had about 600 men in four companies, dispersed around Amersfoort. Its main function in recent times had been to round up shot-down Allied airmen, and as an infantry force it was practically useless. Another unit was Artillery Regiment 184 under *Hauptmann* Breedemann, engaged in training gunners – mostly men caught up in the retreat northwards – at Wageningen, west of Oosterbeek. On 11 September the Regiment received a train shipment of 40 factory-fresh 105 mm howitzers, twelve of which were sent to Doesburg with accompanying personnel for further training.

Had these, together with a few scratch units composed of *Luftwaffe* personnel, police and pioneers, formed the only resistance when the British 1st Airborne Division dropped on Arnhem, then the story of the campaign in north-west Europe might have taken a different turn. But battles are sometimes won or lost on the intervention of an imponderable element called chance, and on 7 September, virtually unnoticed by Allied Intelligence, it arrived in the Dutch province of Gelderland in the form of the battered II SS *Panzer* Corps under the command of *General der Waffen-SS* Paul Hausser.

II SS *Panzer* Corps had fought a hard and bloody road back from France. Its two principal components, the 9th SS *Hohenstaufen* and the 10th SS *Frundsberg Panzer* Divisions, had retreated into the Low Countries via Valenciennes, Mons and Sittard; now, clear at last of the fighting zone, decimated by the carnage of Falaise, they were to reorganize.

The evening of 7 September found the 9th SS *Panzer* Division assembling in the Sittard area north of Maastricht. It was ordered to detach a *Kampfgruppe* including a battalion of infantry and a battery of artillery, to Valkenswaard to reinforce the *Kampfgruppe* Walther; the remainder of the divisional battle group passed through Venlo and Nijmegen to its prepared assembly areas north and east of Arnhem. What was left of the 10th SS *Panzer* Division was already there, having detached one *Kampfgruppe* to establish a rearguard bridgehead west of Maastricht.

Both divisions had collected a considerable quantity of abandoned equipment during the retreat, including most of 40 105-mm guns found on a deserted train in Arras, but in terms of personnel they had lost up to 60 per cent of their original strength. Model's intention had been to re-equip both divisions at the front as quickly as possible in order to form an Army Group reserve, but because of the severe personnel losses it was decided to replenish only the 10th SS *Panzer* Division on the spot and sent 9 SS back to Germany after handing over its heavy equipment to its sister division. Another reason for the decision to leave 10 SS at Arnhem was that it was scheduled to be re-equipped with new Panther tanks; in fact, these did not arrive until after the Arnhem battle was over, so in terms of effective fighting strength the Division had only one battalion of Mk IV *Panzers* and a battalion of *Jagdpanzer* IV tank destroyers. Some of the latter were despatched to reinforce *Kampfgruppe* Walther at the Neerpelt bridgehead, as the *Kampfgruppe* Heinke, which comprised SS *Panzergrenadier* Battalion 21, a battery of artillery, and reconnaissance and engineer companies.

The commander of 10 SS, *Obersturmbannführer* Heinz Harmel, energetically set about reorganizing his battle group. His leading priority was to organize balanced combat teams capable of dealing with any eventuality. He ordered his only remaining infantry group, *Panzergrenadier* Regiment *Frundsberg*, to form a twelve-gun anti-tank company and drafted experienced anti-tank gunners from other units into it. Similarly, self-propelled gun drivers from the artillery regiment were transferred to the division's tank regiment. The *Panzergrenadier* Regiment's armoured half-tracks were allotted to the reconnaissance battalion, and all available anti-aircraft guns were concentrated in the Flak Regiment. At the end of the reorganization 10 SS had what amounted to a brigade-strength battle group comprising three *Panzergrenadier* battalions at Deventer, Diepensen and Rheden, a tank HQ with Mk IVs at Vorden, and artillery in Dieren. Numbering about 3,000 men, it was henceforth referred to as the *Kampfgruppe Frundsberg*.

Meanwhile, *Obersturmbannführer* Walter Harzer's 9 SS *Hohenstaufen*, after transferring its heavy equipment to 10 SS, had been reduced to a series of small units scattered over the Apeldoorn–Arnhem–Zutphen triangle. The advance parties, comprising administrative and technical personnel, began entraining for Germany on 12 September. A new *Hohenstaufen* Division was already being formed in the *Reich* and in normal circumstances the movement from Holland would have been completed in just a few days, but Allied fighter-bomber activity made rail movement by daylight prohibitive. Also, on Model's orders, the shift to Germany was to be completed gradually, the fighting echelons to be transferred last of all. On 16 September, therefore, Harzer still had about 2,500 troops in Holland, spread over twelve locations within, on average, a ten-mile radius of Arnhem. From 17 September, what remained of 9 SS was referred to as the *Kampfgruppe* Harzer. In theory, these men could form up to nineteen quick-reaction groups of company strength.

Because of several factors, not least of which was the widely-scattered disposition of the newly-arrived SS units in the Arnhem area, air reconnaissance failed to reveal their presence. But to state that this presence was unknown to Allied Intelligence – and this has been claimed in several accounts of the operation – is erroneous. On 14 September, the following message was transmitted from the Dutch *Kees* Resistance cell: 'SS divisie Hohenstrufl (sic) langs IJssel, onderdelen hiervan waargenomen van Arnhem tot Zutphen, en langs de weg Zutphen–Apeldoorn. De staf wellicht in Eerde. Langs de IJssel bouwt men thans veldversterkingen.' (SS Division Hohenstrufl along Yssel. Units from this division observed from Arnhem to Zutphen–Apeldoorn. HQ perhaps at Eerde. Field fortifications are being built along Yssel.).[23]

This message contained inaccuracies, as did a second one from Resistance cell *Albrecht* which stated that *Hohenstaufen* SS Division was stationed along both banks of the Yssel between Zwolle and Arnhem, that Divisional HQ was probably at Doetinchem with sub-HQs at Beekbergen and Epse, and that 1,900 troops of the Division were located north of a line Loenen–Zutphen. Both these messages were received and recorded by British Intelligence in London on 15 September, and on that day the *Kees* cell sent another: 'At Arnhem *MELDEKOPF HOHENSTAUFL*. This is assembly place of members of the SS Division previously reported. Also at Arnhem *MELDEKOPF HARZER* presumably forming part of a unit situated south of Arnhem.'[24]

The report was inaccurate, but at least it confirmed the presence of the *Hohenstaufen* Division in the Arnhem area. The problem with this and the other

Troop trains travelling on raised embankments in the vicinity of the Rhine were vulnerable to air attack by day.

messages lay not in their content, but with the filtration process to which they were subjected, first at Dutch Resistance HQ in Rotterdam – where incoming reports from the Resistance cells were sometimes dismissed as being outdated – and then by British Intelligence in London before the information reached SHAEF, where it was subjected to further filtration and assessment before being passed on to the appropriate subordinate commands. The fragmentary reports from the Dutch Resistance did in fact reach HQ I Airborne Corps – but not until 20 September. By that time, 1st Airborne Division already knew what it was up against.[25].

CHAPTER 5

Final Preparations, 16–17 September 1944

There had been little change, since June, in the disposition of the troop-carrier units that were to carry the airborne forces into action. The location of the RAF's transport squadrons, in fact, had not changed at all; they were positioned in pairs at eight bases, six of which were grouped about 80 miles west of London and 30 miles north-west of Greenham Common. The others, Keevil and Tarrant Rushton, lay respectively 30 and 60 miles south of the rest. At these eight airfields, the men of the 1st Airborne Division had been standing by since Operation *Linnet* was ordered on 2 September, their gliders loaded and ready to go. The ritual of an evening briefing, an 0500 hrs morning call, and then the cry of 'it's off!' was becoming familiar.

IX Troop Carrier Command's 53rd Wing and its component groups were also still on the bases they had occupied during the Normandy invasion. Their task, as before, was to lift the 101st Airborne Division into battle. Similarly, the 52nd Wing, occupying airfields which had been its home since March, was to lift the 82nd Airborne Division as well as elements of the British 1st Airborne Division and the Polish Brigade.

The only real change had affected the 50th Troop Carrier Wing, part of which was to help lift troops of the 82nd Airborne Division. On 8 September, the 50th Wing had been ordered to France to conduct air supply operations for the ground forces, and 48 hours later the 439th and 441st Groups were operational in the Reims area, with most of the Wing's equipment either in France or in transit. Then, at 2230 hrs on 10 September, the 50th Wing was ordered back to its English bases – Balderton, Langar and Fulbeck – and given 24 hours to get ready for *Market*. The deadline was met, a remarkable achievement in view of the fact that the airfields were being deactivated in readiness for their return to the RAF.

A further change involved the move of the C-47s of IX TCC Pathfinder School, early in September, from North Witham to Chalgrove, twenty miles north of Greenham Common. Redesignated the Pathfinder Group (Provisional), it now occupied an airfield previously used by the 10th Tactical Reconnaissance Group, which had moved to the Continent in August.

On 16 September, IX Troop Carrier Command had 1,274 operational aircraft, all C-47s. No 38 Group RAF had 321 Albemarles, Stirlings and Halifaxes, and No 46 Group 164 Dakotas. On this date, IX TCC also had 2,160 Waco CG-4A gliders, thanks to the herculean efforts of the 26th Mobile Repair and Reclamation Squadron at Crookham Common, whose 900 personnel had proved capable of assembling 60 Wacos per day against a target figure of 40. On one occasion, they assembled 100 in 24 hours. The British airborne forces had 812 Horsa gliders and 64 Hamilcars; the Americans also had 104 Horsas but did not intend to use them, having acquired a dislike of the British glider.[26]

The General Aircraft Hamilcar glider had considerable load-carrying capacity, as shown by this photograph of one disgorging a Tetrarch tank. The British airborne forces used 64 during the Arnhem operation.

On 16 September, with all personnel in position on their assigned bases, detailed briefings were held. These were as comprehensive as possible, but were hampered by a lack of photographic intelligence on the zones. Large-scale maps were also in short supply and, as it would be discovered later, those provided for the airborne troops were often woefully inaccurate.

There remained the question of the weather, that most unpredictable of all factors governing air operations in north-west Europe. Everything depended on it, for *Market* needed three consecutive days of good weather if the operation was to succeed. Weather evaluation was made by the Staff Weather Officer of IX Troop Carrier Command and the Senior Meteorological Officer of No 38 Group, acting jointly at Ascot as weather officers for the Airborne Army. Long-range weather forecasting conferences were held twice a day, drawing on the advice and experience of the many weather experts who had been assembled in England since long before the Normandy landings, and a four-day forecast was issued daily, in addition to a 24-hour forecast sent to the troop-carrier units. Daily weather reconnaissance flights were made over the Low Countries by de Havilland Mosquito XVIs of the Eighth Air Force's 25th Bomb Group (R), operating from Watton in Norfolk as a component of the 325th Photographic Wing.

At 1630 hrs on 16 September, the weather experts reported that weather conditions over the coming four-day period would be favourable. A high pressure system was approaching Belgium from the south-west and would be over it the next day. Fair weather with little cloud and light winds would prevail until the 20th. There would be some fog on and after D plus one, but only in the early morning. Armed with this encouraging information, General Brereton issued orders, at 1900 hrs on 16 September, that *Market* would take place as planned on the following day, with H-Hour set for 1300 hrs.

Offensive air operations in support of *Market* began on the night of 16/17 September when 200 Lancasters and 23 Mosquitoes of Nos 1 and 8 Groups bombed four *Luftwaffe* day-fighter airfields at Leeuwarden, Steenwijk-Havelte, Hopsten and Rheine, and 54 Lancasters and five Mosquitoes of Nos 3 and 8 Groups attacked a flak position at Moerdijk. According to the war diary of *Luftflotte* 3, the most damage was caused at Rheine where the

airfield was put out of action for 24 hours. This was important, because *Kampfgeschwader* 51 was working up at Rheine with Messerschmitt Me 262 jet fighter-bombers, aircraft which presented a very serious threat to Allied air superiority. The attack on the flak positions at the Moerdijk bridge – which crossed the Maas near its mouth – was disappointing, achieving only near misses for the loss of two Lancasters. The bombing operations were supported by six B-17 Fortresses of No 214 (Radio Countermeasures) Squadron, RAF, and five of the 803rd (Countermeasures) Squadron, US Eighth Air Force.

These attacks were followed up, at 0620 hrs on 17 September, by six Mosquitoes which strafed Steenwijk-Havelte airfield. Then, after a 30-minute delay caused by early morning fog, the softening up of the German defences continued with attacks by 852 Eighth Air Force B-17s on 117 targets, mostly known flak positions, along the airborne forces' routes. Because of the small size of their targets the bombers flew in formations of four to six aircraft and in the main dropped 260 lb fragmentation bombs (2,888 tons, against only 29 tons of high explosive) from altitudes of between 10,000 and 20,000 feet. Visibility was good, no enemy fighters were encountered, and there was little flak except in the vicinity of Arnhem, where it was reported to be moderate but inaccurate. That was also a reasonable description of the bombing results; only 45 per cent of the bombs came within 1,000 ft of their targets, and only 43 of the flak sites were seriously affected. Two bombers were shot down and 112 damaged, most of them lightly. Area support during the operation was provided by 147 P-51 Mustangs, and one of these also failed to return.

A further operation on the morning of 17 September involved attacks by 112 Lancasters and 20 Mosquitoes of Nos 1 and 8 Groups on German flak positions in the Flushing (Vissingen) area of Walcheren as a diversionary measure; all the aircraft returned safely.

Then, shortly before 1100 hrs, 32 Mosquitoes of Nos 107 and 613 Squadron took off from Lasham, in Hampshire, to attack barracks in the Arnhem area, while seventeen of No 21 Squadron left Thorney Island to attack similar targets at Nijmegen. The Arnhem Mosquitoes attacked from heights varying between 800 and 1,500 feet, each aircraft dropping four 500 lb bombs. The raid caused considerable

ABOVE:
Heavy softening-up attacks were carried out by the Allied air forces prior to the airborne operation. Here, 8th AF B-17s release their bombs.

BELOW:
8th Air Force P-51 fighters flew perimeter patrols around the landing zones and kept the *Luftwaffe* at bay.

damage to the military accommodation, and an ammunition dump was destroyed. Two Mosquitoes were shot down and the flak was reported to be intense. At Nijmegen, five Mosquitoes claimed to have bombed barracks as detailed, three attacked secondary targets and seven other crews reported that there were so many aircraft in the area that they were unable to attack. One Mosquito was lost to flak.[27]

In conjunction with these raids, 48 B-25 Mitchells and 24 Bostons of Second TAF also set out to bomb military barracks at Ede. Because of cloud conditions and other difficulties only 30 Mitchells and thirteen Bostons made the attack, but the 63 tons of HE bombs they dropped caused many casualties, the full extent of which was only revealed when German reports were examined after the war.

Now, literally minutes in advance of the transport serials, it was the turn of the fighters and fighter-bombers. As the transports approached the Low Countries, Eighth Air Force P-51s provided a buffer between the transport columns and the *Luftwaffe's* fighter force. They flew in two layers, one at 5,000 feet and the other at 2,500, sometimes dropping lower down in cloudy areas in order to stay below the cloud base. Six groups were involved, one of which flew back and forth on perimeter patrol between Hasselt and Wesel, with a second covering a semicircular line between Wesel and the Zuider Zee. The only attempts by the *Luftwaffe* to interfere with the airborne operation on D-Day were frustrated by these two groups. The 4th Fighter Group, patrolling north-west of Wesel intercepted fifteen aggressive Focke-Wulf FW 190s and claimed the destruction of five of them, with a sixth probably destroyed, for the loss of one Mustang, while the 361st Fighter Group had a skirmish with fifteen Messerschmitt 109s south-west of Wesel and shot one of them down.

In the Eindhoven sector, flak suppression operations were entrusted to four Ninth Air Force fighter groups, two with P-38s and two with P-47s. The first attack was made at 1230 hours by the P-38s of the 474th Fighter Group, each aircraft armed with two 500 lb bombs, and was the most effective; its pilots reported the destruction of seven flak positions, with eighteen more probably destroyed. The next two groups claimed only nine positions destroyed, and the last group arrived at 1350 hrs as the last transports were leaving the area. Pilots found that low cloud and haze, together with the small size of the objectives, made dive-bombing almost impossible; in fact, the first three groups dropped only 61 bombs between them, relying on strafing to neutralize their targets. Two P-38s were shot down.

In the Nijmegen sector, besides the P-51 perimeter patrols – which protected both routes – escort and area cover from England to the Initial Point was provided by eighteen Spitfire squadrons from ADGB. One of these, No 504 Squadron, had earlier carried out a series of armed reconnaissances along the route with the object of drawing flak to pinpoint enemy batteries. Between the IP and Nijmegen the escort task was taken over by two Eighth Air Force P-51 groups; their pilots sighted a few enemy aircraft, but there were no engagements.

Flak suppression from the coast to the IP was undertaken by five Tempest, three Typhoon, three Mustang and two Spitfire squadrons of ADGB, all of which did an excellent job. One of the most important tasks was assigned to the Tempests of Nos 80 and 274 Squadrons; their targets were four flak ships in the Hellegat, whose multiple cannon were capable of inflicting considerable damage on the low-flying transport columns. The eight Tempests attacked with their 20 mm cannon in the teeth of intense flak and sank all four boats, then turned inland in search of more anti-aircraft sites around the Ooster Scheldt estuary. One Tempest was shot down and another had to return to base with damage; the others continued their attacks until they were relieved by rocket-firing Typhoons. Almost all the returning aircraft had taken hits. One Mustang was also lost on a flak suppression sortie.

Beyond the IP, the flak suppression task was given to the P-47s of the 78th Fighter Group, Eighth Air Force. The 50 Thunderbolts went into action about half an hour before the transport columns arrived; flying low to draw anti-aircraft fire, then attacking with guns and bombs, the American pilots knocked out an estimated eight guns and silenced six more. They also hit other targets, including a flak barge, and destroyed a Messerschmitt 110 on the ground at Gilze-Rijn. Subsequently, the 78th Group made rendezvous with the troop-carrier formations and escorted them to their drop zones. One P-47 was lost and several more damaged.

In the Arnhem sector, which had earlier been

subjected to considerable 'softening up' by the bombers of No 2 Group RAF, gun positions were attacked by Typhoons of 2nd TAF, which despatched 107 sorties against these targets. The major part of 2 TAF's fighter-bomber effort, however, was committed to the advance of XXX Corps.[28]

For the average person today, who has never seen more than a few aircraft in the sky at any one time, it is difficult to visualize the sheer magnitude of the air armada that left England on that sunny morning on Sunday, 17 September 1944. From 24 airfields, a mightly assembly of 1,545 paratroop aircraft, 451 glider tugs and 451 gliders assembled over the English coast and set course for Holland. Weaving a protective screen over and around the transport and glider serials were, 1,130 Allied fighter aircraft.

As a demonstration of Allied air power, it was awesome.

The flight over the North Sea provided a spectacle that no-one who was there will never forget. As far as the eye could see there were planes and gliders all travelling on a dead straight course. Weaving in and out, up and down, were the fighters; there seemed to be hundreds of them . . . Somehow Sunday seemed to be a strange day for such a trip but most of us felt a great elation now that we were finally committed to an operation. This one would not be aborted now. We were all raring to go, superbly fit and full of the feeling that we were invincible . . . [29].

CHAPTER 6

D-Day, 17 September 1944

THE PATHFINDERS

The first pair of American pathfinder C-47s took off from Chalgrove at 1025 hours, followed by the other two pairs at ten-minute intervals. The aircraft were escorted by P-47s as far as the Belgian coast.

The leading pair of C-47s, carrying the 82nd Airborne Division's pathfinders, had an uneventful trip as far as Grave, when anti-aircraft guns opened up on them. The flak grew more intense as the aircraft approached their objective, DZ 'O'; luckily, Thunderbolts of the 78th Fighter Group were on hand and the enemy guns were quickly silenced. The American crews made their drop from 500 feet, the two pathfinder teams landing side by side in open fields about 500 yards north of DZ 'O'. While the second team took up defensive positions, the

first set up its equipment, and within three minutes the pathfinders had deployed their identification panels and brought their radio and radar homing beacons into operation. It was now 1250 hours.

The other two pathfinder serials crossed the front line at Gheel, locating the orange marker smoke set out by XXX Corps' forward troops, and almost at once the leading pair, bound for DZ 'Z', ran into heavy AA fire. Forbidden to take evasive action, the best the pilots could do was increase their speed to 180 mph in an attempt to clear the danger zone as quickly as possible. It was not enough. Over Ratie, one of the DZ 'A' pair was hit in the port engine and wing tank and crashed in flames – the first casualty, over the battle area, in Operation *Market*. The event was witnessed by the British troops in the forward area, including Syd Martin of the 2nd Battalion the Gordon Highlanders, who saw two parachutes open. At the time, Martin and his comrades could not understand why the transport aircraft was flying low over the enemy lines, all alone; the second aircraft, unseen, was some distance away.[30]

This second C-47 flew on to Veghel, sighted the railway which bounded the zone to the north, and flew parallel to the line until it reached DZ 'A', dropping its troops at 1247 hours. Here, too, the direction-finding equipment was functioning within three minutes.

The pair of C-47s assigned to DZs 'B' and 'C' arrived at their zones without trouble, the pilots reducing speed to 90 mph to make an extremely accurate drop. The *Eureka* beacon was in action in less than a minute, and the other equipment was ready within four. There were some enemy troops in the area, but they were quickly eliminated after a short firefight.

Douglas C-47s and Waco CG-4A gliders assembled at an airfield in southern England just before the start of *Market*.

Meanwhile, the twelve pathfinder Stirlings of No 38 Group RAF had taken off from Fairford carrying six officers and 180 other ranks of the 21st Independent Parachute Company under Major B.A. Wilson. The crews located their zones – LZ 'S' and DZ 'X' –without difficulty and made accurate drops at about 1240 hours. The teams assembled quickly, accepted the surrender of fifteen Germans, and had their equipment functioning in time for the arrival of the main force.[31]

D-DAY: EINDHOVEN

It was shortly after 1000 hours that the C-47s of the 53rd Troop Carrier Wing, lifting 6,695 paratroops of the 101st Airborne Division, began taking off from their bases in the Greenham Common area. Their pathfinders had not yet departed, but the latter, flying a more direct route and not needing to sacrifice time in any assembly process, would still make their drops twenty minutes ahead of the main force.

In all, 424 aircraft of the 53rd TCW were involved – eight less than originally planned – and the take-off and assembly procedure was accomplished very professionally. One serial of the 442nd TCG got its 45 C-47s airborne in five minutes, and within a quarter of an hour had formed up and was on its way to Hatfield, the Wing assembly area. The 435th Group also managed to get a serial of 32 aircraft airborne, formed up and en route within a quarter of an hour.

The southern route into Holland was supposed to be much safer than the northern one, but this was far from apparent to the men of the 101st Airborne Division and their transport crews. As the serials crossed the German lines near Rethy they began to encounter intense flak and small-arms fire. Much of the flak came from concealed positions in woodland which had escaped the earlier attentions of the defence suppression fighter-bombers.

The first three serials comprised 90 aircraft of the 434th TCG and 45 of the 442nd, carrying the 2,050 men of the 501st Parachute Regiment destined for DZs 'A' and 'A-1'. These serials encountered flak from some batteries on the banks of the Wilhelmina Canal as they began their run-in from Oirchot, twelve miles south-west of the zones. In an attempt to avoid the denser pockets of flak, the lead serial, carrying the 1st Battalion of the 501st Regiment to DZ A-1, detoured some distance to the west of its planned track and dropped 42 sticks of paratroops in fields some three miles north-west of the zone. Despite this error, the drop pattern was good and the battalion succeeded in assembling 90 per cent of its men and equipment within three-quarters of an hour before marching on Veghel, preceded by an advance party in requisitioned trucks and on bicycles. Some resistance by about 30 rear-echelon troops was easily overcome, and by 1600 hours the battalion had taken its objectives, the two bridges over the Aa south-east of the town.

The second serial dropped five minutes after the first, at 1306 hours, the 2nd Battalion of the 501st Regiment going down in a tight pattern at the western end of DZ A. The third serial's drop, at 1311 hours, was equally good, the 3rd Battalion landing about 1,500 yards west of the zone. There was no enemy opposition, and 95 per cent of the men were assembled inside 45 minutes. By 1515 hours, the 2nd Battalion had secured the road and railway bridges over the Willems Canal, while the 3rd Battalion captured the village of Eerde and established positions south of the drop zone on the Eindhoven–Arnhem highway. An hour later, the 1st and 2nd Battalions made contact in Veghel. At the close of the day, the 501st Parachute Infantry Regiment had taken all its D-Day objectives, together with 32 prisoners, at a cost of ten casualties, none of which was attributable to enemy action.

The three serials assigned to DZ 'B', a mile north-west of Zon, encountered heavy flak on their run-in, particularly around the village of Best, a mile to the south-west. There was also much light flak and small-arms fire around the DZ itself, but although many of the troop-carriers – comprising 45 aircraft of the 442nd TCG and 90 of the 436th – received damage, only one was shot down. The serials began dropping 2,200 men of the 506th Parachute Infantry Regiment at 1312 hours, and completed the drop at 1324 hours. Only 24 men were injured in the drop, and 80 per cent of the Regiment was assembled within an hour.

As soon as the main body of the 1st Battalion was assembled, about 45 minutes after the drop, it set off quickly through the woods south of the DZ, leaving any stragglers to follow in small groups. Passing through the woods without incident, the paratroops reached the Willems canal and turned left along its bank towards Zon, where their priority task was to take the highway bridge and two smaller bridges.

However, the Battalion's progress was spotted by the enemy and it was halted by fire from two 88 mm guns.

Meanwhile, the 2nd Battalion, scheduled to advance from the eastern edge of the zone along the road to Zon, had got off to a slower start, not least because of confusion with assembly signals on the adjoining DZ 'C', where four serials – two of 36 and 28 aircraft respectively from the 435th TCG and two of 45 each from the 438th Group – began dropping 2,434 men of the 502nd Parachute Infantry Regiment, the advance echelon of Divisional HQ, and a company of engineers at 1324 hours. One C-47 was shot down on the run-in, but the remainder made a successful drop, even though the first serial of the 435th TCG had to drop from between 900 and 1,200 feet because of a danger of collision with the last serial of the 438th, which was slightly off course and four minutes late.

The task of the 502nd Regiment was to form a connecting link between the 501st to the north and

the 506th to the south of its DZ, as well as providing a divisional reserve. Assembly of the Regiment was virtually complete within an hour.

Another factor that delayed the movement of the 506th Regiment's 2nd Battalion was the arrival of the first glider serials; many of the paratroopers ran to assist in the unloading of the Wacos, or to help the occupants of those that had made bad landings.

The Wacos, which were towed to the Zon area by two 35-aircraft serials of the 437th Group, carried 43 jeeps, eighteen trailers, and 311 airborne troops, mostly from the 101st Division's signals company and reconnaissance platoon. There were also some headquarters, artillery and medical personnel, plus a British liaison and combat communications unit known as a *Phantom* Detachment.

The gliders ran into trouble even before they cleared the English coast. Two broke loose from their tugs and landed safely, but a third was forced to cast off when a bolt holding its tail strut cable broke. Seconds later, the tail folded and the Waco spiralled down to crash, killing all fourteen men on board. Another was forced to ditch in the Channel when its fuselage canvas began peeling away, all the occupants being rescued, and two more made forced landings on friendly Belgian territory.

The real trouble began when the glider serials crossed into Holland. Six C-47s were mortally hit, causing their glider tugs to make emergency releases. These, together with a seventh Waco, came down between the IP and LZ 'W'; one of the gliders crashed, killing passengers and pilot. The first serial released its gliders over LZ 'W' at 1348 hours, and the second at 1355 hours. Three Wacos – two of which collided in mid-air – made crash landings, killing one pilot and injuring five men; the remaining 53 landed safely to disgorge 252 troops, 32 jeeps and thirteen trailers.

In all, the 53rd Troop Carrier Wing lost 24 aircraft on the Eindhoven mission, sixteen of them during the paratroop drop, and many more were damaged. The glider tugs were particularly hard hit, no fewer than 64 aircraft receiving damage – a staggering 70 per cent. The human cost to the Wing was 44 aircrew killed and eighteen wounded.

The CG-4A glider was cheap and easy to mass-produce, but it was not as robust as the British Horsa and was sometimes prone to structural failure. This one lost a wing during a demonstration flight in the USA.

Some pilots displayed great courage in ensuring that the paratroops reached the drop zones; at least four – Major Dan Elam, 1st Lieutenants John Gurecki and Robert S. Stoddart, Jr, and 2nd Lieutenant Herbert E. Schulman – are known to have stayed at the controls of their blazing aircraft, sacrificing themselves in order to drop their paratroops in the right place. There were to be many such individual acts of heroism in the days that followed.[32]

With the gliders on the ground, the 2nd Battalion of the 506th Infantry Regiment at last set out along the road to Zon, half an hour late. The only sign of the enemy was a pair of Mk IV tanks, knocked out by P-47s earlier. It linked up with the 1st Battalion in Zon and was also held up for a time by enemy fire. German resistance was overcome at about 1600 hours and the two battalions advanced on the bridges over the Wilhelmina Canal. As they advanced on the road bridge, their principal objective, the Germans blew it up. The other bridges had already been destroyed, but some paratroops

A flight of C-47s, towing Waco CG-4A gliders, over the Dutch landscape en route for Eindhoven.

swam across the canal and established a foothold on the far bank while engineers laboured to build a footbridge across the waterway. This was completed by 1730 hours, but was so narrow and frail that it was not until the early hours of the following morning that the whole of the 506th Regiment had passed over. The Regiment then halted for the rest of the night about 1,500 yards south of the canal and prepared to resume its advance on Eindhoven – which, according to the plan, it should have taken by 2000 hours on D-Day – the next morning. Meanwhile, the airborne engineers dropped with the 506th Regiment worked flat out all night to repair the centre trestle of the Zon highway bridge, the piers and underpinnings of which had not been badly damaged by the demolition charges, to prepare a crossing for the leading echelons of XXX Corps.

While the 506th Regiment headed for Zon, the 1st Battalion of the 502nd marched north to St Oedenrode, halfway between Zon and Veghel, which it reached at nightfall and made contact with units of the 501st Regiment. A bridge over the Dommel in St Oedenrode was taken intact. A company of the 3rd Battalion, despatched to seize a bridge over the Wilhelmina Canal about a mile south-west of DZ 'C', enjoyed less good fortune. Setting out at 1440 hours, it took the bridge without much trouble but was then driven off it by a German counter-attack, being almost cut off in the process. The rest of the battalion came up at 1845 hours and saved the situation, but efforts to recapture the bridge were frustrated by the German force, which was unexpectedly strong. The battalion dug in for the night, the rest of the 502nd remaining close to the DZ.

D-DAY: NIJMEGEN
The mission carrying the paratroops of the 82nd Airborne Division to its zones in the Nijmegen area involved six groups of the 50th and 52nd Troop Carrier Wings, all based in the Grantham area of Lincolnshire: 480 aircraft in eleven serials, bearing 7,250 men. The aircraft took off at five-second intervals on average and assembly went smoothly, although the official USAAF history mentions that one soldier went violently insane after take-off and

had to be landed (whether in the aircraft or underneath his parachute is not recorded).

Weather conditions were much the same as those prevailing on the southern route, except that at Langar overcast compelled the 441st TCG to climb above 2,500 feet before assembling. Cloud cover along the route varied between four-tenths and eight-tenths, and haze over the Dutch coast limited visibility to three or four miles. Closer to the DZs, the cloud base was above 2,500 feet and visibility more than seven miles.

The flak suppression aircraft had done their job well, and the troop carriers encountered no trouble until they reached the Grave area, when they ran into anti-aircraft fire. One C-47 was shot down and several others damaged. The fire grew more intense as the aircraft neared their dropping zones and two more C-47s were hit, one going down to crash and the other making a forced landing, but all the paratroops made a fast exit from both aircraft.

The first drops were made on DZ 'N', south of Groesbeek, by three serials of 45 aircraft, two from the 313th TCG and one from the 316th. These carried 2,281 paratroops, mostly from the 505th Parachute Infantry Regiment, and 756 containers amounting to 70 tons of supplies and equipment.

Because of a marshalling error the serials heading for DZ 'N' were not in their correct order, the second serial of the 313th Group having accidentally changed places with the first. The pilots of the leading serial sighted smoke and marker panels on DZ 'O', a little to the west of Blankenberg, and headed for the unmarked DZ 'N', but strayed some distance to the north of track and climbed to 900 feet in an attempt to avoid intense small-arms fire and light flak. As a consequence, they dropped almost all of the 2nd Battalion of 505th PIR between one and a half and three miles north-east of DZ 'N'; only six pilots, their aircraft carrying regimental head-quarters and signallers, located the zone and dropped their troops on or near it.

The next seven pilots of the 313th Group's other serial –the one that should have been in the lead – followed their predecessors and, at 1308 hours, dropped regimental headquarters between two and three miles north of DZ 'N', so compounding the original error. Had DZ 'N' been marked by path-finders, the mistake would not have happened at all, but because of the excellent visual navigational references on the approach to the zone it had been decided to dispense with markers – not a wise move, as had now been demonstrated.

The rest of the serial redressed the situation by making an excellent drop of the 3rd Battalion on the zone. So did the 316th Group's serial, carrying the 1st Battalion and Divisional Headquarters, although this serial had gone a long way off track to the south – so far, in fact, that it passed over the lead serial of the 53rd Wing which was making its drop north-east of Veghel. The 316th's pilots quickly made good their error and map-read their way to DZ 'N'.

Despite the inaccuracy of its drop, the 2nd Battalion had come down in a fairly tight pattern near the village of Kamp, about a mile north-east of Groesbeek, and at 1415 hours a strong nucleus set out to take its assigned objectives. The 2nd Battalion's task was to occupy the western side of the Regiment's perimeter, make contact with the 504th PIR along the Maas–Waal Canal, reconnoitre a railway bridge over the Maas between Molenhoek and Mook, and occupy the high ground west of Groesbeek. This latter task it achieved at 1545 hours, having met with only light opposition as it pushed through the northern part of Groesbeek. The town was taken at about 1500 hours by two companies of the 3rd Battalion; the other company pushed on towards the edge of the Reichswald, where it had some inconclusive skirmishes with hastily-assembled units of the German 406th Division.

The task of the 1st Battalion of the 505th PIR was to hold the 82nd Airborne Division's southern perimeter from the railway bridge – which a 2nd Battalion patrol had discovered to be destroyed – to the Reichswald. Assembling about 90 per cent of its men within twenty minutes, the 1st Battalion set out at 1330 hours to occupy positions at the southern end of the Groesbeek ridge and sent detachments to Mook, where 30 prisoners were taken, south to Riethorst and east to the Reichswald. At Riethorst, on the main road running along the Maas to Gennep canal, the Americans were attacked by company-strength units of 406 Division, but these were beaten off with considerable loss to the enemy.

By 2100 hours, the 505th PIR had taken all its objectives and held a strong semicircular perimeter from the canal on the west to Riethorst in the south and Heikant in the east. The Regiment was at 95 per cent full strength; only fourteen men had become casualties during the drop, and combat losses had been minimal.

Close behind the first three troop-carrier serials came three more, also of 45 aircraft each, carrying 2,031 men of the 504th PIR. One aircraft (of the 315th TCG) was lost over western Holland; the remainder flew on to their objective, DZ 'O', and made very accurate drops, beginning at 1315 hours. The first serial, flown by the 316th TCG, carried the 1st Battalion of the 504th, which had the task of taking the bridges over the Maas–Waal Canal. The Battalion was dropped in a good pattern on and around the DZ, a mile and a half west of the canal and a mile north-east of the village of Overasselt. The 315th TCG, flying the other two serials with the 2nd and 3rd Battalions, dropped all 78 sticks within 1,500 yards of the pathfinder beacons on DZ O; the only exception was one company which was detailed to drop in heavily ditched fields on the far side of the Maas to take the southern end of the Grave bridge.

Company A of the 1st Battalion assembled within fifteen minutes and set off quickly for its objective, Bridge 8, only to suffer the frustration of seeing it blown up as they came within sight of it. Company B had better luck; advancing on Bridge 7 at Heumen unseen, they laid down such a withering fire that the Germans were unable to detonate the charges, and at about 1800 hours the Americans took the bridge intact. Company C, approaching Bridge 9 at Hattert, had the same experience as their colleagues in Company A; the bridge blew up as they came within striking distance of it.

Only one bridge over the canal had been taken, but it was enough. Much depended now on the efforts of the 2nd Battalion's Company E, dropped in the ditched area close to the 640-foot bridge structure over the Maas at Grave. This was the most important objective, for it was the road the armour of XXX Corps would take to Nijmegen. Speed was paramount, and the platoon of E Company dropped nearest the bridge quickly assembled and the paratroops worked their way along drainage ditches until they were in a position to engage the defences. They raked the approaches with machine-gun fire and used a bazooka to knock out a flak tower at the south end of the bridge; then they rushed the tower and took control of the gun. They held their positions until the rest of the 2nd Battalion arrived at the northern end of the bridge, which was soon in American hands. The Battalion then attacked Grave, dislodging a garrison of several

hundred Germans, and before the end of the day the paratroops had established a perimeter about a mile in radius around the south end of the bridge. The 3rd Battalion, meanwhile, had been held back as a regimental reserve and carried out some clearing operations in the area north-west of DZ 'O'. At midnight on D-Day, the 504th PIR was at 95 per cent strength and had fulfilled its mission. Casualties, sustained during the drop and in combat, amounted to 57 men.

The three troop-carrier serials assigned to DZ 'T' – two of the 441st TCG, with 45 aircraft each, and one of the 440th TCG with 42 – encountered the worst of the anti-aircraft fire in the Nijmegen sector on D-Day. These serials began dropping 1,922 men of the 508th PIR and 40 pathfinders of the 325th Glider Regiment at 1326 hours. Despite the intense fire the drop was very accurate, two battalions going down just outside the northern edge of the zone and the 3rd battalion within its eastern end. Two C-47s were shot down on the approach, their sticks jumping clear short of the zone, and four more were shot down as they turned away over the Reichswald. Two more aircraft went down over Holland on the return flight as the result of a collision and one had to ditch, the crew of the latter being rescued.

Once on the ground, the first task of the 508th Regiment was to clear the area around the DZ. Two anti-aircraft batteries, one on the edge of the zone and one near the village of Wyler, 1,000 yards to the north-east, were quickly overcome; the crew of the latter battery were rather unfortunate in that two sticks of paratroops had been dropped practically next to them when their aircraft overshot the zone.

With the DZ secure, the 508th PIR set about seizing the northern portion of the Groesbeek ridge and establishing roadblocks on either side of the ridge in the hamlets of De Ploeg and Berg en Dal. The paratroops encountered only light resistance, and these tasks were accomplished by 1900 hours. This left the way clear for a swift move on the Nijmegen bridge, a five-span steel structure 1,960 feet long with a 35-foot roadway suitable for heavy vehicles and tanks. The Germans had erected a pontoon bridge alongside it. There was also a railway bridge across the Waal west of Nijmegen, but this had only a ten-foot roadway and was unsuitable for vehicles.

General Gavin attached the utmost importance to the speedy capture of the Nijmegen bridge; the river at this point was between 800 and 1,800 feet across, and to build a bridge across it capable of supporting tanks and artillery would be a slow business requiring a great deal of labour and huge quantities of engineering equipment.

Gavin therefore directed the 1st Battalion of the 508th PIR to take the Nijmegen bridge, despite reports that there were up to 4,000 SS troops in the town itself. There were indeed substantial numbers of enemy forces in the Nijmegen area, but unknown to Gavin they were as yet disorganized and widely scattered; they would not be ready for action until the following day.

At 2030 hours, the 1st Battalion set off northwards along the road from De Ploeg, their right flank covered by G Company of the 3rd Battalion, advancing from Berg en Dal. Guided by members of the Dutch underground, A and B Companies reached Nijmegen at 0015 hours on 18 September and penetrated to within 400 yards of the bridge when they were halted by hastily-assembled German forces. Although they were unable to move forward, the paratroops frustrated enemy plans to destroy the bridge by seizing and destroying the building which housed the demolition controls.

Meanwhile, further serials in support of 82nd Airborne Division's mission had been arriving at Zone N during the afternoon of D-Day. The first of these, and seventh overall, involved 30 C-47s of the 439th TCG, which dropped 47 headquarters artillery personnel and 388 men of the 307th Engineer Battalion, beginning at 1321 hours. Twenty minutes later, 48 aircraft of the 440th TCG dropped 544 men and 42 tons of equipment, including twelve 75 mm howitzers, of the 376th Parachute Field Artillery Battalion. The battalion was assembled – at a cost of 24 men injured during the drop or wounded by enemy fire – within an hour, and ten of the howitzers were ready for action.

Next came 50 C-47s of the 439th TCG, each towing a Waco CG-4A. The first 22 gliders carried 86 men of Battery A, 80th Airborne Anti-tank Battalion, with eight 57 mm guns, nine jeeps, and two trailers of ammunition; the remainder carried elements of divisional headquarters, divisional artillery headquarters, and divisional signal company, the reconnaissance platoon, and an air support party, the whole comprising 130 men and eighteen jeeps. The progress of this serial was by no means trouble-free; two gliders broke their tow-ropes on take-off

and had to be hitched up again, while a third, brought back to base when its load began to shift, made a lonely flight to the LZ later on. One glider, carrying a jeep, began to disintegrate over the Channel and was released, but ditched safely. One tug and its glider were shot down over Schouwen Island, and five C-47s were damaged by AA fire.

The first gliders were released at 1347 hours. Only six Wacos landed on LZ 'N', but 40 came down only a mile or so to the west. Two were destroyed on landing and fourteen damaged, but injuries were minimal and the guns were undamaged. The premature release probably saved the 439th Group from taking losses, for it enabled the C-47s to make their turns clear of the Reichswald and its concealed flak positions.

Shortly after 1400 hours, a further glider serial reached LZ 'N'. This comprised 29 Horsa gliders (out of 32 despatched, the other three having broken their tow-ropes) and six Wacos, towed by aircraft of No 38 Group RAF. The gliders carried General Browning and Headquarters, I Airborne Corps, together with a substantial amount of equipment. By 1530 hours, A Corps command post had been established in woodland on the northern slopes of the Groesbeek ridge near the northern edge of DZ 'N'. The Corps signals staff soon established radio communications with rear HQ in England and with Second Army, but no effective contact was made with either the 1st Airborne Division or the 101st Airborne Division. At this crucial juncture, General Browning was completely ignorant of the situation in and around Arnhem.

D-DAY: ARNHEM

The D-Day plan called for the British airborne forces to be delivered to Arnhem in three lifts. First, 130 aircraft of No 46 Group and 23 of No 38 Group were to release Horsa gliders on LZ 'S' beginning at 1300 hours, then 167 aircraft of No 38 Group would deliver 154 Horsas and thirteen Hamilcars to LZ 'Z'. The gliders carried the men of the 1st Airlanding Brigade and an anti-tank battery with 17-pounder guns. Finally, 143 C-47s of the 52nd Troop Carrier Wing were to drop the 1st Parachute Brigade on DZ 'X' at 1355 hours.

The glider operation got off to a poor start. Twenty-three Horsas broke their tows while still over England and another was damaged before take-off. Most of the premature releases occurred

ABOVE:

Men of the 1st Airborne Division, wearing Denison smocks, enjoy a 'brew' before emplaning in US Troop Carrier Command C-47s.

RIGHT:
Horsa gliders on LZ 'Z', 17 September 1944.

BELOW:
En route at last: men of the 1st Airborne wave off a Horsa glider bound for Arnhem.

The tugs and gliders over Holland. In this case, the tugs are Halifaxes.

when the combinations encountered low cloud at 2,500 feet; the American serials, flying at a lower altitide, avoided this hazard. (The loads of 22 of these gliders, in fact, were recovered and transferred to a subsequent lift).

Visibility improved over the sea, and apart from five gliders which were forced down due to tow rope or tug engine failure – four of them ditched successfully and their occupants rescued by the Royal Navy MTBs which were on station for just this purpose – the great stream of aircraft flew steadily on towards the objectives. Only slight opposition was encountered over Holland – a light flak barrage near the coast was soon silenced by fighter-bombers – but eight more gliders slipped their tow en route to Arnhem, probably because of difficulties caused by the slipstream ahead. In all, 39 gliders were unable to reach their assigned zones.

Because visibility en route to Arnhem was good, the majority of the glider-tug pilots found it unnecessary to use either *Rebecca* or *Gee*. Pilots who did use their *Rebecca* to interrogate the *Eureka* beacons on the LZs reported good results from LZ 'S', but less satisfactory responses from LZ 'Z'. Nevertheless, Major B.A. Wilson's 21st Independent Parachute Company had done their work well; the coloured panels, smoke and lights displayed by the pathfinders were easily visible.

A Stirling/Horsa combination crossing the Dutch coast. Note the position of the glider, above and to one side of the tug's slipstream.

Heavy and light flak was encountered near the landing zones, but although six aircraft were damaged none was lost and the landings took place without serious mishap. Of the 134 gliders assigned to LZ 'S', 132 landed on or near the zone, while of the remaining 150 destined for LZ 'Z', 116 made accurate landings and 27 landed close by. There was a tendency for the gliders to overshoot in the light wind, causing close concentrations on the north end of LZ 'Z' and the west end of LZ 'S'. A few gliders were damaged, including two Hamilcars which overturned in soft ground on LZ 'Z', involving the loss of two 17-pounder guns.

ABOVE:
The air armada en route: Stirlings and Horsas over the North Sea.

BELOW:
Horsa gliders scattered over LZ 'S' near Arnhem. Despite the congestion, there were few landing accidents.

The task of those components of the 1st Air Landing Brigade which reached Arnhem on D-Day – the 1st Battalion of the Border Regiment, the 2nd Battalion of the South Staffordshire Regiment, and the 7th Battalion of the King's Own Scottish Borderers – was to secure and hold the landing and dropping zones so that the second lift might arrive safely on D plus 1. The Brigade's arrival was described by Lieutenant-Colonel R. Payton-Reid, commanding the Borderers.

The first glider came down at 1.30 and we all moved off at three o'clock. Everything was unloaded by then. We had no local help. There were one or two crashed gliders. We couldn't get out the motor-bikes and one anti-tank gun. A lot of the gliders' undercarriages came up through the bottom because we landed on very soft ground. Eight gliders didn't arrive, otherwise we were complete, just over 700 men and forty officers. The battalion landed to the tune of its regimental march, *The Blue Bonnets over the Border*, played by a piper who continued to march up and down the rendezvous until all the men had reached it.[33]

Hard on the heels of the glider landings came the paratroops: three battalions of the 1st Parachute Brigade under the command of Brigadier Gerald

Lathbury. The paratroop mission to Arnhem was flown by two serials of the 314th Troop Carrier Group and two from the 61st TCG, flying from Saltby and Barkston Heath respectively. Slight flak was encountered as the serials entered Holland and there was more near Elst and Wageningen in the Arnhem area, but only five aircraft were damaged. Between 1353 hours and 1408 hours, the American crews dropped 2,279 men of the Brigade and the 1st Parachute Squadron, Royal Engineers with a very high degree of accuracy from between 700 and 900 feet on DZ 'X'. The aircraft also dropped 645 containers; 34 more became stuck and stubbornly refused to be released, although the pilots made several passes over the zone as they attempted to get them loose.

The 3rd Battalion dropped first, its task to protect the DZ while the 2nd and 1st Battalions followed at five-minute intervals. Accompanying the 1st Battalion was Brigade HQ, the 16th Parachute Field Ambulance and the 9th Field Company, Royal Engineers.

The medical plan, which had been very carefully worked out, was an important feature of the Arnhem operation and one that is sometimes overlooked. The first medical unit to arrive, with the Air Landing Brigade, was the 181st Air Landing Field Ambulance under Lieutenant-Colonel A.T.

Lt-Col W.F.K. Thompson of the Royal Artillery (left) supervising the unloading of a Horsa after landing near Arnhem, 17 September 1944.

ABOVE:
Parachutes blossom from Dakotas as the transports fly low over the DZ to make sure of an accurate drop.

BELOW:
Discarded parachutes litter the DZ. They provided an unexpected windfall for Dutch women, who used the silk to make clothing.

Marrable; its task was to establish a dressing station in the area of Wolfheze which was to remain open until the evening of D plus 1, when it was expected that the Air Landing Brigade would withdraw inside the Arnhem perimeter. This dressing station was to deal with casualties from all dropping and landing zones and from 1st Air Landing and 1st Parachute Brigades in their initial tasks. As the dressing station was only to be kept open for 36 hours, surgery was to be kept to a minimum. On arrival in Arnhem a dressing station was to be opened at the Deaconess Hospital. The 16th Parachute Field Ambulance (Lieutenant-Colonel E. Townsend) was to establish casualty clearing posts as required, and was to evacuate casualties to 181st Air Landing Field Ambulance in the early stages. It was to establish a dressing station in Arnhem, probably at the Saint Elisabeth Hospital, as soon as the town had been captured. On D plus 1, the 133rd Parachute Field Ambulance (Lieutenant-Colonel W.C. Alford) was to arrive with the second lift and establish a dressing station in the Arnhem area on arrival, probably in the Municipal Hospital. Finally, the Polish Parachute Field Ambulance, landing with the Polish Parachute Brigade Group on D plus 2, was to open casualty clearing posts as required.[34]

Thanks to the high level of accuracy in the drop, the paratroops were assembled and ready to move by 1500 hours. The original plan envisaged the armoured jeeps of Major C.F.H ('Freddie') Gough's 1st Airborne Reconnaissance Squadron striking rapidly for the Arnhem road bridge in a *coup de main* assault; the 2nd Battalion of the 1st Parachute Brigade under Lieutenant-Colonel John Frost would allow on foot to reinforce this advance party.

In the event, the *coup de main* attack never materialized. Most published accounts of this part of the battle state that the failure of this part of the plan was due to the non-arrival of some gliders carrying the unit's jeeps. However, No 38 Group's records show that only two gliders (Nos 355 and 364) from the 22 in serial B.15 which were scheduled to lift the Reconnaissance Squadron, were forced to abandon their missions, and it is known that 28 out of the 31 Jeeps earmarked for it were in fact mustered. So what went wrong?

The glider element of the Reconnaissance Squadron, carrying jeeps and other essential equipment and under the command of Captain David Allsop, reached its LZ at about 1330 hours; the remaining 160 personnel of the Squadron dropped with the 1st Parachute Brigade half an hour later. But, despite a successful assembly at the designated RV, the Squadron was not ready to move until about 1540 hours, and it appears that the main reasons for the delay was the difficulty experienced in unloading some of the jeeps from their gliders, some of which had been badly damaged in crash landings on the boggy ground or in nearby trees. Removing the Horsa's tail for unloading could be a tricky job at the best of times, and damage could turn it into a nightmare task, as Trooper Ken Hope recalls:

Troops of the Air Landing Brigade, armed with Lee-Enfield rifles and Sten guns, assemble after landing near Arnhem.

The impact of the landing had distorted the tail unit of our glider, and the tail release mechanism refused to function. The glider pilots, Henry (Sgt Henry Venes) and I hacked and battered for hours, or so it seemed, but the tail stubbornly refused to budge. To the right of us there was a huge Hamilcar glider, completely overturned, with the weight of a 17-pounder gun crushing the pilots' cabin . . . Eventually, a colonel, resplendent in full Highland military outfit (Lt-Col Murray of the Glider Pilot Regiment) arrived on the scene with his staff . . . we now attacked the Horsa tail with renewed energy. Soon it was torn away and the anchor chains on the jeeps released. One of our vehicles had sustained a fractured exhaust pipe; the noise it created as it emerged from the ramps would not have disgraced a Sherman tank. Now, at last, we had arrived.[35]

The Squadron eventually set out for its objective, with C Troop leading followed by HQ Troop, D Troop and Support Troop. A Troop was left in reserve at the DZ. The Support Troop towed a pair of 20 mm Polsten guns; lighter versions of the Swiss Oerlikon, these had a rate of fire of 450 rounds per minute and were a formidable addition to the Squadron's firepower, which comprised the usual array of infantry and anti-tank weapons common to the airborne forces.

The events of the next few hours are recalled by Trooper Des Evans, a member of C Troop.

We joined our sections; mine was No 9 under 2nd Lt Bowles. Our driver was Bill Edmond, a likeable Scot . . . Setting off on our various routes the Troops split up. C Troop headed towards the railway crossing at Wolfheze station. Before crossing the line we turned left on to a track which was parallel with the railway. The first German we saw looked as if he was snoozing in the sun, sitting down against a fence post. The hole in his helmet, through which the blood still dripped, shattered the illusion. There was an ack-ack train of Bofors (sic) guns on the railway line that had been hammered by our fighters the day before. It was just so much scrap metal. We were startled when another German, who had been hiding in a ditch nearby, jumped up with his hands in the air. The Dutch Commando, attached to our Troop, got hold of him, hustled him into the woods and shot him.[36]

Within minutes of this happening firing broke out ahead of us and we heard the order for dismounted action. Leaping off our jeeps we sought cover. Most of the firing seemed to be coming from the woods at right angles to the track and immediately ahead of us, and some of our lads were caught out in open ground.[37]

What had happened was this: at Wolfheze, following the Reconnaissance Squadron's practice of 'leapfrogging', in which sections took it in turn to

Men of the 1st Airborne Reconnaissance Squadron in position at Wolfheze. The man on the left is armed with a PIAT.

take the lead, No 9 Section had pulled aside to let Nos 8 and 7 Sections pass through, in that order. It was these sections, moving along a road called the Johannahoeveweg that ran eastward from the station, that ran into trouble.

The opposition came from the 16th SS Training and Replacement (Reserve) Battalion under *Sturmbannführer* Sepp Krafft. This battalion was the largest self-contained unit nearest to the airborne landing zones, and it so happened that it had been carrying out exercises in the woods near Wolfheze. The masses of transport aircraft roaring overhead clearly indicated to Krafft that a major Allied airborne operation was in progress, but the landing and dropping zones were obscured by the woods and Krafft did not know their precise location. He therefore directed No 2 Company to make a reconnaissance towards the suspected landing zones, No 4 Company to set up defensive positions near the Hotel Wolfheze, and No 9 Company to come up from Arnhem to create a battalion reserve.

No 2 Company's reconnaissance was brief. Emerging from the woods on the eastern side of LZ 'Z', their heavy machine-gun section opened fire on some gliders that were landing, without causing any appreciable damage, and then – stunned by the scale of the landings – fell back to dig in alongside No 4 Company on the Wolfheze road. Sepp Krafft had no doubt at all that the Arnhem road bridge was the principal Allied objective, and he quickly deployed his blocking force along the eastern side of the Wolfhezerweg from its junction at Utrechtseweg northwards almost as far as Wolfheze station. As part of his defence, he detached his Reserve Platoon and positioned it in the woodland to the north of the railway in order to protect the Battalion's right flank, and also to cover the railway itself. It was this platoon that now engaged the 1st Reconnaissance Squadron.

Number 8 Section took the brunt of the enemy fire.

Scene on the Utrechtseweg in the afternoon of 17 September. Hastily-assembled German forces prepare to oppose the airborne landings.

One man was killed and all the others wounded. Pinned down, facing the prospect of being picked off one by one, the men of No 8 Section had no alternative but to surrender.

Lieutenant Ralph Foulkes, commanding No 7 Section, pulled his two jeeps into the shelter of some trees and went forward to find out what had happened. As soon as he had assessed the situation, he moved back and reported to the Troop Commander Captain John Hay, who decided that No 7 Section should move up to the scene of the action on foot while No 9 Section deployed on the south side of the railway to protect the Squadron's right flank.

No 7 Section advanced as directed, but almost at once came under heavy attack from mortars, small arms and heavy machine-guns. It was now more than an hour since the action had started, and Captain Hay, anxious to break the stalemate, ordered No 9 Section to relieve Foulkes and his men, who had suffered serious casualties. However, the enemy fire was growing steadily more intense, and it was soon clear that a breakthrough was impossible. Captain Hay therefore issued orders for the recovery of the wounded, and for a withdrawal of Wolfheze.

Trooper Evans:

At this juncture I was still wearing my steel helmet and lying down facing the enemy. I was surprised to see our MO (Captain Douglas Swinscow) stand up waving the Red Cross flag. There was a shot from somewhere on my right and he went down. The weight of my helmet caused an ache in the back of my neck, so I rested it for a while with the front of the helmet on the ground. As I raised by head again a bullet whizzed in front of my face, shattering a small twig near by left hand – I'd just looked up in time. I couldn't make out where the shot had come from but assumed it came from the same man who had shot the MO.* As the place was getting too hot for comfort I scrambled to my knees; he fired again and this shot hit the bandolier of ammo swung across my chest. Two close calls in as many minutes . . . Hearing movement behind me I turned to see members of the Glider Pilot Regiment who had been sent to relieve us. Those big chaps came up and asked casually if anything was happening. I was quick to tell them that there was a sniper busy on our right and that he'd shot the MO. They didn't take very kindly to this, and after a look round they headed across the railway to the opposite side. As soon as I saw where they were going I realised where the sniper was hiding and kicked myself for not realising sooner. There was a large bush beside the railway and as the pilots approached it a German emerged with a rather sickly smile on his face and his hands in the air.

C Troop withdrew back to Wolfheze. Taking our wounded with us we placed them in the care of our MO who, in spite of his own wounds, started work right away.

A Dutch house had been taken over for this purpose with the enthusiastic consent of the lady who lived there. Bill Edmond, my jeep driver, had been killed during the action. I'll always remember him as a man who was extremely fond of his wife and was never reluctant to say so. He was buried in a temporary grave opposite the house that held the wounded. A little later a Dutch lady approached us with the suggestion that our dead be buried in her garden. We were pleased to do this, so Bill was disinterred and moved. Later I used his original grave as a slit trench . . . [38]

The 1st Reconnaissance Squadron held its positions near Wolfheze until 1830 hours, having endured heavy mortar fire for much of the time. It was then ordered to disengage by Divisional HQ, and relieved by men of the Glider Pilot Regiment.

Ironically, at about the same time Sepp Krafft also began withdrawing his units from their blocking positions, believing that they were being encircled. With the arrival of No 9 Company the 16th

Battalion's strength had risen to thirteen officers, 73 NCOs and 349 men; their directive now was to break out under cover of darkness.

Earlier, when the fighting was at its height, Major Freddie Gough, who was with Squadron HQ a few hundred yards to the rear of the leading elements, had received a message that General Urquhart wished to see him at Divisional HQ, which had been set up at the DZ. Gough duly went back to find that Urquhart had left a few minutes earlier with Brigadier Lathbury and Brigade HQ.

The instruction to Major Gough to report personally to Divisional HQ resulted directly from a breakdown in radio communication between Division and the forward operational units. The radio transceivers in use had a range of not much more than three miles, but the main problem was that the heavily wooded territory acted as a screen against the reception of signals from sets transmitting on simple rod aerials.

The problem was compounded by an extraordinary rumour which reached Divisional HQ – and to this day no-one knows how or where it originated – that the 1st Airborne Reconnaissance Squadron had lost most of its vehicles. With no means of establishing by radio whether the rumour was true or not, Urquhart left Divisional HQ at Renkum Heath and set out in the wake of Lt-Col. John Frost's 2nd Battalion.

Following assembly, the 2nd Battalion moved off from Heelsum, south of Renkum Heath, having had a brief skirmish with the enemy there and taken twenty prisoners. The time was about 1530 hours, and the Battalion faced a six-mile march before it reached the Arnhem bridges. Conscious of the urgency, Frost's men maintained a fast pace as they progressed along the southernmost route into Arnhem; designated *Lion*, this ran from Heelsum via Heveadorp and Oosterbeek, roughly following the line of the Neder Rijn. The Battalion encountered some enemy fire from the woods at Doorwerth – probably from an isolated unit of 16th SS Battalion – but was soon on the move again. There was more fighting as the spearhead of the Battalion passed through the southern suburbs of Oosterbeek; this time, the opponents were a pioneer section of 9 SS, part of one of the Division's quick-reaction companies which had rushed towards the sounds of battle using every available means of transport. The Dutch population, overjoyed by the

---

* Captain Swinscow, in fact, had not been hit by the sniper, but had been wounded in the back by mortar bomb fragments. Displaying great gallantry, he and his orderlies had recovered the wounded, under constant fire.

Troops of Lt-Col John Frost's 2nd Parachute Battalion set out on the long approach march to the Arnhem Bridge.

prospect of liberation, crowded into the streets, ignoring the danger.

We came down the long slope into Oosterbeek, and the people met us with baskets of apples and pears. We filled up our smocks as they kept pressing them on us and pouring them into the men's helmets. Others brought us jugs of water and beer, while one farmer was dipping out milk from a churn . . . Those Dutch men and women, in their overwhelming enthusiasm, showed complete disregard for danger. Every now and again a sniper's rifle would crack quite alarmingly near and be answered by the clatter of a vigilant Bren, but no-one paid the least attention. There was heavy firing to the north, but to them it was merely the prelude to peace. We munched apples down the quiet suburban avenues but kept a wary eye open as we pushed on with all speed . . . [39]

Beyond Oosterbeek, C Company detached from the line of march and followed a cart track across some fields towards the river. Its objective was the railway bridge. On the way, the Company passed an abandoned 40 mm gun, with rifles and a box of grenades lying nearby. The lane ended in a large disused brick-kiln near the river; the bridge and the fifteen-foot railway embankment lay some 200 yards ahead.

The leading platoon climbed up the embankment and passed a flak emplacement, shattered by rocket-firing Typhoons earlier in the day. German dead still lay around it. The platoon reached the bridge and advanced on to the first span, but was halted by small-arms fire from some stragglers – a mixture of infantry and anti-aircraft gunners – from 10 SS. A few moments later the German demolition commander fired his charges and the bridge's main span curled up in the air and then collapsed on itself with a terrific explosion. After a brief engagement with some enemy trucks that came along the embankment road, Major V. Dover led his company back along the track to the main road, following the rest of the 2nd Battalion into Arnhem.

The Battalion, meanwhile, had been delayed by German resistance near some high ground called Den Brink, on the approach road to the Arnhem road bridge, where another mixed bunch of enemy troops had been assembled under the command of a 10 SS *Unterscharführer* (the equivalent of a lance-corporal) named Helmut Buttlar. This small force inflicted a number of casualties on B Company, which took and held the high ground after a fierce fire-fight; Buttlar then withdrew his surviving men deeper into the Den Brink park.

While this action was in progress, A Company

skirted the Den Brink position to the south and pushed on towards the road bridge, keeping close to the river and meeting with small, scattered parties of Germans who were killed or captured. At about 2000 hours, Frost's men came within sight of the bridge.

The German plans to defend the Arnhem road bridge were in disarray. The officer responsible for securing and co-ordinating its defence was *Generalmajor* Kussin, and Kussin was dead.

The chain of events leading to his death, and the subsequent confusion over who was to defend the vital bridge, had begun at about 1400 hours, just as the British paratroops were descending on their dropping zones. At that time, *Feldmarschall* Walther Model, commanding Army Group B, was just about to sit down to take lunch with his officers in the Tafelberg Hotel in Oosterbeek when the news came – accompanied by the crump of anti-aircraft fire – that Allied airborne landings were taking place two or three miles to the west.

Model at once ordered his staff to dismantle their HQ in the hotel and report to their various assignments in Arnhem. Model himself, grabbing a suitcase of personal belongings, set out for Doetinchem and the headquarters of II SS *Panzer* Corps. On the way he called at the *Feldkom-mandantur* (Area Command HQ) in Arnhem and instructed the area commander, General Kussin, to radio the latest events to Hitler's HQ in East Prussia. He also mentioned that he had escaped from Oosterbeek by the skin of his teeth, a fact that Kussin dutifully relayed. Kussin then decided to drive westwards to assess the situation for himself. A few hours later he and his two aides lay dead in the bullet-riddled wreck of their staff car, having been ambushed by the 3rd Parachute Battalion.

It was some time before the news of Kussin's death reached his Chief of Staff, Major Ernst Schliefenbaum. He at once telephoned Model, who made him responsible for the defence of Arnhem and the bridge. Schliefenbaum was well aware of the problems facing him; only half an hour earlier, he had been conferring with Walther Harzer, commanding the *Kampfgruppe* of 9 SS, making arrangements for the deployment of the German forces converging on Arnhem and for the defence of the bridge.

Harzer was nervous about the bridge defences, which then comprised only a couple of dozen

---

General Kussin, the German area commander at Arnhem, lies dead beside his bullet-riddled staff car after being ambushed by the 3rd Parachute Battalion.

guards, either elderly or very young, and a few police units. One unit could have been immediately diverted to strengthen the defences; this was the 9th SS Reconnaissance Battalion, numbering 400 men and equipped with armoured half-tracks, under the command of *Hauptsturmführer* Viktor Gräbner. It was based at Hoenderloo, ten miles north of Arnhem. But on the orders of SS General Wilhelm Bittrich, now commanding II *Panzer* Corps, Grabner's unit was to make with all speed for Nijmegen. At about 1800 hours on 17 September, with 30 armoured cars and half-tracks, the Reconnaissance Battalion passed through Arnhem and crossed the bridge, bound for its assigned objective.

When the Battalion had passed over, the bridge seemed strangely deserted. A Dutch police constable named van Kuijk later reported that he had walked across it at 1930 hours without seeing a soul – doubtless because the defenders were in their bunkers, waiting apprehensively for the coming onslaught.

The bridge that loomed up in the gathering dusk before the eyes of John Frost's 2nd Parachute Battalion was an impressive sight. The great, curving single span, superbly designed, was approached from the north by a huge concrete ramp, which carried bridge traffic up and over the riverside roads that ran between the supporting pillars. Around the approach to the ramp, houses were clustered in narrow streets. As the leading platoons of the 2nd Battalion ran towards the bridge they could see German transport still crossing over from north to south.

At this time the 2nd Battalion consisted mainly of A Company; C Company had become blocked by a force of Germans near the railway station and B Company, having driven the Germans from the Den Brink rise, had gone on to investigate the pontoon bridge over the river – which it found to be useless, the Germans having removed several sections.

While part of A Company set about establishing defensive positions in the buildings around the bridge ramp, one of the Battalion's officers, Lieutenant McDermont, led a detachment in an attempt to take the south end of the bridge. Advancing on to the structure, the men were pinned down by fire from a bunker mounting a twin 20 mm anti-aircraft gun on the north-west side of the bridge and also from an armoured car that appeared on the south side. This vehicle, also armed with a 20 mm cannon, was one of several belonging to No 1 Company of 10 SS Reconnaissance Battalion under the command of SS *Obersturmführer* Karl Ziebrecht; the Company had been ordered up to the bridge to reconnoitre the situation while the rest of the Battalion covered the east bank of the Rhine, Emmerich and Wesel. It arrived just as Frost's A Company was attempting the *coup de main* assault and exchanged fire with the paratroops. In the dusk and general confusion Ziebrecht was not certain about the scale of the opposition, but he radioed HQ 10 SS and reported what he had seen.

While A Company went about clearing the enemy bunkers on the north side of the bridge with PIATs and flame-throwers, other British troops began arriving in the bridge area. They included Brigade HQ and its Defence Platoon, a platoon of the RASC, the 1st Parachute Squadron Royal Engineers and a small party of the 1st Airborne Reconnaissance Squadron, led by Major Gough. The Reconnaissance Squadron's weapons, which included Vickers K guns, were a welcome addition to the Battalion's firepower, as were the flame-throwers carried by the Sappers.

In the absence of Brigadier Lathbury, Lt-Col. Frost assumed command at Brigade HQ, which established its base in a house with a high flat roof about 50 yards from the bridge overlooking the Eusebius Binnensingel. HQ 2nd Battalion was set up alongside on the corner of the Marktstraat. At this time, Frost's signallers were making repeated efforts to contact B and C Companies, with no success. In fact, the only radio contact that could be established was between a radio set in Brigade HQ and another in 2nd Battalion HQ, a mere 30 yards away.

In the meantime, another very gallant attempt to reach the southern side of the bridge had been thwarted. This was led by Lieutenant J.H. Grayburn, a platoon commander with the 2nd Battalion. He led his platoon on to the bridge and began the attack, but encountered intense fire from the 20 mm guns in the *flak* bunker and also from an armoured car at the other end of the bridge. Grayburn was wounded in the shoulder almost at once, but despite his injury he pressed forward until his casualties became so severe that he had no option but to withdraw. Grayburn personally directed with withdrawal from the bridge, and was the last man to leave the ramp. We shall hear more of him later.

Men of the Royal Engineers Parachute Squadron were detailed to try and knock out the troublesome 20 mm installation with a flame-thrower. Creeping up as close to it as possible, they took cover in a three-storey house overlooking the bridge and gave the bunker a good squirt before igniting the fuel. They missed the slit in the bunker, but hit one of an adjacent row of huts and set it on fire. Unknown to the paratroops, the huts contained 20 mm ammunition. Within a short time the whole lot went up in a tremendous explosion, and the resulting fire quickly spread to the bridge itself, burning away the paintwork and damaging some electrical cables. Under cover of the conflagration, Lieutenant Vlasto of the 2nd Parachute Battalion went forward and knocked out the bunker with a PIAT.

The fire had an unexpected consequence, for the electrical cables it damaged – if the testimony of a German officer who was captured later is to be believed – were part of the bridge's emergency demolition system. Some mystery, in fact, surrounds the failure of the Germans to blow the bridge. According to Sapper Ron Hall – who had served with the 2nd Battalion in North Africa and Sicily, and who had been awarded the Military Medal for his part in making safe the demolition charges on the Primosole Bridge – the arrangements made by the Germans for destroying the Arnhem bridge were incomplete; the primary system was not operational.[40] But, in any case, the Germans were more concerned with holding the bridge than demolishing it; if the bridges further up the Rhine were in Allied hands, the Arnhem bridge would be the only means of extricating German forces remaining to the north.

Meanwhile, more German units – mostly under orders from HQ II SS Corps to push on to Nijmegen and reinforce the garrison there – were converging on the Arnhem bridge from various points of the compass. The one unit that did receive specific orders to secure the bridge was the 10th Reconnaissance Battalion of 10 SS, which was attached to 9 SS to compensate for the removal of Grabner's battalion to Nijmegen. Formed into the *Kampfgruppe* Brinkmann, this battalion set out for Arnhem at about the same time as the *Euling* Battalion of 10 SS, to which it had been transferred from 9 SS a few days earlier. Commanded by SS

Hauptsturmführer Karl-Heinz Euling, this battalion had orders to go to Nijmegen. Other rapid-reaction units were also heading for the Arnhem bridge; the most important of them was No 3 Company of *Panzergrenadier* Regiment 21, also of 10 SS, commanded by an NCO named Rudolf Trapp.

As mentioned earlier, the first of these units to make contact with the 2nd Parachute Battalion was Karl Ziebricht's No 1 Company of 10 SS Reconnaissance Battalion. Next to arrive was the *Euling* Battalion, whose troopers, on reaching the northern end of the bridge, found themselves involved in a vicious fire-fight without having any real idea of what was going on. A little while later, Rudolf Trapp's No 3 Company of 21 *Panzergrenadier* Regiment arrived on the northern outskirts of Arnhem, the men having made their way from Deventer by bicycle. They then advanced through the town on foot, making for the bridge, by way of Ryn Kade on the lower Rhine road. They were, in fact, moving behind Frost's battalion, and at dusk they exchanged fire with British paratroops – probably men of B Company – near the Oosterbeek-Laag church. It was dark by the time they reached the bridge area, where they came under heavy fire from the defensive positions set up by the 2nd Battalion in the buildings around the ramp. Initially, the Germans on the south bank of the river did not seem to realize the strength of the 2nd Battalion's defences; attempts to force the bridge by lorry-borne infantry were broken up at heavy cost to the attackers, the vehicles exploding in flames on the northern ramp and their occupants being cut down as they jumped clear.

The paratroops were by now very tired. The act of making a parachute drop is in itself a physically demanding experience for a soldier in battle gear, and on top of that there had been the six-mile march followed by the strain of combat. It was a relief when the fighting died away as the night progressed; the men took it in turns to keep watch and sleep, and to snatch their first bite of food – discounting titbits pressed on them by grateful Dutch civilians – since leaving England.

On the bridge vehicles were still burning. One was obviously an ammunition lorry. Every now and again it shuddered as the fire reached a further box of bullets or shells and they exploded . . . A pall of thick black smoke from the burning trucks hung over our positions. Although it smelt bad, it did help to conceal us from the enemy. On the road . . . a sentry from one of the rifle companies paced up and down, his heel-plates clinking softly on the street – one indicating of the measure of control we had established around the northern end of the bridge.[41]

The 2nd Battalion, or at least part of it, had reached its objective, but had not succeeded in taking it. All Lt-Col. Frost could do now was hold on to await the arrival of his missing companies and the other two parachute brigades. When these reinforcements reached him, he would be in a position to attempt a further assault on the southern end of the bridge.

But the other battalions would not reach him. The chain of events that would culminate in the overall disaster of Arnhem was being forged, link by link.

Lieutenant-Colonel David Dobie's 1st Parachute Battalion had set off at about 1600 hours to follow the northernmost route –*Leopard* – into Arnhem. Its first task was to reach Wolfheze station and then advance into Arnhem along the Ede–Arnhem road, securing the high ground to the north of the town and closing the route leading into it from Apeldoorn and Zutphen.

The 1st Battalion reached Wolfheze to find the 1st Airborne Reconnaissance Squadron in action with elements of Sepp Krafft's 16th SS Battalion. Major Gough informed Dobie that there was enemy activity along the railway line that ran eastward to Arnhem, and on the road that led northward from Wolfheze to join the Ede–Arnhem route. It was on this stretch of road that the 1st Battalion ran into serious trouble.

The German unit that stood in the path of the 1st Battalion was the *Kampfgruppe* Allworden. SS *Hauptsturmführer* Klaus von Allworden had commanded *Panzerjäger Abteilung* 9, the tank-destroyer battalion of 9 SS Division; the remains of this unit formed the nucleus of Allworden's quick-reaction force. It comprised 120 men – mostly former SP gun crews – in three companies. There were also two self-propelled guns and a number of 75 mm anti-tank guns at Allworden's disposal.

The *Kampfgruppe* Allworden established a blocking line along the Dreyenseweg, north of Oosterbeek, and sent out probes along the Arnhem–Ede road in the direction of Wolfheze. The *Kampfgruppe* was very well armed; in addition to the Mk IV *Jagdpanzer* SP guns, it possessed a considerable number of MG 42 machine-guns. Horst Schueler, who served with a *Kampfgruppe* at

Arnhem, remembers this excellent weapon with affection:

In 1944–45 this was the ultimate MG regarding firepower; it had a rate of fire of 1,200 rounds per minute and you could literally fell trees with it. We called it the Hitler Saw (*Hitlersäge*). It needed three men to operate it; one ammo feeder, one on the gun and one to change barrels. These were quick fit and we had five to play with. After every fifth change of barrel we changed places, so everyone got a chance to fire. Firing engagements lasted about 15–20 minutes, and after each one we changed position by a few hundred yards. When we were being mortared we used to move into fresh craters; they seldom got hit again.[42]

The fearsome efficiency of the *Hitlersäge* was demonstrated as the leading element of the 1st Battalion, R Company, moved north through woodland towards the Ede–Arnhem road. The Company walked straight into an ambush from enemy positions laid on wooded high ground and was hard hit, suffering 50 per cent casualties. Despite this, the Company fought its way through to the Ede–Arnhem road junction, where it encountered a force of enemy armour and half-tracks, which took up positions in the woods. It was now about 1900 hours, and radio contact between R Company and the rest of the battalion was lost. Lt.-Col. Dobie despatched one of his officers to find out what had happened, and – aware now of the strong enemy opposition to the north – decided to try to by-pass the German positions by taking a more southerly route.

As the battalion advanced through the woods towards the Dreyenseweg, the route running north from Oosterbeek and crossing the railway before joining the Ede–Arnhem road, it encountered stiffening resistance not only from Allworden's *Kampfgruppe*, but also from Sepp Krafft's 16th SS Battalion and from a new *Kampfgruppe* which was beginning to deploy in the Arnhem area. This was the *Kampfgruppe* Spindler, named after the SS *Sturmbannführer* who commanded the artillery regiment of 9 SS Division. The nucleus of the *Kampfgruppe* was Spindler's own regiment, which no longer had any guns and which had been reduced by earlier casualties to two companies numbering some 150 men. At about 1730 hours, these were ordered to march to Arnhem from Dieren, five miles away.

Bittrich's principal order to Spindler was to form a *Sperrlinie* – blocking line – along the Dreyenseweg,

A German half-track, mounting a 20-mm cannon, in action in the woods north-west of Arnhem.

bringing under his command those scattered units of 9 SS Division which were already in action. The blocking line was to extend from the Ede–Arnhem road south to the lower Rhine. To achieve this was an incredibly difficult task, given the general confusion, communications difficulties and the onset of darkness; the fact that it was achieved in an astonishingly short time was a fine example of German Army discipline and organization at their best.

Spindler's *Sperrlinie* was already beginning to firm up by 2000 hours, the first units to arrive establishing themselves north-south along the Dreyenseweg and north-west to south-east along the Ede–Arnhem railway from the point where the road intersected it. On the Germans' right flank, Krafft's 16th SS Battalion fell back along the Ede–Arnhem road under pressure from the 1st Parachute Battalion and joined up with Spindler's troops. So did the remnants of the 9 SS Pioneer Battalion, which earlier in the day had engaged the 2nd Parachute Battalion on the outskirts of Oosterbeek; this was now reduced to about 100 men, supported by a few armoured half-tracks and commanded by SS *Hauptsturmführer* Hans Möller. Another unit that was brought into the defensive line, and one that provided a valuable firepower

addition, was a 9 SS anti-aircraft battery under SS *Obersturmführer* Gopp; this was equipped with 20 mm guns mounted on half-tracks, formidable weapons when used ground-to-ground at close range. Another valuable unit contributing to the *Sperrlinie* was *Kampfgruppe* Harder, formed from the original *Panzer* Regiment 9 and comprising three infantry companies, one composed of dismounted tank crews, one of fitters and supply personnel, and the third of naval personnel. This *Kampfgruppe* formed a secondary line of defence running through the western suburbs of Arnhem, from the railway station via the Nieuwe and Roermonds Plein to the lower Rhine; in so doing it cut off access to Lt.-Col. Frost's force at the bridge, 800 yards to the east.

Throughout the late evening of 17 September, and through the night, Dobie's 1st Parachute Battalion launched determined and costly attacks against the *Sperrlinie* in the woods near Johannahoeve, but to no avail. At 2200 hours, the officer who had been sent to R Company returned and reported that it had suffered casualties amounting to 50 per cent of its strength. Dobie sent orders that the Company was to disengage and rejoin the rest of the battalion.

Lieutenant-Colonel J.A.C. Fitch's 3rd Parachute Battalion, meanwhile, had fared no better. From Heelsum, the 3rd Battalion had set off after Frost's battalion, passing to the north of the Heveadorp woods to follow the line of the Utrechtseweg – *Tiger* route – towards Oosterbeek and Arnhem. It had been on the road for less than an hour when, about half a mile from Oosterbeek, it was halted by a counter-attack from No 9 Company of Krafft's 16th Battalion, supported by two armoured cars. The encounter, which took place at the Utrechtseweg-Wolfheze crossroads, took B Company of the 3rd Battalion – forming the advance guard – by surprise. The Company had no PIATS, and its sole six-pounder anti-tank gun was pointing the wrong way when the enemy armour appeared; it was knocked out as the paratroops were trying to turn it around. The men went to ground and engaged the armoured cars and infantry positions round the Bilderberg Hotel with small-arms fire.

The time was about 1700 hours. At that moment, the paratroops were astonished to see a lone staff car driving at speed along the Utrechtseweg towards the crossroads. The paratroops let it come on, then poured Sten fire into it, killing all four occupants. One of them was General Kussin, who, against the advice of Sepp Krafft – whose headquarters he had just visited – had decided to return to Arnhem by this route instead of the safer northern one, parallel with the railway.

The 3rd Battalion's leading companies were now subjected to a fierce mortar bombardment by Krafft's No 2 Company, well dug in near the Bilderberg Hotel; this held the paratroops up for at least an hour. By this time, Fitch had been joined by General Urquhart and Brigadier Lathbury, who – in the absence of adequate radio communications – had gone off personally to try to speed progress along the southern route. Soon after his arrival, Urquhart had a lucky escape; as he was returning to his jeep to try to raise Divisional HQ on the radio, the vehicle was hit by a mortar bomb and his signaller seriously wounded. As there was considerable fire from enemy mortars and snipers, inflicting many casualties on the 3rd Battalion, Urquhart and Lathbury decided that it would be too dangerous to return to Brigade HQ and elected to stay with the Battalion.

The position at the crossroads was clearly becoming untenable. At about 1800 hours, with Brigadier Lathbury's concurrence, Lt.-Col. Fitch decided to initiate a flanking movement with C Company to the left as far as the railway line and then follow that line to the Arnhem bridge. C Company accordingly advanced through B towards the railway, and this was the last the rest of the battalion saw of it. As C Company moved down a small by-road the platoons became separated. The leading one fought an action against a captured British jeep filled with Germans and continued on; the other two platoons eventually caught up with it, having attacked an ammunition truck and set it on fire. At dusk, all three platoons, now much reduced in numbers, reached the railway station at Arnhem and then moved on towards the bridge through streets that seemed deserted except for a couple of Dutch policemen.

Major-General Roy Urquhart, commanding the 1st Airborne Division, seen outside his HQ at Hartenstein. The photograph was taken at the height of the battle.

The Company walked down a main street towards the bridge, the leading platoon destroying an enemy half-track with a Gammon bomb just before it reached its objective. There was a confused fight in the darkness, and eventually what was left of C Company fought its way through to the school house, where the Sappers of the 1st Parachute Squadron were already installed.

The rest of the 3rd Battalion, meanwhile, dug in for the night near a restaurant called De Koude Herberg on the outskirts of Oosterbeek. By now, patrols were reporting enemy activity to both east and west, making it impossible for Fitch to evacuate his wounded – 35 men, some seriously hurt – either back to the 1st Air Landing Brigade's HQ at Wolfheze or forward to St Elisabeth's Hospital in Arnhem. Fitch resolved to rest his men for a few hours, then resume his advance shortly before dawn, following the route the 2nd Battalion had taken.

While the three battalions of the 1st Parachute Brigade were trying to reach the Arnhem bridge by three different routes, the three battalions of the 1st Air Landing Brigade had remained behind to secure and guard the dropping and landing zones in readiness for the second lift. The 2nd Battalion The South Staffordshire Regiment (less two companies due to arrive with the second lift) was deployed at Reijerscamp, the 7th Battalion The King's Own Scottish Borderers at Planken Wambuis (Ginkel Heath) and the 1st Battalion The Border Regiment at Renkum Heath. Unlike the other zones, Ginkel Heath had not been used on 17 September.

The task of opposing the airborne forces in this north-western sector of the operational area fell to *Generalleutnant* Hans von Tettau, commanding the reception screen that had been set up to deal with German forces withdrawing into Holland. Von Tettau had no clear idea of what was going on, and to confuse matters even further he was receiving persistent – and completely false – reports of airborne landings at Utrecht, Tiel, Dordrecht and Veenendaal.

Krafft's 16th SS Battalion had already made some weak probes towards the landing zones in the course of the afternoon, but when that withdrew to form part of the eastern blocking force von Tettau had to make do with whatever forces could be scraped together at short notice.

The formation immediately available to him was *Hauptsturmführer* Paul Helle's Dutch SS Surveillance Battalion (*Wachbattalion* 3). This was now instructed to proceed from Amersfoort to Ede, with vague orders to infiltrate the woods to the north of the zones and attack the enemy. The first unit to set out, at about 1700 hours, was the Battalion's so-called *Jagdkommando* (raiding detachment); composed mainly of bandsmen, its usual job was to round up Allied airmen who had been shot down.

Helle went on ahead and set up his Headquarters in the Langenberg Hotel on the Ede–Arnhem road to the north-west of Ginkel Heath. Soon afterwards the *Jagdkommando* arrived, led by Drum-Major Sakkel, in the only available trucks. Helle ordered Sakkel and his men to follow the road skirting Ginkel Heath and reconnoitre the enemy positions on the western side. They did so, and were ambushed by a platoon of the 7th KOSB. Sakkel fell, seriously wounded, he was brought in and died later in hospital in Apeldoorn. The rest of the *Jagdkommando* scattered in panic, and many subsequently deserted.

Some time afterwards, a second probe was made by the *Wachbattalion*'s No 4 Company, commanded by SS *Obersturmführer* Bartsch, newly arrived at Ginkel Heath after commandeering transport. Approaching the British positions at about 2100 hours, the Dutch SS were beaten off by a withering fire from A Company of the 7th KOSB, astride the Arnhem road, and D Company, entrenched in the woods a short distance to the south. Number 3 Company under SS *Obersturmführer* Hink, advancing on No 4 Company's right and a little to the rear, met the same fate. Many of these men, who were concentration camp guards, also took the opportunity to desert in the confusion.

A third company arrived, commanded by *Obersturmführer* Fernau, and attempted to outflank the British positions, advancing cautiously through the woods on Hink's right. Fernau moved south-east towards the area where – unknown to him – Lt.-Col. Payton-Reid, commanding the 7th KSOB, had established his Battalion HQ. This was flanked on the right by Headquarters Company, covering a woodland track. Fernau also encountered strong opposition and reported back to Helle that no further progress was possible.

Eventually a fourth Dutch SS company reached the northern edge of the heath and its commander, *Obersturmführer* Kuhne, was ordered to occupy the sector between Hink and Fernau. As luck would have it, right in the middle of this sector stood a wooden hut which was occupied by a platoon of D Company of the 7th KSOB; after a short fight these men were surrounded and captured. The commander of D Company initiated a counter-attack to try to rescue them, but the attempt failed.

This was the only success registered by the Germans against the 1st Air Landing Brigade on 17 September, but stronger forces were already beginning to assemble against it. By mid-evening, HQ 9 SS Division had established that the principal airborne landing areas were Arnhem and Nijmegen, and by 2230 hours German Intelligence officers, sifting through documents found on the body of an American officer killed when his first-wave Waco glider crashed near General Student's Headquarters in Vught, were able to provide Army Group B with a clearer picture of the Allies' intentions. By midnight, Army Group B alerted its subordinate commands that

101 Airborne Division has the task, according to captured papers and interrogations of prisoners, of occupying the roads and bridges between Veghel–Oedenrode and Zon. These are to be kept open for British troops – XXX Corps – who are to attack through Holland and Germany.[43]

Armed with all available information on the 1st Airborne Division's deployments, scant though it still was, HQ Army Group B directed von Tettau to attack the Arnhem landing areas from the west and north. This would be accomplished with the help of troops drawn from the Waal screening force, which in reality meant *Obersturmbannführer* Hans-Michael Lippert's SS NCO School, now expanded to regimental status with the addition of personnel from other units. Reporting to von Tettau's Headquarters at Rhenen, Lippert was ordered to advance to Renkum Heath via Wageningen and attack the enemy. His men began their approach march just before midnight, reinforced by a Naval *Kampfgruppe* (*Schiffsturmabteilung* 10, supported by detachments from Naval Battalions 6 and 14), a *Fliegerhorst* Battalion and an infantry battalion formed from Artillery Regiment 184.

Lippert's forces would soon come into contact with the 1st Battalion The Border Regiment, defending Renkum Heath. As was the case with the 2nd Battalion The South Staffordshire at Reijerscamp, the Borders had spent an uneventful

day, with patrolling their main activity. As the South Staffordshire's war diary later commented,

It was a strange sensation to be deep in enemy territory and miles from one's own troops. However, the Huns either did not know where the battalion was, or were being kept too busy to come and cause any trouble. There was spasmodic fighting in the direction of Arnhem during the night, but as it did not come any nearer most of the men were able to get what was to be their only real night's sleep during the operation.[44]

There was no indication, yet, of the cauldron that would soon engulf them.

THE ADVANCE OF XXX CORPS

From a vantage point on the roof of a factory overlooking the Meuse–Escaut canal, Lieutenant-General Brian Horrocks watched the airborne armada pass overhead and issued the final orders which, at 1400 hours, sent his armoured divisions and their supporting infantry smashing through the German crust around the Neerpelt bridgehead and along the road to Valkenswaard and Eindhoven.

The breakout, spearheaded by Lieutenant-Colonel J.O.E. Vandeleur's Irish Guards Group, was preceded by an hour-long artillery bombardment and by attacks along the Valkenswaard road delivered by medium bombers of 2nd Tactical Air Force. This softening-up mainly affected the three battalions of the Regiment von Hoffman and destroyed all of its towed anti-tank artillery, so that the infantry were left initially with only *Panzerfaust* anti-tank weapons with which to engage the leading elements of the Irish Guards. The Germans' defensive measures were greatly helped by the terrain; the ground on either side of the road was sandy and boggy, quite unsuitable for tanks, and this fact –together with fears that the ground might have been mined – led to the armour advancing down the road in closely echeloned columns.

The German infantry had sited their anti-tank positions well. They waited until the leading squadron of the Irish Guards Group rolled past and then opened fire, hitting the rearmost tanks and those leading the second squadron. In all, *Panzerfaust* ambushes knocked out eight tanks and two armoured cars during this initial phase of the assault, but now that the German positions were identified they were quickly wiped out by fire from the armoured fighting vehicles. The Typhoons of

No 38 Group also provided support on the road to Eindhoven, flying 116 sorties against targets identified by the Guards Armoured Division's forward air controllers.

By 1700 hours the British armoured column, supported on the left flank by XII Corps operating against *Kampfgruppe* Chill, had reached a point about two miles south of Valkenswaard. Here it suffered further casualties inflicted by the 88 mm anti-tank guns of SS *Kampfgruppe* Röstel; this unit also had eight Mk IV *Panzerjäger* SP guns, which made occasional forays from the woods to snipe at the British tanks. Because of the dense vegetation bordering the road, and the softness of the ground, it was virtually impossible for the tanks to take evasive action; however, once an 88 mm gun had given away its position by firing it was inevitably destroyed.

So, fighting small and vicious actions against scattered and desperate groups of German soldiers, the Guards Armoured Division punched its way to Valkenswaard, which it reached at 1930 hours. And there it halted – the first of several halts that would prove fatal for the 1st Airborne Division at Arnhem.

CHAIN OF COMMAND AND ORDER OF BATTLE: *GARDEN*

21st Army Group:	Field-Marshal B.L. Montgomery (Commanding)
	Major-General Francis de Guingand (Chief of Staff)
Second British Army:	General Miles Dempsey (Commanding)
XXX Corps:	Lt-Gen Brian Horrocks (Commanding)
Guards Armoured Division:	Major-General Allan Adair (Commanding)
	Brigadier Norman Gwatkin (Chief of Staff)
Irish Guards Group:	Lt-Col J.O.E. Vandeleur (Commanding)
2nd Battalion:	Lt-Col Giles Vandeleur
Scots Guards:	One Company (X Coy Infantry)
Grenadier Guards:	2 Battalions (Armoured and Infantry)
Coldstream Guards:	2 Battalions (Armoured and Infantry)
2nd Household Cavalry Regiment	(Armoured and Scout Cars)
43rd Wessex Division:	Major-General Ivor Thomas (Commanding)
129th Infantry Brigade:	(Brigadier G.H.L. Mole)
4th Somerset Light Infantry	(Lt-Col C.G. Lipscomb)
5th Wiltshire	(Lt-Col W.G. Roberts)
4th Wiltshire	(Lt-Col E.L. Luce)
130th Infantry Brigade	(Brigadier B.B. Walton)
7th Hampshire	(Lt-Col D.E.B. Talbot)
4th Dorset	(Lt-Col G. Tilley)
5th Dorset	(Lt-Col B.A. Coad)
217th Infantry Brigade	(Brigadier H. Essame)
7th Somerset Light Infantry	(Lt-Col H.A. Borradaile)
1st Worcestershire	(Lt-Col R.E. Osborne-Smith)
5th Duke of Cornwall's Light Infantry	(Lt-Col G. Taylor)
Princess Irene Brigade	(Col A. de Ruyter van Steveninck, commanding)
	(Maj Johkheer Jan Beelaerts van Blokland, Chief of Staff)
50th Northumbrian Division	(Corps reserve: Major-General D.A.H. Graham, commanding)

52nd Lowland Division, Airportable (to have been flown to LZs in Arnhem area)

1st Airborne Division, Land/Sea Element (the 'Seaborne Tail')
Comprised about 1,000 vehicles despatched to France about six weeks before *Market Garden*. Carried supplies and ammunition for replenishing the whole Division. Reached Nijmegen with the Guards Armoured Division; maintained survivors of 1st Airborne Division after their withdrawal across the Rhine.

CHAPTER 7
D plus One, 18 September 1944

On the night of 17/18 September, ten aircraft of RAF Bomber Command dropped dummy parachutists and explosive devices to simulate small-arms fire west of Utrecht, while ten more carried out a similar operation near Emmerich in an attempt to divert enemy forces from the *Market* area. These 'spoof' operations failed to achieve the desired result, but they did initiate rumours – which persisted up to D plus 4 – that airborne forces were landing in small numbers at various points in Holland.

As the aircraft returned to their bases, there were already signs that the weather was taking a turn for the worse. Since late the previous afternoon, the Airborne Army's meteorological advisers had been predicting that there would be fog over the troop carrier bases on the morning of the 18th, and that low cloud and rain would persist over the Channel and the Low Countries until about noon. At about 1800 hours on D-Day, General Brereton accordingly

decided to postpone H-Hour on D plus 1 from 1000 to 1400 hours, and to send all the missions over the southern route. The decision to use only this route was made in the hope of reducing flak casualties; if all went according to plan by the end of D-Day, the air corridor would be in friendly hands as far as Nijmegen.

Early on 18 September, weather reconnaissance flights reported that dense cloud was starting to build up over the western sector of the southern route; the northern route, on the other hand, remained relatively clear, so Brereton reversed his earlier decision and instructed all missions to use this route. H-Hour was left at 1400 hours. The northern route had been planned to accommodate three-lane traffic, so there would be no unacceptable congestion. The serials for the 101st Airborne Division would use the right-hand lane, turning right at the IP for the run-in to LZ 'W'; those for the 82nd Division would fly in the centre, while the

Preparing to hook up a Horsa glider to a Stirling tug at a base in the UK.

Men of the 1st Airborne Division and Stirlings of No 38 Group RAF preparing for a mission to Arnhem.

American transport aircraft bringing in the second lift for the 1st Airborne Division would use the left-hand lane as far as the IP, when they would turn left for Arnhem. Overhead, at 2,500 feet, glider tug combinations of No 38 Group, also heading for Arnhem, would in effect create a fourth lane of traffic. The whole operation would involve the despatch of 1,336 American troop-carriers, 340 British troop-carriers and 1,205 gliders. The airborne force would be followed by 252 USAAF B-24 Liberators flying the bomber resupply mission. In theory, the resupply aircraft would benefit from the anti-flak operations preceding the passage of the airborne force.

Fighter escort for the troop-carriers between England and the IP was to be provided by sixteen squadrons of Spitfires, while three squadrons of Spitfires, five of Tempests and three of Mustangs undertook flak suppression operations from Schouwen Island to the IP. The whole RAF fighter force assigned to D plus 1 missions amounted to 277 aircraft. The US Eighth Air Force, for its part, assigned 397 P-51s and P-47s to the second day of operations; again, two P-51 groups were to fly perimeter patrols on a line curving from Hasselt through Wesel to the Zuider Zee, while area cover between the IP and the zones was to be provided by six P-51 groups flying at and above 2,500 feet. To deal with flak batteries and other ground targets, the Ninth Air Force loaned two groups of P-47s and one squadron of Thunderbolts equipped with air-to-ground rockets.

The flak suppression task proved far more difficult than on D-Day. Haze and low cloud hampered identification and impeded bombing; of the 95 P-47s committed, only 45 dropped bombs. Because of poor intelligence on the exact positions of the Allied airborne troops, the Thunderbolt pilots were told to attack only when fired upon, which tended to compound their problems; the German gunners, realizing what the Americans were up to, held their fire until a P-47 had flown past and then gave it a quick burst from astern. Despite the handicaps, the Allied pilots claimed the destruction of 33 flak positions, together with four damaged and 37 silenced, for the loss of three aircraft.

It was on 18 September that the Germans made their first determined attempt to interfere with the transport serials by the use of fighter aircraft. The first attempt came shortly before 1500 hours, when 35 FW 190s were sighted fifteen miles north-east of Arnhem, heading for the zones. They were intercepted and driven off by 57 Mustangs of the 359th Fighter Group, which shot down three Germans for the loss of two of their own number. But the biggest success of the day came a few minutes later when 52 Mustangs of the 357th Fighter Group, covering the Eindhoven area, were vectored to a point on the perimeter about 40 miles south-east of Eindhoven to meet an incoming attack by about 60 enemy aircraft, a mixed force of Focke-Wulf 190s and Messerschmitt 109s. The Americans claimed 26 Germans destroyed for the loss of two of their own aircraft.

The perimeter patrols were so effective, in fact, that the only enemy aircraft to succeed in breaking through them on 18 September were one or two Me 262 jets; at least one of these aircraft dropped a couple of bombs near the 615th Field Squadron, Royal Engineers, during the Guards Armoured Division's advance on Eindhoven. Apart from these isolated incidents, Allied air supremacy was as near total as possible.

EINDHOVEN

Ground operations in the Eindhoven sector began before dawn, when the 506th Parachute Infantry Regiment of the 101st Airborne Division marched south to the town. Reaching the outskirts of Eindhoven at 0900 hours, the 2nd Battalion met and overcame resistance by units of 18 Flak Brigade (*Kampfgruppe* Köppel). By noon, most of the town was in American hands; shortly beforehand, an officer telephoned HQ 1st *Fallschirmjäger* Army and reported that

Enemy has penetrated into the north of Eindhoven. Street fighting. Further contact with unit not now possible. The insertion of infantry reinforcements has been ruled out. Anti-tank group *Grünewald* requests further orders from Army -

At that point, the telephone message was abruptly cut off.[45]

The 506th PIR found the Eindhoven bridges undamaged; it only remained for them now to hold on until the arrival of XXX Corps. Of the 101st Airborne's other regiments, the 501st PIR found no difficulty in repulsing four or five attacks made by weak German forces from the direction of Schijndel and 's Hertogenbosch; these were mounted by improvised units of the *Kampfgruppe* Chill.

The 502nd PIR, however, was having a much harder time. In the early hours of 18 September, its 3rd Battalion became involved in a heavy firefight with *Flak Abteilung* 424, part of Flak Brigade 18, at a road junction east of Best of the edge of the Zon forest. As the hours passed, the German force was strengthened by the arrival of advance units of *Generalleutnant* Poppe's 59th Infantry Division. The remainder of the 502nd PIR, with the exception of the 1st Battalion, which remained at St Oedenrode, came up to assist the 3rd Battalion and was also pinned down. By mid-morning the situation was desperate, and one particularly heavy attack, supported by tanks, was only beaten off when the enemy was bombed and strafed by five P-47s which put in a timely appearance.

The constant attacks against the 502nd PIR, whose sector lay less than a thousand yards west and south-west of LZ 'W', presented an unexpected hazard to the glider missions scheduled for that afternoon.

The plan was for the 101st Division to be reinforced by 2,656 troops, 156 jeeps, 111 trailers and two bulldozers transported in 450 Waco gliders towed by C-47s of the 53rd Troop Carrier Wing. The troops were mainly from the 327th Glider Infantry Regiment (minus the 1st Battalion) commanded by Colonel Joseph P. Harper, the 326th Airborne Engineer Battalion, and the 326th Airborne Medical Company. Among the remainder was a detachment of Divisional Headquarters including the divisional artillery commander, Brigadier-General Anthony C. McAuliffe, who flew in the lead glider of the lead serial.

This began its take-off at about 1120 hours, the fog having at last burned away as the sun rose higher. The serials assembled over the Greenham Common area, took up their en route stations over Hatfield, and then flew the 83 miles north-east to Aldeburgh. From there they followed the northern route to the IP near 's Hertogenbosch, where they turned on to a south-easterly heading for the final run to LZ 'W'. The weather was good, although in places a thick haze reduced visibility to only a couple of miles.

Not all the Wacos reached the LZ. Five had structural failures and another five broke their tow-ropes while still over England; two of these crashed. Three more ditched in the sea, but efficient rescue work by the Royal Navy's MTBs saved all their occupants. Another became uncontrollable over the

Dutch coast and had to be released; it crash-landed in the middle of a fortified position on Schouwen Island, and all on board were taken prisoner by German flak crews.

One Waco pilot, Flight Officer Roy C. Lovingood, had an extraordinary experience. Ever since take-off his glider had been flying left wing heavy, and it had needed all his strength to keep the wings level during the sea crossing. As the combination crossed the Dutch coast a flak shell tore through the troublesome wing and water poured out through the hole. It turned out that someone had failed to replace an inspection cover on the upper surface of the wing during a safety check, and the wing cavity had filled with a considerable volume of rainwater. The rest of the flight was uneventful, a vast relief to the pilot's aching arms. [46]

Two C-47s in the lead serial were hit by light flak as they approached the LZ and crashed after releasing their gliders; 21 more were damaged. One of these was the aircraft towing the Waco in which General McAuliffe was a passenger. The fact that the tug's starboard engine was on fire was of no concern to McAuliffe, who was fast asleep in the co-pilot's seat. He woke up just before the glider was released, its pilot taking it down for a near-perfect landing only yards from the spot – a schoolhouse – previously selected by the general.[47]

The other eleven serials in the mission lost only two C-47s. One of these was hit about fifteen miles short of the zone, caught fire, released its glider and crashed; the other ditched on the homeward flight and its crew was rescued. Ninety-one aircraft from these serials were damaged, although all but four were repairable. Seven more Wacos were lost; one was hit by flak three miles from the LZ and disintegrated, three others were prematurely released over enemy territory and not heard of again, and three more crashed on landing at the zone.

Despite a good deal of confusion caused by serials arriving out of sequence, and gliders being released at higher than the planned altitude in order to avoid flak, the landings generally went very well, 428 gliders mostly concentrating on the western end of LZ 'W'. Some gliders overshot, landing too far to the west, and their troops were pinned down by fire from units of the 59th Infantry Division. This formation was still arriving piecemeal in the battle area, together with hastily-organized battle groups. One of these, *Kampfgruppe* Rink – a mixture of trainee infantry, police and anti-aircraft personnel – launched a half-hearted attack on the 502nd PIR as the airborne landings were taking place, but it was easily beaten off. The Americans also held on to their positions at St Oedenrode, despite a more determined assault by *Fallschirmjäger* Battalion Ewald.

Meanwhile, at 1230 hours, two scout cars of the 2nd Household Cavalry Regiment, probing ahead of XXX Corps on a reconnaissance, had established contact with the 506th PIR at Eindhoven. The bulk of the Corps was still five miles to the south, fighting its way from roadblock to roadblock. The advance was falling seriously behind schedule.

NIJMEGEN

At Nijmegen, General Gavin's 82nd Airborne Division found itself face to face with a potentially dangerous situation on D plus 1. The divisional perimeter was developing nicely, the 508th PIR having extended its lines westward to make contact

German infantry in action against the US 82nd Airborne Division at Groesbeek. The fight for the Nijmegen airhead cost both sides dearly.

with the 504th PIR at the site of Bridge 9, and the 508th was mustering its forces for a renewed and stronger attack on the vital bridge at Nijmegen.

So far, German resistance to American operations in the Nijmegen sector – with the exception of that at the main bridge – had been negligible, but any complacency was quickly shattered when, at about 0700 hours, a major German attack developed from the Kleve–Kranenburg area towards Beek, Eyler and Groesbeek. The main direction of the attack was west and north-west, across the landing zones, towards the Groesbeek Heights.

All through the night of 17/18 September, *Generalleutnant* Scherbening's 406th Infantry Division, which had consisted of nothing more than his Headquarters and a few training units when the 82nd Airborne Division descended on Nijmegen, had been strengthened by the arrival of quick-reaction groups from *Wehrkreis* VI, the military district just across the German border. By first light on 18 September, the equivalent of four battalions of infantry – composed mainly of *Luftwaffe* 'fortress' personnel – and three batteries of artillery had been assembled in the Groesbeek–Zyfflich area.

The attack was launched by three *Kampfgruppen*, named Stargaard, Fürstenberg and Greschick after their commanders; each was roughly of battalion strength and the whole attacking force was supported by a *Kampfgruppe*, commanded by *Hauptmann Freiherr* von Fürstenberg, which had at its disposal five armoured cars and three half-tracks mounting 20 mm flak guns. Another *Kampfgruppe*, Goebel, attacked from the south, near the village of Mook.

The attack registered some early successes; the enemy thrust from Wyler pushed back the single company of the 508th PIR which had been left to guard LZ 'T', and also seized an ammunition dump. General Gavin had to act quickly, and he was lucky in one respect; the postponement of the second lift meant that he had time in which to secure the landing zones before the vulnerable glider serials arrived.

Fortunately, the Germans – mostly untrained conscripts – were no match for the veterans of the 82nd Airborne, who made them pay dearly for every inch of ground they gained. But Gavin knew that he had to prevent the enemy from breaking through the defensive perimeter into the woods around Groesbeek, from which it would be virtually impossible to dislodge them. He accordingly threw his only available reserve, two companies of the 307th Engineers, into the gap between the 505th and 508th Regiments. He also ordered the two regiments to hold their lines along the Groesbeek Ridge at all costs and, when they were able, to retake the two compromised landing zones, 'T' and 'N', before the glider missions came in.

The 508th Regiment quickly pulled back its companies from the Nijmegen area and redeployed them on the ridge, and at 1310 hours it launched a counter-attack on LZ 'T'. Within an hour the paratroops had cleared the zone, taking 149 prisoners. Meanwhile, the 1st Battalion of the 505th PIR was ordered to attack eastward and clear LZ 'N'; since most of the Battalion was engaged in heavy fighting at Mook and Riethorst, the counter-attack was carried out by Company C, which charged downhill across the zone and put the enemy to flight. Less than half an hour later, at 1415 hours, three companies of enemy infantry attacked out of the Reichswald with the support of eleven armoured vehicles; the attack was beaten off by the 3rd Battalion of the 505th PIR with the help of artillery fire, which destroyed five of the AFVs.

The landing zones were once more in American hands, but they were far from secure. Fighting was still going on around their perimeters, and they were well within range of mortar and small-arms fire. When the second lift's leading serial appeared overhead at 1431 hours, it was clear that the glider-borne troops could expect a rough reception.

The reinforcement lift to the 82nd Airborne Division, flown by the 50th and 52nd Troop Carrier Wings, comprised eleven serials with a total of 454 C-47s, each one towing a Waco glider. The emphasis was on providing the 82nd Airborne with artillery; of the 1,889 troops in the gliders, nearly three-quarters belonged to the 319th, 320th and 456th Field Artillery Battalions, Battery B of the 80th Anti-tank Battalion, and Headquarters Battery of Divisional Artillery. The gliders also carried 206 jeeps, 123 trailers and 60 guns.

Fog and low cloud over the Grantham area delayed the start of the mission by 50 minutes, and it was not until 1109 hours that the first combination was airborne. Assembly took almost two hours, being impeded by the weather conditions, but once clear of the coast the pilots found that the weather was good, although a little hazy.

Two gliders made emergency landings in England, one after its airframe started to break up and another when a soldier went berserk, ran forward to the cockpit and pulled the release handle. Two more ditched in the sea when their tow ropes snapped in turbulence caused by the slipstream of aircraft ahead; one of these accidents was blamed on a four-engined tug of No 38 Group RAF, flying at a lower altitude than it should have been. Three more gliders were released over Holland because of tow breakages or flak damage, and another came down by mistake on LZ 'W', the pilot of the tug aircraft having become mixed up with a serial of the 53rd TCW.

Many of the glider pilots who did complete the mission found the flight to the LZ hard going. Unlike the British, the Americans did not make use of co-pilots, and in some cases pilots were virtually exhausted by the time they had completed the three-hour flight. There were also cases where the Waco's windscreen failed and blew out, admitting a 100 mph blast of air into the cockpit and fuselage. Pilots also reported that over 20 per cent of the intercom phones between tug and glider either failed or did not work properly.[48]

Aircraft losses on the mission amounted to ten C-47s. One was shot down by flak after the pilot went off course and strayed over the defences of Schouwen Island, and another that went missing was probably brought down in that area. Opposition between the coast and the IP was slight, but flak near 's Hertogenbosch tore the wing off a C-47. Two more were brought down by light flak and machine-guns in the Schijndel-Uden area, and another two were shot down just after releasing their gliders over LZ 'T'. The remaining three were destroyed after a serious navigational error took them several miles south-east of the zone. About 100 aircraft were damaged, but all were repairable.

The lead serial was flown by the 313th Troop Carrier Group (29th, 47th, 48th and 49th Troop Carrier Squadrons) from Folkingham, Lincolnshire. The 313th had dropped paratroops of the 82nd Airborne Division during the Normandy operations and had subsequently been stationed at advanced airstrips in France; this was its first combat glider mission, although on 17 September it had participated in the 1st Airborne Division's drop at Arnhem.

As it approached the release area, the formation split into two well-spaced columns so that the tugs could make a left turn without causing too much congestion. The first glider was released at 1431 hours, turning to land into a gentle north-east wind that blew across LZ 'N'. Some glider pilots, seeing fighting in progress at the edge of the zone, elected to come in fast, but most landings were made slowly and accurately at 60 or 70 mph. About half the gliders in this and subsequent serials had been fitted with arrester parachutes, which brought the Wacos to a halt in as little as 50 feet. Of the 212 gliders assigned to LZ 'N', 150 landed within a circle a half-mile radius centred on the hamlet of Knapheide a mile south-west of the zone; the remainder landed either within a mile and a half of Knapheide or on the zone itself.

The serials destined for LZ 'T' encountered more problems, at least some of which were caused by confusion over landing signals. Panels and smoke markers had been laid out on the western edge of the zone, but it seems likely that some of these were removed to a safer distance when the German attacks developed from the Reichswald.

Of the 242 gliders intended for LZ 'T', 90 landed on it and another 52 within a mile of its western boundary. Nineteen more were concentrated just over a mile to the west, and a further nineteen scattered in German-held territory up to four miles to the north-east.

The main problems arose in three serials, starting with the third, which was flown by the 316th TCG. The flight leader, who was responsible for navigation, released his glider prematurely over LZ 'O', and half the pilots in his serial followed suit. This error was not particularly damaging, as the airborne troops were able to assemble in safety and set out on the four-mile march to the other zones.

The rest of the serial reached LZ 'T', but only six released their gliders there. The other eight flew on in error and released their Wacos, carrying men of the 319th Field Artillery Battalion and various items of cargo, between Wyler and Zyfflich. The gliders landed almost on top of Replacement Battalion 1/E6, which was supported by a 20 mm flak gun. Some Americans managed to escape and join up with the division, but the cost to the 319th Battalion was five officers and 40 men killed or captured. The gliders' cargoes, needless to say, were all lost, and the Germans acquired an unexpected supply of jeeps.

The eighth serial, flown by the 61st TCG and carrying Battery B of the 320th Glider Field Artillery, ran into trouble 45 miles short of the zone, when a Waco was hit by flak and was cut loose. The tug pilot circled to watch the glider land, then turned and went home. The problem was that he was a flight leader, responsible for the serial's navigation; the pilot of the C-47 that took the lead did not have the benefit of radio navigational aids and, relying on visual navigation alone, got lost. Followed by eight other combinations, he missed the zone and the gliders went down twelve miles inside Germany, their occupants being either killed or taken prisoner.

The lead elements of the other squadron in this serial also overshot the zone, and nine of its gliders came down in the Wyler area. Realizing that they were in enemy territory, the airborne troops scrambled clear and took cover; the gliders were quickly destroyed by shellfire, but most of the Americans managed to hold out until nightfall and then work their way back to the Groesbeek area. The other 21 gliders in the serial all landed on or near the zone.

The following serial also had problems of navigation, this time because its *Gee* sets were being subjected to enemy jamming and its *Rebecca* receivers were not picking up signals from the *Eureka* beacon on the landing zone. As the 38 glider-tug combinations in this serial reached the Grave–Veghel area, 24 – and possibly as many as 30 – went off course to the south and the gliders were released in the Gennep area between three and five miles south of LZ 'T'. These gliders ran into close-range fire from anti-aircraft batteries and all kinds of small arms. Three C-47s were shot down and two gliders crashed; others were wrecked on landing as their pilots made frantic efforts to get down quickly by side-slipping or diving steeply. Those that did land safely were immediately attacked by German infantry, and the surviving troops had to fight for their lives until dark and then attempt to work their way into the 82nd Division's airhead. The fact that 22 glider pilots and 160 artillerymen, together with ten jeeps and two howitzers, were rescued in this way was a tribute to the fine leadership displayed by the officers and NCOs of the 320th Field Artillery, who organized their men into four separate groups for the breakout. Only four glider pilots and nine of the airborne troops were missing.

Of the other gliders in this serial, one came down on LZ 'O' after a flak hit, half a dozen more landed on or near LZ 'T' and another overshot to land in the Wyler area. The occupants of this glider reached friendly territory in due course.

THE BOMBER RE-SUPPLY MISSION

During the night of 17/18 September, 252 B-24 Liberators of the 2nd Bombardment Division, Eighth Army Air Force, were made ready for the mission to drop supplies to the 82nd and 101st Airborne Divisions. Each aircraft had its ball turret removed to save weight (in any case, it was designed for downward defence and would be superfluous on this low-level mission) and 2 tons of supplies packed in 20 containers were loaded in the bomb racks, bomb bay and fuselage. A trained dropmaster of the 2nd Quartermaster Battalion (a unit specializing in dropping supplies to resistance groups) was assigned to each aircraft to supervise the pushing of containers through the ball turret well and the rear hatch.

The B-24s were to fly in V formations of nine aircraft, each one separated by a 30-second interval. From Orfordness on the Suffolk coast, the departure point, the aircraft were to fly to the Initial Point at 1,500 feet, maintaining an indicated airspeed (IAS) of 165 mph, reducing to 300 feet and 150 mph for the drop. All formations were to follow the northern route so as to benefit from the marker boat, anti-flak operations and air-sea rescue facilities provided for the troop-carriers. After making the drop, the formations would make a climbing turn back to 1,500 feet for the flight home.

The mission was to be led by 131 aircraft of the 20th Bombardment Wing, dropping supplies for the 82nd Airborne Division on DZ 'N'; following on were 121 Liberators of the 14th Bombardment Wing, heading for DZ 'A' and DZ 'W' with supplies for the 101st Airborne Division.

Close escort for the mission was flown by two groups of P-51s and two of P-38s, which accompanied the bombers from the Dutch coast to the DZs, while area cover in the Nijmegen and Eindhoven areas was provided by four P-51 groups. The most difficult and dangerous task in the supporting air operations was performed by the P-47 Thunderbolts of the 56th, 78th, 353rd and 356th Fighter Groups; theirs was the flak suppression role, and in 88 sorties – attacking under a 1,000-foot cloud base and in haze – the 56th FG alone lost 21 aircraft and had many more damaged. Escort sorties were also flown by Spitfire, Mustang and Tempest squadrons of the ADGB.

USAAF B-24 Liberators were pressed into service for a major re-supply mission to the US airborne zones on D plus 1.

The mission got away to an unfortunate start: some staff officer at 2nd Air Division HQ sent the 14th Wing's target and en-route data to the 20th Wing and vice versa, and this was used at the briefings. The Wings received the correct data shortly before take-off, with the Liberators already warming up, and the pilots and navigators had to familiarize themselves with the route literally as they went along.

There was more confusion over the Channel when the 20th Wing made a 360-degree turn to the left in order to avoid a delayed serial of the 442nd Troop Carrier Group. The 14th Wing, whose crews were anxious to maintain their assigned position, turned with it; the result was delay and disorder, particularly in the 20th Wing, whose 448th Group became separated from the rest in the haze and proceeded independently. Five crews of the 93rd Group also got lost and returned to their base at Hardwick, in Norfolk.

The rest, however, all reached the IP, thanks mainly to good visual navigation. The 489th Group made a successful drop on DZ 'N' on the third try, having previously overshot it, and although the 448th Group dropped five miles short, close to DZ 'O', about 80 per cent of the 258 tons of supplies fell within the 82nd Airborne Division's perimeter and were recovered. The 446th Group's drop, which was also successful, completed the 82nd Airborne's resupply; the cost to the 20th Wing was four Liberators, with 38 more damaged.

The drop by the 14th Wing to the 101st Airborne Division on DZs 'A' and 'W' was ragged, the B-24 formations having become broken up in the haze. About 238 tons were dropped in the vicinity of DZ 'W' by 108 Liberators, but only about 20 per cent of the total was recovered; most fell into the hands of the enemy in the Best sector. The drop to the 501st PIR on DZ 'A', carried out by thirteen aircraft, was better placed, and in this case about 50 per cent of the supplies were recovered.

As they made their climbing turn away from DZ 'W', the 14th Wing's B-24s came under intense fire from the German positions around Best. Three were shot down in flames, one crash-landed at Brussels and 36 more were damaged, four so badly that they had to be scrapped. These losses were particularly unfortunate in the light of the failure of the 14th Wing's mission, which left the 101st Airborne Division seriously short of food and other essential items.

ARNHEM

Monday, 18 September, dawned with a chill mist curling along the banks of the Rhine where A Company of John Frost's 2nd Parachute Battalion still clung tenaciously to their positions around the northern end of the Arnhem bridge, reinforced by a badly mauled platoon of Lt-Col Fitch's 3rd Battalion. These men – the survivors of three platoons which had set out to force their way through to the bridge – joined the Sappers of the 1st Parachute Squadron RE at their positions in the school house to the east of the bridge. They had done their best to make it as secure as possible:

All the containers that could hold water were filled and obstacles placed at the foot of the stairs. We were then assigned to defensive positions covering areas around the school. My first position was at a circular window overlooking a park, and as the window was quite high I pushed a school desk up against the wall and rested my Bren gun on the window ledge and prepared myself for whatever was about to happen. Syd Guerran, my number two on the Bren did likewise so that he was close to me and could pass the magazines as I needed them. There was a lot of noise –rifle fire, machine-guns, explosions – and in the early hours a very loud bang as the house next door to us was blown up. It had been occupied by most of A Troop of our Squadron, and what was left of them came into our building led by Captain Eric Mackay, their Troop Commander. Our Troop Commander had been wounded early in the battle and we had been commanded by our stick officer, Lieutenant Simpson, known as 'Stiffy'. (Lt D.R. Simpson, MC). He now handed over to Mackay. As dawn broke, enemy attacks started with offensive patrols, no doubt to gauge the strength of the opposition. The school was situated beside the ramp that led up to the bridge, the ramp actually being level with the second floor, so we had a good view of the approach to the bridge and could cover it from the top floor, where most of us were. It was not long before the Germans started attacking in earnest . . . [49]

Meanwhile, Lt-Col Frost's position had been further reinforced by the arrival at about 0500 hours, of the 2nd Battalion's B Company, returning from its mission to the pontoon bridge. The new arrivals occupied buildings on the west side of the ramp. Of C Company, which had been despatched to the railway bridge, there was no sign.

At least Frost could rely on some artillery support. Major Dennis Mumford, commanding the 3rd Light Battery RA, had become separated from his unit – which was positioned south of Wolfheze – and was at Brigade HQ, close to the bridge. Shortly before dawn he despatched Captain Harrison, one of his officers, to try to contact the Battery and, if possible, have the guns brought within range of the bridge. Harrison successfully accomplished this difficult and dangerous task, and made contact with Lt-Col W.F.K. Thompson, commanding the 1st Air Landing Light Regiment RA. As a result, the guns were brought up to a position near Oosterbeek Laag church, about three miles away, and Mumford – eventually securing a reliable 22 set link – was able to direct their fire on to enemy positions around the bridge. The guns remained in action until the 2nd Battalion was eventually overwhelmed.

While darkness persisted, much of the fighting for control of the northern end of the bridge took place on the eastern side of the 2nd Battalion's positions, which were being contested by units of *Hauptsturmführer* Karl-Heinz Euling's 10 SS Battalion. The fighting to the west of the bridge, in the houses near the ramp and bordering the Great Market, mainly involved the hastily-assembled battle groups of *Panzergrenadier* Regiment 21, in particular its No 3 Company. All these units came under the command of the *Kampfgruppe* Brinkmann, which at dawn began to step up its attacks in preparation for a full-scale assault.

Euling's battalion had taken a severe battering in its attempts to infiltrate the British positions at the northern ramp. The close-quarter fighting was savage and confused, with luckless Dutch civilians suffering death and injury as they tried to flee from their burning homes.

The first substantial German reinforcements arrived shortly before dawn in the shape of the *Panzergrenadier* Training and Replacement Battalion Bocholt. Commanded by Major Hans-Peter Knaust, this included four companies of infantry composed mainly of troops who were recovering from wounds and who were not yet classed as fit for front-line service. Knaust himself was fitted with a wooden leg, replacing a limb lost on the Russian front. But Knaust was bringing some armour with him: eight Mk III and IV tanks from the 6th *Panzer* Replacement Regiment Bielefeld. Knaust's force was placed under Brinkmann's command and ordered to relieve Euling's battalion at once, even though it would be some time before the tanks arrived.

At first light, the paratroops were subjected to an intense artillery and mortar attack, the preliminary to an armoured assault from the east by Brinkmann's reconnaissance battalion. A column of light tanks, armoured cars and half-tracks swept under the northern bridge ramp, firing into the houses on either side, and burst into the Markt Straat, where the leading tank was brought to a blazing standstill by two six-pounder anti-tank guns emplaced in the open streets. The half-tracks following the tank were forced to slow down in order to squeeze past the wreck and were picked off one by one, their occupants being shot down as they baled out and scattered for cover.

At about 0900 hours, Frost's men, still battling against sporadic attacks that developed from the factory district that lay to the east of the northern bridge ramp, saw signs of activity on the southern side of the bridge. What they were seeing was Viktor Gräbner's 9 SS Reconnaissance Battalion, back at Arnhem after its reconnaissance of the Nijmegen road. At his disposal Gräbner had a mixture of 22 fighting vehicles: armoured cars and half-tracks, some mounting 75 mm guns and all mounting machine-guns. At this stage, it was the biggest concentration of armour that 9 SS could muster, and Gräbner planned to use it for a *coup de main* assault on Frost's positions.

The expression 'courage and dash' fitted Gräbner well. A fine officer, liked and respected by his men, he had established a reputation for bold action in battle, and he had been awarded the *Ritterkreuz* (Knight's Cross) for a spectacular series of armoured counter-attacks against the British at Noyers Bocage, Normandy, when his battalion was in support of 277 Infantry Division. His *modus operandi* was to strike hard and fast, achieving the maximum element of surprise, and he doubtless believed that these tactics would work now, in a sudden thrust across Arnhem bridge.

The armoured vehicles assembled in column a few hundred yards beyond the southern bridge ramp, shrouded in exhaust fumes as the drivers gunned their engines. At a few minutes after nine o'clock the column set off, with *Puma* armoured cars in the lead; behind them came the half-tracks, with a few truckloads of infantry bringing up the rear. Gräbner, as usual was well to the fore, riding in a captured British Humber staff car.

The leading armoured cars rolled over the crest of the southern ramp and opened up with their cannon and machine-guns as they roared across the centre span at top speed. Behind them, the half-tracks made slower progress, being capable of only about 25 mph with a full load of troops on board.

Still firing, the first five armoured cars plunged on past the smouldering wrecks of the trucks destroyed during the night's fighting and continued unscathed down the northern ramp and into the town. A sixth lost a wheel when it struck one of a necklace of Hawkins mines laid across the road earlier and was disabled, although it continued firing until knocked out by a PIAT round.

So far, the British firing had been intermittent; but now, as the half-tracks clattered down the ramp, they received its full fury. As the leading pair came abreast of the school house Captain Mackay's Sappers hurled grenades into them, causing fearful carnage among the occupants. The paratroops made use of all their available weapons in breaking up the attack, which stalled completely when two half-tracks collided and burst into flames. One after another the following vehicles, plunging on through the smoke, piled into the wreckage. Soon the road was blocked, with Gräbner's SS troopers desperately seeking whatever shelter they could find among the bridge girders as Frost's men poured a merciless fire into them. The six-pounders of the 1st Air Landing Brigade's anti-tank troop were also able to set their sights on the enemy column; these and the PIATS were later credited with having destroyed two armoured cars, eight half-tracks and five or six trucks. To complete the column's destruction, Major Mumford called down fire from the light artillery position at Oosterbeek-Laag.

The fight continued for more than two hours, and when it was over more than half the attacking force had been destroyed. Among the dead, somewhere, was Gräbner himself, the victim of his own suicidal confidence. Again and again, SS troopers tried to break out of the trap at the northern end of the bridge, and were slaughtered; many, desperately trying to escape the withering fire, leaped over the bridge balustrades into the lower Rhine.

So, as noon approached on Monday, 18 September, the remnants of 9 SS Reconnaissance Battalion straggled back to the south bank of the river, and the firing gradually died away.

Elsewhere in the Arnhem sector, the remainder of the 1st Airborne Division was slowly but inevitably being boxed in. The sides of the box were, to the west, the *Kampfgruppe* von Tettau, and to the east the *Kampfgruppe* Spindler; the lower Rhine was the bottom of the box; and its lid, about to be closed, was Sepp Krafft's 16th SS Battalion, which had withdrawn through the woods during the night after being relieved and which, early on the 18th, was regrouping to the south of Deelen airfield.

General Bittrich, commanding II SS *Panzer* Corps, was issued the following orders.

II SS *Panzer* Corps will resolutely direct its main effort against the enemy who has landed at Nijmegen (US 82nd Airborne Division). For this purpose further forces will be ferried across the Neder Rijn (at Pannerden) and a firm bridgehead will be maintained south of the Waal at Nijmegen. The 9th SS *Panzer* Division will also destroy as speedily as possible the enemy parachutists who have established themselves at the bridge, continue to attack, and reduce the area held by the 1st Airborne Division and, after the arrival of fresh reinforcements, destroy it.

The task of Sepp Krafft's battalion, once it had reorganized at Deelen, was to move towards Oosterbeek, push the British paratroops back to the northern edge of the town, and establish contact with the western side of the 'box' – the *Kampfgruppe* von Tettau. At the same time, the Spindler *Kampfgruppe* would continue its attacks against Oosterbeek from the east on a broad front. The urgent goal was to consolidate Spindler's front to such an extent that no supplies or reinforcements could reach Frost's battalion fighting at the bridge – the only battalion outside the box. It would then be possible for the Germans to calculate, roughly, when that battalion was likely to run out of ammunition.

With the progress of the 1st and 3rd Parachute Battalions at a virtual standstill, much now depended on the second lift. This was to drop Brigadier John W. Hackett's 4th Parachute Brigade on DZ 'Y' (Ginkel Heath) while the remaining elements of the 1st Air Landing Brigade Group on LZ 'X' and LZ 'S' (Renkum Heath and Reijerscamp). A resupply mission was also to be flown to LZ 'L' north-east of Wolfheze. All these objectives were freshly marked out by the pathfinders of the 21st Independent Parachute Company, whose war diary notes that:

Platoons moved out during the morning to mark DZ and LZs for the second lift. No 1 Platoon to LZ 'L', No 2 Platoon to LZ 'X' and No 3 Platoon to DZ 'Y'. HQ remained on 'S' to supply aids. Enemy opposition was encountered in all landing areas and platoons had stiff fighting to drive the enemy back and to hold them while the second lift landed, also having to put out ground aids under fire. [50]

The position on and around the drop and landing zones on the morning of 18 September was indeed precarious. In the south, Lippert's experienced troopers of the SS NCO School were making steady progress towards the western edge of Renkum Heath and had penetrated Heelsum, where they were engaged in fierce fighting with the 1st Battalion The Border Regiment as they strove to break through to LZ 'Z'; in the north, Helle's *Wachbattalion* 3 had actually crossed Ginkel Heath and was fighting with the thinly-stretched screen of the 7th KOSB at the edge of the woods on the eastern side of DZ 'Y'.

Only in the centre, opposite DZ 'X', did the German advance fail to make progress. Here, the *Luftwaffe* personnel of the Soesterberg *Fliegerhorst* Battalion were pinned down by D Company of the 1st Border Regiment and had to be reinforced by

two companies of Lippert's SS NCOs. The *Fliegerhorst* Battalion's morale rose a little with the appearance of half a dozen tanks which emerged from the woods to the west of Renkum, but the relief was short-lived. The AFVs, belonging to *Panzerkompagnie* 224 of II SS Corps, were old French Renault *Char* Type Bs, 32-ton tanks mounting a 47 mm gun in the turret and a hull-mounted 75 mm for close support. They were part of a group of eight brought back from France by II SS Corps.

Now, as they trundled along the road at their top speed of about fifteen miles per hour, they proved easy targets for the Air Landing Brigade's anti-tank guns. All six were quickly knocked out, their surviving crew members – and the troops who had been using the tanks as cover – running the gauntlet of intense machine-gun fire as they sought safety.

Lippert, an officer of much the same mould as the ill-fated Gräbner, now decided that desperate measures were necessary if his troops were to make further progress. Driving on to DZ 'X', roughly at the point where it joined LZ 'Z', he raced on at speed in his *Kubelwagen* – Volkswagen's equivalent of the Jeep – firing signal flares as he went to draw the weight of the British fire. His ruse succeeded and his men, inspired by their commander's courage and initiative, stormed on to the zone in a wild charge,

---

At the beginning of the Arnhem battle, II SS Corps was so short of tanks that it had to use captured French Renaults of 1940 vintage. All of them were knocked out by the Air Landing Brigade's anti-tank guns.

rushing on through the smoke from fires started on the heathland during earlier fighting. They suffered heavy casualties, but they broke through the Border Regiment's defensive screen and surrounded D Company, which managed to fight its way out of the trap and withdraw towards Wolfheze and Oosterbeek minus its supporting weapons.

Lippert's assault was halted some distance east of the zone by heavy British fire from the western edge of Oosterbeek. Meanwhile, Helle's *Wachbattalion* 3, swinging to the south-east, was exerting pressure on the 7th KOSB; bitter fighting ensued as Payton-Reid's men counter-attacked with the bayonet, and for the time being Helle's drive was also halted.

The Air Landing Brigade, its numbers already badly depleted by casualties, had been further weakened during the morning by Brigadier Hicks' decision to send a half battalion of the 2nd South Staffordshires to join the two airborne battalions attempting to break through to Lt-Col Frost at Arnhem bridge. Hicks had assumed the duties of divisional commander at about 0730 hours when General Urquhart had still not rejoined Divisional Headquarters, which had now moved to the crossroads on the Utrecht road a mile south of Wolfheze Station.

The decision meant that the task of holding LZ 'S' at Reijerscamp until the arrival of the second lift now devolved upon what was left of C Troop of the 1st Airborne Reconnaissance Squadron, a platoon of the 21st Independent Parachute Company and about 50 men of the Glider Pilot Regiment. Their positions were not yet under serious threat, although they had been subjected to some weak probing attacks, but as the day wore on and there was no sign of the second lift – due to come in at 1000 hours – their anxiety naturally increased.

It has been suggested that, if Urquhart had returned to Divisional HQ that morning – having seen for himself the growing effectiveness of the *Sperrlinie* blocking the approach march of the 1st and 3rd Parachute Battalions to the bridge – he might have decided upon a drastic change of plan. He might, for example, have recalled Frost's battalion – if that was still possible – and concentrated his six original battalions, together with the three battalions of the 4th Parachute Brigade due to arrive with the second lift, in an attempt to establish a firm bridgehead somewhere else on the north side of the Neder Rijn, perhaps

between Heveadorp and Oosterbeek with the high ground at Westerbouwing, dominating the Driel ferry, at its centre.

But Hicks could not be expected to implement such a sweeping alteration to the original plan. Urquhart was merely missing; he might return to his headquarters at any moment. So Hicks decided, in keeping with the original plan, to take measures designed to enforce the speedy capture of the Rhine bridge by making a maximum effort to breach the German blocking line. As soon as the remainder of the 2nd Battalion, The South Staffordshire Regiment, arrived it would also be despatched to reinforce the 1st and 3rd Parachute Battalions; so, too, would the 11th Parachute Battalion of Brigadier Hackett's 4th Parachute Brigade.

There could be no question, however, of the 11th Parachute Battalion undertaking a rapid reinforcement role. It was scheduled to make its drop on Ginkel Heath, a full eight miles from Arnhem – but its transport was to be landed by glider two miles to the east, at the Reijerscamp zone. There would be a considerable delay while the battalion assembled, marched to Reijerscamp and collected its transport – and delay was a luxury Hicks could not afford.

Because of the prevailing adverse weather conditions, the second lift had already been postponed by four hours. It was not until 1123 hours that the first serials began taking off. The mission was led by 126 C-47s of IX Troop Carrier Command: two serials of 36 aircraft each from the 314th TCG and two of 27 from the 315th Group. They carried 2,119 paratroops of the 4th Parachute Brigade, destined for DZ 'Y', together with 51 tons of supplies.

Me 262 jet fighter-bombers made sporadic attacks on the Arnhem airhead, and also on XXX Corps.

While the second lift was en route, the zones near Arnhem received some attention – for the first time – from the *Luftwaffe*. The war diary of the 21st Independent Parachute Company records that LZ 'L' and LZ 'S' were both strafed at about noon by Messerschmitt 109s, which came in from the east to make their attack. They caused no casualties, but on LZ 'L' they came very close to hitting the *Eureka* beacon which, in order to function, had to be sited out in the open clear of trees which surrounded the LZ. Sergeant Walter Langham of the Glider Pilot Regiment, who had brought in a Horsa on the first lift and who was now helping to hold LZ 'S', also recalls an attack by a solitary Me 262 . . . 'which stafed us in the wood. It was the first jet plane we had ever seen, and luckily there was only one, as several of us stood up to get a better view!'[51]

As it was, the *Luftwaffe* made no attempt to interfere with the second lift, but there was plenty of flak opposition. The flight along the northern route went smoothly until the serials reached Oss, six miles beyond the IP. There, one C-47, apparently hit by small-arms fire, crashed with all on board, and another was hit by flak and burst into flames; its occupants all jumped clear and in due course made their way to the Allied lines. Ten miles further on flak claimed a third aircraft, which began to burn;

Men of the 1st Airborne Division making last-minute checks of their equipment before departing for Arnhem.

the paratroops and at least one of the crew got out and were picked up by the Dutch Resistance, who guided them to Nijmegen.

The most intense fire, including a lot of 20 mm flak, came up as the serials passed Wageningen, about five miles short of the DZ. The pilots of two C-47s which were set on fire attempted emergency landings, but one exploded when it struck some power lines and the other disintegrated on impact. Fortunately, their paratroops had been preparing to jump and most were able to get out, but all except one of the American crew members perished.

At Wageningen the serials turned north, then made a 90-degree turn to cross DZ 'Y' heading east. Another C-47 was hit and set on fire as it crossed the edge of the DZ, but its pilot held his course until the paratroops were clear; the aircraft plunged into the line of trees bordering the zone and exploded.

All the surviving C-47s cleared the zone, although at least 24 were damaged. No more losses were sustained during the flight home, but many of the returning troop-carrier crews were bitterly critical of the lack of Allied fighter-bomber activity around Arnhem – unaware, perhaps, that the 2nd Tactical Air Force's flak suppression aircraft were forbidden to operate in the vicinity of the zones while air landings were in progress. Fighter cover had, however, been provided as far as the IP by nineteen Spitfire, five Tempest and three Mustang squadrons, and these had attacked a number of flak positions at a cost of two Tempests and four Spitfires.

Minutes before the 4th Parachute Brigade descended on Ginkel Heath, a spirited bayonet charge by Lt-Col Payton-Reid's 7th King's Own Scottish Borderers, attacking from the woods to the east, threw Helle's Dutch SS Battalion into confusion. The confusion quickly turned to panic when they discovered that an entire brigade was dropping in their rear. Nevertheless, enemy forces on and around the DZ put up an intense fire as the sticks of paratroops dropped from their aircraft. Some men were killed when they drifted into the tree line before a stiff breeze that had risen and had become entangled, presenting easy targets; but the breeze undoubtedly saved many more lives, resulting in a fast descent that gave the Germans little time to set their sights on the men in the air.

Disorganized as it was, Helle's battalion continued to offer resistance, and the 10th Parachute Battalion had to fight its way through to the

ABOVE, LEFT:
British paratrooper in typical combat dress. Note the fighting knife at his right thigh.

ABOVE, RIGHT:
A soldier of the Air Landing Brigade using a compact radio transmitter. These sets proved almost worthless in the woods north and west of Arnhem-Oosterbeek.

RIGHT:
Under an overcast sky, paratroops cascade from USAAF C-47s over an Arnhem DZ.

rendezvous point. The enemy, however, surrounded on all sides by the paratroops and the KOSB's counter-attack, soon began to surrender or to withdraw to the north, filtering away through the woods. Brigadier Hackett himself accepted the surrender of ten Germans within a couple of minutes of shedding his parachute harness.

SS *Obersturmführer* Fernau, commanding the most southerly of Helle's companies, was soon captured, and the other companies quickly collapsed. Only one, the heavy weapons company under *Obersturmführer* Einenkel, appears to have conducted anything resembling a fighting withdrawal, pulling away to the north in reasonably good order. Helle himself narrowly escaped capture when his command post was overrun; many of the Dutch SS troopers under his command who did manage to get away took the opportunity to desert.

A combination of good landmarks and the navigational aids set out by the pathfinders made it relatively easy for most of the troop-carrier pilots to locate DZ 'Y'. The drop of the 4th Parachute Brigade took place 'in a shower of tracers' between 1406 and 1420 hours from heights of between 800 and 1,000 feet. Only six paratroops failed to drop, either because of wounds or snarled equipment. Most of the drops were right on target; only one flight of nine C-47s, having become separated from the last serial, made its drop a mile or two short of the zone, the men landing roughly in bushes and trees.

One of the signallers who arrived with the second lift, Bill Carr – a member of a three-man team from K Section Signals attached to the 11th Parachute

Paratrooper with a Type 22 wireless set. The Type 22 had a limited range and was ineffective in the Arnhem terrain.

Battalion – describes the problems that could attend a combat drop by a paratrooper festooned with equipment.

Usually, the kitbag attached to one's leg made for an easy exit as one simply swung the leg through the door and the weight pulled one down like a stone. However, on this occasion I was also carrying a long wireless aerial in my hands and somehow this became jammed in the door as I jumped. Fortunately, someone behind pulled it clear and I was able to drop clear still clutching the aerial rods.

As Horsa gliders are unloaded, paratroops of the 1st Airborne Division drop into LZ 'S'.

I landed with a bump, due to the wind, and my Sten gun, which was slung around my neck, swung up and clouted me on the nose, causing it to bleed profusely. One of our team had been knocked out on the jump, so the corporal and I shared the equipment between us and set off for the rendezvous. As we were crossing a rise, a machine-gun opened up from a small wood and the corporal, who was carrying the wireless set, was hit in the leg at the side of the knee. I pulled him into a hollow in the ground and put a field dressing on the wound.

We discussed the situation and agreed that I should leave him there and continue to the rendezvous with all the equipment. Before leaving, I fired a couple of bursts from my Sten gun into the wood without actually being able to see the target. Later, I found two dead Germans there beside a Spandau gun. They were dressed in RAF blue-coloured uniforms with forage caps, and for an awful moment I thought I had killed some of our own men. I passed some stretcher bearers and gave them the location of my colleague, and they set off to attend to him.

I was having to struggle along with the wireless set on my back, carrying two heavy dry batteries, the aerial and all the ancillary equipment. I thought back to an occasion a few months previously, when I had demonstrated the 22 Set to King George the Sixth. In answer to his question, I told him that it required three men to carry all the necessary equipment. Now I was having to manage alone. It was with great relief that I finally joined up with 11th Battalion.

The wireless set frequencies were pre-set by means of a crystal which was inserted in the set before operation. To my utter disgust with myself, I now found that the crystal had been left in the breast pocket of my wounded colleague. By now he would have been moved by the stretcher bearers, and the wireless set was useless without the pre-set frequency. It was dumped on a jeep and taken away to be fixed. Without the rest of my crew and a working set, I joined up with an infantry platoon of the 11th Battalion. [52]

Meanwhile, a second mission had been despatched to Arnhem. This comprised 295 four-engined aircraft of No 38 Group, towing gliders to LZ 'S' and LZ 'X'; the gliders carried the second echelon of the 1st Air Landing Brigade Group. The glider column was supposed to fly at 2,500 feet, but ran into dense cloud (five-tenths to ten-tenths) with its base as low as 2,000 feet; nine gliders broke their tows and made forced landings in England, while two more were forced to ditch in the sea. Flak over Holland was heavy, particularly in the 's Hertogenbosch area, where heavy batteries were in action; fifteen gliders were lost during this stage of the mission, at least nine of them because of ground fire. One pilot of a No 295 Squadron Stirling remembers how flak shot the tail off the glider he was towing: 'The glider pilot

The crew of a 38 Group Stirling with their station commander after returning from a resupply mission to Arnhem.

released the tow rope and we saw him spiral like a leaf down to the land near the coast.'[53]

The navigational accuracy of the No 38 Group aircrews was once again very good. All the pathfinders' beacons and markers worked well, but the *Rebecca/Eureka* equipment produced poor results; less than half of the crews interrogating the *Eureka* on LZ 'X' received responses. Of 73 glider-tug combinations sent to LZ 'S', 69 reached the landing area, and at least 67 put their gliders on or near the zone. Of the 223 despatched to LZ 'X' 203 crews reported a successful mission, and reconnaissance photographs showed 189 gliders either on or close to the zone. Only one tug aircraft was lost.

Landing accidents at both zones were infrequent, but once on the ground the glider-borne troops came under heavy fire from enemy forces just outside the landing areas and many gliders were destroyed by mortar fire – fortunately, in the majority of cases, after the troops had disembarked and the supplies offloaded. One glider co-pilot described a scene of confusion:

. . . Everywhere we saw groups of men cursing, sweating and heaving to get the tails off their gliders. Some were even using saws and axes, and when we looked at our watches we found that we had done the job in twenty minutes, which made us feel very pleased with ourselves. To get to our first rendezvous we had to follow a narrow, sandy lane through low brushwood, small fields and single rows of trees. Everywhere we saw gliders; in the fields, some even on the trees, there was an odd wing wedged between two big branches of an oak, a tail unit sticking right up in the air, and pieces of gliders distributed everywhere. We passed a large meadow with gliders parked in a more orderly fashion; obviously this was the real landing zone of Sunday's lift. We joined more and more jeeps and trailers, all filing to their various RVs. Ours was not so difficult as it was Wolfheze Station, and from there to the lunatic asylum . . . all the while we were sniped at; sometimes a mortar would go over and everyone seemed to disappear, but after a few seconds the confusion returned. Everyone was spreading out maps and asking everyone else if they had seen or heard of their respective units.[54]

Meanwhile, at about 1500 hours, 35 Stirlings of No 38 Group from RAF Harwell approached DZ 'L' on the first re-supply mission to the 1st Airborne Division. One returning crew admitted that they had dropped by mistake on LZ 'S', about a mile to the west of 'L', but all except two of the remainder believed that they had made accurate drops from a height of around 500 feet. In fact, the panniers and containers they dropped were widely scattered and drifted south-west of the zone into enemy territory. Of the 87 tons of supplies dropped, only twelve tons were recovered.

As far as the RAF aircrews were concerned, one in particular showed outstanding initiative during the glider mission on D plus 1. Their aircraft, a Dakota of No 575 Squadron, was hit by flak over Holland; the pilot was killed and the first navigator, Flying Officer McKinley, was wounded. The second navigator, Warrant Officer A.E. Smith, took over the controls and at first attempted to complete the mission, but this had to be abandoned when the glider's ailerons were shot away. The glider was released over friendly territory and its pilot made a crash landing. Afterwards, WO Smith attempted an

emergency landing at Brussels, but failed because of low cloud; with the help of the injured first navigator, Smith flew the aircraft back to England and made a safe landing at Martlesham Heath. Both Smith and McKinley were awarded the Distinguished Flying Cross.[55]

This report of No 38 Group's operations for D+1 (on page 93) is reproduced exactly as it came off the teleprinter at the time. There would be no further optimistic final paragraphs in later summaries.

At about 1515 hours on 18 September, Lieutenant-Colonel C.B. Mackenzie, GSO 1 (Operations) of the 1st Airborne Division, met Brigadier Hackett on the dropping zone and informed him of the change of plan decided upon by Brigadier Hicks in the light of the increasingly strong opposition that 1st Parachute Brigade was meeting. Hackett at once ordered the 11th Parachute Battalion to move off in the wake of the two companies of the South Staffordshires which had also come in with the second lift. It was some solace to learn that the gap left by the loss of the 11th Battalion was to be filled by the 7th KOSB, which would be attached to the 4th Parachute Brigade. But the KOSB was a weary battalion, having been in action for twenty-four hours, and it had still to perform another major task: protecting the arrival of the Polish Parachute Brigade's equipment on LZ 'L' at Johannahoeve during the third lift, scheduled for Tuesday.

Brigadier Hackett's 4th Parachute Brigade also had a major task ahead of it: the capture of the high ground to the north of Arnhem. There were problems enough attending this, and they were compounded by several others, not least of which was the confusion prevailing at Divisional Headquarters. By the late afternoon of Monday 18

Losses from flak become increasingly severe. This Stirling crash-landed in Allied territory en route to Arnhem.

NO 38 GROUP INTELLIGENCE SUMMARY FOR D + 1

38 GP OPERATED 210 A/C COMPRISING HALIFAX/HAMILCAR, STIRLING/HORSA AND ALBEMARLE/HORSA & WACO COMBINATIONS OBJECT STRENGTHENING AND RESUPPLY OF AREAS CAPTURED. 88 A/C SUCCESSFUL DROPPED LOADS COMPRISING TROOPS, JEEPS, CARS, BREN CARRIERS, 17LB GUNS, HOWITZERS, M/C, CYCLES, PANNIERS, STRETCHERS, COMPRESSORS, W/T SET, CHARGING SET, MINE DETECTORS, HOSES, AMMUNITION AND RMLS.

19 A/C UNSUCCESSFUL, 9 TOW-ROPES BREAKING, 4 MECH FAILURE, 1 MISSING, 1 HIT BY FLAK, 1 BAD LOADING AND 3 SLIPSTREAM DIFFICULTIES FALLING INTO SEA. REPORTS OF A/C IN DISTRESS, STIRLING WITH SMOKE COMING FROM IT, SECOND HIT BY FLAK SEEN TO CRASH AND EXPLODE, THIRD BURNING ON GROUND, FOURTH CRASH-LANDED, FIFTH HIT BY FLAK AND ONE MEMBER OF A/C SEEN TO BALE OUT, SIXTH (NO2) ST/BD TANK LEAKING AND DAKOTA SEEN GOING DOWN AND FOUR CHUTES SEEN TO OPEN. LARGE SILVER ROCKET TOWING SILVER COLOURED KITE, SPEED EST 200 MPH TRAVELLING DUE WEST.

GRATIFYING TO NOTE OPERATION HAS GONE SO SMOOTHLY AND THAT GEN DEMPSEY'S 2ND BRITISH ARMY HAS ALREADY CONTACTED FORCES WE DROPPED ON D-DAY.

September General Urquhart was still missing, as was Brigadier Lathbury, and Divisional HQ was in the process of moving to a new location at the Hartenstein Hotel in Oosterbeek.

Having despatched 11th Parachute Battalion towards Arnhem, Brigadier Hackett ordered the 156th Parachute Battalion to lead the advance of his brigade along the line of the railway to the high ground north of the town. The 10th Parachute Battalion was to remain where it was for the time being in the area of South Ginkel on the Arnhem–Ede road. Brigade Headquarters was to move as soon as possible to a track junction in the woods half a mile east of this location, and 133rd Parachute Field Ambulance was to follow along the axis of advance as soon as the casualty situation permitted.

During the evening, the 4th Parachute Brigade gradually took over the protection of the dropping and landing zones from the King's Own Scottish Borderers, who reverted to command of the 1st Air Landing Brigade. By nightfall, 156th Battalion had reached Wolfheze Station, 10th Battalion had halted at the track junction a mile north-west of Buunderkamp, and Brigade Headquarters had moved up to the railway halt immediately south of Buunderkamp.

Both battalions had set out with a fair degree of confidence. By about 2000 hours they had acquired their glider-borne transport and weapons, and appeared to be in a strong position. Both, however, soon began to encounter opposition; the 10th Battalion was held up by 20 mm fire and also encountered SP guns and tanks, leaving its

companies little choice but to dig in on either side of the Arnhem–Ede road; the Battalion was, in effect, stuck in the angle created by Sepp Krafft's SS Battalion and Spindler's *Sperrlinie*, running north-south along the Dreyenseweg. The 156th Parachute Battalion's advance along the railway line was also blocked by the *Sperrlinie*, and its commander, Lt-Col Sir Richard des Voeux, decided to establish a firm base in the woods until first light with the intention of entering Arnhem from the north-west the next morning. By this time, communication with 4th Parachute Brigade HQ had broken down.

The 7th KOSB, meanwhile, had set out from Ginkel Heath at 1900 hours, following the same route along the railway as the 156th Parachute Battalion, which caused some confusion until the force reached the area of Wolfheze Station, where the two battalions separated. Moving on through the darkness towards its objective – the ground near Johannahoeve Farm, where the gliders supporting the Polish Brigade were to land the next day – the KOSB Battalion found that the positions it was supposed to occupy were already in the hands of the enemy, who had set up MG posts on and around them. As it was impossible to locate and deal with these in the darkness, the Battalion, after suffering a number of casualties, took up a position before dawn based on Johannahoeve.

While these movements were in progress, the 1st Battalion The Border Regiment, still under pressure from Lippert's *Kampfgruppe*, took up positions, each held by a company, at Graftombe north-west of Hartenstein, the crossroads between Oosterbeek church and Heveadorp, astride the Utrecht road south-west of Hill Oek, and at Zilverenberg south of Hill Oek. These positions had been allotted in the original plan, and they were to remain practically unaltered throughout the battle.

Brigadier Hackett and his staff, in the meantime, had followed a route parallel to and north of the railway line until they reached the Buunderkamp Hotel, where Brigade HQ was established. Hackett asked the proprietor to bring all available mattresses downstairs and most of his staff officers spent the night outside on them, sleeping in the garden near the wreckage of a glider, its dead pilot still trapped in the cockpit. Hackett himself went to Divisional Headquarters and, with other senior officers, discussed operations for the following day. It was decided that the 4th Parachute Brigade should secure the high ground at Koepel, a mile north-west of the outskirts of Arnhem, and retain a firm left flank on the Arnhem–Ede road.

The offensive would have to be mounted into the teeth of an enemy whose strength was growing all the while, and who possessed absolute superiority in tanks, armoured cars and self-propelled guns. Few brigade commanders must have faced a task from such an unenviable position.

Long before the 4th Parachute Brigade even set off for Holland, the situation of the 1st and 3rd Parachute Battalions, desperately trying to fight their way through to the Arnhem bridge, had become not only unenviable but impossible. Time after time, their attacks were blunted by the stiffening wall of the *Sperrlinie*, stretching from the Arnhem–Ede road along the Dreyenseweg to the railway line and junction and from there to the Neder Rijn. The northern sector, before which Brigadier Hackett's battalions halted after nightfall, had been initially held almost entirely by Krafft's battalion, but as the day went on this was strengthened by the injection of other units: part of the *Kampfgruppe* Bruhns, a *Wehrmacht* battalion, and some of von Allworden's SS *Panzerjäger*. South of the Arnhem–Ede road was Spindler's artillery *Kampfgruppe*, reinforced by a combat team drawn from *Panzergrenadier* Regiments 19 and 20 occupying the line as far as the Neder Rijn; on the other side of the river, remnants of Gräbner's 9 SS Reconnaissance Battalion occupied the brickworks, where they had sited quick-firing anti-aircraft artillery. Behind the *Sperrlinie*, rapidly building up a defence in depth, troops of the newly-formed *Kampfgruppe* Harzer occupied positions from the railway station due south to the river.

Against this opposition, attempts by the 1st and 3rd Parachute Battalions and their supporting troops from 1st Air Landing Brigade to continue the advance to the bridge on Monday morning degenerated into a series of confused and isolated actions between pockets of friend and foe. In general, the 3rd Battalion was engaged in the residential suburb west of St Elisabeth's Hospital, while the 1st Battalion was fighting south of the Utrechtseweg.

It was the confused nature of the fighting that prevented General Urquhart and Brigadier Lathbury from returning to Divisional HQ on the morning of the 18th. Having taken refuge in a house during the night, they remained pinned down until the afternoon. Urquhart later wrote,

There was good deal of small-arms fire across this area, and I was told that there were Germans in the upper rooms of the houses across the gardens. My prospects of returning to Divisional HQ appeared for the present more remote that I would have liked . . . Our situation quickly took on the appearance of a siege.[56]

Finally, sometime between 1500 and 1600 hours on Monday afternoon, Urquhart and Lathbury decided to make a break for it. Making a quick exit through the back door of the house in which they had been sheltering, their dash covered by smoke bombs, they climbed over the garden fence. As they did so, Lathbury accidentally discharged his Sten gun, narrowly missing the general. Accompanied by Captain Cleminson of the 3rd Parachute Battalion and Captain Taylor of 1st Parachute Brigade HQ, they cut through a narrow alley and ran eastwards down Alexanderstraat towards St Elisabeth's Hospital. Suddenly, an MG 42 opened up and Lathbury fell, hit in the back. Temporarily paralysed, he was carried into No 135 Alexanderstraat, where he was left in the care of a Dutch couple. While they were in the house, a German soldier looked in through the window and Urquhart shot him dead. Then Urquhart and the other two officers left by the back door and ran across to Zwarteweg, a short street close to the west side of the hospital. They managed to reach a house – No 14 –just as Germans swarmed into the street; the Dutch occupants quickly showed them up some stairs to an attic. Through a small window they could see lots of enemy activity outside, and in due course an SP gun rattled up and stopped almost directly under the window. Urquhart later wrote,

I was frustrated at my inability to influence the battle, and the minutes dragged through the evening and night. If I had known just how badly the battle was going elsewhere, I would certainly have attempted to reach my HQ. It is doubtful, however, if I could have succeeded.[57]

Amid all the confusion there were curious lulls in the fighting, but they were illusory, as Trooper Des Evans of C Troop, 1st Airborne Reconnaissance Squadron remembers.

In the afternoon (of the 18th) we drove up the main Arnhem road from Wolfheze and were just remarking on how quiet it was when there was a loud bang very close to us. Looking away to our right we saw an enemy mortar which had been firing on our troops elsewhere; it had been turned around and was now firing at us. The Troop OC was all for getting out of it but I thought 'bugger this,' and steadying my rifle against a tree I tried a shot. It was a long shot for a rifle, and the mortar was still firing at us; in fact we'd abandoned another of our precious jeeps as a result of its accuracy. Raising the muzzle slightly, I fired. One of the mortar crew grabbed his chest and staggered back into the trees behind him. I began running through the trees at the side of the road, my idea being to get close enough for another shot at the mortar crew. I became conscious that I was not alone and, still running, looked round. Five other lads had joined me; I remember Fred Brawn, Alan Baker and Jim Salmon, all from my jeep crew. I do not remember who the other two were.
Drawing level with the mortar, without any discussion or plan we ran across the road towards it, shouting like lunatics *Waho Mohammed*, the famous battlecry of the 1st Airborne Division carried from its origins in North Africa. The two remaining members of the mortar crew looked rather uncertain as to what to do next, but this uncertainty was resolved when six more Germans came out of the woods to join them. I tripped and dropped my rifle and saw a bayonet coming at me; automatically I lashed out with my right hand and my thumb hit the blade. My hand then came down swiftly to the fighting knife on my right leg and I lunged upwards with it. There was a grunt and the German soldier almost collapsed on top of me. One enemy soldier was running back into the woods, the remainder lay at our feet . . . [58]

The probing activities of the Reconnaissance Squadron failed to find any gaps in the enemy's blocking line, which was growing stronger by the hour. By the late afternoon of 18 September, attrition had reduced Lt-Col Fitch's 3rd Parachute Battalion to about 140

men who were still fighting fit; on the other side of the Utrechtseweg, Lt-Col Dobie's 1st Battalion was in even worse shape, down to about 100 men after bitter fighting in the area between Den Brink and Klingel-beeksweg. The 2nd Battalion The South Staffordshire Regiment had managed to penetrate to a distance of about 500 yards east of the Oosterbeek crossroads, and there it too was halted. Some forward elements of the South Staffordshires made contact with the 1st Parachute Battalion west of the Onderlangs road fork at about 2000 hours. Well after dark, Lt-Col George Lea's 11th Parachute Battalion also made contact with the 1st Battalion, having had a relatively trouble-free approach march. The whole force, under no organized command, dug in for the night and prepared to resume the advance the next morning.

At the Arnhem Bridge, meanwhile, Frost's 2nd Parachute Battalion was being attacked by the Knaust and Brinkmann *Kampfgruppen* from three directions and more reinforcements, including artillery, were being brought up to the south bank of the river. Throughout the day, the battalion area was heavily and continually mortared, and during the late afternoon and early evening a strong attack developed along the river bank from the east. It was supported by heavy mortar fire and two tanks, one of which was knocked out by a PIAT round and the other by a six-pounder anti-tank gun.

The attack was contained, although at considerable cost to the defenders of the positions east of the bridge. The Brigade Defence Platoon in particular suffered heavy casualties and had to abandon its positions. By now, the Germans had adopted new tactics. As their attacks withered against the 2nd Battalion's strongpoints, they determined to burn out the paratroops.

Soon after dark the Germans made their first attempt to burn the sappers out of the school buildings. It started with a hail of rifle-grenades from the neighbouring houses into all the windows of the northern face. These small bombs caused enough confusion to allow a German flame-thrower to go into action, and this set fire to the half-tracks resting up against the two wings of the school. As these blazed away the walls became very hot, floorboards began to char and sparks threatened to set the wooden roof alight. Anyone moving outside the building was silhouetted against the flames and came under heavy fire, but eventually two brave men crawled out with large explosive charges and blew each vehicle to pieces. The concussions shook the school to its foundations, but it did the trick.

The enemy now fired the office building immediately to the north, and the strong wind blew showers of burning fragments over the school. All available men were rushed up to the attic with sand, shovels and extinguishers, and a long battle against the flames ensued. The whole area was bright as day and these parties came under constant fire, though covering fire was provided as far as possible from below. At last, after three hours, the flames were under control. Everyone was exhausted from lack of sleep and from working feverishly in the intense heat.[59]

The Sappers' determination had saved their building for the time being, but others had been irretrievably lost. Of the eighteen buildings originally occupied by Frost's men, only ten were left in British hands at the end of the second day. There was still no sign of XXX Corps, and – in Arnhem at least – no news of its progress. There were still hopes that the 2nd Parachute Battalion would be reinforced by the other battalions of the 1st Parachute Brigade, but as the hours went by that prospect became increasingly remote.

Long before dawn on Tuesday, 19 September, it was clear that this would be the decisive day.

THE ADVANCE OF XXX CORPS
After being held up at Valkenswaard by the *Kampfgruppe* Rostel's road block during the night of 17/18 September, the Guards Armoured Division at last resumed its advance towards Aalst and Eindhoven. South of Aalst, the British armour encountered yet another blocking position. Commanded by *Major* Kerutt, the defence here comprised the remnants of the 1st and 3rd Battalions of the Regiment von Hoffmann, a 20 mm anti-aircraft platoon, and eleven 75 mm anti-tank guns with no tractors. South of Aalst, the surviving *Panzerjäger* IV SP guns of the *Kampfgruppe* Rostel were dispersed in the woods bordering the road.

Contact with Kerutt's road block was made at about 1020 hours, and several tanks and armoured cars were knocked out by the *Panzerjäger* IVs and the 75 mm guns before the position was bypassed at noon and Kerutt forced to withdraw to the eastern side of the corridor. The road to Eindhoven was now open and the advance pushed on under sporadic attack by the *Luftwaffe* – mainly by Me 262s, operating singly – and sniping by small numbers of German AFVs, which were quickly dealt with by the British tanks and by RAF Typhoons, which were still providing effective air support for XXX Corps. As one eye-witness recalled:

German convoys heading for the Allied corridor by day ran the continual risk of air attack. This one is being strafed by a Typhoon.

We slowed to a stop and the wireless crackled. The tank commander stuck his head out. 'Royal Tiger tanks a mile ahead. Get under cover. Tiffies have been called.'

His calm words were immediately drowned by the scream of aircraft engines as our Typhoon fighter 'cab-rank' peeled off from their constant circling above our heads. They skimmed overhead, steadied themselves by the huge bulk of the Philips works and let fly with their rockets. They banked and let fly again. The projectiles, like foreshortened lamp-posts with plumes of smoke bursting from the back, vanished behind the works. Seconds later came a dull explosion and a dirty plume of black smoke jetted up. A black object sailed lazily upwards and disappeared into the smoke. It was a tank turret, complete with gun.

Our tank commander swallowed hard. We moved on.[60]

At 1900 hours, the leading tanks of the Guards Armoured Division rumbled into Eindhoven to a rapturous welcome from the population, even though the town had already been liberated by the Americans. To the people of Eindhoven, the arrival of the tanks meant one thing: the Germans were gone for good. Dutch housewives unstintingly turned over their homes to the British troops, and pressed their meagre rations upon them – rations which, in many cases, had been hoarded for years in expectation of this moment.

We were stowing our gear on the tanks and talking about the excellence of our several bedrooms the previous night, when a young, dark-haired man stopped beside *Avenger* and smiled at me. I remember seeing him at the tea-drinking ceremony the previous night and, in fact, had addressed most of my remarks through him, for he spoke very fluent English.

'Good morning,' he said cheerfully. 'Did you enjoy your tea last night?'

'Yes, indeed,' I said. 'Very nice tea.'

He nodded and turned to walk away; then he hesitated and came back to me.

'The housewife bought that tea five years ago,' he said quietly. 'It was the last in Eindhoven. And she swore she would keep it for when the English came, because the English so love tea. Goodbye!'

He waved his hand quickly and then strode away. I thought how near I had come to saying 'No, thank you,' and mopped my brow in relief. But before we rolled out of Eindhoven we broke several different kinds of regulations by thrusting upon the reluctant housewife several tins of the best bully beef.

'It's pretty rough,' commented McGinty. 'But it's not so rough as all that. So what's she crying for, sir?' [61]

CHAPTER 8

D plus Two, 19 September 1944

As Monday, 18 September drew to a close, it was apparent that the weather conditions expected on Tuesday morning would be a good deal worse than those prevailing 24 hours earlier. The forecasters were predicting extensive fog over northern areas and almost unbroken cloud further south; it was expected however, that the fog would disperse by early afternoon and the clouds begin to lift. The adverse weather forecast brought about the first change in the plan for D plus 2; General Brereton decided that all airborne missions would use the southern route and that the drops and landings would be postponed from 1000 to 1500 hours.

The second change was for tactical reasons, and was dictated by unexpected enemy pressure on the 101st Airborne Division's area. Monday's operations had shown the 101st to be seriously deficient in artillery, and the Divisional Commander, General Maxwell Taylor, decided that artillery reinforcement should take precedence over supplies on the third lift. The five serials originally tasked with dropping supplies were therefore transformed into glider serials, carrying guns and artillerymen. The size of the lift would be greatly increased from 191 to 385 Wacos (including three carrying the loads of gliders which had aborted on the second lift).

The number of gliders assigned to the 82nd Airborne Division on the third lift was increased by a smaller margin, from 209 to 219, while the number of resupply aircraft for that division was increased from 142 to 167. More aircraft were also made available to carry the Polish Parachute Brigade to Arnhem – 114 instead of 108. In addition, 163 aircraft of Nos 38 and 46 Groups RAF would undertake a parachute resupply mission to Arnhem, and 52 aircraft would bring in gliders. The increase in the numbers of aircraft and gliders available for the third lift was made possible by the relatively low attrition experienced so far.

Tuesday dawned grey and overcast, with fog and low stratus drifting over the IX Troop Carrier Command's airfields around Grantham and masses of low cloud piled up over the Channel and North Sea. As the day progressed, it became clear that the Airborne Army's weather forecasters had been wrong: the conditions were far worse than they had predicted. Over much of the troop-carrier route, visibility was reduced to half a mile or less; only on the approach to Arnhem did conditions improve, and then to a very moderate extent.

The bad weather also severely disrupted air support missions on D plus 2. Fifteen Spitfire squadrons of ADGB had been earmarked to provide escort along the route between southern England and the IP near Gheel, but only one squadron was able to complete its mission in full and only 68 Spitfire sorties were flown in total. Seven groups of Eighth Air Force P-51s were also assigned to perimeter patrols and area cover; of these, five groups totalling 180 sorties reached the battle area, and two of them had combats with enemy fighters.[62]

In the first of these, the 364th Fighter Group engaged more than 30 enemy aircraft near Wesel at 1445 hours and claimed the destruction of five of them for the loss of one Mustang. The 357th Fighter Group, patrolling the Arnhem area with 54 Mustangs, had four separate engagements, the first at 1610 hours with about 25 Messerschmitt 109s, the second ten minutes later with 30 Focke-Wulf 190s, the third at 1705 hours with a mixed bunch of Me 109s and FW 190s, and the fourth with fifteen Messerschmitts at 1720 hours. The Group's pilots claimed to have shot down eighteen enemy aircraft for the loss of five of their own number.[63]

The Eighth Air Force had also assigned two groups of P-47s and one rocket-firing squadron for flak suppression work south of 's Hertogenbosch, but the weather prevented these from mounting any sorties. Beyond 's Hertogenbosch, on the final run to

For the German troops, food was scarce. These men are receiving a handout of boiled potatoes during a lull in the battle.

Nijmegen and Arnhem, flak suppression was the task of Ninth Air Force units based in northern France; these despatched 171 sorties, but few of them reached the front line and none, in conditions of low cloud and thick haze, attacked any targets.

EINDHOVEN

The *Luftwaffe* was also in evidence in the Eindhoven sector on the night of 18/19 September, when the town itself was heavily bombed. Luckily, the raid inflicted few casualties on the Allied forces or the civilian population.

With the arrival of the Guards Armoured Division the situation was greatly improved, but the 101st Airborne Division still had to defend the lengthy stretch of corridor from Veghel to Eindhoven – a distance of some fifteen miles – and enemy pressure continued to mount. The German 59th Infantry Division was still being inserted piecemeal into the battle, but its attacks were growing stronger with the arrival of each rail transport. However, the biggest potential threat to the 101st Division's airhead – although the Allies did not yet realize it – was the 107th *Panzer* Brigade, which was being routed to the battle area from Aachen. Completely armoured and mechanized, the 107th Brigade was built around a nucleus of a battalion of Mk V Panther tanks, supported by a *Panzergrenadier* infantry battalion mounted in armoured half-tracks, a self-propelled assault gun company, an engineer half-track company, and various supply and transport units. The Brigade had just re-equipped and was about to be loaded on rail transports bound for the eastern front when it received orders to move to Eindhoven. Its armoured columns thundered on

through the night towards Helmond, their assembly area. From there, sometime on Tuesday, the Brigade would attack in conjunction with the 59th Division, its objective to take St Oedenrode and cut off the spearhead of XXX Corps' advance on Grave. That was the urgent order issued to the Brigade Commander, *Major Freiherr* von Maltzahn. With the resources at his disposal – which included a good deal of mobile 20 mm *Flakvierling* batteries – he saw no reason why he should not fulfil his mission.

Even with the arrival of XXX Corps, the 101st Airborne Division's resources were thinly stretched. At first light on 19 September, the 506th Parachute Infantry Regiment, reinforced by two squadrons of British tanks, held the sector south of Zon; the Regiment had suffered a few casualties during the previous night's air raid, but was well dug in and prepared to resist further enemy attacks. At Veghel, the 501st PIR continued to have a relatively easy time, and in the early hours of Tuesday morning sent out a company-strength patrol to Dinter, four miles to the north-east.

The heaviest fighting of the day in the Eindhoven airhead involved the 502nd PIR. At 0600 hours, the 2nd Battalion was despatched to make another assault on the bridge at Best, but again the attack was beaten off. At 1415 hours the whole regiment, with the exception of the 1st Battalion which was defending St Oedenrode, made a co-ordinated attack on the bridge with the support of a squadron of British tanks. This time, the overstretched defences of the 59th Infantry Division, which by now was very short of ammunition, collapsed. By 1600 hours the paratroops had taken the bridge and with it fifteen 88 mm guns and 1,056 prisoners; 300 German dead were found on the battlefield.

Meanwhile, the third lift for the 101st Airborne Division – 385 glider-tug combinations in ten serials, flown by the 53rd Troop Carrier Wing and the 442nd Troop Carrier Group – had taken off from their bases in southern England between 1130 and 1230 hours. On board the gliders were 2,310 troops of the 81st Anti-tank Battalion, the 327th and 907th Field Artillery Battalions, and the 3rd Battalion of the 327th Glider Infantry. Also on board were 136 jeeps, 68 howitzers, 77 trailers of ammunition, and over 500 drums of gasoline.

The weather over the assembly area around Greenham Common was very bad, with poor visibility and a cloud base of about 1,200 feet. Beyond Hatfield it was even worse, and before reaching the coast the serials ran into deep, dense cloud in which visibility was zero. The glider pilots, unable to see their tugs, had to try to keep straight and level by observing the tilt of their towropes, or alternatively by following telephoned instructions from the C-47s' crews. Over the Channel, it was possible to break clear of the cloud by descending to less than 200 feet, but even then horizontal visibility was under half a mile.

The whole of the last serial was recalled when it was well out over the Channel. Of these gliders, 80 landed in England without serious mishap and two collided over their base, killing their pilots and six troops. Of the gliders in the other serials, seventeen were forced to ditch in the Channel; again, Royal Navy MTBs and RAF air-sea rescue launches came to the timely aid of their personnel, all of whom were saved. Thirty-one more gliders broke loose or were released over Belgium; three of these crashed, killing five men and injuring four. The rest made good landings, and all the personnel and equipment on board joined the 101st Airborne Division within a few days. The main problem facing the glider pilots who lost sight of their tug in the overcast was that if they failed to keep station with it in a turn the glider had a tendency to roll over on its back and go out of control; in these circumstances, the only procedure was to carry out an emergency release.

Because of confusion caused by the bad weather, and also because the Allied salient had not been extended in width as much as had been anticipated, the serials followed a route that ran a little to the west of the corridor. As a result, they ran into intense light flak and small-arms fire from Rethy, Moll and Best. As the official US Air Force history comments:

The troops on LZ 'W' could see the formations approaching over the battlefield between Best and the zone and could certainly have saved some losses by recommending a detour if a ground-to-air radio had been provided.[64]

As it was, seventeen aircraft – seven per cent of those fulfilling the mission – were shot down, the low altitude at which they were flying making it impossible for their crews to parachute to safety. Thirty-one aircrew were killed. Twenty-two more aircraft diverted to airfields in Belgium, and five of these had to be scrapped after making forced landings. Of the returning aircraft, 170 suffered damage, although in most cases this was slight.

About half of the pilots whose aircraft were shot down managed to release their gliders on or close to LZ 'W'. According to the US official historian,

Among the bravest and luckiest, were 1st Lt Jesse M. Harrison of the 435th Group and his co-pilot. Although their aircraft was already on fire, they brought their glider over the zone for a good release, then jumped through the flames, and lived.[65]

Many of the gliders were shot loose, broke loose or had to be released prematurely as a result of enemy action. Again, quoting the official historian, 'Since the ceiling in the release area was about 600 feet and visibility less than a mile, the wonder is not that they went wrong, but that so many went right.'[66] Sixteen gliders came down safely in enemy territory, their crews and much of their cargoes eventually reaching the 101st Division, but 26 more were unaccounted for, their occupants killed or captured after coming down in hostile territory.

Other missing crews were helped by the Dutch. One Waco, piloted by Flight Officer George F. Brennan, had to be released short of the zone when both tug and glider were badly hit; Brennan was seriously wounded by 20 mm fire but managed to get the glider down in one piece. With enemy troops in the vicinity, Brennan and another soldier, Sergeant Brasil Thompson – who was also wounded – took cover while the other glider troops set off for Zon, several miles away. Twelve German soldiers came up to loot the glider; Brennan and Thompson killed them all with submachine-gun fire from their hiding place in a ditch, 50 yards away. The two Americans managed to reach a barn, about a mile from the spot where the Waco had landed, and both passed out from exhaustion and loss of blood. They were found that night by members of the Dutch Resistance, who concealed them in the secret compartment of a farm cart laden with cow manure, and by this means they were smuggled to the St Lidwinia Maternity Hospital in the German-occupied town of Schijndel, where their wounds were treated. Thompson, the more slightly injured of the two, was placed in a locked storeroom where the Dutch staff could keep an eye on him; Brennan, disguised as an expectant Dutch housewife, was moved to a ward filled with pregnant women. Both men were hidden by the Dutch for nearly two months, until the town was finally liberated by the British.[67]

Of the 213 gliders that reached the LZ, one was shot down, three crashed, and 209 made good landings with very little damage. The landings began at 1437 hours and ended about 1600 hours. In summary, the lift could only be described as a disaster; of the 2,310 men assigned to the mission, only 1,341 reached the zone safely. Eleven were dead, eleven injured, and 157 missing; the rest had either returned to England or had landed somewhere outside the zone. Equipment losses were also high: 57 out of 136 jeeps and 28 out of 77 trailers. The most serious losses were suffered by the artillery; although 40 out of 68 guns reached the zone, they did not include any of the twelve 105 mm howitzers of the 907th Field Artillery Battalion.[68] Only 24 men of this battalion reached the LZ, and they had been carried by a flight of the seventh serial; the remainder had been airlifted by the ninth and tenth serials, the last of which had totally aborted. The 81st Anti-tank Battalion arrived with only fourteen of its 24 guns, but the 377th Field Artillery had all twelve of its 75 mm howitzers in position and ready for action by 1710 hours, an hour and forty minutes after it landed.

The artillery reinforcements, such as they were, arrived just in time to counter the attack by *Freiherr* von Maltzahn's 107th *Panzer* Brigade. The vanguard of the 107th, comprising dismounted infantry of the 1034th *Panzergrenadier* Regiment supported by Panther tanks, pushed carefully through the woods from the south-east towards Zon and its bridges. Von Maltzahn had some 40 Panthers at his disposal, but the majority of these remained concealed in the woods, ready to be thrown into action when the spearhead force seized its initial objectives: the main road bridge over the Wilhelmina Canal, its centre span now repaired by a Bailey bridge laid in place by XXX Corps engineers, and the smaller bridge about three-quarters of a mile to the east.

At 1715 hours, the leading Panthers opened fire on the church tower and school in Zon, which von Maltzahn suspected would be used as observation posts; the schoolhouse was, in fact, General Maxwell Taylor's command post. The tanks continued firing with main armament and 7.92 machine-guns as the *Panzergrenadiers* advanced across the open fields between the woods and the village. A tank shell struck a British truck from 'Q' Battery of 21st Anti-Tank Regiment as the vehicle was crossing the Bailey bridge and it exploded.[69] By now the leading tanks were within a few hundred yards of the bridge, and might have overwhelmed it had it not been for the timely arrival of a 57 mm anti-tank gun belonging to the 81st Battalion. The gunners fired no more than a couple of rounds before the Panther caught fire and ground to a halt beside the canal. A second Panther was hit by Bazooka fire from men of the 502nd PIR and it also began to burn, its fuel and ammunition exploding. With two of his tanks destroyed von Maltzahn called off the attack, withdrawing his armour to the south and the infantry to the north. By this time it was growing dark, and the German commander decided to launch a full-scale assault at first light. The irony was that, had he been in a position to launch his initial attack just an hour or two earlier, he might well have succeeded in his mission, because then the bridge was only lightly guarded by the 502nd PIR – the majority of its paratroops being engaged at Best or defending the landing zones – and the vital artillery reinforcements had not yet arrived. When the threat did develop, the 502nd PIR had sufficient resources to counter it.

NIJMEGEN

At dawn on Tuesday, Lieutenant-General Browning and General Gavin were eagerly awaiting the arrival of XXX Corps; indeed, on the previous evening Browning had indicated to the commander of the 82nd Airborne Division that the Nijmegen bridge had to be taken on Tuesday, or very early on Wednesday at the latest. Gavin's problem was that he could spare only one parachute infantry battalion to attack the bridge; the rest of his force had a 25-mile perimeter to defend. Meanwhile, the great road bridge stood tantalizingly intact, for reasons which are still not clear. Gavin later claimed that this was due to the efforts of the Dutch Resistance, which prevented the defending Germans from placing demolition charges. There was certainly a great deal of Resistance activity, but there is little doubt that the Germans could have destroyed the bridge had they wished to do so. According to some accounts, the task of preparing the road and rail bridges for demolition was given to a company of 10 SS engineers which reached Nijmegen on the morning of 18 September via the river ferry at Pannerden. The charges, however, were only to be fired on the orders of Army Group B; it seems likely that *Feldmarschall* Model believed that the Nijmegen bridges could be held.

The 82nd Airborne Division was to have been reinforced on Tuesday by the 325th Glider Infantry Regiment, but the glider mission, assigned to the 50th and 52nd Troop Carrier Wings, was postponed because of the weather; the few glider-tug combinations that did take off were recalled almost immediately.

A resupply mission to the 82nd Airborne Division, although it got off the ground – the bases of the 53rd TCW responsible for it being in southern England – ended in failure. One serial of 25 aircraft put up by the 439th Group became dispersed in dense cloud before it reached the Belgian coast and most returned to base; only one aircraft got through to drop its load near LZ 'W', its pilot following a glider serial ahead of him. Another C-47 attempted to get through, but turned back after being hit by flak. Another serial, comprising 35 aircraft of the 61st TCG, crossed the Channel at an altitude of less than 200 feet in dense haze and encountered heavy flak over Holland. Two aircraft were shot down, one west of Veghel and another just after making its drop, and fifteen were damaged. The other 32 got through to DZ 'O', which the 82nd Airborne's commander had decided to use as both a drop and landing zone following Monday's struggle for the other zones, and made a high, fast drop. Bundles were discharged from as high as 2,500 feet at speeds

of up to 135 mph, with the result that most of them were widely scattered over enemy-held territory. The amount recovered was less than 20 per cent, and a very small fraction of the 265 tons General Gavin had been expecting. The failure of the mission left the 82nd Airborne Division critically short of food and ammunition.

Meanwhile, attempts by the Germans to push armoured reinforcements through to the Nijmegen area continued to be frustrated by British 2nd Parachute Battalion's dogged defence of their positions around the northern end of the Arnhem road bridge. *Obersturmbannführer* Heinz Harmel, commanding the 10th SS *Kampfgruppe* Frundsberg, and General Wilhelm Bittrich, commanding II *Panzer* Corps, were both convinced that the destruction of the Nijmegen airhead was crucial to the outcome of the battle, and sought an alternative to the Arnhem crossing point. They found it at Pannerden on the lower Rhine, where on 18 September a ferrying operation was set in motion by the 10 SS Engineer Battalion. It was a slow business; anything that would float was pressed into service to get the men and material across; Mk IV tanks being loaded on to huge rafts and then manhandled across the river with ropes. It was primitive and laborious, but by noon on Monday the badly-needed reinforcements were on their way to Nijmegen.

The first of these, in fact, crossed the lower Rhine via the ferry at Huissen, and comprised 100 men under *Hauptsturmführer* Karl-Heinz Euling, who had just disengaged from the fight for the Arnhem bridge. They reached Nijmegen on Monday afternoon, joining the *Kampfgruppen* Reinhold and Henke in the defence of the town, a task made easier by the fact that the US force attacking the Nijmegen bridge had been withdrawn to defend the landing zones. The Germans took advantage of the temporary withdrawal of American troops to strengthen the defences at the southern end of the Waal road bridge with the aid of a few *Panzerjäger* Mk IV SP guns; 88 mm flak guns were placed among the houses on the other side of the river, covering the bridge and the approach to it. The approaches to both the road and rail bridges were heavily mined, and 20 mm cannon sited to cover the access roads. By dawn on 19 September the Germans were well established in the Hunner Park that flanked the Arnhemsche Weg, the road that led to the southern ramp of the bridge. All the while, reinforcements continued to trickle in from Pannerden; but whether they would be strong enough to hold the line when the Allied attacks were renewed, this time with the probable support of British armour, was open to question.

ARNHEM

A strange, almost eerie silence hung over the shattered streets of Arnhem in the small hours of Tuesday, 19 September. Sounds were muffled by the mist that curled through the town from the Neder Rijn. Through it, phantom-like, moved the remnants of Lieutenant-Colonel Dobie's 1st Parachute Battalion, setting out on what was to be their final attempt to reach the 2nd Battalion at the Arnhem Bridge. They advanced along the Onderlangs, the flat road that followed the bend in the lower Rhine beside the river and harbour. The time was 0400 hours.

Meanwhile, unknown to Dobie, what was left of Lt-Col Fitch's 3rd Parachute Battalion had also been filtering down to the bank of the Neder Rijn under cover of darkness. Bogged down and decimated in the previous day's fighting near St Elisabeth's Hospital, the remains of the Battalion had become split in two, each part occupying a block of houses. At about 0230 hours, Fitch – still determined to do all he could to break through to the 2nd Battalion at the bridge – ordered his officers and NCOs to extricate their men and, in complete silence, rendezvous at the Rhine Pavilion, a building on the bank of the river almost due south of St Elisabeth's Hospital. When Fitch arrived at the Rhine Pavilion, he set off along the Onderlangs with the first party to rendezvous, unaware that the 1st Battalion was ahead of him. It was now 0500 hours.

An hour earlier, in parallel with the advance of the 1st Battalion, the 2nd South Staffordshires and the 11th Parachute Battalion had also begun their attack eastward along the Utrechtseweg, the higher and more northerly route. The whole advance proceeded along a very narrow front; barely 200 yards separated the upper and lower routes at the widest point.

On the lower road, the 1st Parachute Battalion, with the survivors of the 3rd Battalion some distance behind, at first made relatively good progress under cover of the mist and darkness. Then the leading troops made contact with the *Sperrlinie*, manned in this sector by the *Kampfgruppe* Spindler, which occupied the houses along the Onderlangs

and the steep embankment to the left of it. Soon, the darkness was torn by the crack of grenades and the crump of mortar bombs, the harsh, tearing note of MG 42s, the rattle of Sten and rifle fire, all blending into a hideous cacophony magnified a hundred times as it echoed from the walls of the houses, punctuated by the screams and moans of stricken men. Within minutes, the 1st Battalion's advance had broken down into a series of confused, bitterly-contested actions.

Dawn broke, and for the first time, through the mist and smoke, the course of the battle became visible to the survivors of Gräbner's SS Reconnaissance Battalion, positioned in the brickworks on the other side of the river. The sight that confronted them was almost unbelievable: the 1st and 3rd Parachute Battalions, pinned down under heavy fire and strung out along an unprotected strip of ground only 30 or 40 yards wide.

The Germans at once opened fire, traversing the open stretch of road with 20 mm and 30 mm cannon. What followed was little short of a massacre; Dobie's battalion was cut to pieces, hemmed in between two sources of enemy fire. Small groups of paratroops fought vicious hand-to-hand combats with the enemy:

> . . . Major Perrin-Brown led T Company, the parachute war cry *Waho, Mohammed!* bursting from their throats, in a bayonet charge which reduced their strength to eight men. A little later Major Timothy led R Company in a similar charge and fought on till only six were left. Their pertinacity had brought them to within a thousand yards of the bridge, and they could do no more . . . [70]

The 1st Battalion battle report described the disaster in stark terms:

> R Coy six men left. S Coy fifteen men left (approx) . . . T Coy eight men left. Bn HQ about ten left (CO went forward to make recce, position very bad). 0630 T Coy were cut off and could not disengage. Enemy grenading us from houses (on the higher road) we were trying to get into. Managed to force entry (CO wounded) but had only six men. Enemy in rear also . . . Tanks outside our house. Many civilians in cellar with us. Nothing more to be done. Four wounded in our party . . . 0730 SS entered house. Party taken.[71]

Lieutenant-Colonel Dobie, wounded in the eye and arm, was taken to hospital, where his wounds were dressed. He was determined not to remain a captive for long.

The PGEM house in Arnhem was the scene of fierce fighting between the Germans and the 1st Parachute Battalion.

Shortly after arriving at the hospital, my German guard took my watch and while he was showing it to a nurse, I managed to make my escape and hid in the bushes in the hospital grounds. After being stopped once by a German soldier and allaying his suspicions by saying *"Guten Morgen"* I decided not to risk crossing the road and spent the rest of the day in hiding. That night (Tuesday evening) I crossed the street into a house, which had been bombed, and managed to find a bed where I slept very soundly indeed until awakened by somebody, trying to get in at the door. It proved to be a (Dutch) doctor . . . He dressed my wounds once more and found me another bed in the house.[72]

Later, when Arnhem was evacuated on German orders, Dobie was smuggled out and lodged with some friendly Dutch people at Ede. Much later, in possession of vital information about escape routes,

he managed to cross the Rhine with the utmost difficulty and made contact with 21st Army Group.

With Dobie's battalion destroyed, the full weight of the enemy fire now turned on Fitch's 3rd Battalion, which was quickly cut to pieces. John Fitch ordered the survivors to make their way back to the Rhine Pavilion as best they could. Soon afterwards, he was killed by a mortar bomb. Very few of his men reached the Pavilion, where they were joined as the morning wore on by stragglers from the 1st Battalion. Of that Battalion, only 40 men remained.

Meanwhile, the advance of the 2nd South Staffordshires and the 11th Parachute Battalion along the Utrechtseweg had been making much slower progress than the attack along the lower road. As they emerged from the cover of the St Elisabeth Hospital, the South Staffordshires were raked by flanking fire from SS *Obersturmführer* Gropp's anti-aircraft *Kampfgruppe*, installed in houses on the other side of the marshalling yards to the north of the line of advance, and from *Hauptsturmführer* Hans Moller's SS Engineer *Kampfgruppe* on the right flank and in front. The engineers fought the British troops with small arms, mortars, flame-throwers and even *Panzerfaust* anti-tank projectiles, which proved to be quite devastating anti-personnel weapons.

Nevertheless, at 0630 hours a company of the South Staffordshires succeeded in occupying a museum on the high ground, which the troops

German armour, supported by infantry, advancing slowly along the Utrechtseweg during the battle for the *Hexenkessel*.

nicknamed 'The Monastery', and the attack progressed in fits and starts until about 0800 hours, when it came to a standstill. At this point the battalion was in something of a bottleneck, with less than 300 yards separating the enemy troops on either flank. In fact, the Germans were so close that it was very difficult for them to use mortars; 'They were shooting almost straight up in the air.'[73]

The Battalion reached a fork in the road, and the CO, Lieutenant-Colonel W.D.H. McCardie, decided to take the right-hand branch. At 0830 hours he conferred with Lieutenant-Colonel George Lea, commanding the 11th Parachute Battalion, who agreed to support the South Staffordshires' advance by moving his battalion up from the rear to protect the left flank, advancing in parallel along the southern edge of the marshalling yards. Lea returned to his Battalion, and, at 1000 hours he

. . . Informed 2 South Staffords that GARBLED message had been received from Div, which appeared to indicate that 11 Bn was to stand fast in present area. Attack therefore off, positions being taken up till Div intention was clear. 1030–1100 Div Staff officer with orders to 11 Bn to secure Heyenoord–Diependaal.[74]

This line was well to the west of the Battalion's present position – further west, in fact, than the St Elisabeth Hospital, where the attack had started – and the message from Division effectively meant that the 11th Battalion was to withdraw. Lea sent word of this new development to McCardie by runner, but the man never got through. McCardie, still assuming that Lea was coming up to protect his left flank, prepared to renew the attack; Lea, meanwhile formed up his Battalion in column with all available weapons and prepared to march back to the newly-assigned position.

By 1100 hours the South Staffordshires had reached the furthest point on their line of advance, the PGEM (75) building just beyond the Municipal Museum. They were now under attack by the *Sturmgeschütz* III SPs of *Wehrmacht* Assault Gun Brigade 280, which had recently arrived in Arnhem from the north and had been assigned to the *Kampfgruppe* Spindler; each SP mounted a 75 mm gun. The South Staffordshires, lacking anti-tank guns, could only engage them with multiple Bren gun fire and, when the opportunity arose, with PIATS. In this way they managed to keep the enemy armour at bay until 1230 hours; then the PIAT

ammunition ran out. The SP guns now rolled into the British positions virtually unopposed and the South Staffordshires had no alternative but to disengage and withdraw in scattered groups about half a mile to the west. There, an attempt was made to reorganize and attacks were made on enemy positions at Den Brink, the idea being to secure a pivot for the expected attack by the 11th Parachute Battalion. But the 11th Battalion was in the process of withdrawing, and was just getting under way when the German counter-attack from the east fell upon it. What had started as a fairly orderly move quickly degenerated into a series of confused and savage engagements, the survivors of both British battalions being pushed steadily back to the west of the St Elisabeth Hospital. During these actions, Lieutenant-Colonels McCardie and Lea were both wounded and captured.

The order for the 11th Parachute Battalion's withdrawal had come as a result of a chain of circumstances set in motion earlier in the day, when the attack of the 2nd South Staffordshires overran the houses where the Divisional Commander, General Urquhart, was hiding. When the British attacked, the German SP gun that had remained in position throughout the night suddenly withdrew, and the owner of the house ran upstairs to tell Urquhart that British troops were in the street. Within minutes, the Divisional Commander was on his way by jeep to his HQ in the Hartenstein Hotel.

There, he found a situation of growing confusion and unease. Brigadier Hicks briefed him as best he could on the battle situation; there was no doubt about the growing strength of the enemy opposition in the east, where the *Sperrlinie* blocked the access roads to the bridge; fighting around the landing zones appeared to indicate that the enemy was also being reinforced substantially in the north and west, presenting a potentially serious threat to the planned operations of Brigadier John Hackett's 4th Parachute Brigade and to the Division as a whole, which faced the grim possibility of being boxed in.

Urquhart was in urgent need of more intelligence on the German dispositions to the north and west, and accordingly despatched the various troops of the 1st Airborne Reconnaissance Squadron to scout those areas. The Squadron's A Troop set off to reconnoitre the Heelsum–Renkum road, and as Lance-Corporal Ken Hope recalls:

We were deployed, men and vehicles, at a T junction with trees lining the road and open heathland on our right. There were two or three trim villas with neat gardens adjacent to the junction on the left. Suddenly, there was a long burst of 1mg firing at the front of the column. From my position I could not observe any target to engage. After a brief interval I heard Lieutenant Wadsworth call for Sergeant Ray Hewer and myself to join him. We crouched in a ditch on the right of the road. The officer told us that we were to move forward and round up the party of Germans which had just been fired on. Now I could see a confused jumble of bicycles heaped in the roadway, a German NCO stretched out dead under one of the machines, and another German soldier groaning beside him. The three of us automatically adopted the 'Western gunfighters' crouch as we stole along the ditch. It seems instinctive for soldiers to assume this hunched attitude when they know they may come under fire at any time.

We spotted the rest of the cycle party hiding amongst the foliage near the garden fences. I seem to remember there being three of them, all *Waffen* SS men. I recollect myself shouting the most execrable schoolboy German phrases, advising them to come out and surrender or they would be shot. They emerged from cover in very nervous and agitated fashion with hands raised. One of the Germans had extended one arm only and I thought: "My God, the bastard's giving us the Nazi salute!" However, I could see he was shot through the shoulder and upper arm. They were directed to join the Troop at the T junction.

The German NCO was dead, shot through the head . . . The wounded German was groaning and moaning piteously, calling for his mother. A Dutch civilian joined us from one of the nearby houses and offered his services as a doctor. He spoke very soothingly in German, rather like a mother comforting her child, and the German's groaning ceased. I remember feeling hostile at first towards the Dutchman –the German, after all, was an SS man – then I realised, of course, that he was behaving as any humanitarian doctor must, irrespective of nationality. The belly of the field grey uniform was stitched with bullet holes. I think it was Sergeant Ray Hewer who gave the doctor morphia ampoules which we carried with our field dressings. Later in the day, on the same road, we bumped another German patrol, a larger one, trundling a heavy machine-gun. As I recall it, a perfect ambush opportunity was lost because someone in A Troop opened fire prematurely. The Germans had abandoned the gun in the middle of the road. They attempted to disable it with stick grenades. Then they retired and escaped apparently unscathed.

During this reconnaissance, Heelsum Heath to our right was suddenly and dramatically swept by a flight of six Focke-Wulf 190s. They came roaring in at ground level, the head and shoulders of each pilot perfectly outlined under the aircraft canopy. I remember that I was walking across the road as the *Luftwaffe* attack was mounted, though not at our column. There was a rising crescendo of noise, aero-engines, cannon shells and machine-guns. It was all over in seconds and what damage they inflicted, if any, was not visible to me. But when I came to analyse my own apprehension afterwards I felt embarrassed to realise that I had been attempting to shrink and compress my whole body into my steel helmet. The effect of almost naked isolation in the middle of the road had induced a psychological reaction to perform this impossible feat of self-preservation.[76]

The Squadron's C Troop, meanwhile, had run into trouble. Following the road that ran past a home for the blind, they proceeded to the railway crossing at Wolfheze and then moved down a cobbled road which petered out into three tracks after three or four hundred yards. They followed the right-hand track, which led to a farmhouse where 30 or 40 Germans surrendered. Trooper Des Evans recalls what followed.

As we drew level with the farmhouse some of the surrendering enemy pointed out one of their fellows. He was sitting with his back to the farmhouse wall and was clearly very badly injured. Both legs and arms were broken and he had sustained other injuries. Out of nowhere, it seemed, a lieutenant wearing a khaki beret detached himself from a jeep, bent over the wounded man and, with his pistol, shot him through the head. The other Germans were obviously stunned by this cold-blooded act and all made a move to get as far away from the officer as possible. Making them understand that they must keep their hands above their heads we ushered them back unguarded, along the route we had covered. I cannot recall having seen the officer before the patrol began, nor did I see him at all later on.

Passing the farm we took a sharp left turn on to a rougher track that led through wooded country. Jim and I were still leading on foot. Proceeding with extreme caution the Troop began to make its way through this ideal ambush country. Then came the order to start 'leapfrogging', with two men jumping off the jeep that was then leading. I began to feel a most intense pain in my left foot, which was aggravated by my jumping on and off the vehicle. The radio (Type 22) was situated on my side of the jeep; this meant that it was three or four inches higher than the other side and I was having to sit on it. Approaching the main road, which by this time could be seen through the trees, I asked Jim if he would change places with me. He agreed to do so, and this act spared my life.

Bursting out of the woods on to the road we turned right and were soon going flat out. Looking ahead, I saw a tree trunk lying across the road and thought that we'd be caught trying to turn round, but we were able to steer round the left end of it. Then I saw another tree further ahead and thought that we'd really 'buy it' at this one. Again, we were able to drive round it, but then an intense burst of firing came from our left and everyone on the jeep was hit. The engine was hit too, and Lt Bowles managed to steer the jeep over to the far right of the road. L/Cpl

Baker, who had been firing the 'K' gun with its hundred-round magazine, was already dead when he fell sideways and was hit full in the face by a tree. I'd lost my rifle somehow and had to jump off in order to avoid the same tree smashing into my legs.

Lt Bowles was wounded in the foot and the hand, I was wounded near the left elbow, Jim was dead – stitched right across the chest – and Fred too was dead, still lying across the pannier. On recovering my balance I saw that Fred's Bren gun had contrived to land in front of the jeep. Running to pick it up I was bending down when I noticed that the magazine was no longer in place. Lt Bowles was taking the long way round the jeep so I reached for the 'K' gun and covered him as he ran into the trees behind me. There was almost half a magazine left and I fired it all in the direction where I thought the enemy to be. A bullet coming under the jeep hit me in the left leg but not badly enough to impair movement. Turning, I followed Bowles into the woods and caught up with him just before we emerged on the road leading to Wolfheze. Bowles leaned on me; there was a shot from the left, then silence.

I supported him all the way to the Blind Home. On reaching it, we were met by a nurse who bandaged our wounds and then, giving us two blankets each, showed us into a crude air-raid shelter outside. It is quite impossible even to guess how long we were there. There were bouts of intense pain and one day just seemed to follow another. I have no doubt that the good lady must have fed us, but I don't have any memory of what we ate or when. The nurse did apologise profusely for not having any pain-killers and would stand there wringing her hands in her frustration.[77]

Reports filtering in from the north and west left General Urquhart in no doubt about the seriousness of the situation. Of primary concern was the threat to Brigadier Hackett's brigade, which early on Tuesday morning had begun the advance towards its objective, the high ground to the north of Arnhem. All three battalions – the 10th on the left flank, the 7th KOSB in the centre and the 156th on the right – soon encountered strong resistance from the *Sperrlinie* along the Dreyenseweg. Ferocious company attacks by the 10th Parachute Battalion on the northern wing were broken up by intense fire from mortars, tanks and SP guns, but the paratroops succeeded in beating off attacks by enemy infantry.

The exploits of one soldier – Captain L.E. Queripel – serve to illustrate the ferocity of the fighting in the 10th Battalion's sector. Queripel had assumed command of the Battalion's A Company after the company commander, Major Ashworth, was mortally wounded. At 1400 hours on Tuesday, Queripel was leading his Company into action under heavy medium machine-gun fire along a road which ran along an embankment. The Company took many casualties and the advance was halted, the survivors taking cover on either side of the road. In order to reorganize his men, Queripel crossed and re-crossed the road several times, always under fire; during one such dash, he picked up a wounded NCO and carried him to cover, but was himself hit in the face. Despite his extremely painful injury, Captain Queripel led a party of men against a strongpoint that was holding up the advance; the strongpoint, comprising a captured British anti-tank gun and two machine-guns, had been responsible for many of the Company's casualties. The enemy gunners were killed and the anti-tank gun recaptured.

As the Germans harassed the withdrawing party, Queripel and his men took cover in a ditch. By now Queripel was also wounded in both arms. His position was subjected to heavy mortar and MG fire, and Queripel encouraged his men to resist with all the weapons at their disposal – rifles, pistols and Mills bombs. As the Germans closed in, they tossed stick grenades into the ditch; Queripel and his men tossed them back. Soon, most of the men who had shared Queripel's last stand were either dead or wounded, and he ordered the survivors to get clear while he covered their exit with a final bout of grenade throwing. He was last seen alone and still fighting in the ditch.

Captain Lionel Queripel, in fact, was taken prisoner, but died of his wounds while in captivity. On 1 February, 1945, he was gazetted for the award of a posthumous Victoria Cross.

While Lieutenant-Colonel Kenneth Smyth's 10th Parachute Battalion was brought to a halt astride the Amsterdamseweg, the 156th Parachute Battalion under Lieutenant-Colonel Sir Richard des Voeux launched an unsuccessful attack on the *Sperrlinie* along the Dreyenseweg early on Tuesday morning. At about 0700 hours C Company, with B Company in support, succeeded in overrunning strong outlying German positions, but while this action was in progress enemy reinforcements – a battalion of twin and quadruple 20 mm flak guns mounted on half-tracks – arrived to strengthen this sector of the blocking line, which was held principally by a *Waffen*-SS company also equipped with SP anti-aircraft guns. These weapons inflicted appalling casualties on the 156th Battalion when it attempted to resume its attack:

0830 hours. A Company put in an attack on the line of defence on the road running from Arnhem to Utrecht. The company met very heavy opposition including SP guns and armoured cars and suffered heavy casualties, including all officers.

0900 hours. B Company put in an attack on the same line moving round the north of A Company and met with the same heavy opposition. Its commander was wounded and heavy casualties were sustained.[78]

At 0930 hours, C Company and Headquarters Company also launched an attack, and it met with the same fate. Only 30 men got through the storm of 20 mm cannon and MG fire and reached the Dreyenseweg. The exhausted survivors stumbled back through the trees and began to dig in near the start line, immediately behind which Brigadier Hackett established his Headquarters in a copse. In the course of its attacks the 4th Parachute Brigade was also subjected to dive-bombing by Messerschmitt 109s, which inflicted further casualties, particularly on B Company.

Meanwhile, General Urquhart, now aware of the criticality of the situation, had decided to take drastic measures. He would transfer the 4th Parachute Brigade to a different position, occupying a north–south line running from the Utrecht–Arnhem railway to the Neder Rijn, about halfway between Oosterbeek and Arnhem.

On Tuesday afternoon, Urquhart went to Brigadier Hackett's HQ by jeep and, after the two officers had conferred, it was decided to withdraw the 4th Parachute Brigade as quickly as possible, the troops using the railway crossing at Wolfheze and the vehicles being manhandled over the railway embankment several hundred yards to the east. This measure was taken because the crossing at Wolfheze was under artillery fire from the *Kampfgruppen* to the west, and this might prevent the passage of the vehicles. The task was to be undertaken by the 4th Parachute Squadron, Royal Engineers, which had dropped with the 4th Parachute Brigade and was now fighting as part of it.

The 11th Parachute Battalion, meanwhile, had already been ordered to carry out a left flank attack and join up with the remainder of the 4th Brigade – an order which, as we have seen, caused much confusion between that battalion and the South Staffordshires. Urquhart proposed that the 11th Battalion should occupy the Heyenoord–

Diependaal area, apparently unaware that this position was actually to the rear of Spindler's *Sperrlinie*. Even the Arnhem–Utrecht railway, where – according to his own account – Urquhart intended the 4th Brigade to reorganize 'before they went for the Bridge' formed part of the *Sperrlinie*.

On Brigadier Hackett's orders, the withdrawal of the 10th and 156th Parachute Battalions got under way at 1630 hours, the move to the railway crossing being covered by the 7th KOSB, which also had the task of covering the landing of the glider elements of the Polish Brigade near Johannahoeve. Lieutenant-Colonel Payton-Reid of the Borderers, who had also been in conference at Brigadier Hackett's HQ, returned to his battalion to find

. . . a hell of a fight going on. 'Before he could withdraw the battalion, German attacks had to be contained.' This we did successfully . . . Major Cochran, who was afterwards killed, killing twenty of the enemy, and Drum-Major Tate the same number . . . All the Boches who weren't killed turned and went back into the woods, so I took the opportunity of going south.

Eventually the battalion, now reduced to fewer than 300 men, got into a position in two large houses near a small wood just south of the railway.

That plan (for withdrawal) was, as we now see, forced on our higher command, but its execution had the most disastrous consequences. It is against text-book teaching to break off an engagement and withdraw from the battlefield in broad daylight, but that is what we, and the two battalions of 4 Para Bde had to attempt – and without delay. As a result, this fine Scottish Borderer Battalion which at four o'clock in the afternoon was a full-strength unit, with its weapons, transport and organization complete, was reduced, within the hour, to a third of its strength . . . [79]

The 10th Parachute Battalion diarist is in full agreement.

This retreat was to prove a dangerous step as the Battalion was in close contact with the enemy and it meant moving back across about one thousand yards of open ground which was well swept by small-arm guns. It had to be carried out, however, and the companies got back to the level crossing at Wolfheze. Very heavy casualties were suffered crossing the open ground . . . [80]

We were given orders to leave the wood. It was every man for himself, for by then we were all split up. The top of the wood was occupied by fifty or sixty Germans . . . Sergeant Sunley and Sergeant Houghton were terrific. We ran across a playing field and found several men showing yellow triangles . . . We had by then lost about two-thirds, but the men were still in good heart though they had no more support weapons.[81]

Tuesday was also a day of feverish activity for the pathfinders of the 21st Independent Parachute Company, and in particular for No 1 Platoon, which had to set out the navigational aids for the Polish glider element.

The distance from Company HQ to where the platoon set up its landing aids was about a mile and a half and rather more than a mile to the point where a culvert under the embanked railway gave access to the strip of woodland bordering the LZ just north of the line . . . The same dispositions were made as for the previous day, save that the *Eureka* team found an accommodating dung heap under cover of which to operate! Half an hour before the estimated time of arrival of the gliders, Tommy McMahon and his mate were out and ready to operate. The rest of the platoon were in defensive positions and, in view of yesterday's strafing, began digging in . . .

The morning dragged on past 1000 hours and was enlivened by further visits from Messerschmitts who beat up the platoon's positions in three or four waves . . . After the second or third wave a few bold souls lay on their backs in their slit trenches and fired their weapons straight up in the air in the forlorn hope that the odd bullet might prove unlucky for some German pilot. As far as is known, neither side damaged the other . . . The third lift arrived late, as on the previous day, about mid-afternoon. Just before the Polish gliders arrived a message was received from Divisional HQ, instructing the pathfinders to get out on the LZ as soon as the gliders landed and redirect the Poles to Oosterbeek.[82]

The plans for the Third Lift had fallen into almost complete disarray. All 114 C-47s of the 52nd Troop Carrier Wing which were to have dropped the bulk of the Polish Parachute Brigade on DZ 'K' south of the Arnhem bridge were grounded by the impenetrable overcast in their area. Had the Poles landed at 1000 hours that morning, as planned, they might conceivably have saved the bridge or at least rescued what was left of the 2nd Parachute Battalion. It was not until the afternoon that the Germans moved up sufficient armour to begin the systematic destruction of the Battalion's positions at the north end of the bridge; the strongest opposition on the south side was provided by what remained of Gräbner's 9th SS Reconnaissance Battalion, occupying the brickworks.

One mission was not thwarted by the weather. At bases in southern England, 80 American and ten British glider-tug combinations stood ready to airlift the 878th US Aviation Engineer Battalion to LZs 'X' and 'L'. The task of the Battalion was to prepare landing strips so that the 52nd Lowland Division could be flown in by Dakota to reinforce the Arnhem airhead. But the sites selected for the airstrips were still in enemy hands, and the engineer support mission was never flown.

Although the mission to drop the bulk of the Polish Parachute Brigade was postponed, the weather over southern England was clear enough to allow the airlift of the Polish Brigade HQ and supporting artillery. Forty-four combinations were despatched: 35 to LZ 'L', eight to LZ 'X' and one to LZ 'S'. Of these gliders – all Horsas – five broke loose over England, two came down in the sea and five more were released prematurely over Belgium and Holland. Despite considerable flak none of the tug aircraft were lost, but nine were damaged.

The pathfinders had done their work well, and 28 pilots reported the release of their gliders on LZ 'L'. Unfortunately, the glider landings coincided with the withdrawal of the 4th Parachute Brigade; the arrival of the gliders caused violent enemy reaction, a great increase in the volume of fire, and considerable confusion. As the history of the 21st Independent Parachute Company records:

On LZ 'L' the Germans unleashed a vicious attack with MG and mortar fire on hapless Poles and glider pilots who had left England expecting to push straight into Arnhem and who now were the survivors of the flak storm . . . Few of the gliders landed unscathed. Some broke up in the air, scattering already wounded men on to the LZ. Some, their pilots killed or wounded, crashed into each other or crashed on landing. Others, riddled with flak, disintegrated with the impact of landing.

Through all this and the withering MG and mortar fire the men of No 2 Platoon hared around among the surviving Poles and pilots directing them south of the strip of woodland bordering the railway line which at that point was embanked. Here, more confusion reigned. Troops were streaming alone the railway below the embankment going westward towards Wolfheze – away from Arnhem! It looked like a retreat.[83]

The landing of the Polish glider element was also opposed by enemy fighters, although this is mentioned in only a few accounts. One of them, however, was provided by Polish war correspondent Marck Swiecicki, who was on the scene:

Cast off from the tugs, they (the gliders) would be landing in a moment. But at that very moment something happened which we had not expected. From the north other tiny dots . . . grew and grew . . . Messerschmitts! Their machine-guns snapped and barked . . . Several gliders caught fire and . . . dived in a mad flight to the ground . . . One of the gliders broke up in the air like a child's toy, and a jeep, an anti-tank gun and people fell out of it . . . When they (the Messerschmitts) stopped, the forest opened up. Skirmishing Germans, looking in the distance like rabbits jumping . . . moved forward. The German infantry fired at the gliders which had escaped the Messerschmitts . . . The bullets tore through the gliders' wooden walls, over the jeeps and guns which had been brought out, and then over the men, throwing more and more of them to the ground. The men who had escaped whole fled. Yes, they fled; for it could not be called a retreat or a defence.[84]

The increasing activity of German fighters in the Arnhem area is simply explained: the 1st *Jagddivision* (Fighter Division) had been temporarily released from the defence of the *Reich* for offensive operations at Arnhem. This division operated a mixed force of about 300 Messerschmitt 109s and Focke-Wulf 190s, but not all were available for operations against the Allied airhead. Neither were they capable of establishing air superiority in the face of overwhelming Allied fighter cover. But when that essential cover was absent, as we shall see later on, the impact of fighters on slow, unarmed transport aircraft could be devastating.

Once the initial element of surprise had been lost, the Germans had plenty of warning of subsequent incoming airborne missions. Speedy action by *Luftwaffe* signals specialists led to the establishment of a radio link between II SS Corps HQ at Arnhem and the fortress town of Dunkirk, which was still in German hands; the Dunkirk garrison was therefore able to signal the passage of transport aircraft and gliders over the Channel a full hour before they reached the zones, allowing plenty of time for flak and fighters to be alerted.

A further important element in the German air defence system at Arnhem was the arrival, on 19 September, of a flak brigade commanded by *Oberstleutnant* von Swoboda. This formation, comprising five battalions of 88 mm flak and also some 20 mm, 37 mm and 105 mm guns, were redeployed to Arnhem from static defence sites in the Ruhr. Three of the 88 mm battalions were in position by mid-afternoon on Tuesday, and all flak assets in the Arnhem area were placed under the command of von Swoboda's brigade HQ.

This heavy anti-aircraft reinforcement compounded the misfortunes that befell the 19th September resupply mission to Arnhem. The original drop point for this mission, DP 'V', had been selected on the assumption that the 4th Parachute Brigade would be well on the way to establishing a secure defence on the high ground north of Arnhem on D plus 2, but for reasons already explained this had not been achieved. Attempts were made by radio and carrier pigeon to advise HQ Troop Carrier Command in England that DZ 'V' was compromised, and that the resupply drop should be switched to a safer location south of Hartenstein, but the messages were never received. The official history states that:

The airborne set up a *Eureka* in a tower at the new point, but that could be used only intermittently for fear of exhausting the battery. Although about half of the pilots interrogating it reported success, it seems to have done them singularly little good. This may have been partly due to the set being turned on late and partly to the tendency of blips on a *Rebecca* screen to merge when it was within about two miles of its *Eureka*. The old drop point was less than a mile and a half north-east of the new one. Smoke, panels and Very lights were also used, but because of the trees surrounding the new DP an aerial observer would have had to be almost directly overhead to see them. Almost none of the pilots on the mission did pass close enough to the spot to sight the visual aids.[85]

Consequently, when the D plus 2 resupply aircraft – 100 Stirlings of No 38 Group and 63 Dakotas of No 46 Group – flew towards Arnhem on their mission, they approached a DP that was now in enemy hands. Making their run through intense flak at about 1,000 feet – although reports suggest that some crews went as high as 4,000 feet because of the intensity of the fire – the transport crews dropped their loads into enemy hands in the Koepel area. Out of 388 tons of supplies dropped, only 21 tons – less than six per cent – were recovered; these probably came from five aircraft which dropped their cargoes by mistake near Wolfheze and from two Stirlings which dropped on DZ 'L'. Apart from the loss of vital supplies, the tragedy was that the RAF crews showed enormous courage and self-sacrifice in completing the mission.

The resupply mission of Tuesday, 19 September 1944 resulted in the award of RAF Transport Command's only Victoria Cross. The citation is reproduced in full here, and is a tribute not only to the recipient, but to the thirteen crews that failed to

The grave of Flt Lt David Lord, VC, in the Arnhem-Oosterbeek war cemetery.

return and to the dead and injured on the 97 aircraft that were damaged.

The King has been graciously pleased to confer the Victoria Cross on the under-mentioned officer in recognition of most conspicuous bravery:–

Flight Lieutenant David Samuel Anthony Lord, DFC (49149), RAF., No 271 Squadron (deceased).

Flight Lieutenant Lord was pilot and captain of a Dakota aircraft detailed to drop supplies at Arnhem on the afternoon of the 19th September 1944. Our airborne troops had been surrounded and were being pressed into a small area defended by a large number of anti-aircraft guns. Aircrews were warned that intense opposition would be met over the dropping zone. To ensure accuracy they were ordered to fly at 900 feet when dropping their containers.

While flying at 1,500 feet near Arnhem the starboard wing of Flight Lieutenant Lord's aircraft was twice hit by anti-aircraft fire. The starboard engine was set on fire. He would have been justified in leaving the main stream of supply aircraft and continuing at the same height or even abandoning his aircraft. But on learning that his crew were uninjured and that the dropping zone would be reached in three minutes he said he would complete his mission, as the troops were in dire need of supplies.

By now the starboard engine was burning furiously. Flight Lieutenant Lord came down to 900 feet, where he was singled out for concentrated fire of all the anti-aircraft guns. On reaching the dropping zone he kept the aircraft on a straight and level course while supplies were dropped. At the end of the run, he was told that two containers remained.

Although he must have known that the collapse of the starboard wing could not be long delayed, Flight Lieutenant Lord circled, rejoined the stream of aircraft and made a second run to drop the remaining supplies. These manoeuvres took eight minutes in all, the aircraft being continuously under heavy anti-aircraft fire.

His task completed, Flight Lieutenant Lord ordered his crew to abandon the Dakota, making no attempt himself to leave the aircraft, which was down to 500 feet. A few seconds later the starboard wing collapsed and the aircraft fell in flames. There was only one survivor, who was flung out while assisting other members of the crew to put on their parachutes.

By continuing his mission in a damaged and burning aircraft, descending to drop the supplies accurately, returning to the dropping zone a second time and, finally, remaining at the controls to give his crew a chance of escape, Flight Lieutenant Lord displayed supreme valour and self-sacrifice.[86]

Out of the seven crew on board the stricken Dakota – three RAF personnel and four Army despatchers – the sole survivor was the navigator, Flight Lieutenant Harry King. He landed in no-man's land and joined up with the airborne forces, fighting alongside them until he was taken prisoner at the end of the battle.

While Brigadier Hackett's 4th Parachute Brigade disengaged with the utmost difficulty, under constant fire and sustaining very heavy losses in the process, the remnants of the three battalions that had tried to break through to the Arnhem bridge were filtering back to Oosterbeek. As they made their way westwards, the survivors – mostly NCOs and men, the majority of the officers having been killed or captured – were intercepted by Lieutenant-Colonel W.F.K. Thompson, commanding the 1st Airlanding Light Regiment, Royal Artillery, whose guns were occupying positions along the Neder Rijn near Oosterbeek–Laag Church. Thompson ordered the troops to take up defensive positions in the vicinity of his artillery. The men were in a pitiful state, as one eye-witness described:

Inside (the church) we saw a group of very weary, wet and wounded men. These were the remains of the three battalions who had made the attack on the bridge at Arnhem. There could not have been more than two hundred left, and these had escaped by crawling through ditches half-filled with drainage water. Almost everybody was wounded and wet and covered with mud. By looking out of the big shattered church window towards the open field which ran down to the river, you could see the wounded and dead lying where they had

---

NO 38 GROUP INTELLIGENCE SUMMARY FOR D+2

OBJECT RESUPPLY AND STRENGTHENING AND CAPTURE OF ANOTHER DZ NW OF ARNHEM. 144 A/C ENGAGED, 120 SUCCESSFUL. 10 A/C REPORTED MISSING. SOME MAY HAVE DELIVERED GLIDERS BEFORE BECOMING CASUALTIES. OPERATIONS NO LONGER HAVING ELEMENT OF SURPRISE, PRODUCED CONSIDERABLY STIFFER OPPOSITION FROM ENEMY. AGAIN MOST NOTICEABLE FEATURE WAS NON-INTERFERENCE BY LUFTWAFFE WHO WERE TAKEN CARE OF BY OUR FIGHTER COVER.[87] CREWS REPORT FLAK OPPOSITION EXTREMELY ACTIVE ALONG ROUTE TO DZ RANGING FROM SMALL ARMS FIRE TO 40MM. WATERBORNE FLAK ENCOUNTERED ALONG RIVER WAAL.

STIRLING SEEN TO CRASH AND EXPLODE ON DZ L. N-NAN 299 SQN SEEN BY X9Y/299 TO FALL IN FLAMES. THREE OF CREW BALED OUT BUT CHUTES FAILED TO OPEN. STIRLING LETTERS FFT SEEN TO FORCE-LAND CREW SEEN TO BE SAFE.[88] DAKOTA BURNING ON GROUND S OF EINDHOVEN. SOME HORSAS BURNING ON DZ X. DINGHY SIGHTED 5122N/0143E CREW PICKED UP BY ASW WALRUS.

CAPTAINS OF A/C REPORT SUCCESSFUL TRIPS BUT OBSERVE FIGHTERS NOT ON HAND TO DEAL WITH FLAK POSITIONS. THEY ALSO REPORT LOADS BEING DROPPED FROM AS HIGH AS 4000 FT AND OVER WIDE AREA BECAUSE OF STIFF FLAK OPPOSITION.

---

been struck down by mortar and machine-gun fire while trying to escape. It was a terrible sight in the church. Each man was weary to his bones, and miserable, and most were wounded. Yet they were filled with such great spirit that they could never be defeated. There was only one officer left from my battalion (the 1st Parachute Battalion).[89]

To alleviate the problem of command, Brigadier Philip Hicks, who inspected the artillery positions near the Oosterbeek–Laag Church as the remains of the 1st Parachute Brigade started to filter in, sent a number of officers to Lt-Col Thompson's assistance. They included Major Richard Lonsdale, deputy commander of the 11th Parachute Battalion, who now assumed tactical command of the survivors numbering no more than 500, who had escaped the massacre that followed the abortive attempt to relieve the 2nd Parachute Battalion at the bridge. The commander of Lonsdale Force, as it became known, had himself been wounded in the face three times.

John Frost's 2nd Battalion, meanwhile, was still clinging to its positions around the north end of the Arnhem bridge, although its perimeter defence had now shrunk to ten houses which were under continual attack from three directions by the Knaust and Brinkmann *Kampfgruppen*. The infantry assaults were preceded by heavy mortar and shellfire; one particularly devastating weapon brought into action by the Germans in the early hours of Tuesday morning was an 88 mm gun that fired a 20 lb shell originally designed to penetrate the armour of the latest generation of Russian tanks. The gun was mounted on a Tiger tank chassis, and it was the Van Limburg Stirum School, adjacent to the ramp approaches and held by the Royal Engineers, which came in for most of its attention:

They . . . brought up a Tiger tank and positioned it on the road leading up to the bridge. It stopped when it was opposite us. The gun slowly turned until it pointed straight at the top floor of the school so we quickly nipped down the stairs to the second floor and waited for the tank to open fire. The tank could only depress its gun to an angle parallel with the road so it couldn't shoot at the second floor, but the noise as the shell went through the top floor and the ceiling of the second floor was like standing on the Underground platform as a train goes through, plus a hell of a lot of dust and flying brickwork. After he had fired a half dozen rounds at us he packed up and went away whilst we trudged back up to what was left of the top floor.[90]

The defenders had not returned fire while this attack was in progress, and this may have led the Germans to believe that resistance in the school was at an end. At about 0300 hours, a force of about 60 infantry approached the wrecked building; the Sappers, still commanded by Captain Mackay, opened up a withering fire on them with all available weapons, inflicting severe casualties.

Attempts to infiltrate the 2nd Battalion's positions began at about 0700 hours on Tuesday, but the ferocity of the paratroops' defence had made the Germans cautious and their attacks were not pressed home with much determination. In any case, it would not be long before the British were literally blasted out of their positions by tanks, artillery, mortars and *Panzerfausts*.

It was not as simple as that, as an extract from the 2nd Parachute Battalion's battle report indicates. The numbers refer to buildings shown on the map.

At midday three tanks got into position near the river and shelled house 10 at close range, making it temporarily untenable. McDermont's platoon suffered some casualties and were evacuated under the bridge. A group armed with two PIATS scored three hits on tanks and then observed two more tanks. Their officer (Captain A. Frank) returned after obtaining more bombs to see the tanks pulling out.[91]

Lieutenant McDermont's platoon, meanwhile, counter-attacked and reoccupied the house from which they had recently been dislodged. Lieutenant Grayburn then led an attempt to recapture houses 12 and 13, but the attackers sustained casualties and the attempt was abandoned. Later in the morning Focke-Wulf 190 fighter-bombers attempted to attack the British positions, but without success. On the ground, German troops fired white flares from their forward positions as recognition signals, a practice the British defenders quickly imitated, much to the confusion of the enemy pilots. One FW 190, coming in very low, was met by concentrated Bren and Vickers fire; its pilot took violent evasive action, struck a church steeple and flicked into the ground.

Tanks and heavy artillery were a much more serious problem; in the afternoon the positions on the eastern side of the bridge were attacked by eight Mk III *Panzers* and four more modern Mk IVs which had advanced through the centre of Arnhem; the tanks provided cover for *Panzergrenadiers* who flushed a number of British troops from the cellars of houses as they approached the bridge. In addition, a big 150 mm howitzer was brought into action, lobbing shells on to Brigade HQ from a range of only 200 yards; as a result Brigade HQ rapidly became a pile of rubble. The 150 mm gun ceased to be a problem when a 3-inch mortar round apparently scored a direct hit on ammunition stacked beside it.

Nevertheless, the situation of Frost's battalion was becoming increasingly desperate.

Early in the afternoon the tanks drew off to replenish their ammunition but renewed the battle in still larger numbers at about three o'clock. The school came under heavy mortar fire, tank shelling and an intense machine-gun barrage through the eastern windows which, as before, stopped all movement between the floors. The mortar bombs had delayed fuses, so that they penetrated the roof and caused havoc inside the building. Almost every man had received a wound of some kind by this time. Many suffered terribly owing to the absence of skilled attention but made no complaint. The more serious cases were kept in a state of coma with morphia.[92]

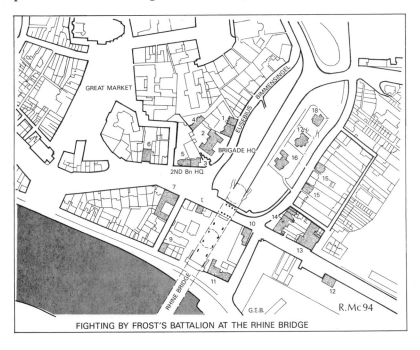

FIGHTING BY FROST'S BATTALION AT THE RHINE BRIDGE

Under cover of this assault, block 8 and house 10 were set on fire, forcing the defenders from these buildings, which were near the crossroads to the east of the bridge ramp, and to seek cover in the ruins of house 11 and block 7. Late in the afternoon, two Tiger tanks, one covering the other, pushed their way through the streets to the north of the bridge, one covering the other as they advanced. One engaged the school with high explosive and then armour-piercing shot, which tore through the building from end to end and knocked a four-foot hole in every room, causing ceilings to collapse and the whole structure to totter precariously. The other clattered down the road opposite houses 1, 2, 3, 5 and 6, firing 88 mm shells into each building in turn while its machine-gun raked the six-pounder anti-tank gun positions.

Battalion HQ stopped three shells before we could all get out . . . Meanwhile houses 14 and 16 were set on fire . . . Our position was now greatly weakened. We had suffered heavy casualties . . . Ammunition was getting fairly short and we had been burnt out of the key position each of the bridge, house 10. The enemy was occupying all houses to the north and west of our positions. Although they did not attempt infiltration from this direction, they were able to keep us under automatic fire – to which we could not afford to reply. The number of wounded was reaching serious proportions. They were all evacuated to the cellars of the Brigade HQ.[93]

With desperate courage, small parties of paratroops stalked the Tigers with Gammon bombs, sustaining terrible casualties as they did so. The bombs had little effect on the tanks, but the impact of their explosions must have shaken the battened-down crews; the Tigers withdrew after dark.

Utter exhaustion now laid hold of our men after three days and two nights of continuous battle. No one had had more than a few fitful snatches of sleep in the whole period, and there could be no rest now for the few still capable of fighting. Nor could they be revived with food and water – their last bite and drop had gone. Instead, benzedrine was issued all round, and thus drugged, the men set about repairing their posts and looking to their weapons. In their conditions the benzedrine had peculiar effects. Some saw double as though drunk, while others had queer hallucinations which caused many false alarms during the night. Although there was no attack there were sounds of great activity, and the ever-changing lights on the pall of smoke over the city gave the illusion of movement.[94]

Last light on 19 September therefore saw Lt-Col Frost's dwindling battalion holding precariously on to positions that were rapidly becoming untenable, while the few survivors of the 1st Parachute Brigade that had tried so hard to relieve the bridge force had fallen back on Oosterbeek. The 4th Parachute Brigade had become split up as it disengaged; when darkness fell the 10th Parachute Battalion and the 4th Parachute Squadron, RE, had reached Wolfheze station, and the 156th Parachute Battalion, approximately 270 strong, was on the railway immediately west of Johannahoeve. Two companies of this battalion became separated and did not cross the railway. They were attacked and overrun during the night, and only the quartermaster and six men ever reappeared. Brigadier Hackett's HQ was near the railway, north-east of Wolfheze Hotel. Meanwhile, the 7th KOSB, after considerable difficulty, had concentrated at their rendezvous north of the Wolfheze Hotel; at midnight the Borderers were ordered by Divisional HQ to revert to command of the 1st Air Landing Brigade and occupy a position in some woods at Ommershof. Prior to this, the Air Landing Brigade consisted only of Brigade HQ, established at Bilderberg, the 1st Battalion The Border Regiment in the area of Bilderberg to Heveadorp, and the glider pilots in the area of Graftombe.

There was still no news of XXX Corps.

THE ADVANCE OF XXX CORPS

The medium tanks of the Guards Armoured Division, in fact, had advanced over secondary roads to the Maas–Waal Canal and at 1000 hours on Tuesday crossed the bridge at Grave into the 82nd Airborne Division's airhead. An hour later, a battalion of tanks, supported by a company of motorized infantry from the 43rd (Wessex) Division and the 2nd Battalion of the 505th Parachute Infantry Regiment, moved north to make a renewed bid for the Nijmegen bridges. Attacking early in the afternoon, they penetrated to the centre of the town without opposition – except for some artillery fire – and then split up, one paratroop company and seven tanks heading for the railway bridge while the rest attacked the road bridge. The attacks lasted well into the night and produced nothing but heavy losses. Once again, the advance of XXX Corps was stalled; and the way would soon be open for German reinforcements to pour into the Nijmegen area by the direct route – across the Arnhem bridge.

CHAPTER 9

D plus Three, 20 September 1944

EINDHOVEN

Undeterred by the failure of his reconnaissance in force to take the Bailey Bridge at Zon on Tuesday, *Major Freiherr* von Maltzahn decided to launch his 107th *Panzer* Brigade into a second assault on the 101st Airborne Division's airhead on the morning of 20 September. The risk of mounting such an attack in broad daylight was considered acceptable, as the Brigade was able to put up a formidable weight of anti-aircraft fire.

The attack was launched at 0630 hours, and once again the bridge at Zon was the objective. As on the previous day, the German armour came close enough to halt bridge traffic and the defences were initially slow to react, the Americans not having expected a second assault at the same place. A possible enemy breakthrough was foiled by the timely arrival of ten British tanks, which knocked out four Panthers as they approached the canal and compelled the rest to withdraw. Von Maltzahn decided to pull out his force and choose a more suitable place to attack the Allied corridor, hopefully with strong infantry support. A battalion of the 506th PIR, mounted on British tanks, tried to intercept the 107th Brigade's retreat, but von Maltzahn escaped with the loss of about ten per cent of his armoured strength.

In the Veghel area, the 1st Battalion of the 501st PIR occupied Dinter and pushed on to Heeswijk, about five miles to the north-east. During these operations the 501st PIR killed 40 Germans and captured 418; these were mostly *Luftwaffe* personnel assembled into improvised *Kampfgruppen*, a fact that led the Americans to believe that they had destroyed the German forces in this sector. They were wrong; the 101st Airborne Division was to experience further heavy fighting in the days to come, even though it had a relatively easy time on 20 September.

NIJMEGEN

It was a different story in the 82nd Airborne Division's airhead, which in mid-morning was subjected to determined attacks by three *Kampfgruppen* that emerged from the Reichswald. The first of these, led by *Major* Karl-Heinz Becker, comprised 800 men drawn from the 5th, 8th and 9th Regiments of the former 3rd *Fallschirmjäger* Division, supported by some artillery mounted on half-tracks and a small number of anti-aircraft guns; its mission was to advance in a north-westerly direction, attack the American positions around Wyler and reach the Maas–Waal Canal, after which it was to clear the east bank of the Waal as far as the Neerbosch bridge.

The second *Kampfgruppe*, commanded by *Major* Greschick, comprised three under-strength battalions – no more than 500 men – of newly-conscripted infantry, and was supported by fourteen 20 mm cannon mounted on half-tracks. Its task was to carry out a pincer movement around the Groesbeek Heights, push on to the Maas–Waal Canal, and join up with the *Kampfgruppe* Becker in consolidating the east bank. Finally there was the *Kampfgruppe* under *Oberstleutnant* Hermann, formed from survivors of the 5th *Fallschirmjäger* Division and the *Kampfgruppe* Goebel, which had suffered heavily in the attempt to capture Mook. It was supported by a few anti-aircraft guns and a battery from *Fallschirmjäger* Artillery Regiment 6, and its mission was to secure the southern bank of the Waal between the Pontveen road bridge and the Maas–Waal Canal. The entire operation by the three battle groups was co-ordinated from General Feldt's Corps HQ at Kleve, and was intended to buy time until the arrival of reinforcements from 10 SS *Panzer* Division.

The approach march of the three *Kampfgruppen* through the Reichswald began at about 0800 hours, somewhat later than planned, and was preceded by

German infantry reinforcements marching towards Mook, in the US 82nd Airborne Division's airhead, on 20 September 1944. Mook was the scene of savage fighting.

a barrage of 88 mm, *Nebelwerfer* and mortar fire that varied in intensity. In the north, the initial attack by the *Kampfgruppe* Becker was pinned down by artillery fire as the troops emerged from the forest on to open ground, but after regrouping the *Fallschirmjäger* succeeded in driving two platoons of the 508th PIR out of Wyler after a vicious firefight. Further attempts by the Germans to advance to the canal, however, were frustrated by the American defences on a high feature called the Teufelsberg, and although attacks were made on this at intervals throughout the day the Germans were unable to dislodge the defenders. Becker's force did, however, succeed in penetrating the American strongpoint at Beek, and by early evening savage fighting was in progress in the village. The Americans managed to contain the thrust, but only just; as General Gavin later remarked, 'If the Germans had had the wit to more even several hundred yards to the right, they could have walked into the outskirts of Nijmegen almost unmolested.'(95) As it was, attack and counter-attack swayed to and fro into the night, with both sides receiving small reinforcement.

In the centre, too, the *Kampfgruppe* Greschick also made some progress, penetrating into the outskirts of Groesbeek amid bitter street fighting, but here too the attack was contained. The greatest German success of the day was achieved by the *Kampfgruppe* Hermann, attacking from the south-east with strong artillery support. By mid-afternoon Hermann had driven the 505th PIR from Mook after a fierce battle and was within sight of his objective, the Heuman bridge. The situation in this sector became so critical that General Gavin was compelled to reinforce the line with 300 glider pilots who had been helping to guard prisoners and command posts; their injection into the battle, and the support of six Sherman tanks of the Irish Guards, enabled the Americans to launch a counter-attack that threw the Germans out of the shattered village.[96] With this the German effort collapsed, and Hermann withdrew his battle group to Riethorst under cover of darkness.

Meanwhile, in Nijmegen itself, there was bitter fighting as the spearheads of XXX Corps, with US paratroops in support, attempted to force their way through to the Waal bridges. On the night of the 19th, Lt-Gen Browning, General Gavin and Lt-General Horrocks, commanding XXX Corps, had formulated a plan to take the Nijmegen road bridge from the rear by sending the 504th Parachute Infantry Regiment across the Waal in assault boats about a mile downstream of the town; this was to take place in conjunction with a frontal attack by the 2nd Battalion of the 505th PIR supported by Sherman tanks and infantry of the Grenadier Guards.

Early on 20 September, the 504th PIR, which had been holding the bridges at Grave and Heumen, were relieved by armour and infantry of the Coldstream Guards and moved to an assembly area in woods to the east of the Honinghutie bridge. This was close to the local power station, where there was a small harbour. Here the 3rd Battalion of the 504th, commanded by Major Julian A. Cook, waited for the arrival of the assault craft which had been promised by the Royal Engineers. One British eyewitness, Sapper A.C. Sanders of the 615th Field Squadron RE, recalls the Americans' disbelief when they had first sight of the 26 folding assault craft.

Their first question, when they saw the flimsy canvas boats was: Where were the engines? We had to tell them that there were none: the boats were only supplied with paddles. I personally thought this was a suicidal effort, and that's what it turned out to be.[97]

During the morning, British and American forces pressed home a series of attacks towards the Waal bridges in Nijmegen, meeting with strong resistance as they probed against a shrinking enemy perimeter. By noon, the 10 SS bridgehead had been reduced to an area about 1,000 yards in extent and 300 yards in depth, stretching from the railway bridge to a point about 100 yards east of the road bridge. The strongest point of this line was in the area of the road bridge and Hunner Park, which was held by *Hauptsturmführer* Karl-Heinz Euling's 10 SS *Kampfgruppe*, about 100 strong and supported by four assault guns.

At 1400 hours, the 2nd Battalion of the 505th PIR and the Grenadier Guards launched further determined attacks on Euling's positions, forcing him to withdraw from part of the Hunner Park. At 1500 hours, 40 Sherman tanks, 100 artillery pieces and Typhoon fighter-bombers began to pound the enemy positions on the north bank of the Waal opposite the power station. As a smoke screen began to drift over the river, the men of the 504th PIR's 3rd Battalion pushed their frail craft into the water of the little harbour and began to paddle frantically out into the fast-flowing current. On the southern bank, the 1st and 2nd Battalions awaited their turn to cross.

The Waal at this point was some 300 yards in width, and on the far bank the Americans had to cross 600 yards of flat, open terrain, overlooked by a high dyke road, to reach the northern end of the road bridge. First, they would have to overcome the defences of the railway bridge, immediately on their right.

The boats reached the deep water of the main channel, where they were thrown into some confusion by the swift current. As the paratroops tried desperately to sort themselves out and resume their course for the far bank the Germans opened up, first with small-arms fire and then with mortars and artillery. Luckily, only one battery of heavy artillery was available to oppose the crossing, the others being ranged on targets in Nijmegen; the sole battery, however, together with 20 mm and heavy MG fire, caused havoc as the Americans fought to get across the river. Shells and bullets churned the Waal into a bloody froth, ripping boats to shreds and hurling their occupants into the water.

'They were sitting ducks, and I felt extremely sorry for them,' says Sapper Sanders. 'We had very few of the boats returned, and they contained bits and pieces of bodies.'[98] In fact, only eleven of the 26 boats in the first wave got back to make a second trip, but the paratroops in that wave, made almost inhuman by the carnage they had experienced during the crossing, fell on the defenders with a terrible fury. The Germans, mostly elderly reservists and teenage conscripts, were wiped out without mercy as their outposts were overwhelmed one after another. More paratroops came across until a force of roughly battalion size was on the north bank. By 1600 hours they had established a beach-head 1,000 yards deep, and by 1700 hours they had taken the northern end of the railway bridge.

The American force now split into two, one force advancing north-westwards along the bank of the Waal towards Oosterhout while the other attacked Lent, north of the road bridge. The dyke road along the Waal between these two points was now occupied by the 504th PIR.

At about 1830 hours, with enemy defences at the northern end of the road bridge under fire from small groups of the 504th PIR who had penetrated into Lent, a combined tank and infantry attack was mounted on the bridge from the south. A troop of four Shermans of the Grenadier Guards ground their way through the rubble that clogged the southern approach to the bridge, advancing through the smoke of burning houses, their crews conscious that ahead of them lay the carcases of other tanks which had attempted an earlier *coup de main* only to fall victim to *Panzerfausts*.

Two tanks were hit and halted, but the others churned along the Arnhemsche Weg and on to the main span of the bridge, raking the structure from end to end as they went. They encountered some opposition from flak guns on the northern bank of the Waal, but most of the enemy artillery had been abandoned, its crews killed by the fierce artillery barrage.

The passage of the British tanks across the road bridge marked the end of the German defence at Nijmegen. Surviving defenders to the west of the road bridge tried to make their escape over the railway bridge, only to run into heavy machine-gun fire from H and I Companies of the 3rd Battalion, 504th PIR, who were in position on the north side. When the battle was over, 267 German dead were recovered from the railway bridge.

On the other side of the Hunner park from the Arnhemsche Weg, the 60 or so survivors of the *Kampfgruppe* Euling found themselves surrounded in their positions around the battle group's command post. They held out until 2230 hours, under constant fire from Sherman tanks and supporting infantry. By this time the command post, a house, was in flames and ammunition had run out. The British troops, believing that the Germans were all dead, moved on, and the resourceful Euling decided to attempt a breakout. Leading what was left of his battalion through shattered back streets, passing columns of British infantry as they went along in the darkness, Euling passed under the ramp of the road bridge and eventually came to a small feeder canal, where his men were involved in a brief and bloody hand-to-hand fight with a British patrol. The Germans broke through, found a crossing-point over the canal and later reached their own lines after crossing the Waal at Haalderen. The escape earned Euling the award of the *Ritterkreuz*.

Nijmegen was in Allied hands, and the armoured spearheads of XXX Corps were rolling across the road bridge. Seventeen miles to the north, however, a German armoured column, intent on cutting off the advance of XXX Corps at the neck, had also begun to roll across another bridge: the bridge at Arnhem.

ARNHEM

Wednesday dawned wet with drizzling rain, but that was the least of our discomfiture. The town was still burning and one of our resupply Dakotas had been hit by anti-aircraft fire and had hit the steeple of the church opposite our street, which resulted in more fire and debris. The Jerries were still active, even more so as they had wiped out most of the pockets of resistance around the bridge. It looked to us as though only we and a few others around the bridge were left; it was fairly obvious that they were taking on one position at a time and only moving on when they had wiped out that one. But it was difficult for them to get at us and so they began mortaring us and dropping high explosive mixed with incendiary bombs so that they could burn us out.[99]

So wrote Corporal John Humphreys, still fighting in the school house close to Arnhem bridge with the survivors of the 1st Parachute Squadron, Royal Engineers. By this time, the school was the only building on the east side of the bridge ramp that was still occupied; the others were mostly piles of burnt-out rubble. No more than 200 men of the 2nd Parachute Battalion – and that included the Royal Engineers and the men of the Reconnaissance Squadron – were still capable of fighting. Most had dug foxholes for themselves in the gardens of the ruined houses, and from this scant cover they continued to beat off every attack the enemy threw at them. Tanks shelled the men entrenched in the gardens of houses 10 and 11, forcing them to withdraw to the western side of the bridge ramp, and in the school building Captain Mackay's engineers fought off three assaults in the course of the morning and early afternoon, as John Humphreys remembers:

We could see the enemy were forming up some distance away with infantry and tanks, and it was obvious who their target was. Mackay got the few of us that were left together and said: 'We'll let them get very close before opening fire and then if they succeed in breaking in we will go up to the first floor and fight from there, moving up until we are on the top floor when we will fight to the last man and the last round.' The thought came into my mind that he must have read *Beau Geste* . . . Then the tanks and infantry started moving towards us, but the tanks were baulked by the trees and the infantry came on only to be decimated at point-blank range. Then a rifle grenade came through the window and killed Jock Grey and two

others. By now there were about a dozen left fit to fight, but with only a few rounds between us there was no way we could hold off another determined attack.[100]

Wednesday's vicious fighting saw the end of many gallant men at the Arnhem bridge. One was Lieutenant John Grayburn, who, despite having been wounded three times, never ceased to rally his men, organizing fighting patrols and setting up new defensive positions, exposing himself time and again to enemy fire until, almost inevitably, he was killed. His conspicuous gallantry throughout the defence of the Arnhem bridge was later recognized by the posthumous award of the Victoria Cross.

At about 1000 hours on Wednesday, one of the 2nd Parachute Battalion's signallers succeeded in making contact with the Divisional forward net, enabling Lt-Col Frost to speak directly to Major-General Urquhart and appraise him of the latest situation at the bridge, with estimates of casualties on both sides. Frost also reiterated his intention to hold on for as long as was necessary.

Not long after this, Frost was badly wounded by mortar bomb fragments and was evacuated to the cellar of the Brigade Headquarters building, now filled to capacity with injured men. Tactical control of the battle at the bridge now passed to Major Freddie Gough of the 1st Airborne Reconnaissance Squadron, although Frost was kept informed of the ongoing situation and continued to make major decisions.

On the eastern side of the bridge ramp, the end was fast approaching. Shortly before 1500 hours, the Germans brought up a Mk VI Tiger tank and a 105 mm Ferdinand self-propelled gun and systematically proceeded to demolish the school house, which was also under mortar attack. With the school collapsing and in flames, Captain Mackay brought the surviving 45 defenders – of whom 31 were wounded – out into the open. Leaving the wounded behind to surrender, the only possible course of action, the others began to make their way through the shattered streets to the east of the bridge ramp. Humphreys, accompanied by the four men of his stick who were still left, dashed across the road to the shelter of the ruins opposite.

As with most continental houses these had cellars and the gutted windows were level with the pavement, allowing us to dive through and land amongst the still hot bricks inside what was left of a row of houses. The houses ran in the direction of the river and were separated by gardens at the back, all of which had walls which we had to climb over. There were four of us now – one having been hit while crossing the road – all scrambling madly over each wall accompanied by odd bursts of fire which cracked as they flew over our heads.

All was going well and I thought that we would make it to the river when I heard Joe Malley shout for help. I looked back to see him caught up in the barbed wire on top of a wall, unable to move back or forwards. I raced back to him, grasped his webbing at the shoulders and was starting to pull him down when, much quicker than I can tell, there was the chattering rasp of an MG 42 and a rash of bright pink bullet holes appeared in the brickwork less than an inch from my left eye. I pushed Joe back over the wall, dived to my right into a flower bed, had a quick pee without standing up, and then flew over the remaining walls, catching up with the other two on the edge of the tram depot only a few hundred yards from the river.

The depot was large, but so was the number of Germans there. I came around the corner of a building, going fast, and almost ran into a group of enemy soldiers, who saw me and ran even faster – away from me. Before any shooting could start I led the other two to a tram. We crawled underneath and got behind the big iron wheels, knowing that the Germans would have to come at us without cover and that in thirty minutes it would be dark enough to make a run for it. We lay there and the minutes ticked by and my hopes were rising, when once again I heard the noise of enemy tank tracks and a self-propelled 105 mm gun clanked up towards us. They were certainly taking us seriously. It stopped about thirty or forty yards away and the barrel was depressed so that I could see the rifling inside it, and then a voice said, in Oxford-accented English: "If you don't come out I will blow you out." I wasn't going to argue with a bloody great gun, so I said we were coming out.[101]

Captain Mackay was also taken prisoner, his small group having encountered a superior German force standing beside two Mk III tanks. 'We stood in a line,' the British officer said, 'with our six machine guns firing from the hip. We pressed the triggers continuously until the ammunition ran out.'[102] Splitting up, he and his men went back the way they had come. Meeting with more Germans, Mackay lay down and feigned death, a pretence that was painfully uncovered when an enemy soldier jabbed a bayonet into his buttocks, down to the pelvic bone. Neither Mackay, Humphreys, nor Lieutenant Simpson, the latter's stick commander, were to remain in enemy hands for long.

Meanwhile, the battle on the western side of the bridge ramp went on. Here, the defences were virtually restricted to the curve of buildings –

houses 2 to 6, house 2 being Brigade HQ – overlooking the Marktstraat. As enemy pressure increased and more severe damage was inflicted on these buildings, Major Gough ordered more slit trenches to be dug in the gardens. In the late afternoon, while fierce fighting continued in this area, four or five German tanks crossed the bridge from north to south, pushing their way past the debris of Gräbner's failed attack. Their passage was unopposed by the British 6-pounder anti-tank guns, which had had to be abandoned by their crews in the face of intense close-range small-arms fire.

Shortly before darkness fell – by which time the British force at the bridge had been reduced to about 130 – the last few houses held by the 2nd Parachute Battalion were attacked with phosphor bombs and flame-throwers and set on fire. Brigade HQ was in flames and attempts to extinguish them failed, placing the 200 wounded in the building's cellar in terrible peril. The lives of many of these men had been saved by a small and dedicated medical team under two RAMC doctors, Captains J. Logan DSO, and D. Wright, MC, working under the most appalling conditions; it was unthinkable that they should now be left to the flames. Some of them were evacuated to house 4, but this too was set on fire and they had to abandon that too. As a result, many wounded were lying out in the open, subjected to gunfire, grenades and mortar bombs. For Frost and Gough, there was no alternative but to surrender them to the enemy.

A cease-fire was negotiated, and German troops came forward to collect the wounded. To quote Major Gough:

The wounded were taken out and, in claiming that they needed transport to do this, the Germans took our Reconnaissance jeeps as well, and we couldn't really stop them. It was the most astonishing situation, with those SS troops going in and out, and us just sitting behind cover or in slit trenches. Nobody said a word – there was complete silence as we watched and waited for them to complete the job so that the battle could start again.[103]

The confused fighting that took place after dark saw Lt-Col Frost's dwindling force broken into small groups that became scattered among the ruins north of the bridge. Some 50 or 60 more men were lost during the night, either killed or captured. Some tried to slip through the enemy net and make their way to Oosterbeek in an attempt to join the Division, but almost all of them were rounded up. Among them was Sapper Ron Hall, MM, one of the demolition experts whose journey to Arnhem had, in the event, not really been necessary. He might have succeeded, had it not been for an unfortunate accident.

I was with this young soldier, and we had to climb over a wall in the dark. I told him to be careful, but he scrambled across without looking to see what was on the other side. There was a loud sound of breaking glass; he had fallen into a cold frame. The next thing, a machine-gun opened up on us.[104]

The MG bullets shattered Hall's right arm. It was saved by German surgeons, for whose skills he retains the utmost admiration to this day.

Elsewhere on 20 September, the whole of the divisional area, with its centre the Hartenstein Hotel where General Urquhart had established his head-quarters, came under heavy shell and mortar fire at about 0600 hours. Meanwhile, the 4th Parachute Brigade was moving towards the divisional peri-meter through dense woodland east of Bredelaan, fighting tenaciously all the way. The 156th Parachute Battalion, in the lead, came under heavy fire as it reached a point north-east of the Wolfheze

Hotel, but by about 1000 hours it had overcome most of the initial opposition and had reached the main road at the junction south of Bilderberg, near the north-west suburb of Oosterbeek. By now the strength of the battalion had been reduced to about 90 all ranks.

It was now obvious that the enemy was attacking from north and west with substantial forces, and Brigadier Hackett, whose orders were to link up with the Division as soon as possible, had no wish to become involved in a major action. He therefore tried another line of approach and ordered the 10th Parachute Battalion to move round to the east of the 156th Parachute Battalion and take the lead, the 156th Battalion now remaining in contact with the enemy as rearguard. In the course of subsequent actions the 10th Battalion became detached from the rest of the 4th Brigade and fought through on its own, encountering stiff opposition from *Obersturmbannführer* Hans-Michael Lippert's SS Regiment, attacking from the west, as it did so. By noon, the Battalion had reached the road passing

German artillery in action north of Oosterbeek. The Germans, in turn, were subjected to very accurate counter-battery fire by XXX Corps artillery.

Graftombe and was continuing to move south under heavy fire from enemy infantry and from two tanks which appeared at 1115 hours; shortly afterwards the survivors broke through to the divisional perimeter with a desperate bayonet charge through the trees, and just after 1300 hours Lieutenant-Colonel Kenneth Smyth and Major Warre, the commanding officer and second in command of the Battalion, reached Divisional Headquarters with about 60 all ranks, all that was left. The exhausted, filthy and bloodstained men were later assigned to defend some houses at the Oosterbeek crossroads, east of the divisional area.

Meanwhile, in the woods to the west, the remainder of the 4th Parachute Brigade continued to try to extricate itself, under heavy and continual pressure from Lippert in the west, the Eberwein Battalion attacking from Wolfheze in the north-west, and a force under *Hauptsturmführer* Sepp Krafft pushing from the north. Krafft's original Training and Replacement Battalion 16, which had played such a vital part in resisting the 1st Parachute Brigade's march on Arnhem on the first day, had now been expanded into a *Kampfgruppe*, reinforced by the 642nd Marine Regiment, the 1st Marine Cadre Regiment and the 10th Company of the 3rd Police Regiment.[105]

It is a tribute to the fighting spirit of the 4th Parachute Brigade that the Germans still did not realize that they were engaging a force that was in retreat. Each attack was contested so fiercely, each pocket of resistance so hard to overwhelm, that the Germans believed they were coming up against new defensive positions. With the fighting so savage, it was inevitable that the 4th Brigade should suffer terrible casualties, which were particularly high among the officers: among those killed were Lieutenant-Colonel Sir Richard des Voeux, 156th Battalion's commander; Major C.W.B. Dawson, the brigade major; Captain James, in temporary command of the Defence Platoon, and Captain G.L. Blundell, the Brigade Intelligence Officer.

The Brigade, or what was left of it, continued to work its way southwards on Valkenburglaan, fighting every yard of the way, until in the afternoon it reached a spot about 300 yards east of the Bilderberg Hotel. Despite its losses, and despite successive enemy attacks, the Brigade had retained its cohesion during the withdrawal. Brigadier Hackett later wrote,

I was very pleased and proud, at the way in which, after each new blow, the pieces so rapidly fell once more into a recognisable shape. But from the time that the enemy's infantry, with a few small tanks, got right in amongst us, it grew increasingly hard to control and towards the end of the day I could only pull in all I could lay hands on, into a small pocket and command them more or less as a company.

The small pocket referred to by Brigadier Hackett was in fact a crater-shaped depression on the west side of the road near its junction with Sonnenberglaan. It was occupied by about 30 Germans, who were attacked with grenades and cleared out by a bayonet charge led by Major G. Powell of the 156th Parachute Battalion. Into this hollow, John Hackett gathered the remnants of his force; they numbered no more than 150 officers and men.

Throughout the remainder of the afternoon, this handful of desperately hungry and thirsty defenders, short of ammunition and many – including Hackett himself – using German weapons, fought off one attack after another. 'I remember,' wrote Hackett, 'using rifle, grenade and bayonet all that afternoon like any infantry private . . . and having to lead a rush or two at close quarters, which is an unusual and stimulating experience for a brigade commander in modern times.'[106]

There was little doubt that the Germans would make a major attempt to liquidate the position before dark, and so Hackett decided to break out and make a dash for the divisional position.

In the evening we made a dash for where we thought the Division would be if it were still functioning. But the interesting thing was that since we had been out of contact ever since mid-morning and only had our experience of the remainder of the day, by which to judge, we could not be certain that the same thing had not happened to them too.

The men, in fact, made no secret of their conviction that the division had been liquidated. They were none the less ready, even after the rough time they had had, to make an effort to rejoin it, and in the event a comparatively short fast dash brought all we had left inside the perimeter. It all seemed wonderfully peaceful by comparison with the day's performance in the woods.'[107]

By 1900 hours, the remnants of the 4th Parachute Brigade – 60 men of the 10th Battalion, 70 of the 156th and 50 of the 4th Parachute Squadron, RE – were in position covering the approaches to Hartenstein along the main road from Arnhem. At this stage, there was little or nothing that could have prevented a German breakthrough if they had launched a strong attack westwards towards Oosterbeek.

AIR RE-SUPPLY

In keeping with a revised plan formulated on the previous day, the air re-supply mission scheduled for 20 September was to be a maximum effort involving the despatch of 1,047 aircraft and 405 gliders, all along the southern route. All the gliders and 317 re-supply aircraft would fly down the centre lane to DZ/LZ 'O' in the 82nd Airborne Division's airhead; 51 aircraft carrying paratroops and supplies would follow the right-hand lane to the 101st Airborne Division's DZ 'W'; 114 aircraft carrying the postponed mission of the 1st Polish Parachute Brigade to Arnhem were to use the left lane; and overhead would fly 160 RAF aircraft with supplies for the 1st Airborne Division. As usual, the Eighth Air Force would mount perimeter patrols between Maastricht, Wesel, Apeldoorn and Zwolle, provide area cover beyond the IP at Eindhoven, and attack flak positions between the IP and Nijmegen.

With a stick of paratroops descending in the background, a soldier strips a container of its contents.

Paratroops open a 'parapack' after a resupply mission to Arnhem. Most supplies fell into enemy hands.

The task of neutralizing flak batteries between the IP and Arnhem fell to the Ninth Air Force; however, it did not receive its assignment until 1430 hours on the 20th, so all flak suppression sorties were flown by Eighth Air Force.[108]

Again, dense fog and overcast forced the postponement of the day's missions, originally scheduled for an arrival time of 1500, to 1700 hours. However, in view of the desperate supply requirements of the British paratroops at Arnhem, it was decided to despatch part of the RAF mission – 67 aircraft – for a drop at 1345 hours, the rest following later in the afternoon. Accordingly, 67 Stirlings took off for Arnhem, climbing through a cloud base down to 1,000 feet. Visibility over the Channel was just over a mile and it was also poor in the Arnhem area, making an accurate drop virtually impossible to achieve; again, almost all the supplies fell into enemy hands, and two Stirlings were shot down by flak. One Spitfire and one Mustang out of a total of 65 aircraft provided by ADGB for escort also failed to return.

Later missions were provided with an escort of seventeen Spitfire squadrons; these flew 173 sorties as far as the IP, encountering no enemy aircraft and sustaining no losses. The five Eighth Air Force P-51 groups on perimeter patrol also had an uneventful day, flying 430 sorties, meeting with no enemy, and losing one Mustang in a landing accident. Eighth AF also despatched four groups of P-47s, plus one rocket-equipped squadron, on flak suppression beyond the IP; they flew 179 sorties, but – hampered by poor visibility and lacking an adequate briefing – the pilots could only claim to have destroyed two gun positions and damaged two more. All these aircraft returned safely to base.

The second wave of RAF re-supply aircraft, despatched later in the afternoon, comprised 34 Stirlings and 64 Dakotas, of which only two Stirlings aborted. Crews reported very heavy flak, especially in the target area; nine aircraft were shot down and 62 damaged. Of the remainder, the crews of 30 Stirlings reported having made a successful drop on DZ 'Z', unaware that the DZ was now in enemy hands. The rest of the force strove to locate Supply Dropping Point 691785, on the western edge of the divisional perimeter. A *Eureka* and visual aids had been set out despite the heavy fighting, and 122 crews reported having dropped successfully.[109] Although only thirteen crews picked up the *Eureka*, 32 reported having seen lamp signals and Very lights, the latter proving the most effective because they rose above tree-top level. The Germans, unfortunately, soon learned what was happening and fired their own decoy flares. Of the 300 (out of a total of 386) tons of supplies intended for this drop point, about 41 tons were recovered by the paratroops, some from enemy-held territory after dark. The amount salvaged was not much – a mere fourteen per cent – but the rations were worth their weight in gold to men who had had almost nothing to eat for 24 hours or more.

Throughout the afternoon, the transport aircraft that were to have carried the Polish Parachute Brigade to Arnhem stood on their airfields around Grantham, fully laden and with their engines warmed up, ready to go immediately if there was the slightest break in the overcast. But the skies remained leaden, and fog continued to drift over the bases. Five minutes before the scheduled take-off time, the Polish mission was postponed another twenty-four hours.

Re-supply missions were also flown to the 101st and 82nd Airborne Divisions on Wednesday, although a big glider reinforcement mission assembled for the 82nd was grounded by fog in the Grantham area. The re-supply mission for the Division, however, was assigned to the 53rd Troop Carrier Wing, whose bases in southern England were fairly clear, and at 1430 hours 310 C-47s of the 434th, 435th, 436th, 437th and 438th Troop Carrier Groups began taking off for Nijmegen, carrying 441 tons of supplies – mostly ammunition. The flight to the objective, DZ 'O', was mostly over friendly territory, and very little flak was encountered; no aircraft were lost and only six received damage. Despite the lack of opposition, however, and taking into account the fact that navigators were by now familiar with the route, the serials arrived over DZ 'O' at irregular intervals and in broken formations, drops being made at varying altitudes from 800 to

---

NO 38 GROUP INTELLIGENCE SUMMARY FOR D+3

38 GP OPERATED 101 A/C/ 34 STIRLINGS 190 AND 620 SQNS FAIRFORD, 34 STIRLINGS 295 AND 570 SQNS HARWELL, 33 STIRLINGS 196 AND 299 SQNS KEEVIL AND 1 A/C FROM 1665 HCU TILSTOCK. 87 A/C SUCCESSFUL DROPPING 2063 CONTAINERS 325 PANNIERS, 3 PACKAGES, 2 KITBAGS AND 1 SACK. 11 A/C MISSING. WHILE REPORTS OF INTERCEPTION BY ENEMY FIGHTERS NIL, GROUND DEFENCES HAVE STIFFENED CONSIDERABLY. IN ADDITION TO A/C LOST, A LARGE NUMBER OF HITS ON OTHER A/C ARE REPORTED.

REPORTS OF ROCKET PROJECTILES BEING FIRED FROM TWO DIFFERENT POSITIONS. RETURNING A/C REPORT SEEING A NUMBER OF A/C IN DIFFICULTY. ASR LAUNCH SEEN TO PICK UP CREW E OF RAMSGATE.

CAPTAINS GENERALLY DESCRIBE THEIR EXPERIENCE AS GOOD TRIP, WEATHER HAZY AND DZ TOO CLEAR. ADDED DANGER OF GOING IN LOW BECAUSE OF CONTAINERS BEING DROPPED FROM HIGH LEVELS AND OFTEN SHORT OF DZ. CONSIDERABLE BUNCHING BY THE STREAM OF A/C WHEN CONVERGING ON DZ TENDED TO SQUEEZE A/C OUT OVER A WIDE DROPPING AREA.

1,800 feet. Although 99 per cent of the bundles were delivered, they were widely scattered over an area six miles long and two miles wide to the north-west of the zone.

The official history states that

The 82nd Division reported recovering 60 per cent of these supplies with Dutch assistance, and according to some estimates 80 per cent was ultimately recovered, but the hunt was long and difficult. It was sheer good luck that most of the supplies landed in friendly territory. The value of the mission was very great nevertheless. The supply dumps of the 82nd were running low, and it had not yet received any supplies by road. Indeed, the first truck convoys for the division had just reached the Meuse–Escaut Canal; some of those first trucks had been loaded with shells of the wrong calibre, and others by some strange oversight were empty.[110]

A drop by 35 aircraft of the 442nd and 439th Groups to the 101st Airborne Division was also inaccurate, only about 30 per cent of the supplies being recovered from the vicinity of DZ 'W'. In a second mission, twelve C-47s of the 442nd Group also headed for DZ 'W' carrying 120 artillerymen and six 75 mm howitzers of Battery B, 377th Parachute Field Artillery. The pilots were not informed of changes that had been made to the southern route and, flying to the west of the Allied salient, they ran into intense light flak and small-arms fire which damaged five aircraft. Despite this, and the fact that the approach to the DZ was made in poor visibility caused by thick haze through which the sun was setting, the crews made an excellent and accurate drop, and the battery was ready for action within an hour.

CHAPTER 10
D plus Four, 21 September 1944

The question has often been asked why, when the Sherman tanks of the Grenadier Guards forced the Nijmegen bridge and thrust on into Lent, did they not keep going. After all, as one author points out, 'All that stood in the way of XXX Corps and Arnhem during much of the night of 20–21 September were a few security pickets.'[111]

This was true; the combat elements of 10 SS *Panzer* Division that had crossed the Neder Rijn at Pannerden were still in the process of forming up, the armour waiting for supporting infantry and artillery. The straightforward answer to the original question, however, is that XXX Corps Commander, General Horrocks, did not know *what* lay ahead of him in the way of enemy opposition. There had already been too many unpleasant surprises during the advance from the Neerpelt bridgehead, and caution was understandably the order of the day.

It was certainly the order of the day in the case of the 43rd (Wessex) Division, tasked with providing infantry support for the Guards Armoured Division; when the Guards' leading tanks reached Nijmegen the 43rd Division was still at Grave, five miles to the rear. It has been suggested that, had the 43rd Division been deployed much further forward, its infantry might have been usefully employed in offensive operations against the German *Kampfgruppen* which, attacking from positions that were inaccessible to tanks, had done so much to slow the advance of XXX Corps. The slowness of the 43rd Division's advance, in fact, has been the subject of much criticism. Such criticism is unfair to the Wessex Division as a whole, and in particular to its commanding officer, Major-General Ivor Thomas. The task of the 43rd Division was to *follow* the Guards Armoured Division and then occupy a line from Apeldoorn (which was to be liberated by the Dutch Princess Irene Brigade) and the 1st British Airborne Division's bridgehead at Arnhem. Another, more daunting task assigned to the

Wessex Division was to force crossings of the Maas, Waal and Rhine if the airborne forces failed to take the relevant bridges and the latter were blown up by the enemy.

Admittedly, Major-General Thomas seriously underestimated the strength of the enemy opposition XXX Corps was expected to meet. As one of his brigadiers later wrote, recalling a conference of 43rd Division's staff officers before the start of the operation, 'He (General Thomas) opened up with the statement that the total German force ahead was quite inadequate to offer a prolonged resistance on any line and that armoured reserves of more than one squadron were most unlikely to be met.'[112]

Thomas, though, was by no means alone in making such an inaccurate statement, and once the true extent of the opposition began to make itself felt he may have felt it necessary to adopt a more cautious approach in the Division's advance from Neerpelt, much of its movement being made under cover of darkness. To state that the Guards Armoured Division was compelled to halt each night so that its supporting infantry might catch up with it, however, is untrue. Throughout the advance, Thomas sent forward those elements of his Division requested by Horrocks. On the night of 20/21 September, for example, batteries of the 59th Anti-Tank Regiment, Royal Artillery – which formed part of the 43rd Division – moved up to Nijmegen very quickly in the wake of the armoured advance and were soon dug in north of the bridge, ready to repel any German armoured counter-attacks.

This defensive posture, unfortunately, made little impression on the men who had captured the Nijmegen bridge at considerable cost.

Now that the Nijmegen bridge was in Allied hands, the American paratroopers expected to see long columns of British tanks racing across it for the final dash up to Arnhem, only 11 miles to the north. But the great herds of tanks did not materialize. The British were holding up their armoured thrust until their infantry units arrived to provide the tanks with some form of flank protection. Darkness fell with no tanks in sight. At this point a wave of bitterness swept through the ranks of the 82nd Airborne's paratroopers who had made the desperate river crossing that day.[113]

The fact was that General Horrocks and his subordinate commanders, notwithstanding the delays that continued to build up, were conforming to the *Garden* plan; and it was the plan itself that was at fault, for the plan had placed XXX Corps, quite literally, out on a limb. Horrocks himself put it very concisely when he briefed the officers of XXX Corps on the day before the offensive.

VIII and XII British Corps will be advancing on our right and left respectively but, as most of the available resources have been allotted to XXX Corps, they will not be able to advance so rapidly, and we shall be out on our own, possibly for quite a long period.

Horrocks might have gone further; he might have stated that most of the available resources – and that, mostly, meant fuel – had been allocated to the Guards Armoured Division. The fuel situation was, at least in part, responsible for the slowness of 43rd (Wessex) Division's advance. At the same time, VIII and XII Corps were able to provide little in the way of effective flank support; advancing through difficult terrain on either side of the main corridor, they inevitably fell behind as XXX Corps' advance gathered momentum, and were slowed even more as they encountered stiffer opposition. One account, written by a gunner serving with the 53rd Division, gives a good idea of the problems encountered.

From this point (the Meuse–Escaut Canal), all the battalions fanned out to attack separate villages. The farthest of these was Middelbeers and the HLI . . . started out on one of their longest marches of the campaign. After the breakout in Normandy the men had travelled in vehicles, but now the enemy had regrouped and were fighting back. Every one of the infantrymen carried something in addition to his rifle and personal kit. The majority had pickaxes or shovels, whilst others had parts of mortars or their bombs. Some had Bren guns and boxes of rounds to feed them. Signallers had portable radios on their backs. I suppose that we were fortunate, riding in a carrier, but anyone who has ridden in one of these vehicles will tell you how unbearably hot they get in the back, especially at slow speeds. I was soon walking myself, just to keep cool.

Eventually we saw Middelbeers in the distance and there appeared to be two church steeples. One had a slender spire, whilst the other had a square, solid tower with just a short, blunt point. I decided that the latter would be the better OP – if we had the choice.

My thoughts were interrupted by the distant noise of a Spandau. These German machine-guns fired so fast that it sounded like canvas tearing – a sound that has never been reproduced in any fictional war film. As we neared the village, mortar bombs started to explode in the fields round about, whilst the Spandau now sounded uncomfortably close. At the end of the village street the enemy had constructed a barricade of furniture, taken from nearby cottages. Anyone who tried to dismantle this came under fire from unseen snipers . . . In cases like this it was usual to call for the help of a friendly armoured vehicle. The passage of time has dimmed my memory as to what arrived. It was either a Sherman tank of a supporting squadron or an armoured car of the 53rd Division's reconnaissance corps . . . In this case the vehicle was knocked out by some anti-tank weapon. A second one was more successful and it pushed through the left side of the barrier, ploughed up some beautiful flower beds and moved forward with a dozen or so infantrymen in its wake.

The church was still half a mile down the bullet-raked street and we made our first OP in a nearby house, peering through a small window on the gable end. To the left were open fields that were too exposed to cross. On the horizon was the spread of the village, with the two church steeples being the only outstanding features. One of the troublesome Spandaus seemed to be firing from the left of these buildings and we sent a few shells from our battery to dislodge it. The view to the right of our window was very different. You could see the Highland Light Infantry, now in force, making their way up the main street, dodging from tree to tree, wall to wall. Already there had been casualties and the MO had established a dressing station in a large barn near the original barricade.[114]

The advance of both flank corps was delayed by small, bitterly-fought actions such as this, with the result that the neck of the XXX Corps body was stretched out in front to a dangerous extent. Rather than plunge on into territory where the strength of the enemy's defence was as yet an unknown quantity, Horrocks – with the agreement of Lieutenant-General Browning – decided to laager for the night at Nijmegen and resume the advance at first light, the idea being to rush the Guards Armoured Division through to Arnhem at dawn to take the Arnhem bridge before the paratroops at its north end were overwhelmed. Neither Horrocks nor Browning, of course, had any idea of what had happened to John Frost's gallant 2nd Parachute Battalion.

A mention must be made at this point of the efforts of a very brave band of men to monitor the action at the Arnhem bridge. They were the aircrews of the 654th Heavy Reconnaissance Squadron of the 25th Bomb Group, USAAF. Based at Watton, in Norfolk, and equipped with de Havilland Mosquito PR XVI aircraft, this squadron was assigned to reconnaissance and air control operations in the Arnhem–Nijmegen area from the start of *Market Garden*. It suffered its first casualty of the operation on 18 September, when a Mosquito flown by 1st Lt Robert A. Tunnel (navigator Staff Sgt John G. Cunney) on a PR mission to Nijmegen crashed on Platlunne airfield, killing both crew. Bad weather during *Market Garden* made regular air reconnaissance impossible, so the 654th Squadron was ordered to despatch a Mosquito to the Arnhem bridge every hour on the hour in the hope of finding a clear patch through which to take photographs, or at least make a visual observation.

Not until Thursday, 22 September, did a crew succeed; a Mosquito piloted by Lt Pat Walker flying over the northern end of the bridge at under 500 feet. Navigator Roy C. Conyers recalls that

We were to dip as low as possible to try to establish by visual observation who controlled the bridge. I thought this was crazy and mentioned it to Edwin R. Cerutti, a 654th navigator. His only comment was that the German Command wouldn't believe we were that stupid.

We could see the Germans running for the anti-aircraft guns and we were put into tracer bullet paths from at least two guns. This action lasted maybe 3–5 seconds. They hit the plane many times. The right engine was completely in flames. Pat turned off the fuel to the engine and the flames went out. The engine was, of course, useless. Thank goodness we were still airborne, and managed to fly back to Bournemouth.[115]

The flight confirmed what XXX Corps already knew: that the only people in control of the Arnhem bridge were the Germans. The first real indication of the situation in Arnhem had come early on Thursday, when the 1st Airborne Division's signallers at last succeeded in making radio contact with an element of the relief column: the 64th Medium Regiment, Royal Artillery. Gunner John Lacey, who served with 212 Battery, describes what happened.

At 0930 hours, 21 September, the Regimental Net picked up an unknown station, who reported they were being heavily shelled and could we help. They claimed to be 'the people we were trying to join up with'. After much checking and exchanging of various names – both Christian and surnames of various senior officers – it was decided that they were, without doubt, the 1st Airborne. By 1035 hours, 211 Battery reported 'ready' with their 4.5s, and although the first two targets were out of range, scale 10 was ordered on the third. 211 Battery now moved up a further 4,000 yards, one troop at a time, and by mid-day had engaged a further six targets. At 1230 hours a second stranger appeared on the Regimental Net; he gave the correct reply when challenged, and turned out to be BMRA Airborne Division. The original stranger was afterwards found to be FOO Control, who now stated that the link with us was their only contact with the relieving formations.

Concern was felt about losing radio contact, especially at night, so a relay station was despatched up the road. Our crew consisted of the Lieutenant, Command Post Bombardier, the driver, myself and another signaller. The officer on board was told to go as far as possible without going into the bag.

We set out for Nijmegen a few hours after the original radio contact, our transport being 212 Battery Commander's X-Car half-track which, I suppose, we classed as our 'armour'.

On arrival at Nijmegen we had to make several enquiries as to the location of the bridge, which we eventually found after picking our way through heavy debris and lots of dislodged overhead cables. By this time it was almost dark and we could see about half a dozen 'brew ups' just over the bridge, along with a sprinkling of tracer shells which appeared to be going in all directions and were, we presumed, part of a tank skirmish going on. We were now with the armour and after another 2–300 yards joined the leading elements. Our officer's enquiries as to how much further we could go were answered by tracer shells which appeared to come from a SP gun. The shells came from a point about 6–800 yards down the elevated highway, passing over our heads at tree-top height. We felt a little naked standing next to the Shermans in our half-track with its canvas canopy. I think our driver had similar thoughts as he moved a little, putting the armour between us and the SP gun.

Eventually we moved off the road into a site with some cover, along with the armour, which lined up on the opposite side of the road about 40 yards away. There, we settled down for the night to relay messages, fire orders etc, all five of us packed into the half-track at the ready for a quick move if necessary.[116]

The plan for the Irish Guards to break out of the Nijmegen bridgehead and make a lightning thrust to Arnhem was foredoomed to failure. For five hours during the night of 20/21 September there would have been nothing to stop the tanks if they had pushed on; but by the early hours of Thursday the Germans were well on the way to establishing a strong defensive line along the Waal south of

Ressen, its right flank resting on the 21st Artillery Battery under *Hauptsturmführer* Schwappacher, supported by odds and ends of infantry and well established in a hedgehog defence at Oosterhout, and its right on Bemmel, where the *Kampfgruppe* Reinhold – comprising elements of the 10th SS *Panzer* Regiment and the 22nd SS *Panzergrenadier* Regiment – had arrived from Pannerden late on Wednesday. This force was supported by a number of assault guns and about sixteen Mk IV *Panzers* and SPs. Worse still for Allied aspirations, Thursday morning saw the arrival in the Nijmegen sector of the spearheads of the *Kampfgruppe* Knaust from Arnhem.

As these reinforcements moved into place south of Elst, rapidly setting up artillery and anti-tank positions, *Obersturmbannführer* Heinz Harmel's 10th SS Battle Group, having assembled west of Pannerden, struck at the eastern flank of the XXX Corps attempted breakthrough. The blow was relatively weak – three battalions, supported by the sixteen Mk IVs and some artillery firing from the east bank of the Pannerden Canal – but it was sufficient to slow the breakout from a would-be dash to something more akin to a crawl. The Guards Brigade's problems were compounded by the fact that the road and railway running from the Waal to the Rhine ran on embankments bordered by marshy, heavily-ditched land impassable to armour.

Near Ressen, barely three miles north of Nijmegen, the Guards encountered Knaust's carefully-sited anti-tank guns, and there they were stopped. Every attempt to move up the causeway was smashed, and the tanks could not divert from the causeway to get at the enemy guns. There were no supporting infantry to deal with the German positions on the flanks, and the radio of the Guards' air support party was out of action, so they could not call in No 83 Group's Typhoons to do the job. In the Betuwe, the so-called 'island' of land bounded by the Waal and the Rhine, XXX Corps' operations on Thursday, 21 September, degenerated into bloody chaos.

ARNHEM

By the morning of 21 September, all hope that the 1st Airborne Division might still be capable of fulfilling its original mission had long since been abandoned. All that Major-General Urquhart could hope for now was a miracle by which the remains of the

By 21 September, the 4th Parachute Brigade had virtually ceased to exist. Here, paratroops carry a wounded comrade into captivity.

Division might be rescued. For all practical purposes, the 4th Parachute Brigade had ceased to exist, and there was no question of any further offensive operations. Urquhart therefore decided to stand firm on the perimeter which had been slowly forming in Oosterbeek, and to build this up with the maximum numbers that were available.

Urquhart divided his troops into two forces, one under Brigadier Hicks to be responsible for the defence of the west side of the perimeter and the other, under Brigadier Hackett, for the east side. The forces under Hicks' command were the 1st Airborne Reconnaissance Squadron on the main road at Hartenstein; the King's Own Scottish Borderers to the north in the woods at Ommershol; the 21st Independent Parachute Company on the high ground south of Ommershof; the Glider Pilots on their left at Graftombe; the 1st and 4th Parachute Squadrons and the 9th Field Company, Royal Engineers, in the woods south of Graftombe, and the Borders from there to Heveadorp.

Under Brigadier Hackett's command was what remained of the 156th Parachute Battalion at the crossroads south-east of Ommershof; the remnants of the 10th Parachute Battalion, supported by some glider pilots, at the crossroads east of Hartenstein; Lonsdale Force at Oosterbeek Church, and the 1st Air Landing Light Regiment, now combined with the survivors of the South Staffordshires and known as Thomson Force, to the west of the church.

From about 0700 hours, all defensive positions in Oosterbeek were subjected to heavy shelling and mortaring and to limited penetrations by SP guns and tanks, against which the defenders could do little. The armoured penetrations were a preliminary to enemy infantry attacks, which began on the eastern side of the perimeter about noon. Ken Hope, installed with other members of the 1st Airborne Reconnaissance Squadron in a combined house and bakery on the north corner of Paul Krugerstraat, tells how he

. . . was stationed in the store attic at the top of the building. Lieutenant Wadsworth and I had constructed an emplacement of flour bags on which I had sited my Bren and a rifle. He had his Sten machine-carbine and grenades. The storehouse was approached by steeply-angled steps. I had the 1mg trained on some trees across the road, about 30 yards distant.

I became aware of coal-scuttle helmets just visible above a ditch flanking the road. Very slowly and cautiously one German straightened up and stood at the edge of the road. I thought, 'Now, if I give him a quick burst with the Bren, the other bastards will spot the flame from the flash eliminator against the dark background of the store-room'. I preferred using the rifle to levering 'single shot' on the Bren. I fired two shots from the rifle which rested on the flour bags. The first one missed, but the second shot struck him somewhere below the waist, for one leg crumpled and he fell to the ground. One of the German's pals appeared to grasp him by a boot and hauled him into the ditch . . .

Then there occurred a very strange and uncanny incident which puzzled me at the time, and has done so ever since. A large, powerfully-built Alsatian dog ran across the road, loped up and down directly below our gun position, wheeled round and returned to the trees where the Jerries were deployed. The animal's approach was direct, purposeful and, one might imply, disciplined. Shortly after this, the building was hit by HE and set on fire, and we scrambled out to find another base.[117]

Hope's theory is that this was a specially-trained German infantry dog, rather than a stray; in any case, those poor, panic-stricken creatures had vanished from the streets some time earlier. It may

have been, for the Germans were making extensive use of dogs to locate British soldiers who were hiding in ruined buildings outside the perimeter.

For the assault on the perimeter, the Germans had laid their plans carefully.

During the night of 20–21 September the various 9 SS *Kampfgruppen* were ordered to regroup to include small penetration groups of assault pioneers (*Sturmpionieren*) and attack in echeloned units one after the other on a selected but reduced sector. The aim was to form narrow but deep penetration points in the British front. Assault guns and armoured half-tracks mounting heavy weapons trundled up to forward staging areas in the half-light of dawn, to assist in shooting a way through these 'roll-over' assaults. Constant attacks were to concentrate on a small front, with reserves standing by in echelon to follow through immediately on success. *Schwerpunkt*, or the main focus of effort, was to remain in the *Kampfgruppe* Spindler's sector. Spearheads were tempered by the inclusion of the three SP batteries belonging to Assault Gun Brigade 280. The brigade which had only just refitted in Denmark, was briefed under 15th Army command before being despatched to Arnhem where it had swung the balance in the German favour on 19 September. Major Kurt Kühne (subsequently awarded the Knight's Cross for his unit's contribution), had penny-packaged his batteries of three *Sturmgeschütz* III each to the *Kampfgruppen* Spindler, Harder and von Allworden . . . The brigade included its own integral heavily-armed infantry. Each battery had eight light machine-guns and seven *Panzerfaust*. Many of its personnel were still lacking in combat experience.

This regrouping of resources achieved some deep penetrations but at considerable cost. Pockets containing trapped enemy troops are referred to as *Der Kessel* – the cauldron – in German military parlance. This particular battle was embellished with a more meaningful term by German soldiers, who referred to their situation as *Der Hexenkessel* – the witches' cauldron . . . [118]

What was left of the 10th Parachute Battalion, astride the Utrechtseweg east of Hartenstein, was subjected to a series of fierce assaults and overrun, most of the houses it occupied being set on fire. The commanding officer, Lieutenant-Colonel Kenneth Smyth, was mortally wounded and the remaining officers killed or wounded. Very few men were left, but those who survived the onslaught went back into their former positions and held them under constant attack for two more days, a fine tribute to the determination and fighting qualities of the 4th Parachute Brigade. The commander of that brigade, Brigadier John Hackett, was himself wounded on this day, though not seriously, and his second brigade major, Major D.J. Madden – normally on the air staff at Divisional HQ – was killed by the same shell. Lieutenant-Colonel W.F.K. 'Sheriff' Thompson of the 1st Air Landing Light Regiment RA was also wounded.

The 7th Battalion, the King's Own Scottish Borderers, came under particularly fierce attack. On the extreme north of the perimeter, the Battalion was dug in around the Hotel Dreyeroord, a large rambling building known to the British troops as the White House. In the words of Lieutenant-Colonel Payton-Reid, the Battalion Commander:

I do not think that any who were there will forget the White House and its surroundings. When I knocked at its door about 9 pm on 19 September all was peace and quiet, since we had, temporarily, broken contact. Had I dropped from Mars, I could scarcely have aroused more interest and I was immediately greeted as a liberator by the numerous occupants – it was, I found, a small hotel. Never have I felt such a hypocrite. I had come to announce my intention of placing soldiers in the grounds and vicinity and the delight with which this news was received was most touching – but at the same time most pathetic, as I knew I was bringing them only danger and destruction.

By the next night the building was reduced to a shell and its inmates were crouching uncomfortably in the cellar. It was then garrisoned by a section of men who were living in the eerie atmosphere of a haunted house. The moon shone through shot-holes in the walls, casting weird shadows, prowling footsteps could be heard on the enemy side and one felt that faces were peering through every window. There was, too, every reason to expect unwelcome visitors . . . [119]

On Wednesday, the KOSB suffered heavy casualties from sniper fire, and the Medical Officer, Captain Devlin, asked Payton-Reid's permission to evacuate the Regimental Aid Post and the walking wounded to another house. This was outside the Battalion perimeter, and in the process of evacuation the wounded encountered a German patrol and were taken prisoner – which was probably just as well, as they were well cared for by German doctors.

Our final episode before leaving here was what has come to be known as the 'Battle of the White House' (Payton-Reid's account continues.) 'By this time we had, because of diminishing numbers, evacuated the house itself . . . During the afternoon of the 21st the enemy infiltrated close to our position, through the house and woods and under cover of a mortar barrage. When he finally came into the open to attack, the stolid patience with which we had endured his constant pin-pricks gave way to a ferocious lust for revenge, which was reflected in our

greeting to him. Everything opened up. Riflemen and Bren gunners vied with each other in production of rapid fire; mortars, their barrels practically vertical, lobbed bombs over our heads at the maximum possible range, anti-tank guns defended our flanks and Vickers MGs belched forth streams of bullets as only a Vickers can. The consequent din was reinforced by a stream of vindictive utterances in a predominantly Scottish accent.

The German attack was stopped but they went to ground and returned the fire hotly, displaying, in several cases, marked bravery. When it was adjudged that we had won the fire-fight, we went for them with the bayonet in the good old-fashioned style, with more blood-curdling yells, and this was too much for them. I have been told that close on 100 German bodies were found and buried there'.[120]

This action cost the KOSB four officers killed and eight wounded. Payton-Reid, however, does not give the whole story. One company of the Borderers was driven from its positions, creating a dangerous gap some 400 yards in extent between these and the 21st Independent Parachute Company, some distance to the west. The KOSBs fell back as far as the Independent Company's lines, then rallied and counter-attacked with the bayonet, disappearing into the dust and smoke of the battle. By the time they had reoccupied their positions, they were reduced in strength to about 150 all ranks.

As a result, reports began to reach Divisional HQ that Payton-Reid's battalion had been wiped out. There was no radio contact with it, and consequently Brigadier Hackett – whose perimeter command included the 1st Airborne Reconnaissance Squadron – ordered a patrol from this unit to go forward and investigate. Ken Hope was a member of that patrol.

I gathered up the spare magazines on the sill, crammed them into my ammunition pouches, and clattered down the staircase. Lieutenant Wadsworth explained to Sergeant Hewer and myself that we had to convey certain information to the Battalion HQ of the 7th King's Own Scottish Borderers . . . the street door was opened and we sprinted across the road to the houses opposite.

Then we began our 'leap-frog' covering progression as we reached an obstacle, perhaps a wooden fence, a garden wall or strands of wire. Sometimes the officer, then the sergeant or myself would be in the lead as we made our way from house to house, passing through gardens, orchards or vegetable patches. We came upon the body of a powerfully-built German lying face down, the rim of his helmet pressed into the earth . . . Beyond him was a narrow passage-way, between houses and leading to a road. I entered cautiously, reached the end wall, and looked left and right up and down the street. A few yards to my right, abandoned in the centre of the road, was a supply container, festooned with rigging lines and parachute.

Suddenly there was a shattering of glass at the bedroom window of a house directly opposite. For a second I stood mesmerised at the sight of a grenade lying near the base of the wall. We turned back and scrambled furiously for cover at the rear of a house just as the grenade exploded. The wall took the force of the blast; otherwise, bunched as we were in the alleyway, the fragmentation effect could only have been disastrous. Lieutenant Wadsworth made a quick appreciation and rapped out an order. He and Sergeant Hewer opened fire with their Stens from the left of our cover and I sprang into the mouth of the alleyway we had so hastily vacated. I opened fire, from the hip, with the Bren. I just clutched the trigger and emptied the contents of a full magazine. For a few brief seconds a torrent of fire poured at the upper windows from three guns. Glass, brickwork and wood frames were splintered and shattered. The effect on the occupants must have been devastating. The fire was not returned. We resumed our patrol. It was inevitable that we should collide with some of the enemy, even within the perimeter, for many houses occupied by British and Germans were inextricably confused.

We could see troops manning trenches in cover at the end of woodland. Lieutenant Wadsworth felt certain that we had reached the KOSB positions. At his bidding we raced across a patch of open ground and flung ourselves into cover. A lance-corporal emerged from a trench dug amongst the foliage of laurel bushes. He was a paratrooper of the 21st Independent Parachute Company.[121]

There was a remarkable sequel to this encounter. About eighteen months after the Battle at Arnhem Ken Hope was an infantry subaltern reporting for duty at the 1st Battalion The South Staffordshire Regiment at Agra, northern India. The first person he met in the Officers' Mess was a lieutenant whose tunic displayed the Military Medal, France and Germany Star, and Parachute Wings. The subsequent conversation established that he – Bill Barclay – was the Parachute Company NCO who

. . . offered to guide us into the KOSB lines immediately to the right flank. We crossed a narrow lane in which was sited a six-pounder anti-tank gun, shrouded in foliage. Lieutenant Wadsworth approached an officer I took to be Lieutenant-Colonel Payton-Reid . . . I dropped into a fairly deep, sandy hole and attempted to take a snooze. The noise was deafening, a constant clattering of machine guns and the roar of exploding mortars and shells. A Borderer captain was thoroughly enjoying himself with a German Schmeisser machine pistol. It might have been the height of the grouse-shooting season . . .

The German 'stonk' was very impressive, and they just poured on the punishment. Eventually, the fury of the

General Stanislaw Sosabowski, commanding the Polish Parachute Brigade, conferring with British and Polish staff officers before the mission to Arnhem. Sosabowski believed that *Market Garden* was a foolhardy venture.

barrage lessened somewhat, and Lieutenant Wadsworth, Sergeant Hewer and myself made our way back to our own A Troop positions. Our return progress was fairly rapid as we now had a better idea of the local topography. There was one occasion when the three of us dived into the black earth of a vegetable garden. Clusters of mortar bombs were passing from the east into the perimeter defences. I remember looking up and watching with amazement as scores of the projectiles were simultaneously visible against the grey sky. The German supply of ammunition seemed inexhaustible . . . [122]

At 1310 hours, with the battle for the perimeter raging with unabated fury, the first serial of the 52nd Troop Carrier Wing began taking off from Lincolnshire, carrying the delayed mission of the 1st Polish Parachute Brigade. The weather was dreadful – layer upon layer of cloud extending from 150 feet up to 9,000 feet, with ground visibility close to zero – but such was the desperate plight of the 1st Airborne Division at Arnhem that the mission was authorized to go ahead. It was arranged in three serials of 27 aircraft and one of 33, the first two flown from Spanhoe by the 315th TCG and the other two from Saltby by the 314th TCG.

The pilots of the lead serial were briefed to climb to 1,500 feet, where a clear corridor had been predicted between layers of cloud. But no such corridor existed, so the pilots were ordered to disperse and try to climb through the overcast. During this attempt, no fewer than 25 crews lost their bearings and aborted the mission, returning to base; the other two broke cloud and, after circling for some time, joined on to a later serial.

The next three serials adopted a different procedure. Instead of assembling below the cloud, they climbed through it in a spiral of individual aircraft and assembled on top at 10,000 feet. In this way, 87 out of 93 aircraft joined formation and set course for Holland. At 1545 hours, however, while crossing the Channel, one flight leader received a garbled radio message which he was unable to decipher; he decided that it must have been a recall signal and led his ten C-47s, all belonging to the 314th Group, back to base.

As a result of all this confusion, the 52nd TCW was now heading for Arnhem with only 998 troops and 69 tons of supplies instead of the planned figure of 1,511 troops and 100 tons. At first, the C-47s flew on at 10,000 feet, but as the serials approached the Belgian coast the clouds began to break up, enabling pilots to make a gradual descent to 1,500 feet. One

aircraft was hit by flak over the Scheldt Estuary, having gone off course, and had to drop its troops near Ghent; it regained its base on one engine. The remainder continued up the west side of the salient towards the revised drop zone, a large area of open, ditched land north-east of the town of Driel on the southern side of the Neder Rijn opposite Heveadorp. It had been impossible to send pathfinders to mark the zone, but the leaders found it with the aid of good visual navigation checked occasionally by *Gee*, which for once was not being jammed.

The mission had no flak suppression support, and no fighter cover was available over Holland. One P-51 group on area patrol beyond Eindhoven departed just before the troop-carriers arrived. Luckily, no enemy fighters appeared to interfere with the paratroop serials, but there was a lot of light flak and small-arms fire as the C-47s approached the DZ; several were hit, but all managed to make their drops. All three serials passed over the DZ within eight minutes at altitudes of between 750 and 800 feet. The Poles, heavily laden with equipment and making their first combat drop, were somewhat slow in getting out, with the result that many came down several hundred yards beyond the zone.

Because of this, some of the troop-carriers turned away from the zone later than intended, and as a consequence they passed over Elst, which was bristling with anti-aircraft guns. The flickering gun flashes reminded one observer as 'a pinball machine gone mad.'[123]

As far as the pilots were concerned, it was every man for himself as they tried desperately to escape the barrage. Breaking formation, they dived to ground level and roared across the Dutch landscape at top speed. Very few aircraft returned to their bases that night, being forced to land in Belgium or elsewhere in England because of damage, darkness and thickening fog. Five aircraft, all from the 315th Group, had been shot down and 33 damaged, fourteen severely.

The drop of the Polish Parachute Brigade took the Germans completely by surprise. About 750 paratroops, including the Brigade Commander, Major-General Sosabowski, landed on the designated DZ and quickly assembled. Although the German troops on the north bank of the Rhine turned their guns on the paratroops, casualties during the descent were much lighter than might have been expected. As soon as they landed, the Poles came under heavy fire from the enemy's 191st Artillery Regiment and from a group of *Nebelwerfer*, but the shooting was fortunately wild and inaccurate. Of the drop itself, Sosabowski later wrote:

I cannot praise too much the perfect dropping, which in difficult weather conditions and in spite of strong enemy anti-aircraft fire over the DZ was equal to the best dropping during any exercise this Brigade Group has ever had.[124]

The Polish Brigade, however, was unable to carry out its mission, which was to seize the Driel ferry and make a crossing of the Neder Rijn to Heveadorp. When they reached the river bank, they found that the ferry had been sunk and that German forces were in possession of the opposite bank at Westerbouwing, a 100-foot rise which, until Wednesday, had been occupied by the 1st Battalion The Border Regiment, or rather one platoon of it. By the time the Poles landed, however, the Borders had been withdrawn further east to form part of the perimeter defence. Once the Germans has captured Westerbouwing they were in a position to enfilade the entire base of the perimeter, which consisted of low-lying polder. Surprisingly, they failed to do so.

The landing of the Polish Brigade presented the Germans with a sudden and unexpected crisis. At this juncture, HQ II SS *Panzer* Corps had no idea what the Poles' intentions were. Their logical move would be to force a crossing of the Neder Rijn and link up with the airborne forces in the Oosterbeek perimeter; on the other hand, they might make a sudden thrust to the north-east, cutting off the passage of 10 SS *Frundsberg* over the Arnhem bridge en route to the 82nd Airborne Division's airhead at Nijmegen. To forestall such an eventuality, General Bittrich, commanding II SS Corps, ordered the *Wehrmacht* Battalion of the *Kampfgruppe* Knaust, supported by a company of Panther tanks from 9 SS and by 10 SS artillery, to defend Elst, midway between Arnhem and Nijmegen; at the same time, *Sturmbannführer* Walther Harzer, commanding 9 SS, was to establish a *Sperrverband*, or blocking formation, along the Arnhem–Elst railway embankment. This improvised force consisted of five battalions: the Battalion Schörken, from the *Wehrmacht*, the Battalion Köhnen, from Marine

Kampfgruppe 642, the Battalion Kauer, composed of *Luftwaffe* ground staff, Coastal Machine Gun Battalion 47, and the 3rd *Landsturm Niederland* Battalion, Dutch territorial SS reserves raised by the Germans. Artillery support was provided by the 191st Artillery Regiment and Swoboda's Flak Brigade, occupying positions at Elden. The whole force, eventually, added up to 2,461 infantry supported by sixteen 88 mm flak guns, eight 20 mm cannon and some 37 mm flak guns. It was, therefore, a very substantial force to be diverted from the fighting at Oosterbeek, and its transfer significantly weakened the assaults on the British perimeter.

Although the paratroop mission to Arnhem – at least, the part of it that actually reached the zones – had gone well, the air resupply missions to the 1st Airborne Division had been disastrous. Resupply operations for D plus 4 called for 117 sorties to a drop point near Hartenstein, about 200 yards east of that used on the previous day.[125] To reduce the flak hazard the aircraft were despatched in four waves, the first timed to arrive at 1315 hours and the last at 1615 hours. The first three waves were to be escorted by six Spitfire squadrons of ADGB, with an Eighth Air Force P-51 group providing area cover. The last wave, flying in parallel with a large American resupply mission to the 82nd and 101st Airborne Divisions, would have an escort of fifteen ADGB squadrons as far as Eindhoven, when fifteen squadrons of the Eighth Air Force would take over.

The morning fog had lifted as the first wave of 64 Stirlings of No 38 Group took off from their bases in southern England at 1100 hours, but there was low stratus between 600 and 1,200 feet and visibility was reduced to about a mile. Over Holland there were better conditions: four- to seven-tenths cloud at about 3,000 feet. However, bad weather kept most of the escorting Spitfire squadrons on the ground; only nineteen aircraft took off, and these did not rendezvous with the Stirlings until after they had left the Arnhem area. The 56th Fighter Group of the Eighth Air Force also despatched 34 P-47 Thunderbolts on area patrol, but these too arrived late.

The absence of Allied fighter protection resulted in tragedy, for it was on this day that the *Luftwaffe* intervened in strength over Arnhem. The enemy fighters involved were the Focke-Wulf FW 190s of *Jagdgeschwader* 2 and 26,[126] and they wrought havoc among the transport aircraft. Pouncing on ten

Stirlings of No 190 Squadron, they shot down seven of them in the space of a few moments. The total loss to the RAF re-supply aircraft was eighteen to fighters and five more to anti-aircraft fire; most of these losses occurred in the third and fourth waves, which had no fighter escort at all. In the other instances, Spitfires drove off FW 190s and claimed to have damaged three, and at 1505 hours the 56th Fighter Group's Thunderbolts intercepted 22 Focke-Wulfs returning from the Arnhem area after attacking the third wave and claimed to have destroyed fifteen of them for the loss of two P-47s.

The Dakotas of No 46 Group, forming the last re-supply wave, lost ten aircraft to flak and fighters. In addition to aircraft destroyed, 38 were damaged. Although 91 crews reported successful drops, only eleven tons of the 271 tons released were recovered by the starving and desperate troops on the ground.

The Polish paratroop mission had a more effective escort, and may have been lucky in that it made its drop between successive attacks on the re-supply aircraft by enemy fighters. ADGB fighters made 118 sorties in support of the troop-carriers and sighted only a few enemy aircraft, which were quickly driven off. As far as the Eighth Air Force was concerned, area patrol during the troop-carrier mission was provided by only one P-47 group, the rest having been recalled because of bad weather.[127] The remaining group, the 353rd

Gunners of the Air Landing Brigade engaging German targets with a 75 mm pack howitzer, the largest artillery piece used at Arnhem.

Fighter Group, patrolled the Eindhoven–Arnhem area from 1610 to 1650 hours, and about five miles south-west of Nijmegen it encountered about 30 Focke-Wulfs, some attacking C-47s while the others provided top cover. The Americans engaged the FW 190s, whose pilots showed a degree of skill that was unusual at this stage of the war, and drove them off, claiming the destruction of six Focke-Wulfs for the loss of one P-47.

The bad weather in England caused the postponement of two American glider missions which were to have reinforced the 101st and 82nd Airborne Divisions. The loss of the first, involving 82 Wacos, was not particularly serious, as the 101st Division was no longer under heavy pressure; in the late afternoon it received a resupply drop by 24 C-47s of the 437th and 438th Troop Carrier Groups, six more aircraft having turned back for various reasons, and about a third of the supplies were recovered. The postponement of the mission to the 82nd Division, which involved 419 gliders carrying the 325th Glider Regiment, was much more serious, as heavy fighting was in progress around the 82nd's airhead and the airborne troops, exhausted after four days' fighting, were hard put to hold on.

At Arnhem, the remnants of the 1st Airborne Division fought on stubbornly in the defence of the perimeter, and it was this phase of the battle that brought the Division the award of two more Victoria Crosses.

On 20 September, as the perimeter was being formed, Lance-Sergeant J.D. Baskeyfield of the South Staffordshire Regiment was in command of a section manning a six-pounder anti-tank gun engaged in repelling a heavy attack by enemy armour. Displaying the utmost coolness and daring, the section destroyed two Tiger tanks and a self-propelled gun, holding their fire to make sure of success until the enemy fighting vehicles were less than 100 yards off. All the gun's crew were killed or wounded, John Baskeyfield himself being badly hit in the leg. Refusing to be carried to the Regimental Aid Post, he remained alone with the gun and soon afterwards repelled a second and even fiercer armoured attack. By this time, Baskeyfield's action alone was halting the enemy advance, as the crews of other guns in the vicinity had been killed, and his own gun was soon destroyed by intense fire. Baskeyfield managed to crawl to another six-pounder, the crew of which was dead, and single-handed brought it into action. He managed to fire two rounds at an SP gun before the six-pounder was destroyed by shellfire, which also killed him. Never, in the annals of the British Army, was the award of a posthumous Victoria Cross more richly deserved.

The award of the VC to Major R.H. Cain came about as the result of a series of actions in the defence of the perimeter over several days, rather than for a single gallant act. On 19 September, Cain was commanding a rifle company of the South Staffordshires in a position north of Oosterbeek Church when the company was cut off from the rest of their battalion. From then on, the Germans mounted repeated attacks on the position in an attempt to dislodge the defenders, who resisted fiercely. On 20 September, Cain went out alone and armed with a PIAT to deal with a Tiger tank that approached the company's position. Lying in the path of the tank, he fired some 50 bombs at it, his fire being directed by Captain Ian Meikle, who continued to carry out this role until he was killed. The tank turned its machine-gun on him, wounding him, and he took refuge in a shed with the PIAT and two remaining bombs. Putting his head round the door, he 'fired at the thing and the bomb went off underneath it.' He then left the shed moments before the tank's main armament blew it apart. The Tiger was eventually destroyed by a 75 mm howitzer.

On the following day three more tanks tried to break into the company's position, and Cain went out into the open to engage them with the PIAT. He fired at one of them immediately when it was less than 100 yards away and the tank fired back, which 'raised a huge cloud of dust and smoke. As soon as I could see the outline of the tank I let it have another. This also raised a lot of dust again, and through it I saw the crew of the tank baling out.' They were dealt with by a Bren gun. Cain fired the PIAT again, but the bomb burst prematurely in the muzzle, wounding him in the face, perforating an eardrum and giving him two black eyes. Despite his injuries, Major Robert Cain fought on for another four days, arming himself with a two-inch mortar when his supply of PIAT ammunition was exhausted. In the words of his citation, 'His coolness

and courage under incessant fire could not be surpassed.'[128]

As darkness fell on Thursday, 21 September, the Polish Parachute Brigade on the south bank of the Neder Rijn set about concentrating its forces in and around Driel; an area, fortunately, where the terrain did not favour tank operations. Had it been otherwise, Major-General Sosabowski's command might have ceased to exist by dawn on the following day.

At about 2230 hours on 21 September, two liaison officers from 1st Airborne Division crossed the river with the help of the Dutch Resistance and made contact with the Poles. They were Lieutenant-Colonel Charles Mackenzie, the Division's GSO 1 (Ops) and Lieutenant-Colonel E.C.W. Myers, the Commander, Royal Engineers. They notified General Sosabowski that 1st Airborne Division was preparing a counter-attack on Heveadorp, which the Germans had captured earlier, in order to regain control of the ferry terminus; boats and rafts would then be assembled to ferry the Polish Brigade across. But the Division was in no position to launch a counter-attack, and the boats never materialized.

In the meantime, General Urquhart had received a message from XXX Corps to the effect that the 43rd Infantry Division had been ordered to take all risks to effect the relief of the airborne troops. The Wessex Division was to push on through the positions of the Guards Armoured Division and break out of the Nijmegen bridgehead in a two-pronged thrust, one force heading for the Arnhem bridge and the other making a westerly flanking movement to join up with the Poles at Driel. But the night wore on, and the 43rd Division made no move except to send up a reconnaissance troop of the Household Cavalry to make contact with the Polish Brigade; from its command vehicle, Lieutenant-Colonel Mackenzie sent a message to XXX Corps, reporting as precisely as he could the desperate situation of the Airborne Division.

Towards dawn, the 43rd Division's main infantry force at last prepared to move. But the Germans were on the move too, and the next 48 hours would see bitter fighting as *Feldmarschall* Model's *Panzers* made their most determined effort yet to sever the head of the Allied drive to the Rhine.

CHAPTER 11

D plus Five, 22 September 1944

Late on 21 September, while II SS *Panzer* Corps applied increasing pressure on the 1st Airborne Division's perimeter at Oosterbeek, *Feldmarschall* Walther Model issued the orders which, he hoped, would result in the Allied corridor being sliced in two between Eindhoven and Nijmegen. The attack was to be carried out simultaneously by General Reinhard's LXXXVIII Corps and General Hans von Obstfelder's LXXXVI Corps, lying to the west and east of the corridor.

Von Obstfelder's Corps was a new formation within General Kurt Student's 1st *Fallschirmjäger* Army, having only assumed control of the 7th *Fallschirmjäger* Division and the 176th Infantry Division on 18 September. Now, in preparation for the coming offensive, Obstfelder was also given command of the *Kampfgruppe* Walther, regrouped and reinforced after the heavy losses it had suffered during the XXX Corps breakout from the Neerpelt bridgehead. Its assets now included *Major Freiherr* von Maltzahn's 107th *Panzer* Brigade, a small 10 SS battle group under *Hauptsturmführer* Friedrich Richter; an artillery battalion of the 180th Regiment with 105 mm and 150 mm howitzers; the 1st Battalion of the 16th Grenadier Regiment, a heavy flak battery; the 1st Battalion of the 21st *Fallschirmjäger* Regiment, and SS *Hauptsturmführer* Rostel's 10th SS Tank-Destroyer Battalion. *Oberst* Walther therefore had an impressive force at his disposal, although the infantry lacked combat experience and the artillery was short of ammunition. His objective was to cut the Eindhoven–Grave road at Veghel, seize the town, and destroy the bridge over the Zuid Wilhelms Vaart Canal. He was also to prevent the passage of reinforcements along the road, and make contact with German forces attacking the corridor from the west.

The assault from the west would be much weaker than that from the east. It was to be mounted by the *Kampfgruppe* Huber, which comprised three infantry battalions of the 59th Division; a battalion of 105 mm howitzers; a battery of 20 mm anti-aircraft guns; seven anti-tank guns and four *Jagdpanther* from the 1st Company of the 559th Tank-Destroyer Battalion. Huber's task was to attack from Schijndel through the villages of Wijbosch and Eerde to Veghel.[129]

The axis of both attacks had been shrewdly chosen. While the British VIII and XII Corps had moved up to buttress both flanks of the Allied corridor as far as the Wilhelmina Canal, their progress had been slow; the former was still south-east of Eindhoven and the latter had been halted south-west of Best. The road from the Wilhelmina Canal to Grave was therefore defended only by the 101st Airborne Division, and by British units escorting convoys moving up the highway. Over most of this stretch, no-man's land began at the edge of the road; the Allies had no control over the woods and farms and obscure back roads where the Germans were marshalling their forces for the pincer attack.

Veghel was also the logical objective, for the destruction of the bridge there would block the road for days, even if the town were re-taken quickly. Moreover, Veghel was only lightly defended by the Headquarters and the 2nd Battalion of the 501st Parachute Infantry Regiment, the 1st and 3rd Battalions having been detached for offensive operations in the Schijndel area. The nearest possible reinforcement was the 502nd PIR at St Oedenrode, but it was needed for the defence of that sector; realistically, any help would have to come from Zon, seven or eight miles away.

During the night of 21/22 September, General Maxwell Taylor, commanding the 101st Airborne Division, received persistent reports – mostly from Dutch civilians – of enemy troop movements on the northern flank of his airhead, and decided to take pre-emptive action. He ordered the 327th Glider

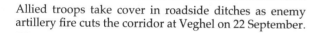

Allied troops take cover in roadside ditches as enemy artillery fire cuts the corridor at Veghel on 22 September.

Infantry Regiment to move to Veghel and the 506th PIR, minus its 1st Battalion, to occupy Uden, four miles to the north of Veghel. At about 1000 hours on Friday morning the Regimental Headquarters of the 506th PIR, followed shortly afterwards by 175 men of the 2nd Battalion, passed through Veghel and drove on to Uden without incident. The rest of the 506th was still south of St Oedenrode, while the 327th Glider Infantry Regiment, which had not received the order to move until 0930 hours, was only just beginning to move out. Only its 3rd Battalion was to go by truck; the others were ordered to march via secondary roads so as not to obstruct traffic on the highway.

By then, the German attack from the east was already on the move, spearheaded by *Major Freiherr* von Maltzahn's 107th *Panzer* Brigade's Panthers. By 1100 hours the tanks and supporting *Panzer-grenadiers* had reached the outskirts of Veghel, the infantry assaulting the town while the tanks swung north to cut the highway between Veghel and Uden. In Veghel, the 2nd Battalion of the 501st PIR under Lieutenant-Colonel Ballard fought desperately to stem the onslaught; it was very nearly overwhelmed, but held on doggedly with the support of some British armour and artillery which had pulled aside in the town earlier that morning to allow unrestricted passage of the 69th Brigade Group.

Meanwhile, west of the corridor, *Major* Huber had been forced to alter his plans somewhat because the 1st and 3rd Battalions of the 501st PIR had taken Schijndel during the night. Leaving one infantry

battalion in contact with the Americans there, he now led his force along back roads and tracks to Eerde, where his *Jagdpanthers* knocked out two British armoured cars just before entering the village at 1100 hours. By 1400 hours, his artillery and tank-destroyers had brought the bridge over the Wilhelms Canal at Veghel under fire.

In Veghel, reinforcements for the hard-pressed defenders arrived at about 1215 hours when the 3rd Battalion of the 327th reached the town, with a squadron of British tanks in support. They were followed some time later by part of the 506th PIR's 2nd Battalion, coming up from St Oedenrode, and a battery of 57 mm motorized anti-tank guns. The latter arrived just in time to meet an attack by von Maltzahn's Panthers, which, having cut the road, had now turned left and were attempting to drive into Veghel from the north-east. The leading tank was disabled and set on fire by a 57 mm round, and those following, caught out in the open, withdrew.

On the western side of the corridor, Major Huber's infantry had begun their push towards the town. Company D of the 506th PIR, which had just entered Veghel, was hastily despatched to stop them, and managed to do so with the aid of British tanks. Huber, having failed to penetrate Veghel, now concentrated his efforts on trying to cut the road to the south. His leading infantry elements were

A British armoured car explodes and burns in the corridor after being hit by shells from a Panther tank of 107 *Panzer* Brigade.

On 24 September, stationary Allied convoys on the highway between Veghel and St Oedenrode were raked with deadly effect by the Jungwirth Battalion. Here, an ammunition truck explodes.

actually starting to cross the road when the remaining battalions of the 327th Glider Infantry arrived, supported by the 321st Glider Field Artillery Battalion. They beat off the German attack and fought their way into the town to join the other defenders. The attack from the west had failed, and the *Kampfgruppe* Huber's fate was sealed when the 3rd Battalion of the 501st PIR, hurrying from Schijndel to the relief of Veghel, fell on Huber's rear echelons and cut them to pieces, occupying Wijbosch and Eerde and cutting off his infantry battalions. Only a handful of stragglers escaped from the trap.

The crisis was over, but for several hours the enemy had been dangerously close to success, and it had needed the concentrated strength of half the 101st Airborne Division, supported by British tanks and artillery, to beat him off. But the road north of Veghel was still blocked and the detachment of the

506th PIR in Uden was isolated and under heavy pressure. During the night the *Kampfgruppe* Walther again tried to break into Veghel from the north-east and again the attack was beaten off. By this time Walther's force had suffered very heavy casualties, particularly among its officers. The battle for Veghel, however, was by no means over.

While the 101st Airborne Division was heavily engaged, the 82nd Airborne had been having a comparatively quiet day, pushing a force along the south bank of the Waal to Pals, about three miles east of Nijmegen, to provide an extended defensive zone around the all-important bridge. The only real resistance was encountered by the 508th PIR, which had to fend off several fierce enemy attacks on a hill it was holding south of Beek; elsewhere, the divisional perimeter was quiet.

No air transport operations were flown on 22 September. There was widespread fog over England and the Low Countries during the morning, and in the afternoon this was replaced by stratus which lowered the ceiling to 300 feet in some areas. Rain spread over the British Isles from the west, with cloud ceilings of 500–1,000 feet and a horizontal visibility of between 1,000 and 2,000 yards. Despite the appalling weather, the US Eighth Air Force despatched two P-47 groups to patrol the Arnhem area; they flew 77 uneventful sorties and all returned safely.[130]

At Oosterbeek, the first major German assault on the 1st Airborne Division's perimeter developed from the west, and was preceded by heavy mortar and artillery attacks on the positions held by the 1st Battalion The Border Regiment. The infantry attacks were directed by *Obersturmbannführer* Hans Michael Lippert and involved four battalions: the Dutch SS *Wachbattalion* 3 under *Hauptsturmführer* Paul Helle, advancing from the area of the Koude Herberg crossroads in the north-west; the SS Battalions Schulz and Eberwein attacking in the centre, along and to the south of the Wageningen–Oosterbeek road; and the Hermann Göring Battalion from the SS division of that title advancing on the right, parallel to the Neder Rijn. Once the perimeter defences had been reached, the Eberwein Battalion was to thrust south and east until it reached the river.

But the defences were not breached; the Border Regiment and other supporting units fought tenaciously in the heavily wooded territory that characterized the western perimeter. The Dutch Battalion was cut to pieces, many more of its men deserted, and by nightfall it had been disbanded, the survivors being assigned to the Eberwein Battalion. The latter also made small progress, its attacks stalling in the course of the day.

From the east, the German attack on the perimeter was carried out by four 9 SS *Kampfgruppen*, all of them involved in desperate street fighting. Astride the Utrechtseweg was *Hauptsturmführer* Hans Möller's badly depleted 9th SS Engineer Battalion; to their right was *Sturmbannführer* Ludwig Spindler's battle group, and to their left von Allworden's, fighting from house to house. Between von Allworden's battle group and the river, SS *Obersturmführer* Harder's *Kampfgruppe* fought savage actions against the remnants of Lonsdale Force as it tried to penetrate to the Oosterbeek–Laag Church, where the Airborne Division's artillery was concentrated.

All around the perimeter, the morale of the defenders was greatly uplifted by the accurate shoots of the 64th Medium Regiment, Royal Artillery. Time and again, from a distance of eleven miles, its 4.5 inch medium guns – supported later by a battery of 7.2 inch 'heavies'[131] – broke up infantry and armoured attacks on the perimeter. Targets – often as close as 100 yards to the British positions – were selected by Brigadiers Hicks and Hackett and the tasks relayed by Lieutenant-Colonel R.G. Loder-Symonds DSO, the 1st Airborne Division's Commander, Royal Artillery, via the tenuous radio link to Lieutenant-Colonel Hunt, the 64th Medium Regiment's commanding officer. And it was not all just a question of providing fire support for the Airborne troops.

We had a varied selection of fire whilst at the position. Apart from our own guns over the top, we had 25-pounders firing in the same direction but dropping behind us on what we believed to be enemy armour cut off to the rear. This was more or less confirmed only on Sunday morning, 24 September, when as reported in the SITRP and 9 am: 'One Boche tank (Tiger) passed through at great speed going north.' We were about 20 yards from the road and the armour about the same distance from the opposite side. As there was no gunfire at the time, we assumed that he made it back to his own lines, even though our infantry had advanced across the road during the night.[132]

The two brigadiers commanding their respective parts of the perimeter defence – and, indeed, Major-General Urquhart himself – were everywhere among their troops, always visible. Lieutenant John Stevenson of the Reconnaissance Squadron, which had been transferred from Hicks's command to that of Hackett the previous evening, recalled:

He (Hackett) came up on a jeep and there was a hell of a rumpus going on at the time, to which he paid not one blind bit of attention. It was just as if it wasn't happening. I remember he sat up on the bonnet of his vehicle, and opened out this map and proceeded to give me the most precise instructions. I cannot now remember what it was that he wanted me to do, but I do know that more than anything else I wanted to get down, because those mortar bombs were going off all around us all the time that he was talking. The briefing lasted for not more than five minutes, but they were about five of the longest minutes of my life.

Another officer of the same unit, Captain David Allsop, remembered how Brigadier Hackett

. . . seemed to have the idea that it was good for the chaps in the slit trenches to see him walking about, and so he tended to ignore the firing. When Hackett came and talked to you, it wasn't crouched down in a hole in the ground –you got out and strolled around, as if you were at Henley![133]

It would not be true to say that appearances such as this by their senior officers lifted the morale of the men, for the morale of the 1st Airborne Division had remained high throughout. What they achieved, rather, was to cement the strong bond that existed between the officers and men of what was an elite fighting force.

The factor that most affected the defenders of the Oosterbeek perimeter, amid all the horror and carnage and misery, was fatigue. Concentration was beginning to falter, and only superb discipline and training kept them going. The problem of fatigue was compounded by hunger and thirst – especially thirst, for the Germans had cut off the water supply. All water that could be spared was used for the comfort of the wounded, who, in the words of the official narrative,

. . . were looked after with great devotion by surgeons who remained at their posts to the last and entered captivity or death with them. The 16th Parachute Field Ambulance, under Lieutenant-Colonel E. Townsend, MC, was established in the St Elisabeth Hospital on the evening of the first day, but the Germans reoccupied the buildings a few hours later and took prisoner all the unit save two surgeons, Major Longland and Captain Lipmann-Kessell, who used the greatest ingenuity in preventing their enforced departure . . . A Regimental Aid Post was established by Captain Martin in Oosterbeek. Conditions in it were very bad, for it was soon housing

Street fighting in Oosterbeek. Men of the Glider Pilot Regiment clearing a ruined school.

upwards of 200 wounded, and little beyond first aid could be given to them. The owner of the house, a Dutch lady, worked without rest or food, helped by a boy of seventeen who did likewise. What water there was had to be brought from a pump close by, until it ran 'red with blood'. Every evening the lady moved from room to room, her bible in her hand, and in the light of a torch read aloud the 91st Psalm, 'for,' said she, 'it has comforted my children and may comfort you.' Lying on mattresses or straw amid the stench of wounds and death, the men heard 'her soft voice speaking most carefully the words of King David,

Troops of the 1st Airborne Division dug in on the Oosterbeek perimeter. The man on the left is a radio operator (note headset).

Thou shalt not be afraid for the terror by night, nor for the arrow that flieth by day, nor for the pestilence that walketh in darkness, nor for the destruction that wasteth at noonday.'[134])

The name of that Dutch lady has passed into legend. She was Kate ter Horst.[135]

Meanwhile, the advance of the 43rd Wessex Division had finally got under way at 0830 hours on 22 September; two infantry brigades – the 129th with the 130th coming up in reserve –heading up the highway from Nijmegen while the third, Brigadier Hubert Essame's 214th, set off on its flanking movement to the west via Oosterhout. By now it was broad daylight, the early morning mist had lifted, the German 88 mm gunners in camouflaged positions along the route had no difficulty in picking out their targets, and the advance proceeded painfully slowly. It took most of the day for the leading elements of 129 Brigade to fight their way through to the village of Elst, where they were stopped by the Knaust Battalion and the *Kampfgruppe* Brinkmann, whose assets included twenty Tiger and Panther tanks and numerous 88 mm guns.

Long before this, the flanking movement had also become bogged down at Oosterhout, which – although only lightly defended – was approached cautiously by 214 Brigade. The village was eventually taken after a six and a half hour delay and the brigade pushed forward, with 130 Brigade now in support. At 1800 hours, with the breakout from Oosterhout at last achieved, Brigadier Essame sent forward two battalions of the Duke of Cornwall's Light Infantry (Lieutenant-Colonel George Taylor), one to seize and hold the village of Valburg and the other to make contact with the Poles at Driel. This, the 5th Battalion DCLI, bringing with it two DUKW amphibious vehicles and supported by a squadron of tanks and armoured cars of the 4/7th Dragoon Guards, covered the ten-mile stretch to Driel in just over 30 minutes.

The DUKWs were laden with supplies and ammunition, which had to be offloaded before they could attempt a river crossing. In the meantime, attempts were made from 2100 hours onwards – under cover of darkness – to ferry at least some of the Poles across the Neder Rijn with the help of half a dozen two-man rubber reconnaissance boats, this task being supervised by the 9th Field Company, Royal Engineers. It was a laborious and painfully slow task. An early attempt to tow the boats across by line failed, the swiftly-flowing current causing the rope to snap. After that, the craft were paddled across individually, which meant that only one man at a time could be deposited on the far bank. To compound the problems, the Germans soon discovered what was going on and subjected the stretch of river between Driel and Heveadorp to mortar and machine-gun fire.

At about 0200 hours on Saturday morning, 23 September, the two DUKWs were at last made ready for the ferrying operation and taken down to the river. The part they were supposed to have played ended ignominiously when the two-and-a-half-ton vehicles slid down the steep bank and became stuck in a ditch at the bottom. The upshot was that, all told, only 50 Poles were ferried across the river that night, many having been killed or wounded in the attempt. Those who did get across – and the number eventually rose to 250 with successive night crossings – mostly went to reinforce the 1st Battalion The Border Regiment in the south-west sector of the perimeter.

Bill Carr, the signaller who was attached to the 11th Parachute Battalion during the latter's abortive attempt to break through to the bridge, now found himself part of Lonsdale Force at Oosterbeek Church. He gives a graphic description of the deteriorating conditions inside the perimeter.

Typical of the spirit with which the tanks were resisted was a fellow from my section who I saw with his left arm in a sling and a Sten gun tucked under his right arm, firing at the turret of a tank and laughing all the time. Sandy, as he was known, was a German who had been in the Hitler Youth Movement before his family moved to England and took British nationality. I met him later in a PoW camp. Though wounded, he tried to escape several times and had to keep his German birth a secret from the guards.

I was with a small group which tried to ambush a tank by hiding behind farm buildings until it passed us on the road. When it got level, the crew must have spotted us for it turned very sharply and came straight at us. The others had enough sense to jump into the ditches at the side of the farm track, but I went straight for a stone barn with an open door, the tank chasing me. As I was passing through the door, a shell from the tank hit the barn just above the lintel. Inside, I could scarcely breathe because of the dense smoke and the stench of burning cordite, but I escaped without a scratch. Someone who had been in the barn was not so lucky and was injured by the falling debris. I helped to carry him out, thankful that the shell had not been a couple of feet lower.

I teamed up with a glider pilot sergeant and together we searched the battlefield for weapons and ammunition with which to fight the tanks. Eventually, we found a two-inch mortar and some bombs and engaged the advancing tanks with that. It was not much use in fighting tanks, but it may have had some effect on the infantry following them.[136]

So, in countless actions such as this, armed with whatever weapons they could find, the hungry, thirsty, battered but undaunted survivors of the 1st Airborne Division held on; and hold on they would, until they were relieved or overwhelmed. Their tenacity was summed up concisely in the SITREP passed by General Urquhart to General Browning at HQ I Airborne Corps as Friday, 22 September drew to a close.

Perimeter unchanged. Positions heavily shelled and mortared during day. Minor attacks defeated. Some SP guns knocked out. Assistance given by supporting artillery forward Div. Intend ferry some Poles over tonight. Shall attack direction ferry first light tomorrow. Morale high.

CHAPTER 12

D plus Six, 23 September 1944

The morning of Saturday, 23 September saw renewed attempts by the Germans to cut the Allied corridor at Veghel, which the 101st Airborne Division had held so doggedly the day before.

On the western side of the corridor, the *Kampfgruppe* Huber, decimated in Friday's fighting, had fallen back in disarray, but its place was taken by *Oberstleutnant* Friedrich *Freiherr* von der Heydte's *Fallschirmjäger* Regiment 6. Its troops, heavily laden with equipment and exhausted after a lengthy forced march, were assembled east of Boxtel and von der Heydte was ordered to throw them into an assault on the American positions south of Veghel, the aim being to take the Veghel bridge. There was to be no respite for the weary troops; the attack would begin at 0700 hours.

It started, in fact, a little behind schedule, the troops advancing along the Boxtel-Coch railway line. There was little cover, and the Germans soon encountered stiffening resistance from well-camouflaged pockets of US airborne troops, forming a defensive screen well to the west of the threatened village. Before long, *Falschirmjäger* Regiment 6 was taking unacceptable casualties and its commander, realizing that the attack had stalled, ordered his men to dig in.

On the opposite side of the corridor, the *Kampfgruppe* Walther made a number of small-scale forays against the Veghel sector during the morning, but no major assault could be launched until reinforcements arrived. Adding to the Germans' problems was the fact that the weather improved greatly on the morning of the 23rd, permitting much increased Allied fighter-bomber activity. Apart from weather considerations, TacAir operations by the Typhoons of No 83 Group were given a boost when, on 22 September, the four squadrons of No 124 Wing (Nos 137, 181, 182 and 247 Squadrons) flew from their base at Melsbroek, in Belgium, to the newly-constructed advanced airstrip B.78 at Eindhoven, much more conveniently placed for operations over the battle area. Three days later No 143 Wing RCAF (Nos 438, 439 and 440 Squadrons) also moved up to Eindhoven, and by the end of the month No 121 Wing (Nos 174, 175, 184 and 245 Squadrons) were settling in at Volkel, further to the north-east. The move of No 124 Wing meant that the Typhoons could now be called upon to react at very short notice, and on 22–23 September they flew 115 sorties against gun positions, tanks and troop movements in the area south of 's Hertogenbosch and Uden, as well as carrying out patrols over the Waal and Maas bridges.[137] Much of this activity took place in the afternoon, when a cold front at last swept away the low cloud that had persisted over Holland, leaving clearing skies and brisk westerly winds.

In England, the weather was fair, with high, broken cloud and only an occasional shower of rain. The delayed supply and glider missions to I Airborne Corps could now go ahead; as it turned out, they would be the last such missions flown by the RAF from the United Kingdom, although IX Troop Carrier Command continued to operate from its English bases.

Whilst analysing the results of the first three days of resupply operations to Arnhem, two outstanding conclusions had been reached. First, the lack of communication had led to inability to obtain up-to-date tactical information of the ground situation at Arnhem; and second, the fact that the transport aircraft and their fighter escort had not operated from within the same UK weather zone had led to a high casualty rate among the transports on D plus 4.

With these problems in mind, Air Commodore Darvall, the AOC No 46 Group – who had witnessed at first hand the German fighter attacks on his transport aircraft during a visit to HQ I Airborne Corps at Nijmegen on 21 September – conferred with the AOC No 38 Group and then returned to the Continent. After consulting with the commanders of 2nd Tactical Air Force and No 83 Group, followed by talks with Lieutenant-Generals Browning and Horrocks, three points were agreed upon:

1 The production of an anti-flak plan for aircraft and medium artillery, the latter to undertake counter-battery fire against known flak positions.
2 The immediate use of Brussels airfield by Dakotas where direct communication with the forward area and the tactical air force was assured, thus permitting the use of fleeting opportunities and facilitating supply.
3 The opening of Grave airfield for Dakota operations.[138]

So, on 23 September, No 575 Squadron, No 46 Group, was redeployed from Broadwell in Oxfordshire to Brussels, from where its Dakotas would undertake re-supply operations under the control of No 38 Group. For the first time, the transport crews would have the latest information on the tactical situation before sorties, and would also have fighter-bomber close support as required. The shorter flights to Arnhem would enable a faster turn-round on the ground, leading to an increased sortie rate, and last-minute changes to the aircraft loads could be made without undue penalty.

While No 575 Squadron set about its re-deployment, transport missions continued from the United Kingdom. They were to have the benefit of massive air cover. Between Bourg Leopold and Eindhoven, escort was to be provided by fourteen Spitfire squadrons of ADGB and four drawn from 2nd TAF, while three ADGB Mustang squadrons were to fly area patrols between Eindhoven and Volkel. The US Eighth Air Force was to provide thirteen fighter groups, plus one squadron; three groups of P-51s, flying at between 2,500 and 5,000 feet, were to operate between Bourg Leopold and Arnhem, with another group of P-51s and one of P-47s flying top cover. Five groups of P-51s and one of P-38s were to fly perimeter patrols between Maastricht, Kleve and Zwolle, while two groups of P-47s and one squadron equipped with rockets were tasked with flak suppression between Nijmegen and Arnhem.

The RAF fighters put up 193 sorties and met with no opposition, although ground fire accounted for a couple of aircraft. Flak also accounted for most of the sixteen aircraft lost by the Eighth Air Force. The Americans mounted 580 sorties and pilots reported sighting at least 185 enemy fighters, generally operating in groups of about 35 aircraft, and claimed to have destroyed 27 for the loss of six of their own. Three of these were Mustangs of the 339th Fighter Group, which fought three separate engagements against enemy fighters trying to break through to the transports over Holland and claimed the destruction of six Messerschmitt 109s. The pilots of the 353rd Fighter Group, flying top cover south-east of Arnhem, also had a hectic battle against a mixed force of Me 109s and FW 190s, claiming to have destroyed nineteen of them for the loss of three P-51s. This battle took place at 1745 hours, by which time the last transport aircraft had left the zones and were on their way home.

The flak suppression aircraft flew 88 sorties, the pilots reporting the destruction of 18 gun positions with 17 damaged. One P-47 was shot down and 22 more returned to base with varying degrees of flak damage. Particularly good work was done by the 78th Fighter Group, which attacked flak positions in the area of the British re-supply drop and probably reduced the RAF's casualties by a considerable margin.[139]

The glider re-supply mission to the US Airborne Forces, which had stood ready on the airfields of the 50th and 52nd Troop Carrier Wings since 19 September, at last began taking off at 1210 hours on the 23rd. A total of 406 Wacos carried the 325th Glider Infantry Regiment, four batteries of the 80th Airborne Anti-aircraft Battalion, two companies of engineers, the 101st Division's reconnaissance platoon, and a military police platoon – in all, 3,385 troops, 104 jeeps, 59 loaded trailers and 25 artillery pieces.

The American glider missions flew in the centre lane of the southern route; 84 gliders were assigned to the 101st Airborne Division and the rest to the 82nd, the two serials carrying the artillery reinforcements for the 101st flying in the middle of the glider column destined for the 82nd. In the left-hand lane, a 42-aircraft serial carried that part of the Polish Parachute Brigade which had been forced to turn back on D plus 4. The ground situation no longer required the Poles to drop at Driel, and so the plan was to drop them at DZ 'O', in the 82nd Division's airhead. Above this skytrain, at 2,500 feet, flew 123

Stirlings and Dakotas of Nos 38 and 46 Groups RAF, bound for Oosterbeek on their desperately vital resupply mission.

The launching and assembly of the whole massive skytrain was a difficult business, and took about an hour to complete, the glider pilots experiencing some difficulty with slipstream – especially when their tug aircraft climbed above their assigned altitude and ran into the propeller wash from the big four-engined Stirlings. However, the operation was well handled, and was helped by the fact that intercom sets worked better than ever before, although 20 per cent still failed to function properly.

One glider broke loose over England, two combinations turned back with technical trouble, and a glider ditched successfully in the Channel; otherwise the missions proceeded smoothly under broken cloud with a visibility of about five miles. For some reason, the lead serial turned north at Gheel rather than at Bourg Leopold, which placed it outside the Allied salient; five gliders were damaged by small-arms fire and had to be released.

It was at Veghel, though, that the skytrain encountered serious trouble. Here, although the enemy had been cleared from the main road, he was massed in strength on both flanks, and the serials had to run the gauntlet of five miles of intense flak – much of it from 107 *Panzer* Brigade's mobile batteries – and automatic weapons fire. Nine aircraft were shot down on this murderous stretch, and 96 more damaged. The first serial suffered badly, three C-47s being destroyed and several gliders being shot loose or having to be cut loose. When this happened to the two leading gliders of the 29th TCS, several behind followed suit, with the result that 21 Wacos came down prematurely between Veghel and Grave. All their occupants and cargo, luckily, were recovered. A similar situation occurred in the fourth serial, when eighteen gliders came down within six miles of Veghel; in this case, six came down in hostile territory and all aboard were lost.

The last three serials were alerted to the danger by radio, and made the necessary course corrections to take them clear of the worst of the flak. These serials lost only one aircraft, two gliders being released prematurely near Veghel. The first serial reached LZ 'O' at 1603 hours and released its gliders from altitudes of between 900 and 2,500 feet. Although some of the serials arrived out of sequence, there was no serious confusion, and by 1717 hours 210

gliders had landed on an oval a mile across and a mile and a half long north-west of Overasselt, a further 100 gliders coming down on an area of similar size on the river bank opposite Grave. Of the rest, all but one were on or close to the zone.

Although LZ 'O' was well clear of enemy interference, landing on it proved difficult because much of it consisted of small fields bounded by fences, hedges and drainage ditches. Also, large numbers of livestock were grazing in the fields. Eight gliders were destroyed through hitting obstacles and 102 were damaged, although the damage toll would certainly have been higher had it not been for the effective use of arrester chutes. Out of 24 guns, 82 jeeps and 47 trailers brought in, only one jeep was unusable, and there were only ten serious casualties among the 2,900 troops landed.

By 1800 hours, the 325th Glider Infantry Regiment, commanded by Colonel Charles Billingslea, had assembled 75 per cent of its effectives and was moving off to the Groesbeek Heights to take up defensive positions in the eastern flank of the 82nd Airborne Division.

Meanwhile, the glider mission to the 101st Airborne Division had taken off from the bases of the 436th and 438th Troop Carrier Groups, the Wacos carrying 395 troops and 100 tons of supplies and equipment, including fifteen guns, thirteen trailers and 23 jeeps. Four gliders aborted over England – one when a soldier pulled the release handle – and another was released over Belgium, but the remaining combinations, flying between Serials 5 and 6 of the mission to the 82nd Airborne, had an uneventful flight to LZ 'W' east of Best. Two gliders crash-landed, killing three soldiers and injuring nine, but the others landed without incident.

The glider mission to the 101st Airborne Division landed between 1632 and 1636 hours. An hour and a half earlier, the Division's 501st Parachute Infantry Regiment had launched a counter-attack towards Uden, meeting only feeble resistance. At 1800 hours it made contact with the 32nd Guards Brigade, which had been diverted down the highway from Grave to the relief of Uden, where the 2nd Battalion of the 501st PIR had been holding on with great determination. The road to Nijmegen was once more open and the convoys that had been piling up to the south once more began to roll. They had been delayed now for 24 hours, and with them they carried the assault craft in which the relieving troops of XXX Corps were to have forced a crossing of the Neder Rijn.

At 1643 hours, 41 C-47s of the 315th Troop Carrier Group, carrying 560 troops and 28 tons of supplies and equipment, arrived over LZ 'O' after a completely uneventful flight from England. All but twelve troops and virtually all the supply packs were successfully dropped on the zone, or very close to it. The Polish paratroops were quickly assembled and moved off to the Groesbeek area to form a reserve for the 82nd Airborne Division.

Early in the morning of 23 September, the Germans launched heavy attacks at all points of the Oosterbeek perimeter, intent on reducing one British strongpoint after another. The infantry assaults were supported by tanks and SP guns, as the War Diary of the 21st Independent Parachute Company records:

0300 hours – 3 Platoon moved up and took up the positions occupied by the 10th Battalion who were withdrawn into reserve.[140] This position is very isolated and I objected to occupying it. The Brigadier, however, insisted as it protects the CCS (Casualty Clearing Station) . . . 0730 hours. 3 platoon position is heavily attacked with 1 Mk IV tank and two SP guns supporting infantry.

Against opposition such as this, the airborne troops fought with suicidal gallantry.

1 Platoon received the overflow of this attack. Sergeant Jerry Thompson, with the remains of his section, rushed wild-eyed into No 1 Section's position, without helmet and looking for Germans. He had been blasted out of his house by SP guns on the main road. The house had literally been brought down about their ears. Before leaving, Jerry had hurled a Gammon bomb of his own concoction into a mob of Germans, who in arrogant confidence had entered his garden. Jerry had killed a lot of Germans and now, quite berserk, was looking for more. He was killed soon after and others of his section were badly wounded in 1 Platoon's sector.[141]

During the morning, the Germans began using flame-throwing tanks and phosphorus bombs. The 1st Battalion The Border Regiment was subjected to a particularly heavy attack; it was checked by artillery fire from south of the river, but not before a number of positions had been infiltrated. Mortaring continued to be the main hazard; the weight of fire increased as the enemy moved up more six-barrelled 15 cm *Nebelwerfer* to the area, so that the defences were literally saturated. Whether one of the many projectiles impacted on a slit trench or not became purely a matter of chance, and with SP guns and tanks roaming the streets and systematically pounding the houses to rubble, slit trenches now provided the most effective cover.

Apart from the enemy armour's activities, the infiltration of enemy snipers and medium machine guns greatly restricted movement within the perimeter, while the blocking of roads and tracks by fallen trees and damaged vehicles made the use of the few surviving vehicles virtually impossible. In an attempt to lower the moraleß of the defenders, the Germans made increasing use of psychological warfare; a tank equipped with a loudspeaker and broadcasting equipment would trundle up to the perimeter defences.

. . . They'd start out with this tune, 'If you go down to the woods today. . .' Then a voice would tell us that we had fought well, but that the 2nd Army couldn't reach us, so we were to walk out of the trenches with our hands up, and come forward to surrender. They always said that we'd be well treated.[142]

These exhortations were answered, in the fashion of the British soldier, with shouts of derision laced with the baser forms of Anglo-Saxon, but there is little doubt that they had a wearing effect on the nerves.

Just after 1600 hours, the last RAF supply mission flown from British airfields to the 1st Airborne Division approached the Oosterbeek perimeter, which by now had contracted to about 1,000 yards in diameter and which was ringed with enemy guns. The mission comprised 73 Stirlings and 50 Dakotas; two aircraft aborted and six were shot down in the target area. The drop point proved extremely hard to locate; the *Eureka* beacon was not working because its batteries had given out, and the Germans had captured the Pathfinders' reserve stock. Enemy fire made it impossible for parties to lay out new marker signals, and although Very lights were fired very few were sighted by the transport crews. Again, the situation was confused when the Germans fired similar signals. It will never be known with certainty what percentage of the supplies was recovered, but it was probably less than ten per cent, even assuming that some packages were picked up by isolated groups of defenders and their contents distributed on the spot.

While these operations were in progress, the Guards Armoured Division was fighting hard to secure the Nijmegen bridgehead and the vital corridor. Brigadier Hubert Essame's 214th Brigade had now swung east to join the battle for Elst, with the Duke of Cornwall's Light Infantry fighting in the outskirts, and by the end of the day the 130th Infantry Brigade, comprising the 7th Hampshires and the 4th and 5th Dorsets, had continued the flanking move to join up with the Polish Parachute Brigade at Driel.

At 2015 hours, General Urquhart once more sent a signal to HQ I Airborne Corps.

Many attacks during day by small parties inf, SP guns and tanks including flamethrowers. Each attack accompanied by very heavy mortaring and shelling within Div perimeter. After many alarms and excursions the latter remains substantially unchanged, although very thinly held. Physical contact not yet made with those on south bank of river. Resup (re-supply) a flop, small quantities of amn only gathered in. Still no food and all ranks extremely dirty owing to shortage of water. Morale still adequate, but continued heavy mortaring and shelling is having obvious effects. We shall hold but at the same time hope for a brighter 24 hours ahead.

At 2020 hours, HQ Second Army gave permission to withdraw the 1st Airborne Division from Arnhem if conditions permitted.[146]

NO 38 GROUP INTELLIGENCE SUMMARY FOR D+6

38 GP OPERATED 73 A/C, 64 REACHING DZ AND DROPPING 1540 CONTAINERS, 235 PANNIERS AND 50 JEEP TYRES. RESULTS OF TWO A/C UNKNOWN BUT PHONE REPORT FROM ONE LANDED AT MANSTON WITH ENGINE U/S CLAIMS TO HAVE DROPPED ON DZ.

INCREASING NUMBER OF AIRCREW FINDING THEIR WAY BACK FROM HOLLAND, TO DATE TEN COMPLETE OR ALMOST COMPLETE CREWS.

NUMBER OF A/C SEEN IN DISTRESS IN AREAS WHERE FLAK WAS ENCOUNTERED. CAPTAINS STATE HAVING SEEN: STIRLING (INTACT) ON GROUND 3 MILES S OF GRAVE. STIRLING SEEN TO MAKE GOOD CRASH LANDING 3 MLS W OF VALKENSWAARD WITH S/1 ENGINE ON FIRE, S/B WING FELL OFF. DZ AREA 4 STIRLINGS SEEN TO CRASH IN FLAMES. 2 SEEN TO BALE OUT OF ONE A/C. STIRLING SEEN ON GROUND W OF NIJMEGEN WITH CREW STANDING ROUND. SW OF ARNHEIM E7W [143] SEEN ON FIRE AND CRASHING. STIRLING WITH ENGINE ON FIRE SEEN TO GO INTO WOOD, THEN FLAMES SEEN FROM WOOD. STIRLING SEEN TO BELLY-LAND W OF DZ. A/C V8G [144] CRASHED SOUTH OF RIVER AND BURST INTO FLAMES. DAKOTA IN RIVER BEFORE DZ, ONLY TAIL SHOWING ABOVE WATER. STIRLING ON GROUND W OF NIJMEGEN, CREW SEEN WAVING. DAKOTA BURNING IN WOODS S. OF EINDHOVEN.[145]

MOST CREWS DESCRIBE TRIP AS SATISFACTORY DESPITE VERY HOT RECEPTION AT DZ. FIGHTER COVER RECEIVES PRAISE VARYING FROM OK TO EXCELLENT. A/C ARE REPORTED AS DROPPING AT 2000–2500 FT CAUSING OTHERS CONSIDERABLE INCONVENIENCE, ENDANGERING LOW FLYING A/C AND RESTRICTING MOVEMENT TO AVOID FLAK.

CHAPTER 13

D plus Seven to D plus Nine, 24–26 September 1944

At dawn on 24 September, squalls of rain driven by winds of up to 30 mph lashed the Continent and the British Isles, and in England the RAF and USAAF transport aircraft stood immobile on their bases under an overcast that lowered to 300 feet. Only No 575 Squadron at Brussels was able to operate, and in the afternoon this unit despatched 21 Dakotas on resupply missions, four to Oosterbeek and seventeen to the US 82nd Airborne Division. The transport sorties were escorted by 36 Spitfires drawn from 2nd TAF squadrons based in Belgium.

The four Dakotas bound for Oosterbeek reached the target area, but the weather was so bad that two did not drop and the other two dropped more or less at random, no signals being sighted at the DZ. All four aircraft were damaged by flak but returned to base safely. Of the aircraft tasked for the 82nd Airborne Division, fifteen made successful drops and the other two unloaded after landing on the newly-acquired airstrip at Grave.

At about 0900 hours on the 24th, the Germans made a further determined attempt to cut the Allied corridor in the 101st Airborne Division's sector, the objective being to overrun the thinly-stretched defences in the Eerde area and capture the road and rail bridges at Veghel. The attack, which developed from the west was spearheaded by *Oberstleutnant* von der Heydte's *Fallschirmjäger* Regiment 6, supported by various scratch units and some *Jagdpanther* tank destroyers, and enjoyed some initial success. An outpost line set up by the 1st Battalion of the 501st Parachute Infantry Regiment in the sand dunes outside Eerde was overrun, and the western suburbs of the town came under mortar fire. Nine Sherman tanks of the 44th Royal Tank Regiment were called up to assist the American infantry and were engaged by the *Jagdpanther*; three Shermans were knocked out within minutes and the remainder were forced to stay outside the range of the tank destroyers' 88 mm guns. The German infantry assault was eventually halted outside Eerde, but it took all three battalions of the 501st PIR and supporting artillery to contain it. Even so, the *Jagdpanther* succeeded in cutting the highway by their gunfire, creating havoc among the soft-skinned vehicles and their escorting armour and bringing the northward advance of the Allied supply convoys to a standstill.

While this action was in progress, a *Fallschirmjäger* battalion of 59th Infantry Division, commanded by *Major* Hans Jungwirth, advanced down a secondary road towards the hamlet of Koevering, between Veghel and St Oedenrode. This sector had been extensively reconnoitred and the weak spots in the American defences were well known, so Jungwirth was able to avoid all contact with the enemy during his approach march. As they came within sight of the highway, the Germans found Allied transport parked bumper to bumper, unable to progress because of the fighting at Eerde. Moving stealthily into position at about 1900 hours, Jungwirth's men opened up with heavy machine-guns, mortars and *Panzerfaust*, raking the stationary columns to deadly effect. Two companies of the 502nd Parachute Infantry Regiment were rushed to the defence of Koevering and managed to keep the German infantry out of the hamlet, but about 50 British vehicles lay wrecked and burning on the highway by the early hours of the next morning.

Throughout 25 September, the Allies made a series of vigorous counter-attacks. More companies of the 502nd PIR came up from St Oedenrode; the 506th PIR counter-attacked from the north-east, and the British 50th (Northumbrian) Division entered the fray with the support of some M10 tank destroyers. A battery of the US 907th Glider Field Artillery Battalion engaged the enemy positions over open sights. None of these efforts succeeded in dislodging Jungwirth's battalion, and there was little in the way of direct tactical air support, but even had this been available the Allied and German positions were so closely interlocked that ground-attack missions would have been virtually impossible to carry out.

In any case, the Allied fighter-bombers were engaged elsewhere. In view of the powerful enemy reinforcements being rushed into the area between Eindhoven and Arnhem, 2nd Tactical Air Force had been instructed to make pre-arranged attacks on the elaborate railway system in southern Holland and the network of lines on the German frontier, particularly around Goch and Kleve. These rail cuts by fighter-bombers, begun on 24 September, were certain to be repaired quickly, but it was thought that at least they might delay the arrival of enemy reinforcements in the threatened area. For the next week or so this type of mission was the principal contribution of 2nd TAF in support of the Army.[147]

The Jungwirth Battalion held tenaciously on to its positions until the night of 25–26 September, when it was forced to disengage under heavy pressure. Above all, Jungwirth had needed reinforcements,

Typhoon target: a castle in Goch, turned into an enemy headquarters, after a rocket attack by 2 TAF Typhoons.

but none were forthcoming. The Germans had shot their bolt. Von der Heydte's *Fallschirmjäger* Regiment 6 had exhausted itself in the attack towards Veghel and could do nothing to help, while reserves – composed mainly of elderly and war-weary troops – marching to the combat area from locations in north-west Holland had no hope of arriving in time to have any impact on the situation. Consequently, General Reinhard, commanding

The town of Kleve (Cleves) seen after a devastating bombing attack by 2 TAF operating in support of the northward drive by 21st Army Group.

LXXXVIII Corps, ordered the troops investing the highway to conduct a fighting retreat to the north-west under cover of darkness.

Jungwirth complied, but not before his men had extensively mined the highway at Koevering. This action, together with the considerable time it took to clear away the wreckage of Allied vehicles, meant that the main road was not open to traffic until 1400 hours on 26 September, some 40 hours after the highway had been blocked.

During those 40 hours, the resistance of the 1st Airborne Division in the Oosterbeek perimeter was slowly strangled to death.

One of the more serious consequences of the German attacks on the highway was that the majority of the assault craft available to XXX Corps for the projected crossing of the Neder Rijn were caught up in the blockage. The formation that succeeded in reaching the Poles at Driel, 130 Brigade, had brought with it enough boats to ferry across a single battalion, and no more. The fact alone made nonsense of the assignment ordered for the night of 23/24 September by Lieutenant-General Horrocks, XXX Corps Commander, which was threefold. The Oosterbeek pocket must be supplied; the 1st Polish Parachute Brigade must be ferried over the river to join the perimeter defences; and the perimeter must be extended westwards by attacking with two battalions of the 43rd Division which also had to be ferried across.

When darkness fell, sixteen assault boats were made ready for the initial ferrying operation, which involved some 250 Polish paratroopers. The ferrying operation was undertaken by 204 Field Company, Royal Engineers, and the 5th Dorsets, and was supported by every weapon 130 Brigade could bring to bear on the opposite bank. It failed to stop the enemy from laying down withering small-arms and mortar fire on the boats as they fought against the fast-flowing current. Several were sunk and the others left on the north bank, where they were shot to pieces the next morning. Altogether about 150 Poles got across the river and were assigned to Brigadier Hicks' part of the perimeter, where they fought valiantly until the end.

The end itself was heralded in the early morning of Sunday, 24 September, with the arrival at Arnhem of 45 60-ton Tiger II tanks of *Schwere Abteilung* (Heavy Battalion) 506. Two companies of these monsters, 30 tanks in all, were despatched to the aid of 10 SS at Elst; the remaining fifteen, commanded by *Leutnant* Hummel, were assigned to 9 SS at Oosterbeek.

In the fighting so far, the tanks and SP guns available to 9 SS had taken a considerable beating. *Panzer* Company 224 had lost all eight of its converted Renault tanks; six tanks had been destroyed and one (a Tiger) damaged in the fighting around Arnhem bridge; and other losses included five Mk IIIs, four *Sturmgeschütz* III SP guns, and two Panthers. The majority of these losses, in the early days, were caused by well-sited and camouflaged British anti-tank guns, picking off enemy armour that was committed to the battle piecemeal and in an unco-ordinated manner. The Germans learned quickly, however, and from 21 September the tanks operated in conjunction with special street-fighting infantry teams, some of which had experienced this type of action in Russia.

Leutnant Hummel's fifteen Tigers went into action at Oosterbeek at first light on 24 September; their 88 mm guns began the systematic destruction of British strongpoints, which were then assaulted by infantry teams spearheaded by pioneer sections equipped with flame-throwers. These terrible weapons proved to be a decisive factor in dislodging the paratroops from their positions; almost all the men had witnessed the horrifying consequences of their use, and few were prepared to stand and face them. Staff Sergeant Walter Langham of the Glider Pilot Regiment recalls that he

. . . looked up and suddenly there was a bloody great tank coming towards me. I managed to get out of the slit trench without touching the sides and got behind a tree just as it let go with the flame-thrower, which engulfed all the trench and all the gear that was lying about. I was very fortunate I wasn't there when that happened.

Yet it was the continual mortar bombardment that had the most telling psychological effect.

Those mortars were horrible things, (says Langham). During our time in the woods you would hear them being fired, then hear nothing else until a tree close to you disappeared when the round struck. They were very, very frightening.[148]

It was the mortars that caused most of the British casualties, which by this time were fearful. One victim, on that morning of 24 September, was Brigadier 'Shan' Hackett, who was in the vicinity of

Sgt Walter Langham of the Glider Pilot Regiment, who survived Arnhem to take part in the Rhine crossing of March 1945.

Walter Langham pictured nearly half a century on, with the Arnhem Bridge in the background.

what remained of his Brigade HQ – now no more than 300 yards from Divisional HQ – when the round struck. Hackett sank to his knees, feeling sick, bewildered and unhappy, but recovered sufficiently to walk back to the Divisional Aid Post at the Hartenstein Hotel. Before seeking attention himself, he organized a stretcher party to bring in a trooper of the Airborne Reconnaissance Squadron who had been acting as his runner; the man's leg had been broken in the mortar attack, and he was sheltering in a slit trench.

Brigadier Hackett was aware that he had been hit in the thigh, but it was not until he was taken by jeep to the St Elisabeth Hospital and subjected to a more thorough medical examination that doctors discovered a second wound: a fragment of shrapnel about two inches square had penetrated his lower intestine. His wound was operated on by that brilliant surgeon, Captain Lipmann Kessel, a South African; Hackett's life hung in the balance for several days, but Kessel's skill – coupled with the British officer's own fortitude and willpower – pulled him through, and he eventually made a full recovery. He was later hidden by Dutch civilians, and in due course made his escape to Allied territory.[149]

The progressive reduction of 1 Airborne Division's perimeter could now be witnessed at first hand by Lieutenant-General Horrocks and the officer commanding the 43rd (Wessex) Division, Major-General Ivor Thomas, from an observation post in the church tower at Driel. It was clear that the most important strategic point, the high ground at

Westerbouwing, was in German hands; the Airborne Division's only link with the Neder Rijn was a flat oblong of ground extending for several hundred yards from the river into the higher, wooded ground at its northern end. It was clear, too, that an enemy east-west pincer movement along the banks of the Neder Rijn was bound, sooner or later, to cut off the Division's access to the river, and therefore its only means of escape.

On the morning of Sunday, 24 September, General Horrocks called a conference of his senior XXX Corps commanders; General Sosabowski, commanding the Polish Parachute Brigade, was also present. The general feeling at the meeting was that the situation on the other side of the Neder Rijn was now so critical, and the strip of land held by 1st Airborne Division now so narrow, that the perimeter would have to be reinforced before the division could be evacuated. At this point, some hope still appears to have been entertained that XXX Corps might yet succeed not only in relieving 1st Airborne Division, but also in establishing a permanent bridgehead across the Neder Rijn, but by mid-afternoon, with the passage of Allied support convoys blocked by the enemy, such hope had vanished. At this time Horrocks was in St Oedenrode, where he had gone after the morning meeting at Driel to confer with General Dempsey, commanding the British Second Army; the two agreed that a final attempt to establish an Allied bridgehead north of the Neder Rijn would be made on the night of 25/26 September, by which time it was expected that support units would have reached the area. The futility of this plan became vividly apparent to Horrocks when, after leaving St Oedenrode at 1630 hours, he almost fell foul of the German attacks on the highway. Driving northwards through Veghel, Horrocks escaped by the narrowest of margins; but behind him the road was blocked, and it was to remain blocked for the better part of two days.

Meanwhile, in the shrinking perimeter at Oosterbeek, the men of the 1st Airborne Division fought on. They were bloodied and bone-weary; most did not even know what day it was, such was their exhaustion. But their spirit was unquenchable, and so was that of the Dutch people who had clung so tenaciously to the ruins of their homes where the men of the Airborne fought; although some could endure no more.

The experience of Trooper Ken Hope of the Airborne Reconnaissance Squadron was typical of many.

Just before dawn (on 24 September) the occupants of the house emerged, a pathetic little group barely discernible in the darkness – husband, wife, daughter about twelve years, and son about nine years. They were carrying whatever they felt should be salvaged in bundles of blankets or sheets. Even the darkness could not conceal the tension one sensed in the movements of the father, mother and daughter. The latter's face was chalk white. But the boy, wearing a Scout or Cub uniform, obviously regarded the sortie as something of an adventure as he cheerily bade us: 'Good morning! Long live General Montgomery.' The little family was swallowed up in the darkness, abandoning their home, resigned to what must happen when daylight revealed out positions.[150]

Dawn, for Hope and his comrades, brought the rattle of tank tracks. There was faint hopes, at first, that the tanks might be the Shermans of XXX Corps, but these were quickly dispelled.

As the light became stronger, shapes gained clearer definition, and snipers began firing into our position with sustained concentration. Soon bullets were thudding with monotonous regularity into the wall near the rear door of the house. I called out to Lieutenant Galbraith and Sergeant Venes to have a care as they emerged from the Troop HQ post. Ron and I had piled a considerable amount of sandy sub-soil behind our trench, and an old, dilapidated table lay particularly buried in the spoil. The table was struck several times and little cascades of disturbed earth fell into the collar of my camouflaged jumping smock. Several times Ron and I peered around the rear mound to try to spot our persistent antagonists. We failed to locate the snipers, for they could have been concealed in any of the nearby buildings, or heavily camouflaged amongst the trees. Bullets sang uncomfortably close, bare inches above our heads, and I hunched lower into the trench . . .

A shattering and violent explosion seemed to shake the house to its foundations. A great belching orange-tinted cloud of dust vomited from the rear door. Stan Southerby, who had been standing just inside the rear doorway at that moment, sank to the ground almost languorously. 'Poor Stan's had it,' Ron exclaimed. Then, incredibly, Stan got to his feet again, rather dazedly, like a boxer pushing himself off the canvas, and reeled and swayed in the doorway. In the next instant Jock Fraser came hurtling towards us from the interior of the house. 'The bloody wall's down!' he cried. He had sustained a face wound and blood was dripping on to my helmet and shoulders. His right eyeball appeared to be dislodged from its socket and was hanging on the cheekbone.[151]

He was trying to take refuge in the restricted space of our slit trench. I had already got one leg hoisted on the lip of the trench for a rapid exit. It was a moment of extreme panic. I remember gazing around wildly, the Bren muzzle describing the frenetic 180-degree arc, and wondering from which direction opponents in field grey would suddenly appear. Apparently some *Panzergrenadiers* had infiltrated our right flank and blasted the side wall with a *Panzerfaust*. The concussion was quite catastrophic.

'Where the bloody hell do you think you are all going? Now just bloody well settle down!' There was no mistaking the Scots accent of Lieutenant Galbraith. The command was compelling, imperious, demanding instant obedience. The effect was instantaneous, a text-book exercise in disciplined response to sustained military training. Control was immediately restored, the panic instantly dissipated; everyone was alert, ready to react. It was a lesson I have often recalled. All those weeks and months of interminable parade-ground drills, kit inspections, battle drill and field-firing exercises had served their purpose.[152]

That night, 24/25 September, a very gallant attempt was made to ferry 250 men of the 4th Battalion The Dorsetshire Regiment across the Neder Rijn. In order to facilitate the crossing, General Urquhart ordered a series of attacks from within the perimeter against enemy positions at the river. With the resources available, this effort was doomed to failure, as Bill Carr of the 11th Parachute Battalion describes:

HQ Company was now reduced to a handful of men. My two pals volunteered to go with them, and with some reluctance I joined them. We formed a group of twelve with a lieutenant in charge.

We met with heavy opposition when past our lines and four of the group were killed, including one of my pals who was shot in the head. During the skirmish, I jumped into a fox-hole. In it was the body of one of our snipers who had also been shot through the head. I knew I was in terrible trouble as the trench was obviously covered and bullets were soon whistling above my head. However, I managed to get out and rejoin the patrol. We were forced to withdraw to the (Oosterbeek-Laag) church.

After about twenty minutes, we were ordered to make a further attempt. Now reduced to eight men, we made our way through our lines by a different route. At the forward trenches, there was a heated altercation between our Lieutenant and another officer who brandished his revolver at us and told us that the German strength in that area was too strong to penetrate and that no-one was to pass through his lines. Our lieutenant was determined to carry out his orders and we pressed on.

On reaching a small copse, he spread his map on the ground and began briefing us on the attack. Just then there was a heavy mortar bombardment of the wood which was, of course, a perfect target for the German mortar crews, who kept up a relentless attack. I was lying shoulder to shoulder with Tom, my other pal from our Signal section. A mortar bomb landed on the other side of him and he had terrible injuries all down his right side. His body shielded me from the effects of the explosion. I turned him over and gave him a morphine injection. He was quite calm but was convinced that his leg had been blown off, since he could not feel it. He had been married shortly before we left and said he did not want to go back a cripple. I tried to reassure him and applied two field dressings where the bleeding was most severe.

I tried to apply a split to his leg with a branch from a tree. Just then, I was hit in the left side by a piece of shrapnel. It was a very small wound but bled freely. All the patrol were now either dead or severely wounded. The lieutenant, who was very badly wounded himself, ordered me to get back to a dressing station and get stretcher bearers. I was glad of the opportunity to get out of the wood as bombs were still falling thick and fast . . . [153]

The planned crossing of the Neder Rijn by the 4th Dorsets was scheduled for 2200 hours on 24 September; if all went well it would bring them to the northern end of the Driel ferry, a little to the west of the perimeter. The Dorsets' right flank was to be protected by elements of the Polish Parachute Brigade, which were also to be ferried across.

Led by their commanding officer, Lieutenant-Colonel G. Tilley, the Dorsets marched to their assembly area along a muddy, slippery road in a miserably cold and wet evening, expecting to find their assault craft already in position there. But there were no boats. Two truck loads had taken a wrong turning and driven into the enemy lines at Elst, and two more had come to grief when they skidded off muddy roads. One truck load arrived at the Poles' assembly area, but the boats were without oars. The Polish crossing was therefore postponed and their boats assigned to the Dorsets, who carried them for 600 yards through an orchard down to the river bank, all the while under mortar and machine-gun fire from across the river. By the time they had reached their positions, and scraped together some means of paddling the craft, it was 0100 hours; an undesirable time to set out, as the Neder Rijn's current always increased in strength after midnight.

Even before the boats were launched, one was destroyed by enemy mortar bombs and others holed by splinters. Still others were swept away by the current. Those that remained more or less on course headed for the glare of burning buildings that lit up the high ground at Westerbouwing. Eventually, elements of four rifle companies reached the northern bank, most of them to be pinned down by close-quarter fighting as soon as they landed; many soldiers, raked by machine-gun fire, lost their lives in the black, swirling water.

Those that did get across, in small parties of no more than platoon strength, fought their way desperately up the 60-degree slope of Wester-bouwing. Lieutenant-Colonel Tilley was last seen leading a platoon along the lower slopes of the hill, urging his men to attack with the bayonet; nothing more was heard of him. By daylight, some of the few dozen men who had survived the river crossing and subsequent enemy action had fought their way up through the woods towards a burning factory on the left flank. On the right, another small party had succeeded in entering the perimeter and in making contact with HQ 1st Airborne Division. Two members of this party were officers, Major J.D. Grafton and Lieutenant D.L. Eccles, who had been briefed to deliver important verbal and written messages to Major-General Urquhart.

The messages concerned the impending evacuation of the 1st Airborne Division. Already, on 24 September, Urquhart had sent the following signal to HQ 21st Army Group:

Must warn you unless physical contact is made with us early 25 September consider it unlikely we can hold out long enough. All ranks now exhausted. Lack of rations, water, ammunition, and weapons with high officer casualty rate . . . Even slight enemy offensive action may cause complete disintegration. If this happens all will be ordered to break towards bridgehead if anything rather than surrender. Any movement at present in face of enemy is not possible. Have attempted our best and will do so as long as possible.[154]

Some uncertainty exists over the actual timing of the final decision to evacuate the Airborne Division. It appears to have been made at HQ I Airborne Corps at Nijmegen sometime around midnight – not in time, unfortunately, to call off the suicidal river crossing by the 4th Dorsets. The timing is really immaterial. The fact is that in the early hours of 25 September, Lieutenant-Colonel Myers, who had remained on the south bank since 22 September to advise possible reinforcements about river crossing procedures, came back across the river and made his way to Urquhart's headquarters bearing a letter from the Commander, 43rd Infantry Division. The letter explained that it was no longer the intention of Second Army to form a bridgehead over the Rhine near Arnhem, and also gave the plan for the

withdrawal of the Airborne Division south of the river on whatever date should be agreed. It did not take Urquhart long to make up his mind. At 0808 hours on Monday, 25 September, he sent a wireless signal to Major-General Thomas informing him that the evacuation must take place on the night of 25/26th. It was to be code-named Operation *Berlin*.

Such was the confusion prevailing in the perimeter that the defence commanders appear to have had no foreknowledge that a relief force from 43rd Division was to attempt a crossing on the night of 24/25 September. As the War Diary of 1st Air Landing Brigade records,

25 September. 04.45 Liaison officer arrived to find out whether we had made contact with follow-up troops, who were said to have crossed the river with supplies and ammunition. No contact had been made and it subsequently transpired that the crossing had taken place about 1,000 yards to the west in the Heveadorp area (opposite ground held by the Germans).

In fact, an attempt had been made to ferry supplies and ammunition across the Neder Rijn at about 0330 hours using six DUKWs; because of the steep embankment only three were launched, and these became hopelessly stuck in the mud on the far side. They were destroyed by enemy action after first light.

Monday, 25 September, saw further operations by the USAAF and RAF transport squadrons. For once, weather conditions over England were favourable, although the cloud base over the Channel and the Low Countries was between 1,000 and 1,500 feet. The English weather began to deteriorate in the afternoon, but conditions held out for long enough to enable a serial of 34 C-47s drawn from the 434th, 435th and 436th Troop Carrier Groups to take-off from Ramsbury, Wiltshire, with 49 tons of howitzer ammunition for the 101st Airborne Division. The aircraft flew up the highway from Hechtel and made a good drop on DZ 'W' at 1600 hours; all the C-47s returned safely, except for one which was damaged in a heavy landing.

From Brussels, No 575 Squadron despatched seven Dakotas to Oosterbeek, also by the southern route, carrying medical supplies and food. One aircraft was shot down by flak; the other six made their drop at SDP 682768, Heveadorp, but none of the bundles were recovered by 1st Airborne. Three more Dakotas sustained flak damage. Both resupply missions were protected by 60 Spitfires and 36 Mustangs of ADGB, which encountered about 50 enemy fighters near Arnhem and 40 near Hengelo and claimed four destroyed for the loss of two Mustangs.

As the survivors of the 1st Airborne Division prepared to evacuate during 25 September, 2nd Tactical Air Force diverted some of its effort away from railway interdiction to try to relieve the pressure on the dwindling Oosterbeek perimeter. Attacks on enemy gun positions were made by seven Typhoons, 54 Mitchells and 24 Bostons. The weight of the bombing attacks fell on the western suburbs of Arnhem, the idea being to block the roads with rubble and so prevent the enemy from launching a major assault on the perimeter from that direction while the evacuation was in progress. The only real effect of this air operation was to cause further massive damage to the buildings of Arnhem and inflict further suffering on its luckless inhabitants.

The plan for the evacuation of 1st Airborne Division was based on those furthest from the river withdrawing first. Two routes were selected and were to be marked as far as possible; these were judged to be the most favourable, although it was not expected that they would be free from enemy interference. Units were to move to the river in parties of fourteen, the approximate size of a boat load. Boots were muffled; if possible, troops were to avoid contact with the enemy during the withdrawal. On arrival at the river, they were to lie down in the mud and await their turn for a boat. A comprehensive artillery programme to cover the whole withdrawal was arranged with XXX Corps, involving the firing of every available weapon from medium machine-guns upwards. The operation was to begin at 2200 hours.

Feldmarschall Model's orders for 25 September insisted on the rapid liquidation of the remaining British forces in the *Hexenkessel*, with simultaneous attacks from east and west by armour and infantry fighting groups, but this task was far from easy to fulfil. Many of the German troops were as exhausted as the defenders, and stunned by the continued ferocity shown by the remaining pockets of resistance. Although a number of serious penetrations were made – at one point, for example, a considerable force of enemy penetrated between the British artillery position at Oosterbeek–Laag

and Divisional HQ, cutting the Divisional area in two – the German troops generally approached their task with great caution, and understandably so, for they had sustained appalling casualties. To avoid further losses as far as possible, Model agreed that the British forces in the dwindling perimeter be reduced by heavy artillery fire, and in the afternoon 110 artillery pieces, aided by the guns of tanks, began to pour a rain of high explosive on to the British positions.

Some of the heavier German armour/infantry attacks were halted by extremely accurate fire by XXX Corps' artillery; there were occasions when British officers had to call down shoots on top of their own positions. It is no exaggeration to claim that the fine work of the artillery almost certainly saved the Airborne from complete annihilation during these final, crucial hours.

By nightfall on 25 September, British infantry and armour of the 43rd Division at last drove the enemy out of Elst, securing the highway between Arnhem and Nijmegen. The 5th Duke of Cornwall's Light Infantry played a prominent part in these operations, which opened the way for the exfiltration of the 1st Airborne southwards through the Betuwe.

At this time, the position inside the perimeter was critical. German forces, advancing from east and west, were only half a mile apart on the line of the river, and in many places snipers and medium machine-guns were in place inside the British lines; most units were to some extent encircled and cut off from their neighbours.

At 2100 hours the British artillery south of the river opened fire, and at 2145 hours the first units to withdraw crossed the start line, which was the road running east-west alongside the Oosterbeek–Laag Church. At this time the enemy was laying down heavy mortar and shellfire, but this slackened at about 2200 hours. Following tapes set out by men of the Glider Pilot Regiment, the small parties of men set off for the river, their movements concealed by darkness, pouring rain and wind. It was a slow, stop-start process, and there were occasional skirmishes with the enemy, but it soon became clear that the Germans were unaware of what was taking place.

The wounded at Divisional Headquarters were left under the care of Lieutenant Randall, RAMC. All doctors and chaplains still alive remained at the

The end at Oosterbeek: exhausted and bloody, men of the 1st Airborne Division march away into captivity.

Dressing Stations and Regimental Aid Posts. For these men of great courage and fortitude, there was now only the prospect of captivity.

The ferrying operation was conducted by 130 Brigade and by two field companies of Canadian engineers. Initially, available water transport comprised fourteen storm boats with outboard motors and some canvas assault craft; most of the latter sank during the operation.

The wait on the bank seemed interminable; men who had fought against all odds for nine days, who had witnessed unimaginable horror and destruction and who were now within sight of salvation, found themselves dangerously close to breaking down as fatigue overwhelmed them and nervous reaction set in. From across the river, a battery of AA guns sent tracer shells stabbing into the darkness to mark the crossing point; they belonged to the Wessex Division and fired a round every minute, alternately in pairs, for seven hours.

Although comparatively calm near the banks, the Neder Rijn ran strongly in the middle, which caused many problems. In the words of one officer:

We got into a boat, pushed off, and soon reached that part of the river where the current was flowing strongly. I thought that, once in its grip, we would be swept along into what seemed to me to be a hellish battle in progress downstream. At that moment the outboard engine cut, so we seized our rifles and paddled with the butts. I beat time. Those without rifles encouraged those with them until they were persuaded to swop.[155]

Some elected to swim the distance; the wiser among them, braving the cold, stripped naked before entering the water. Many others drowned, dragged under by their waterlogged clothes. Still others succumbed to exhaustion and slipped under the surface to oblivion, sometimes with only yards to go before their ordeal ended.

Some reached the far bank in the face of all odds. One of them was Marian Roguski, a young Polish paratrooper who had fought in the defence of the perimeter. Despite being severely wounded by shell splinters in the back and a bullet in the right shoulder, Roguski escaped from the St Elisabeth Hospital via a first floor window and made his way to the river bank. He was helped by a Dutch Red Cross worker, who dressed his wounds (which, although they had been closed by a German doctor, still had shrapnel inside) and lay low for a while, waiting for darkness. Then, although in agony from

Stragglers from Arnhem crossing the Rhine after reaching the Allied lines at Nijmegen.

Marian Roguski, the young Polish paratrooper who fought two battles: one at Arnhem and the other against the British war pensions authorities.

his wounds and with his strength ebbing, he swam across the river.[156]

The evacuation went on all through the night, the troops showing exemplary conduct throughout. Once across the river, all ranks marched to a rendezvous south of Driel, where tea, hot food and a blanket were supplied to all ranks by 43rd Division. By 1200 hours on Tuesday, 26 September, what was left of the 1st Airborne Division was concentrated at Nijmegen, where its welfare was taken over by the Division's land/sea element, the 'Seaborne Tail'. This meant that the great majority of men received their large packs containing a complete change of clothing.

At first light on that Tuesday morning, the Germans resumed their attacks on Oosterbeek, and were astonished by the ease with which they were able to advance through the ruined streets towards the Hartenstein Hotel, where the forces pushing from east and west were to rendezvous. It was some time before the reason for this lack of resistance dawned on them. Oosterbeek was peopled by medical staff, wounded and corpses. The remainder of the 1st Airborne Division had gone, and the battle of the *Hexenkessel* was over.

EPILOGUE

By dawn on 26 September, when the withdrawal operations had to cease, a total of 2,398 men had successfully crossed the Neder Rijn. The figure included 160 Poles and 75 Dorsets. During the nine-day battle the 1st Airborne Division lost 7,212 all ranks killed, wounded and captured; the death toll was 1,130, while about 6,000 went into captivity. A few – not more than 120 – managed to evade capture and reached Allied lines later.[157] The US 82nd Airborne Divison had 215 dead, 427 missing and 790 wounded, while the 101st Airborne Division had 315 killed, 547 missing and 790 wounded. It all added up to a very depressing casualty total for I Airborne Corps, and all there was to show for it was a 50-mile salient that led nowhere.

German casualties – killed, wounded and missing – in the *Market Garden* operation are much harder to assess. *Feldmarschall* Model's own estimate of 3,300 – covering Arnhem–Oosterbeek and the fighting in the corridor – is without doubt too low. More recently, diligent research by historians suggests that the Germans had at least 1,725 killed at Arnhem–Oosterbeek, and that the total casualty figure for this area might be as high as 5,175; a lower estimate puts it at 2,565. An estimate for the fighting in the corridor gives a German casualty figure of 3,750; the lack of accurate records makes this a rough estimate only, but there is no reason to think that it is unrealistic.

Much has been written over the past half century on the reasons for the failure at Arnhem. Without a great deal of unnecessary treading of old ground, the following points are worth summarizing as there is general agreement on them.

There is no doubt at all that the 1st Airborne Division was set down too far from its objective. This was especially true in the case of the 4th Parachute Brigade, which came in on D plus 1 when the element of surprise had been lost.

Allied Intelligence failed to appreciate the extraordinary revival of German fighting capacity brought about by determined and able leadership, from *Feldmarschall* Model down to the commanders of the *Kampfgruppen*. Intelligence reports of overall enemy strength were quite accurate, but as late as 14 September a Second Army estimate described the Germans as weak, demoralized, and likely to collapse entirely if confronted with a large airborne attack. Had that been the case, *Market* would have been assured of success.

Second Army Intelligence failed completely to assess the movement of elements of two *Panzer* divisions into the Arnhem area. Although at that time they were deficient in armour, they had enough armoured fighting vehicles and artillery to render 1st Airborne Division's task virtually impossible with the weaponry available to it. Had the 38 gliders that ferried Lieutenant-General Browning's Corps Headquarters to Nijmegen been used instead to provide 1st Airborne Division with additional anti-tank guns and artillerymen, the *Panzers* might have suffered unacceptable losses.

Next there was the problem of the weather, which delayed the arrival of the Polish Brigade from D plus 2 to D plus 4 and that of the 325th Glider Regiment from D plus 2 to D plus 6. It was Field Marshal Montgomery's belief that if these two formations had arrived on schedule, the Poles would have broken through to Frost's battalion at the Arnhem bridge and the 325th Glider Regiment might have provided the extra infantry needed for the rapid capture of the bridge at Nijmegen, enabling XXX Corps to push through to Arnhem before nightfall on 20 September. But although the weather was a major contributory factor in the eventual disaster at Arnhem, it was not the main culprit. That was an operational plan which, by distributing the delivery of the 1st Airborne Division over three days, put *Market* at the mercy of the weather and tied up valuable troops in guarding

The sacrifice: this young paratrooper, like many more, died in this foxhole defending the perimeter.

dropping and landing zones, as well as providing the enemy with additional time in which to react.

A further consideration was the wholly inadequate level of tactical air support operations in the Arnhem area, but this was not the fault of 2nd TAF or IX Tactical Air Command. The operational plan vetoed the use of fighter-bombers while transport operations were in progress, and the latter were subjected to so many delays and frustrations that it became quite impossible to allocate over-the-target slots to the tactical pilots. Besides, after D plus 1 the fighting at Arnhem was so confused and intermingled that it would have been impossible to use Tac Air without a very fine degree of forward air control, and this did not exist. Each of the airborne divisions had two air support parties; one was equipped with SCR-193 sets to radio requests for TacAir to Second Army, and with VHF SCR-522 sets for direct ground-to-air communication with tactical support aircraft. The problem was that the SCR-193 had insufficient range to reach Second Army, and the support parties failed to make contact with anyone on the SCR-522. One of 1st Airborne Division's VHF sets was inoperative and the other was knocked out by shellfire on D plus 1; the only three well-trained operators had been killed earlier. Yet in other areas, tactical air support was considerable; from 17 to 26 September inclusive 2nd TAF flew 3,547 sorties, 691 on the last day.[157]

In the final reckoning, though, the cause of the 1st Airborne Division was lost in the corridor to the south. The disastrously slow progress of *Garden* condemned the airborne mission at Arnhem to death. General Horrocks, commanding XXX Corps, later wrote that

. . . *Market Garden* was the most difficult and worrying battle I have ever fought. Firstly because of the rigidity imposed on XXX Corps by its long slender axis reaching back some 60 miles which was constantly being threatened and sometimes cut by fresh German formations, and secondly by the difficulty of advancing in the face of increasing German opposition over the low-lying polderland north of Nijmegen (known as the Island)

The war cemetery at Arnhem-Oosterbeek.

The Hartenstein Hotel, Headquarters of the 1st Airborne Division during the nine-day battle.

where the roads ran all along the tops of dykes with wide ditches on either side. This type of country was admirably suited to defence because advancing tanks and vehicles were inevitably silhouetted against the sky and thus fell easy victims to enemy defences concealed in the many orchards.

I have thought over this battle many times and now that I have had an opportunity of studying the German side of the picture, I blame myself for a mistake in tactics. When the Guards Armoured Division was held up just north of Nijmegen Bridge, instead of continuing to attack on a more or less direct axis towards Arnhem Bridge, I should have employed 43 Division on a much wider left hook so as to cross the Neder Rhine in the Randwijk area and thus take the German Forces operating against the Airborne Division in their perimeter at Oosterbeek, from the rear. If we had done this I believe that we could have relieved the Airborne Division earlier, but we could never under any circumstances have reached our final objective on the Zuider Zee. We had made the cardinal mistake of under-estimating our enemy – a very dangerous thing to do

when fighting the Germans, who are among the best soldiers in the word. Their recovery after the disaster in Normandy was little short of miraculous.[159]

Yet, despite the tragedy that befell it, the 1st Airborne Division emerged from the Battle of Arnhem bearing a victor's laurels, and the victory was not an insignificant one. It was a victory of the spirit, and on this point it is fitting that General Sir John Hackett, who witnessed the destruction of his 4th Parachute Brigade in the woods and lanes north of Oosterbeek, should have the final word.

I was lying in my hospital bed, halfway between life and death, when I heard the sound of singing. My first thought, accompanied by immense relief, was that XXX Corps had arrived at last. And then I realised that it was not the relief force; the singing came from our own men as they were marched off into captivity. After all they had endured, they held high their pride and they sang.

In the midst of defeat, they were undefeated.

NOTES AND SOURCES

1 Bradley, General Omar N.; *A Soldier's Story*.

2 Eisenhower, General Dwight D.; *Crusade in Europe*.

3 *Ibid*.

4 Horrocks, Lt-Gen Sir Brian; *A Full Life*.

5 Roskill, Capt S.W.; *The Navy at War, 1939–45*

6 Eisenhower, *Crusade in Europe*.

7 Bradley, *A Soldier's Story*.

8 Early in 1942 the Axis had in fact assembled 30,000 men for an airborne invasion of Malta. They were to have been flown to the island in 300 DFS 230 and 200 Gotha Go 242 gliders towed by 500 Ju 52 transports, also carrying paratroops and supplies.

9 President Roosevelt could promise only indirect help in response to the request for aircraft, because of pressing demands by the US forces. He did, however, indicate that four USAAF transport groups would be positioned in England by the end of July, totalling 208 aircraft, and that these would be followed by two more in November 1942, increasing the total to 416.

10 It must be emphasized that the airborne activities during the invasion of North Africa were not an essential part of the planned campaign, which would have been carried out whether airborne troops were used or not. Hence the use of American aircraft, the RAF being already fully occupied with its allotted task of strategic bombing. (AP 3231, *Airborne Forces*, Air Ministry, 1951).

11 AP 3231, p. 90.

12 The decision to retain No 296 Sqn in the Mediterranean resulted from Major-General Ridgeway's Sicily after-action report of 6 November 1943, in which he stated that 'Both the 82nd Airborne Division and the North African Air Force Troop Carrier Command are today at airborne training levels below combat requirements . . . Troop Carrier Command glider pilots have not had sufficient training to conduct a successful night glider operation.' (Army Air Force pamphlet *I Troop Carrier Command, the Operational Training Program, 1944*, pp 296–297).

13 AP 3231, pp 96–97.

14 The first suggestion that No 38 Wing be formed into a Group had in fact been made in August 1942 by Air Commodore Groom, SASO of the Special Planning Staff for Operation *Round-up* (a proposed cross-Channel operation for 1943). He proposed that the Group be formed under Bomber Command, but the idea was rejected.

15 In practice, Airborne Army initiated planning in response to requests from the Army Group commanders, Bradley and Montgomery, without waiting for a SHAEF directive. Montgomery ceased to be ground commander-in-chief on 1 August when 12th Army Group under Bradley took over control of the American armies from 21st Army Group; however, he continued to exercise some authority over all ground operations as Eisenhower's deputy until the latter moved to France and on 1 September assumed the role of ground commander in addition to that of supreme commander.

16 Conversation between author and General Sir John Hackett.

17 *Air Power in Operation Market Garden*: article by Sebastian Cox, MoD Air Historical Branch, in *Air Clues*, May 1985.

18 Devlin; *Silent Wings* pp. 239–40.

19 Terraine; *The Right of the Line*, p. 670.

20 *Airborne Operations in World War II, European Theater*, p. 97.

21 Recorded in the Proceedings of the Royal Air Force Historical Society, Issue No 9: Joint RAF/USAF Seminar held on 29 October 1990.

22 Extract from report by German Army Group B G2 Intelligence Officer, quoted in Kershaw, *It Never Snows in September*, p. 31.

23 Bauer, *The Battle of Arnhem*, p. 79.

24 Ibid, p. 80.

25 For a very full and comprehensive account of all German units opposing *Market Garden*, see Kershaw, *It Never Snows in September*.

26 *Airborne Operations in World War II*, p. 98.

27 C. Martin Sharp and Michael J.F. Bowyer, *Mosquito*, p. 253.

28 2nd TAF Daily Log Sheet No 1590, quoted in Air Historical Branch narrative on *Market Garden*.

29 Trooper Des Evans, C Troop 1st Airborne Recce Squadron: correspondence with author.

30 Correspondence; S. Martin and author.

31 The Pathfinders also released homing pigeons throughout their zone marking operations at Arnhem, to advise HQ Airborne Army that the task had been successfully carried out. One of these birds was awarded the Dicken Medal, the 'Animals' VC'. Kent, *First In*: History of the 21st Independent Parachute Company.

32 *Airborne Operations in World War II*, p. 103.

33 *By Air to Battle*, p. 107.

34 *The Second World War, 1939–45: Airborne Forces*, p. 290.

35 Correspondence; Ken Hope and author.

36 Dutch Commando: a member of the Dutch Troop, Special Air Service. Members of No 2 (Dutch) Troop SAS were parachuted into Arnhem with the 1st Airborne Division as interpreters and for special Intelligence duties. Although only two were killed, many others were wounded and captured.

37 Correspondence between Des Evans and author.

38 Ibid.

39 Stainforth, Peter; *Wings of the Wind*.

40 Conversation between R. Hall, MM, and the author.

41 Sims, James; *Arnhem Spearhead*.

42 Correspondence; Horst Scheuler and author.

43 *Anlageband Heeresgruppe* B. Ic *Meldungen* 1–30 September 1944. (Army Group B Intelligence Report, quoted in *It Never Snows in September*.

44 War Diary, 2nd Battalion The South Staffordshire Regiment. Imperial War Museum, Department of Documents.

45 War Diary, LXXXVIII Corps, 18 September 1944; *Bundesarchiv*.

46 *Silent Wings*, p.254.

47 Ibid, p. 255.

48 *Airborne Operations in World War II*, p. 121.

49 Correspondence: Lt-Col John Humphreys and author.

50 *First In*; Parachute Pathfinder Company.

51 Correspondence; Walter Langham and author.

52 Correspondence; Bill Carr and author.

53 Correspondence; Oliver Kingdon and author.

54 Hagen, Louis: *Arnhem Lift*, p. 14.

55 *Air Clues*, June 1985: article by Sebastian Cox, Air Historical Branch (RAF)

56 *Arnhem*; Maj-Gen R.E. Urquhart.

57 Ibid.

58 Correspondence; Des Evans and author.

59 *History of the 2nd Battalion The Parachute Regiment*.

60 Wingfield, R.M.; *The Only Way Out*.

61 Foley, John; *Mailed Fist*.

62 Escort duty between 's Hertogenbosch and Arnhem had originally been assigned to the Ninth Air Force, but on the morning of 19 September the task of escorting the transports beyond Gheel was switched to the Eighth AF.

63 Because of the bad weather, two P-51 groups were late in arriving on station; had the *Luftwaffe* launched its attacks earlier, it would have stood a far better chance of breaking through to the transport serials.

64 *Airborne Operations in World War II*, p. 129.

65 Ibid.

66 Ibid.

67 *Silent Wings*, pp. 263–268.

68 The 907th Field Artillery Battalion had been chosen to introduce this weapon into action. The 105 mm howitzer had been substantially redesigned in order to fit into a C-47, having been made lighter and reduced in dimension. The use of light alloys enabled the weight to be decreased from 4,235 lb to 2,500 lb.

69 *It Never Snows in September*, p. 147.

70 *By Air to Battle*, p. 111.

71 Quoted in *The Battle of Arnhem* (Bauer), p. 180.

72 Ibid.

73 *By Air to Battle*, p. 110.

74 Quoted in *The Battle of Arnhem*, p. 182.

75 PGEM: The Gelderland Provincial Electricity Board. By dialling a secret number it was possible to gain access to the public telephone system via the PGEM network of sub-stations. The Germans made widespread use of this facility during the battle, making it possible to dispense almost entirely with unreliable radio communications. The Dutch Resistance also used it to gather information on German troop dispositions, which they tried hard to pass on to the Airborne Forces.

76 Correspondence; Ken Hope and author.

77 Correspondence; Des Evans and author.

78 War Diary, 156th Parachute Battalion.

79 *By Air to Battle*, p. 111.

80 War Diary, 10th Parachute Battalion.

81 *By Air to Battle*, p. 113. The men showing yellow triangles appear to have belonged to the Polish glider element.

82 *First In*, p. 102.

83 Ibid, p. 105.

84 Swiecicki; *With the Red Devils at Arnhem*.

85 *Airborne Operations in World War II*, p. 132.

86 *The London Gazette*, Tuesday, 13 November 1945.

87 It should be noted that the *Luftwaffe* intervened after the tug aircraft had turned for home after release, so strafing attacks on the zones would not be seen by the crews.

88 'Stirling letters FFT'; this does not correspond with the code of any unit involved in the operation and may have been a mis-reading of F7T, the code of No 196 Squadron.

89 Heaps, Leo; *Escape from Arnhem*.

90 Correspondence; John Humphreys and author.

91 The tanks were Tigers; see *It Never Snows in September* p. 177.

92 Stainforth; *Wings of the Wind*.

93 War Diary, 2nd Parachute Battalion.

94 Stainforth; *Wings of the Wind*.

95 Quoted in *It Never Snows in September*, p. 192.

96 *Silent Wings* p. 269.

97 Correspondence; A.C. Sanders and author.

98 Ibid.

99 Correspondence; John Humphreys and author.

100 Ibid.

101 Ibid.

102 Quoted in Fairley; *Remember Arnhem* p. 120.

103 Quoted in *Remember Arnhem* p. 127.

104 Ron Hall, MM; conversation with author.

105 *It Never Snows in September*, p. 202.

106 Quoted in Bauer; *The Battle of Arnhem*, p. 196

107 Ibid.

108 *Airborne Operations in World War II*, p. 134.

109 This is the total for the day's missions, both drops being lumped together in the RAF summary.

110 *Airborne Operations in World War II*, p. 136. The question must be asked: was this really a 'strange oversight', or were essential supplies, contrary to General Eisenhower's orders, being 'diverted' to support the offensive of the American Third Army?

111 Kershaw; *It Never Snows in September*, p. 224.

112 Essame, Maj-Gen H.; *The 43rd Wessex Division at War, 1939–45*.

113 *Silent Wings*, pp. 269–70. See also *Airborne Operations in World War II*, pp. 136–7. The official US historian is scathing in his reference to the 43rd Division, which '. . . had taken three days to move less than 60 miles by truck. One cause of this lagging was the excessive caution

of British drivers, who caused interminable traffic jams by refusing to pull off the narrow roads onto the grass for fear of mines. Sharing the widespread conviction that the war was practically won, they could not sense the need for haste – nor, it seems, could their commanders.' But, the historian admits, 'Other and inevitable delays had been imposed by the *Luftwaffe* night attack on Eindhoven, which blocked the streets for several hours, by the German tank attacks at Zon on the 19th and 20th, and occasionally by shelling at other points.'

114 Brereton, Wallace; *Salford Boy Goes to War*, pub. Neil Richardson, 1992.

115 *Air Pictorial International*, January 1993; article by Martin Bowman on the de Havilland Mosquito in USAAF service.

116 Correspondence; J. Lacey and author.

117 Correspondence; Ken Hope and author.

118 *It Never Snows in September* pp. 238–9

119 Quoted in *The Battle of Arnhem* (Bauer), p. 215.

120 Ibid, p. 216.

121 Ken Hope, Correspondence with author. This incident is also recorded in Fairley, *Remember Arnhem*, p. 141.

122 Ken Hope; correspondence with author.

123 *Airborne Operations in World War Two*, p. 139.

124 Ibid.

125 The new drop point was designated SDP 693785 and was extremely difficult to find; troops on the ground use Aldis lamp signals, but few of the transport crews spotted these.

126 JG 26 was led by the redoubtable *Oberst* Josef 'Pips' Priller, who scored 101 victories in the war and became the *Luftwaffe* Fighter Inspector/West.

127 One group, the 359th, managed to get 20 pilots airborne, but the weather was so poor that they had to be recalled.

128 *By Air to Battle*, pp. 118–9. Attached to the Air Landing Brigade, Major Robert Henry Cain was an officer of the Royal Northumberland Fusiliers.

129 For full details of German assets and deployments, see *It Never Snows In September*, Chapter XXII.

130 *Airborne Operations in World War II*, p. 140. A footnote to the narrative says: 'There are some references to missions being flown on the 22nd, but the weight of evidence is overwhelmingly against them.'

131 Of No 419 Heavy Battery, Royal Artillery.

132 Correspondence; J. Lacey and author.

133 Fairley; *Remember Arnhem*, pp 152 and 163.

134 *By Air to Battle*, p. 125.

135 Kate ter Horst was killed and her husband severely injured in the most tragic circumstances in 1992, when a vehicle careered off the road that ran past their house and crashed into their front garden.

136 Correspondence; Bill Carr and author.

137 2nd TAF Daily Log Sheet No 1611.

138 AP 3231, *Airborne Forces*, p. 170, and Otway, *Second World War 1939–45, Airborne Forces*, p. 286.

139 *Airborne Operations in World War II*, p. 142.

140 By this time, the 10th Parachute Battalion had virtually ceased to exist, its effective strength having been reduced to about 40 men. The 11th had about 70, the 156th less than 60.

141 *First In*, p. 119.

142 Quoted in Fairley; *Remember Arnhem*, p. 168.

143 E7W: No 570 Squadron.

144 V8G: The V8 code was also carried by No 570 Sqn aircraft.

145 The loss total in the 38 Group summary adds up to thirteen aircraft, but some of these wrecks were certainly the same aircraft seen by different crews.

146 AP 3231, p. 171. Although *permission* to evacuate 1st Airborne Division was given by HQ 2nd Army on this date and at this time, the *decision* for the withdrawal was taken jointly by 1st Airborne Corps and XXX Corps on the following day.

147 Up to 22 September, 21st Army Group had requested that railway communications be kept intact because of the rapid advances being made on the ground. On the other hand, 12th

Army Group had demanded railway interdiction on several occasions. It is impossible to say whether intensive railway interdiction by the Allied air forces would have rescued the situation at Arnhem and Oosterbeek, but it would certainly have delayed the ultimate collapse of 1st Airborne Division.

148 Correspondence; Walter Langham and author.

149 For the full account of Hackett's experiences in Holland following his wounding, see *I Was a Stranger* by General Sir John Hackett, Chatto & Windus, 1977. This is a sensitive and often moving story which highlights, above all, the risks run by the Dutch civilian population to help the survivors of the 1st British Airborne Division.

150 Correspondence; Ken Hope and author.

151 Fraser's comrades bound his wounds with field dressings and left him in a cellar. His eye was replaced by a Polish surgeon who was a PoW and, incredibly, his sight was restored.

152 Correspondence; Ken Hope and author.

153 Correspondence; Bill Carr and author.

154 Urquhart; *Arnhem.*

155 Lt-Col M. St J. Packe, the Divisional Supply Officer. *By Air to Battle*, p. 129.

156 After the war, Roguski's courage was 'rewarded' by the constant rejection of his claim for a War Disability Pension by the War Pensions Directorate. He is still fighting for it, with the aid of the Royal British Legion, half a century later.

157 It is outside the scope of this work to follow the adventures of this group. Some of the books listed in the bibliography provide excellent accounts of the way in which these men evaded capture with the help of gallant Dutch civilians. Other accounts tell of the fortunes of the survivors of the Airborne Division in captivity.

158 2nd TAF Daily Log, 17–26 September 1944.

159 Quoted in the foreword to *Arnhem* (Bauer).

BIBLIOGRAPHY

Air Publication 3231: *Airborne Forces*. Air Ministry (AHB), London, 1951

Bauer, Cornelius *The Battle of Arnhem*. Hodder and Stoughton, London, 1966

Bradley, General Omar N. *A Soldier's Story*. Henry Holt, New York, 1951

Brereton, Lieutenant-General Lewis H. *The Brereton Diaries*. William Morrow, New York, 1946

Brereton, Wallace *Salford Boy Goes to War*. Neil Richardson, Manchester, 1992

By Air to Battle; The Official Account of the British First and Sixth Airborne Divisions, HMSO, London, 1945

Davies, Howard P. *British Parachute Forces 1940–45*. Arms and Armour Press, London, 1974

Devlin, Gerard M. *Silent Wings: The Story of the Glider Pilots of World War II*. W.H. Allen, London, 1985

Eisenhower, General Dwight D. *Crusade in Europe*. Doubleday, New York, 1948

Fairley, John *Remember Arnhem: The Story of the 1st Airborne Reconnaissance Squadron*. Pegasus Journal, Aldershot, 1978

Farrar-Hockley, Anthony *Airborne Carpet – Operation Market Garden*. Macdonald, London, 1970

Gavin, Lieutenant-General James M. *Airborne Warfare*. Infantry Journal Press, Washington D.C., 1947

Hackett, General Sir John *I was a Stranger*. Chatto and Windus, London, 1977

Hagen, Louis *Arnhem Lift*. Hammond and Co., London, 1945

History of the 2nd Battalion The Parachute Regiment. Wellington Press, Aldershot, 1946

Horrocks, Lieutenant-General Sir Brian *A Full Life*. Collins, London, 1960

Horrocks, Lieutenant-General Sir Brian *Corps Commander*. Sidgwick and Jackson, London. 1977

Jackson, Robert *Hawker Tempest*. Blandford Press, London, 1989

Jackson, Robert *Mustang: The Operational Record*. Airlife, Shrewsbury, 1992

Kent, Ron *First In: A History of the 21st Independent Parachute Company 1942–46*. Batsford, London, 1979

Kershaw, Robert J. *It Never Snows in September*. The Crowood Press, Marlborough, 1990

Macdonald, Charles *By Air to Battle*. Macdonald, London, 1969

Montgomery, Field Marshal Sir Bernard L. *The Memoirs of Field Marshal the Viscount Montgomery of Alamein*. Collins, London, 1958

Norton, Geoffrey G. *The Red Devils*. Leo Cooper, London, 1971

Otway, Lieutenant-Colonel T.B.H., DSO *The Second World War 1939–45, Army: Airborne Forces*. Imperial War Museum, London

Packe, Michael *First Airborne*. Secker and Warburg, London, 1948

Powell, Geoffrey *The Devil's Birthday: the Bridges to Arnhem, 1944*. Buchan and Enright, London, 1984

Reppert, Leonard, and Northwood, Arthur, Jun *Rendezvous with Destiny – a History of the 101st Airborne Division*. Washington Infantry Journal Press, Washington D.C., 1948

Roskill, Captain S.W. *The Navy at War 1939–1945*. Collins, London, 1960

Ryan, Cornelius *A Bridge too Far*. Hamish Hamilton, London, 1974

Saunders, Hilary St G. *The Red Beret*. Michael Joseph, London, 1950

Sharp, C.M., and Bowyer, M.J.F. *Mosquito*. Faber and Faber, London, 1967

Sims, James *Arnhem Spearhead*. Imperial War Museum, London, 1978

Stainforth, Peter *Wings of the Wind*. The Falcon Press, London, 1952

Swiecicki, Marck *With the Red Devils at Arnhem*. Max Love Publishing, London, 1945

Ter Horst, Kate A. *A Cloud over Arnhem*. Allan Wingate, London, 1959

Terraine, John *The Right of the Line: The Royal Air Force in the European War 1939–1945*. Hodder and Stoughton, London, 1985

Tugwell, Maurice *Airborne to Battle: A History of Airborne Warfare 1918–1971*. William Kimber, 1971

Urquhart, Major-General Roy *Arnhem*. Cassell, London, 1958

Warren, John G. *U.S. Air Force Historical Study No 97: Airborne Operations in World War II, European Theater*. Maxwell Air Force Base, Alabama, 1956

In addition to the above principal works, I have consulted the War Diaries of the British units engaged at Arnhem-Oosterbeek, and those of the principal forces of XXX Corps. One document, however, deserves a special mention. Its author was SS *Sturmbannführer* Sepp Krafft, and it was commissioned by Heinrich Himmler. Its title, in translation, is: *SS Panzer Grenadier Depot and Reserve Battalion 16 in the Battles at Arnhem, 17.9.44–7.10.44*. I am indebted to General Sir John Hackett for the perusal of it.

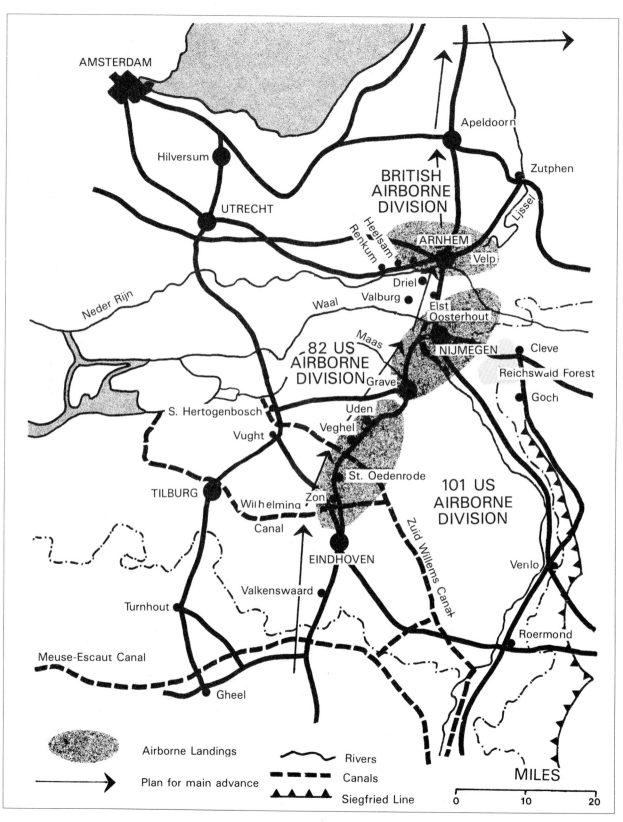

AMSTERDAM

Hilversum

UTRECHT

Apeldoorn

Zutphen

BRITISH
AIRBORNE
DIVISION

Ijssel

Heelsam
Renkum

ARNHEM

Velp

Driel

Neder Rijn

Waal

Valburg

Elst
Oosterhout

NIJMEGEN

Cleve

82 US
AIRBORNE
DIVISION

Maas

Reichswald Forest

Grave

Goch

S. Hertogenbosch

Uden

Veghel

Vught

St. Oedenrode

101 US
AIRBORNE
DIVISION

TILBURG

Wilhelmina

Zon

Canal

Zuid Willems Canal

Venlo

EINDHOVEN

Valkenswaard

Turnhout

Roermond

Meuse-Escaut Canal

Gheel

Airborne Landings

Rivers

Plan for main advance

Canals

Siegfried Line

MILES

0   10   20

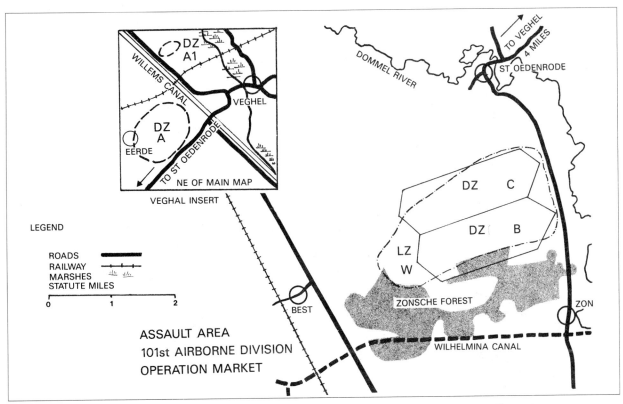

DZ
A1

WILLEMS CANAL

VEGHEL

DZ
A

EERDE

TO ST OEDENRODE

NE OF MAIN MAP

DOMMEL RIVER

ST OEDENRODE

TO VEGHEL
4 MILES

DZ   C

DZ   B

LZ
W

ZONSCHE FOREST

ZON

WILHELMINA CANAL

BEST

LEGEND

ROADS
RAILWAY
MARSHES
STATUTE MILES

0   1   2

ASSAULT AREA
101st AIRBORNE DIVISION
OPERATION MARKET

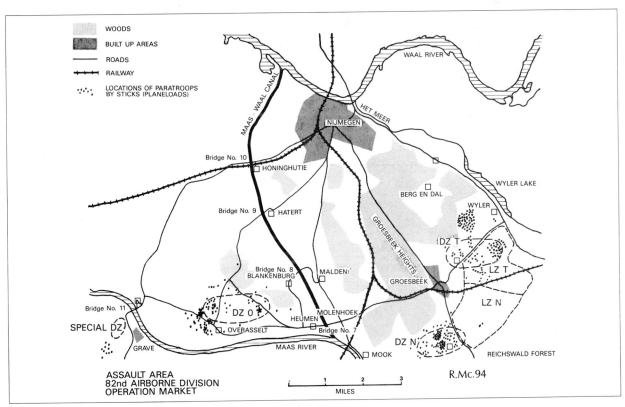

WOODS
BUILT UP AREAS
ROADS
RAILWAY
LOCATIONS OF PARATROOPS
BY STICKS (PLANELOADS)

WAAL RIVER

MAAS - WAAL CANAL

HET MEER

NIJMEGEN

Bridge No. 10

HONINGHUTIE

WYLER LAKE

BERG EN DAL

WYLER

Bridge No. 9   HATERT

GROESBEEK HEIGHTS

DZ T

LZ T

Bridge No. 8
BLANKENBURG

MALDEN

GROESBEEK

LZ N

Bridge No. 11

SPECIAL DZ

DZ O

HEUMEN

MOLENHOEK

Bridge No. 7

DZ N

OVERASSELT

GRAVE

MAAS RIVER

MOOK

REICHSWALD FOREST

R.Mc.94

ASSAULT AREA
82nd AIRBORNE DIVISION
OPERATION MARKET

1   2   3
MILES

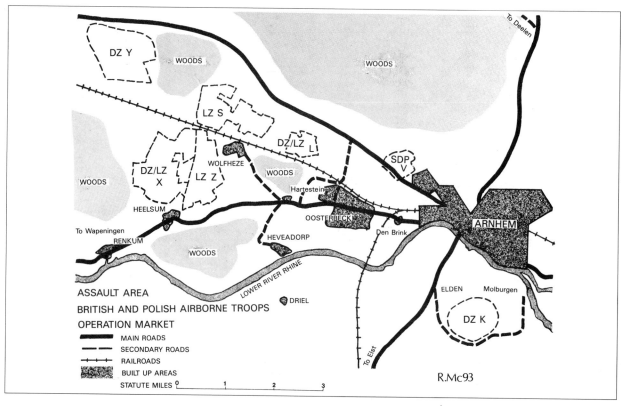

ASSAULT AREA
BRITISH AND POLISH AIRBORNE TROOPS
OPERATION MARKET

▬▬▬	MAIN ROADS
▬ ▬ ▬	SECONDARY ROADS
┼┼┼┼	RAILROADS
▓▓▓	BUILT UP AREAS

STATUTE MILES 0 1 2 3

R.Mc93

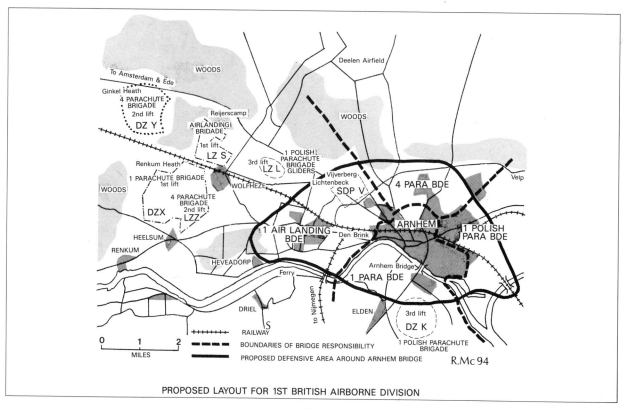

┼┼┼┼	RAILWAY
▬ ▬ ▬	BOUNDARIES OF BRIDGE RESPONSIBILITY
▬▬▬	PROPOSED DEFENSIVE AREA AROUND ARNHEM BRIDGE

0 1 2
MILES

R.Mc 94

PROPOSED LAYOUT FOR 1ST BRITISH AIRBORNE DIVISION

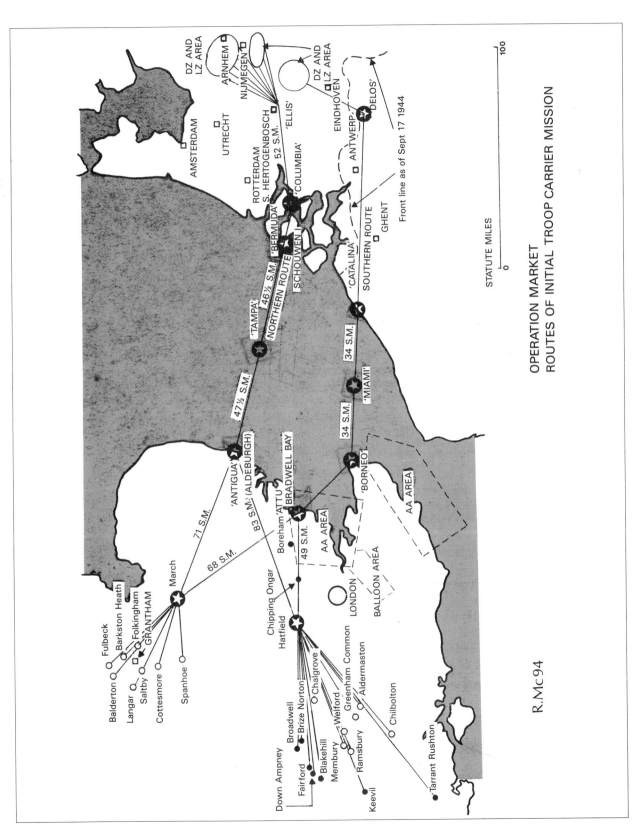

OPERATION MARKET
ROUTES OF INITIAL TROOP CARRIER MISSION

R.Mc 94

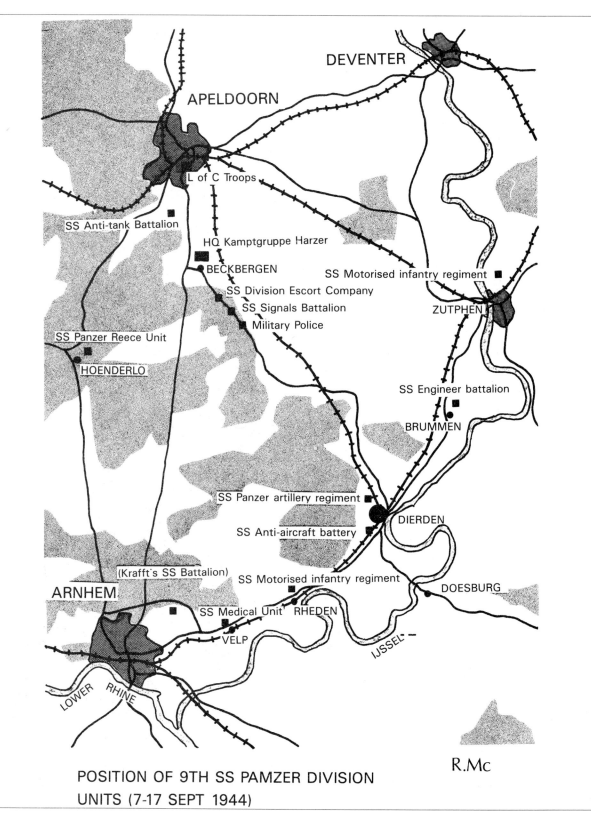

DEVENTER

APELDOORN

L of C Troops

SS Anti-tank Battalion

HQ Kamptgruppe Harzer

BECKBERGEN

SS Division Escort Company

SS Motorised infantry regiment

SS Signals Battalion

Military Police

ZUTPHEN

SS Panzer Reece Unit

HOENDERLO

SS Engineer battalion

BRUMMEN

SS Panzer artillery regiment

SS Anti-aircraft battery

DIERDEN

(Krafft's SS Battalion)

SS Motorised infantry regiment

DOESBURG

ARNHEM

SS Medical Unit   RHEDEN

VELP

IJSSEL

LOWER   RHINE

R.Mc

POSITION OF 9TH SS PAMZER DIVISION
UNITS (7-17 SEPT 1944)

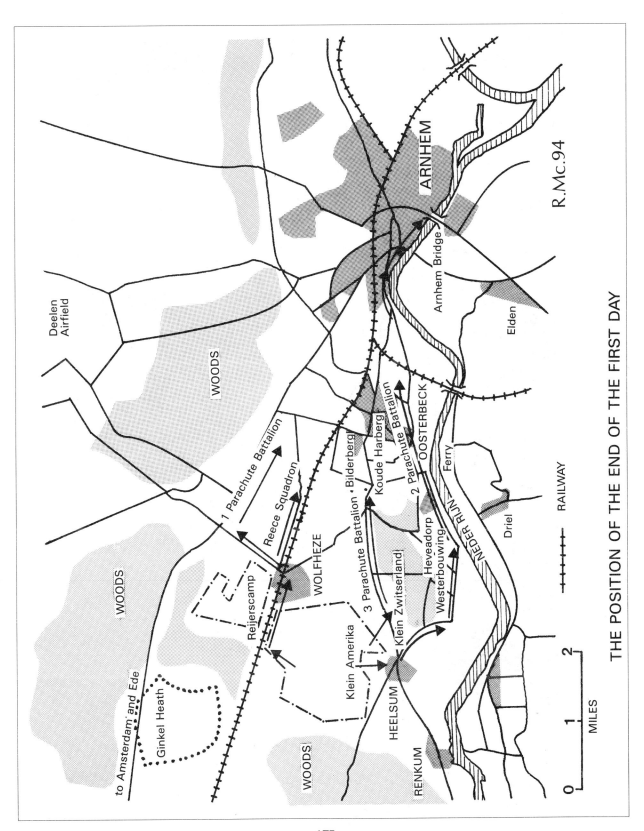

THE POSITION OF THE END OF THE FIRST DAY

R.Mc.94

ARNHEM

Arnhem Bridge

Elden

Deelen
Airfield

WOODS

OOSTERBECK

Koude Harberg

2 Parachute Battalion

Ferry

Heveadorp

Westerbouwing

NEDER RIJN

Driel

1 Parachute Battalion

Reece Squadron

Bilderberg

3 Parachute Battalion

Klein Zwitserland

WOLFHEZE

Reijerscamp

WOODS

Ginkel Heath

to Amsterdam and Ede

Klein Amerika

HEELSUM

RENKUM

WOODS

RAILWAY

0   1   2

MILES

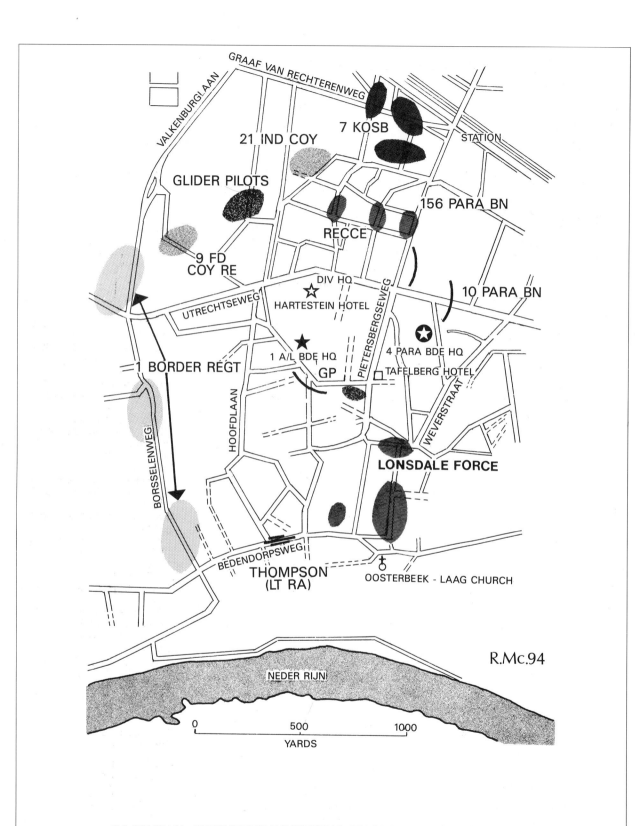

DIVISIONAL PERIMETER POSITIONS THURS 21ST SEPT 1944

Index

Aa River 33
Aachen 3, 29, 38, 41, 99
Aalst 96
Adair, Maj-Gen Allan 75
Air Defence of Great Britain (ADGB) 34–5, 48, 82, 98, 123, 134–5, 146, 156
Airspeed Aircraft:
Horsa 9, 12–14, 23, 33, 45, 56–60, 62–3, 76, 88, 90, 93, 109, 112
Hotspur 9
Aisne River 1
Albert Canal 5–7, 20, 27, 37–9, 41
Aldeburgh 27, 78
Aldermaston, RAF 23
Alexander, General 12
Alford, Lt-Col W C 62
Allied Airborne Army, First 16–17, 19–20, 22, 24, 26, 35, 41, 46, 76, 98
Allied Expeditionary Force 17, 29, 34–5
Allsop, Capt David 62, 141–2
Allworden, SS *Hauptsturmführer* Klaus von 70, 94, 141
Alost 4
Amersfoort 73
Amersfoort Concentration Camp 42
Amiens 4
Amsterdam 30–31
Antwerp 3–8, 25, 37–8, 40
Apeldoorn 43, 70, 73, 123, 126
Ardennes 2–3, 6
Argonne 3
Armstrong Whitworth Aircraft:
Albemarle 12, 14–15, 23, 45, 93
Whitley 9
Arras 4, 19, 42
Arromanches 2
Ashworth, Major 107
Aubigny 4
Auxerre 19
Avesnes 4
Avranches 18
Avrilly 25–6
Avro Aircraft:
Lancaster 46

Baker, L/Cpl 106–7
Baker, Alan 95
Balderton, RAF 23, 45
Ballard, Lt-Col 139
Barclay, Bill MM 132
Barkston Heath, RAF 23, 60
Barrett, AM Sir Arthur 10
Bartsch, SS *Obersturmführer* 73
Baskeyfield, L/Sgt John D, VC 135–6
Beauvais 4
Becker, *Major* Karl-Heinz 115

Beek 79, 117, 140
Beekbergen 43
Beerlingen 6
Beja 11
Belgian Resistance 4
Bemmel 129
Berg en Dal 55–6
Berlin 6–7, 38
Berringen 39
Best 51, 78, 83, 99–101, 137, 147
Betuwe, The 129, 157
Bilderberg 72, 114, 121
Bilderberg Hotel 72, 122
Billingslea, Col Charles 22, 147
Bittrich, SS *General* Wilhelm 68, 70, 85, 102, 134
Blakehill Farm, RAF 23
Blankenberg 54
Bletchley Park 26
Blokland, *Major* Johkeer Jan Beerlaerts van 75
Blundell, Capt G L 122
Boeing Aircraft:
B-17 Flying Fortress 46–7
Bone Airfield 11
Borradaile, Lt-Col H A 75
Bottesford, RAF 23
Boulogne 19
Bourg Leopold 6, 146–7
Bournemouth 128
Bowles, 2nd Lt 63, 106–7
Boxtel 145
Bradley, Gen Omar 2–3, 8
Bradwell Bay 27
Brawn, Fred 95
Bredelaan 121
Bredemann, *Hauptmann* 42
Brennan, Flg Off George F 100–101
Brereton, Lt-Gen Lewis H, DSC 16–17, 19, 22, 24–6, 33, 35, 46, 76, 98
Breskens 5–6
Brielsche Gat 40
British Forces:
Armies
First Canadian Army 1–2, 4, 11
Second Army 1–2, 4, 7–8, 20–1, 24–5, 33, 36, 41, 56, 75, 93, 148–9, 154, 156, 160–1
Eighth Army 13–14
Corps
I Airborne Corps 5, 17, 22, 33, 44, 56, 144–5, 149, 156, 160
VIII Corps 21, 126, 137
XII Corps 4, 6, 75, 126, 137
XXX Corps 4–6, 21, 32, 35, 39, 49–50, 53, 55, 74–5, 77, 79, 96, 99,

101, 114, 117–9, 126–9, 136–7, 148, 152, 154, 157, 160, 163
Royal Army Medical Corps (RAMC) 120, 157
Royal Army Service Corps (RASC) 68
Royal Artillery 13, 22, 60, 62, 83–4, 101, 111, 126, 128, 130–31, 141
Royal Engineers 13–14, 60, 68–9, 77, 108, 112, 114, 117, 119, 122, 129, 136, 143, 152
Divisions
1st Airborne Division 11–20, 22, 24, 29–32, 42, 44–5, 56–7, 74–7, 80, 85, 90, 92, 126, 128–9, 133–7, 141–42, 144, 148, 152–4, 156–63
6th Airborne Division 11, 15–17, 28–9
Guards Armoured Division 4, 6, 39, 75, 77, 96–7, 99, 114, 126–7, 136, 149, 163
7th Armoured Division 4
11th Armoured Division 4–6
5th Division 13
53rd Division 127
51st Highland Division 29
50th Infantry Division 4, 6
52nd Lowland Division 20, 32, 75, 109
50th (Northumbrian) Division 75, 150
43rd (Wessex) Infantry Division 75, 114, 126–7, 136, 143, 152–53, 156–9, 163
Brigade Groups
1st Air Landing Brigade Group 85, 91
24th Guards Brigade Group 10
31st Independent Brigade Group 9
Irish Guards Brigade Group 74–5
Brigades
1st Air Landing Brigade 9, 11–12, 22, 56, 60, 62, 73–4, 85–7, 93–4, 114, 156
6th Air Landing Brigade 12
5th Guards Brigade 4
32nd Guards Brigade 4, 147
129th Infantry Brigade 75, 143
130th Infantry Brigade 75, 143, 149–50, 158
214th Infantry Brigade 143
217th Infantry Brigade 75
1st Parachute Brigade 9–14, 22, 31, 56, 60, 62, 73, 92, 96, 112, 114, 122
2nd Parachute Brigade 10–13

3rd Parachute Brigade 11
4th Parachute Brigade 12, 22, 85, 87–8, 90, 92–4, 105, 108–11, 114, 121–2, 129–30, 160, 163
Regiments
1st Air Landing Light Regiment RA 14, 22, 84, 111–12, 130–1
1st Airborne Light Regiment RA 11
21st Anti-tank Regiment RA 101
59th Anti-tank Regiment RA 126
The Border Regiment 22, 60, 73–4, 86–7, 93, 114, 134, 141, 143, 148
The Coldstream Guards 75, 117
The Dorsetshire Regiment 75, 149, 152, 155–6, 160
The Dragoon Guards 143
The Duke of Cornwall's Light Infantry 75, 143, 149, 157
The Durham Light Infantry 14
The Essex Regiment 12
The Glider Pilot Regiment 9, 63, 65, 87–8, 129, 142, 152, 157
The Gordon Highlanders 50
The Grenadier Guards 75, 117–8, 126
The Hampshire Regiment 75, 149
The Highland Light Infantry 127
The Household Cavalry 4, 6, 75, 79, 136
The Irish Guards 6, 117, 128
The King's Own Scottish Borderers 22, 60, 73–4, 86–8, 90, 92–3, 107–8, 114, 129, 131–32
64th Medium Regiment, RA 128, 141
The Parachute Regiment 9–14, 22, 60, 62, 65–73, 83–5, 87–8, 90–6, 102–5, 107–9, 112–114, 119, 120–2, 127, 130, 143, 155, 160
The Queen's Own Cameron Highlanders 10
The Royal Tank Regiment 150
The Royal Warwickshire Regiment 12
The Royal Welch Fusiliers 10
The Scots Guards 75
The Somerset Light Infantry 12, 75
The South Staffordshire Regiment 22, 60, 73–4, 87, 95, 103–5, 108, 130, 132, 135–6
The Wiltshire Regiment 75
The Worcestershire Regiment 75
The Worcestershire Yeomanry Airborne Light Regiment RA 12
Battalions
Airborne Reconnaissance Battalion 68
1st Battalion The Border Regiment 22, 60, 73–4, 86, 93, 114, 129, 134, 141, 143, 148
4th Battalion The Dorsetshire Regiment 75, 149, 155–6
5th Battalion The Dorsetshire Regiment 75, 149, 152
7th Battalion The Dragoon Guards 143

5th Battalion The Duke of Cornwall's Light Infantry 75, 143, 157
2nd Battalion The Gordon Highlanders 50
7th Battalion The Hampshire Regiment 75, 149
1st Battalion The Irish Guards 6
2nd Battalion The Irish Guards 6, 75
7th Battalion The King's Own Scottish Borderers 22, 60, 73–4, 86–8, 92–3, 107–8, 114, 131
1st Battalion The Parachute Regiment 9, 11, 13, 22, 60, 70–71, 85, 87, 94–5, 103–4, 112
2nd Battalion The Parachute Regiment 9, 11, 13–14, 22, 60, 62, 65–71, 73, 83–4, 95–6, 102–3, 109, 112–13, 119–21, 127, 160
3rd Battalion The Parachute Regiment 10–11, 13, 22, 60, 67, 72–3, 83, 85, 87, 94–5, 103–4
4th (Wessex) Battalion The Parachute Regiment 10
5th (Scottish) Battalion The Parachute Regiment 10
6th (Welch) Battalion The Parachute Regiment 10
7th Battalion The Parachute Regiment 11
8th Battalion The Parachute Regiment 11
9th Battalion The Parachute Regiment 11
10th Battalion The Parachute Regiment 12, 22, 88, 93, 107–9, 114, 121–22, 130
11th Battalion The Parachute Regiment 12, 22, 87, 90–3, 95, 103–5, 108, 112, 143, 155
156th Battalion The Parachute Regiment 12, 22, 93, 107–8, 114, 121–22, 130
7th Battalion The Queen's Own Cameron Highlanders 10
44th Battalion The Royal Tank Regiment 150
10th Battalion The Royal Welch Fusiliers 10
4th Battalion The Somerset Light Infantry 75
7th Battalion The Somerset Light Infantry 75
2nd Battalion The South Staffordshire Regiment 22, 60, 73–4, 87, 92, 95, 103–4
4th Battalion The Wiltshire Regiment 75
5th Battalion The Wiltshire Regiment 75
1st Battalion The Worcestershire Regiment 75
Squadrons
1st Airborne Reconnaissance Squadron 22, 62–5, 68, 70, 87, 95,

105–6, 119, 129–31, 141, 153–5
615th Field Squadron RE 77, 117
1st Parachute Squadron RE 13, 60, 68–9, 73, 83, 119, 129
4th Parachute Squadron RE 108, 114, 122, 129
Companies
9th Field Company RE 60, 129, 143
204th Field Company RE 152
21st Independent Parachute Company (Pathfinder) 14, 22, 28, 51, 58, 85, 87–8, 109, 129, 131–2, 148
Miscellaneous Units
181st Air Landing Field Ambulance RA 60–62
2nd Air Landing Light AA Battery 32
211th Battery 64th Medium Regiment 128
212th Battery 64th Medium Regiment 128
Central Landing Establishment 9
3rd Light Battery RA 83
16th Parachute Field Ambulance RA 13, 60, 62, 142
133rd Parachute Field Ambulance RA 62, 93
Special Forces
Battalions
No 2 Commando 9
No 6 Commando 11
No 2 Special Air Service (SAS) 19
No 11 SAS 9
Brize Norton, RAF 23
Broadhurst, AV-M Harry 35–6
Broadwell, RAF 23, 146
Brooke, Gen Sir Alan 9
Browning, Lt-Gen F A H, DSO 10, 12, 15–18, 22, 33, 36, 56, 101, 117, 127, 144, 146, 160
Bruneval 9

Caen 17
Cain, Maj Robert H, VC 136
Cambrai 4
Camp Claiborne, La 12
Canadian Forces:
II Corps 5
1st Canadian Parachute Regiment 12
1st Canadian Parachute Battalion 12
Cape Passero 14
Carr, Bill 90–1, 143–4, 155
Catania 13
Cerrutti, Edwin R 128
Chalgrove, RAF 45, 50
Chalons 2–3
Cherbourg 2
Chilbolton, RAF 23
Chill, *Generalleutnant* Kurt 38
Christiansen, *General de Flieger* Friedrich 38, 40
Churchill, Rt Hon Winston L S, PM 10
Clark, Gen Mark 10
Cleminson, Capt 94

Coad, Lt-Col B A 75
Cochrane, Major 108
Coningham, AM Sir Arthur 2, 35
Consolidated Aircraft:
    B-24 Liberator 77, 82–3
Conyers, Roy C 128
Cook, Maj Julian A 117
Cotentin Peninsula 2, 18
Cottesmore, RAF 23
Crerar, Lt-Gen H D G 2
Crete 9, 38
Crookham Common, RAF 45
Cunney, Staff Sgt John G 128
Cutler, Brig-Gen Stuart L 17

Darvall, Air Cdre L 22, 145–6
Dawson, Maj C W B 122
De Groote Barrier 6–7, 39
De Havilland Aircraft:
    Mosquito 25, 30, 46, 48, 128
De Koude Herberg 73
De Ploeg 55–6
Deaconess Hospital 62
Deane-Drummond, Maj A J 22
Deelen 29–30, 85
Dempsey, Lt-Gen Miles C 2, 7, 20, 33, 35,
    75, 93, 154
Den Brink 66–8, 95, 105
Depienne 11
Deventer 43, 69
Devlin, Capt 131
Diependraal 108
Diepensen 43
Dieppe 10
Dieren 43, 70
Dinter 99, 115
Dobie, Lt-Col David 22, 70–71, 103–4
Doesburg 42
Doetinchem 43, 67
Dommel River 33, 53
Doorwerth 65
Dordrecht 40, 73
Douai 4, 19
Douglas Aircraft:
    Boston 48, 157
    C-47 Dakota 10–15, 23, 30, 32, 34, 45,
        50–6, 61, 78, 80–1, 87–90, 92, 100,
        102, 109–112, 118, 124–5, 133, 135,
        146–50, 156
Dover, Maj V 66
Down Ampney, RAF 23
Down, Brig Eric 10, 29
Dreyeroord Hotel 131
Driel 87, 133–34, 136, 143, 149, 152–5, 159
Dunkirk 110
Dutch Forces:
    Princess Irene Brigade 75, 126
Dutch Red Cross, 158
Dutch Resistance 43–4, 56, 88, 101–2, 136
    Albrecht Cell 43
    Kees Cell 43
Dutch SS 37, 42–3, 73, 88, 90, 134, 141

Eastcote Troop Carrier Command Post
    27, 35
Eccles, Lt D L 156

Ede 26, 48, 70–71, 93–4, 104
Edmond, Bill 63, 65
Eerde 43, 51, 137–140, 150
Eindhoven 7, 24, 26–7, 30, 32–3, 39, 48,
    51–3, 74–5, 77, 79, 82, 96–7, 99, 112,
    115, 123, 133–5, 137, 145–6, 149, 151
Einenkel, *Oberstürmführer* 90
Eisenhower, Gen Dwight D 2–4, 6–8, 12,
    15–17, 19, 21
Elam, Maj Dan 53
Elden 134
Elst 60, 129, 133–4, 143, 149, 152, 155, 157
Emmerich 34, 68, 76
Enigma Code 26
Epse 43
Escaut Canal 6–7
Essame, Brig Hubert 75, 143, 149
Euling, *Hauptsturmführer* Karl-Heinz 69,
    84, 102, 117–8
Evans, Tpr Des 63, 65, 95, 106–7
Evere 25
Eyler 79

Fairford, RAF 23, 51, 124
Falaise 1, 42
Farello Airstrip 13
Feldt, *General* 115
Fernau, *Oberstürmführer* 73–4, 90
Fitch, Lt-Col John A C 22, 72–3, 83, 95,
    103–4
Flushing (Vissingen) 5, 46
Focke-Wulf Aircraft:
    FW 190 48, 77, 98, 106, 110, 113, 134–5,
    146
Foggia 14
Folkingham, RAF 23, 80
Foulkes, Lt Ralph 64
Frank, Capt A 113
Frankfurt 3
Fraser, Jock 154
French Forces:
    1st Army 2
    2nd Armoured Division 1
French Forces of the Interior (FFI) 18
Frost, Lt-Col J D 9, 11, 22, 62, 65–6, 68,
    70–2, 83–5, 87, 96, 112–4, 119–20, 127,
    160
Fulbeck, RAF 45
Furstenberg, *Hauptmann Frieherr* von 79

Galbraith, Lt 154–5
Gale, Maj-Gen Richard N 9, 11
Gavin, Gen James M 13, 17, 22, 30, 32–3,
    55–6, 79–80, 101–2, 117
Gela 13
General Aircraft Co Aircraft:
    Hamilcar 23, 45, 56, 58, 63, 93
Gennep 54, 81
German Army Units:
    Army Groups
        Army Group B 1, 37–8, 40–1, 67,
        74, 102
        Army Group Centre 37
    Armies
        1st *Fallschirmjäger* (Paratroop)
            Army 1, 37–41, 77, 137

Fifth Panzer Army 1, 6, 39
        Seventh Panzer Army 1, 6, 18, 38
        Fifteenth Army 6, 40–41
    Corps (Korps)
        II SS Panzer Korps 40, 42, 67–9,
            85–6, 102, 134, 137
        LXXXVI Korps 137
        LXXXVIII Korps 38, 137, 152
    Divisions
        3 *Fallschirmjäger* Division 115
        5 *Fallschirmjäger* Division 115
        7 *Fallschirmjäger* Division 38, 137
        Fallschirmjäger Division Erdmann
            40
        59 Infantry Division 78, 99–100,
            137, 150–1
        84 Infantry Division 38
        85 Infantry Division 38, 40
        89 Infantry Division 38
        176 Infantry Division 38, 137
        277 Infantry Division 84
        406 Infantry Division 54, 79
        719 Infantry Division 37
        1st *Jagddivision* 110
        Kranken Division 38
        SS Herman Göring Division 26
        9 SS Panzer Division
            'Hohenstaufen' 42–3, 65, 67,
            69–71, 74, 134, 141, 152
        10 SS Panzer Division
            'Frundsberg' 42–3, 66, 68–9,
            115–7, 126, 134, 152
    Brigades
        280 Assault Gun Brigade 105, 130
        214 Brigade 149
        18 Flak Brigade 77–8
        Flak Brigade Swoboda 110, 134
        107 Panzer Brigade 99, 101, 115,
            137–9, 147
    Regiments
        180 Regiment 137
        184 Artillery Regiment 42, 74
        191 Artillery Regiment 134
        2 *Fallschirmjäger* Regiment 38
        5 *Fallschirmjäger* Regiment 115
        6 *Fallschirmjäger* Regiment 38–40,
            115, 145, 150–51
        8 *Fallschirmjäger* Regiment 115
        9 *Fallschirmjäger* Regiment 115
        21 *Fallschirmjäger* Regiment 137
        16 Grenadier Regiment 137
        59 Infantry Regiment 39
        245 Infantry Regiment 39
        6 Panzer Replacement Regiment
            Bielefeld 84
        9 SS Panzergrenadier Regiment 71
        10 SS Panzergrenadier Regiment
            129
        19 SS Panzergrenadier Regiment
            94
        20 SS Panzergrenadier Regiment
            94
        21 SS Panzergrenadier Regiment
            69, 84
        22 SS Panzergrenadier Regiment
            129

34 SS Panzergrenadier Regiment
101
SS Panzergrenadier Regiment
Frundsberg 42
3 Police Regiment 122
Von Hoffman Regiment 39–40, 74,
96
Battalions
47 Coastal Machine-Gun Battalion
134
Eberwein Battalion 122, 141
Euling Battalion 69
1 Battalion 2 *Fallschirmjäger*
Regiment 38
Fallschirmjäger Battalion Ewald 79
Fliegerhorst Battalion Soesterberg
86
Hermann Göring Battalion 141
Jungwirth Battalion 140
Knaust Battalion 143
Landsturm Niederland Battalion
10
Panzergrenadier Training &
Replacement Battalion Bocholt
84
1/E6 Replacement Battalion 81
10 SS Engineer Battalion 102
21 SS Panzergrenadier Battalion 42
9 SS Pioneer Battalion 71
9 SS Reconnaissance Battalion 68,
84–5, 94, 103, 109
10 SS Reconnaissance Battalion 69,
84
10 SS Tank-Destroyer Battalion 137
16 SS Training & Replacement
(Reserve) Battalion 41–2, 63–5,
70–3, 85, 93–4, 122
3 SS *Wachbattalion* (Surveillance
Battalion) 42, 73, 86–7, 141
Schulz Battalion 141
559 Tank-Destroyer Battalion 137
Wehrmacht Battalion 134
Battle Groups (Kampfgruppen)
KG Allworden 70, 130, 141
KG Becker 115–7
KG Brinkman 69, 84, 95, 112, 143
KG Bruhns 94
KG Chill 38, 75, 77
KG Euling 118
KG Frundsberg 43, 102
KG Furstenberg 79
KG Goebel 79, 115
KG Greschick 79, 115–7
KG Gropp 104
KG Grunewald 77
KG Harder 71, 130, 141
KG Harzer 43, 67, 94
KG Heinke 42
KG Henke 102
KG Hermann 115–7
KG Huber 137–40, 145
KG Knaust 95, 112, 129, 134
KG Koppel 77
KG Krafft 122
KG Lippert 93
KG Reinhold 192, 129

KG Rink 78–9
KG Spindler 70, 85, 94, 103, 105,
130, 141
KG Stargaard 79
KG Von Tettau 85
KG Walther 39, 42, 137, 140, 145
9 SS KG 130, 141
10 SS KG 117, 129, 137
SS KG Rostel 75, 96
Companies
3 Company 21 Panzergrenadier
Regiment 69
224 Panzerkompagnie 86, 152
3 Company Police Regiment 10
1 Company 10 SS Reconnaissance
Battalion 68–9
9 Company 16 SS Battalion 72
Detachments
21 Artillery Battery 129
424 *Flakabteilung* 77
9 *Panzerjäger Abteilung* 70
10 *Panzerjäger Abteilung* 40
506 *Schwere Abteilung* 152
German High Command 37
German Navy Units:
1 Marine Cadre Regiment 122
642 Marine Regiment 122, 134
6 Naval Battalion 74
14 Naval Battalion 74
10 *Schiffsturmabteilung* 74
Gestapo 26
Gheel 6, 34, 39, 50, 98, 147
Ghent 27, 133
Gilze-Rijn 48
Ginkel Heath 73, 85, 87–8, 93
Goch 151
Göring, *Reichsmarschall* Hermann 37
Gough, Maj C F H 22, 62, 65, 68, 70,
119–20
Government Code and Cypher School
26
Grabner, *Hauptsturmführer* Viktor 68–9,
84–6, 103, 109, 120
Graftombe 93, 114, 129
Grafton, Maj J D 156
Graham, Maj-Gen D A H 75
Grantham 53, 80, 98, 124
Grave 7, 20, 24, 27, 32–3, 50, 54–5, 81, 99,
114, 117, 126, 137, 146–7, 149–50
Grayburn, Lt John H, VC 68, 113, 119
Greenham Common, RAF 10, 23, 45, 51,
78, 100
Greschick, *Major* 115
Grey, Jock 119
Groesbeek 24, 32–3, 54, 56, 79–81, 115–7,
147–8
Gropp, *Oberfsturmführer* 71, 104
Guerran, Syd 83
Guingand, Maj-Gen Sir Francis de 19, 75
Gurecki, 1st Lt John 53
Gustrow 38
Gwatkin, Brig Norman 75

Haalderen 118
Hackett, Brig (later General Sir) John W
12, 22, 26, 85, 87, 90, 92–4, 105, 107–8,

111, 114, 121–2, 129–31, 141–2, 152–3,
163
Haddon, Lt-Col Thomas 22
Hague, The 21
Hall, Spr Ron, MM 69, 121
Handley Page Aircraft:
Halifax 12, 15, 23, 30, 45, 58, 93
Harder, SS *Obersturmführer* 141
Hardwick, RAF 83
Harmel, *Obersturmbannführer* Heinz 42,
102, 129
Harper, Col Joseph P 22, 78
Harrison, Capt 83–4
Harrison, 1st Lt Jesse M 100
Hartenstein 93, 110, 122, 129–130, 134
Hartenstein Hotel 93, 105, 121, 153, 159,
163
Harwell, RAF 23, 92, 124
Harzer, *Obersturmbannführer* Walther 43,
67, 134
Hasselt 29, 37–8, 48, 77
Hatfield, RAF 27, 51, 78, 100
Hattert 55
Hausser, *General de Waffen-SS* Paul 42
Hawker Aircraft:
Hector 9
Tempest 48, 77, 82, 88
Typhoon 35, 48–9, 66, 74–5, 96–7, 117,
129, 145, 157
Hay, Capt John 64
Hechtel 6, 39–40, 156
Heelsum 30, 65, 72, 86, 105
Heelsum Heath 106
Heeswijk 115
Heikant 54
Heele, *Hauptsturmführer* Paul 73, 86–8,
90, 141
Hellegat, The 48
Helmond 99
Hengelo 156
Herentals 38
Hermann, *Oberstleutnant* 115–7
's Hertogenbosch 27, 41, 77–8, 80, 91, 98,
145
Heumen 55, 117
Heumen Bridge 117
Heveadorp 31, 65, 72, 87, 94, 114, 129,
133–4, 136, 143, 156
Hewer, Sgt Ray 106, 131–33
Heydte, *Oberstleutnant* Friedrich-August
von der 38–40, 145, 150–51
Hicks, Brig Philip H 22, 87, 92, 105, 112,
129, 141, 152
Hill Oek 94
Hill, Lt-Col S J L 11
Hink, SS *Obersturmführer* 73–4
Hitler, Adolf 1–2, 35, 37, 67, 143
Hodges, Gen Courtney H 2–3
Hoenderloo 68
Hoffman, *Oberst* von 39–40
Hollinghurst, AV-M Leslie N 17, 22, 29
Honinghutie Bridge 117
Hope, L/Cpl Ken 62–3, 105–6, 130–3,
154–5
Hopkinson, Maj-Gen G F 11
Hopsten 46

Horrocks, Gen Sir Brian 5, 21, 37, 74–5, 117, 126–7, 146, 152–4, 161–2
Horst, Kate ter 143
Houghton, Sgt 108
Huber, *Major* 139–40
Huissen 102
Hummel, *Leutnant* 152
Humphreys, Cpl (later Col) John 119–20
Hunner Park 102, 117–8
Hunt, Lt-Col 141

James, Capt 122
Jodl, *Generaloberst* Alfred 37
Johannahoeve 71, 92, 108, 114
Johannahoeve Farm 93
Jungwirth, *Major* Hans 150

Kairouan 12
Kamp 54
Keerans, Brig-Gen Charles L Jr 13
Keevil, RAF 23, 45, 124
Kegler, *Oberst* Gerhard 39
Kerutt, *Major* 96
Kessel, Capt Lipmann 142, 153
King, Flt Lt Harry 111
Kinnaird, Lt-Col Harry W 22
Kitzinger Line 1
Kleve 79, 115, 146, 151
Kluge, *Feldmarschall* Gunther von 1
Knapheide 81
Knaust, *Major* Hans-Peter 84
Koepel 94, 110
Koevering 150, 152
Krafft, SS *Hauptsturmführer* Sepp 41–2, 63–5, 71–3, 85, 93–4, 122
Kranenburg 79
Kuhn, *Obersturmführer* Kurt 73, 130
Kuijk, *Herr* van 68
Kussin, *Generalmajor* 67, 72
Kwaadmechelen 38

Lacey, Gnr John 128
Landau, *Oberst* Christian 38
Langar, RAF 23, 45, 54
Langenberg Hotel 73
Langham, Sgt Walter 88, 152–3
Laon 2, 4
Lasham, RAF 46
Lathbury, Brig Gerald M 14, 22, 60, 65, 68, 72, 93–4
Le Havre 9
Le Mans 18
Lea, Lt-Col George H 22, 95, 105
Leerdam 41
Leeuwarden 46
Leigh-Mallory, AM Sir Trafford 16–7, 34–5
Lens 4
Lent 118, 126
Liege 19
Lille 4, 19
Lindquist, Lt-Col 22
Lippe River 41
Lippert, SS *Obersturmbannführer* Hans-Michael 41–2, 74, 86–7, 93, 121–2, 141
Lipscombe, Lt-Col C G 75

Lockheed Aircraft:
    P-38 Lightning 29, 48, 82, 146
Loder-Symonds, Lt-Col Robert G, DSO 22, 141
Loenen 43
Logan, Capt J, DSO 120
Loire River 2–3
Longland, Major 142
Lonsdale Force 112, 130, 141, 143
Lonsdale, Maj Richard 112
Lord, Flt Lt D S A, VC, DFC 111
Lorraine 6
Louvain 6
Lovingood, Flg Off Roy C 78
Luce, Lt-Col E L 75
Luftwaffe 30, 37–8, 40–2, 46, 48, 79, 86, 88, 96, 99, 106, 110, 115, 134
Luftwaffe Units:
    Kampfgruppe (KG) 51 46
    Jägdgeschwader (JG) 2 134–5
    JG 26 134–5
    Penal Battalion 6 40
    Luftflotte 3 46
Luxembourg 6

Maas Bridge 20, 32, 145
Maas Canal 7
Maas River 20, 26, 32, 40–1, 46, 126
Maas-Scheldt (Meuse-Escaut) Canal 6, 20, 39, 41, 74, 125, 127
Maas-Waal Canal 7, 32, 54–5, 114–5
Maastricht 7, 37–8, 42, 123, 146
MacKay, Capt Eric 83, 85, 112, 119–20
MacKenzie, Lt-Col Charles B 22, 92, 136
Madden, Maj D J 22, 130
Maguire, Maj Hugh 22
Maison Blanche 11
Maison Lafitte 17
Malley, Joe 120
Malta 9
Maltzahn, *Major Freiherr* von 99, 101, 115, 137–9
Manston, RAF 23, 149
Marne River 3
Marrable, Lt-Col A T 60–2
Marshall, Gen George 16
Martin, Capt 142
Martin, Syd 50
Martlesham Heath, RAF 92
Massenhoeven 38
McAuliffe, Brig-Gen Anthony C 78
McCardie, Lt-Col W D H 22, 105
McDermont, Lt 68, 113
McMahon, Tommy 109
Mecklenberg 38
Medjaz 11
Meikle, Capt Jan 136
Melsbroek 145
Melun 4
Membury, RAF 23
Messerschmitt Aircraft:
    Me 109 48, 77, 88, 98, 110, 146
    Me 110 48
    Me 262 46, 87–8, 96
Meubeuge 4
Meuse River 1, 19

Michaelis, Lt-Col John H 22
Middelbeers 127
Mitchell, Col William 16
Mk II Tiger Tank 152
Mk III Tank 84, 113, 120
Mk IV Tank 42–3, 53, 84, 102, 113, 129
Mk V Panther Tank 99
Mk VI Tiger Tank 119
Model, *Feldmarschall* Walther 1, 38, 40–3, 67, 102, 136–7, 157, 160
Moerdijk 46
Mole, Brig G H L 75
Molenhoek 54
Moll 100
Moller, SS *Hauptsturmführer* Hans 71, 104, 141
Mons 4, 42
Montdidier 4
Montgomery, Field Marshal Bernard L 2–4, 6–8, 19–21, 24–5, 33, 35, 41, 75, 154, 160
Mook 54, 79–80, 115–7
Moselle River 1, 3, 7
Mumford, Maj Dennis 83–5
Municipal Hospital 62
Municipal Museum 105
Münster 41
Murray, Lt-Col 63
Myers, Lt-Col E C W 22, 136, 156

Nancy 2
Nantes 2, 4
Neerbosch Bridge 115
Neerpelt 39–40, 42, 74, 126, 137
Netheravon, RAF 9
Newton-Dunn, Maj C F 22
Nijmegen 7, 20, 24, 27, 30–2, 40–2, 46, 48, 53, 55–6, 68–9, 74–6, 79–80, 82, 84–5, 88, 99, 102, 114–8, 123–4, 126–9, 134–7, 140, 143, 145, 147, 149, 156–7, 159–62
North American Aircraft:
    B-25 Mitchell 48, 157
    P-51 Mustang 25–6, 46–8, 77, 82, 88, 98, 123–4, 133–4, 146, 156–7
North Brabant 39
North Foreland 27
North Witham, RAF 23, 45
Noyers Bocage 84

Obstfelder, *General* Hans von 137
Oedenrode 74, 154
Oirchot 51
Ommershof 114, 129–30
Onderlangs 95, 103
Oosterbeek 40, 42, 65–7, 70–3, 85, 87, 93, 95, 109, 111, 114, 120–2, 129–30, 134, 136–7, 141–3, 148, 150, 152, 154, 156–7, 159–60, 163
Oosterbeek-Laag 69, 84–5, 111–2, 141, 143, 155, 157
Oosterhout 118, 129, 143
Operations other than Market Garden:
    Anvil 17
    Beneficiary 18
    Berlin 156
    Biting 9

Boxer 19
Colossus 9
Comet 20–1, 24–5, 30–1, 33–4
Fustian 13–14
Hands Up 18
Husky 12
Ladbroke 12
Linnet I and II 19, 24, 27, 34, 45
Mallard 16
Neptune 16
Overlord 16–17
Swordhilt 18
Torch 10
Transfigure 18, 24
Wallace 19
Wild Oats 17
Oran 10
Orfordness 82
Orleans 2, 18
Osborne-Smith, Lt-Col R E 75
Oss 88
Ostend 27
Oudna 11
Overasselt 55, 147

Packe, Lt-Col Michael St John 22
Pals 140
Pannerden 85, 102–3, 126, 129
Pannerden Canal 129
Parks, Brig-Gen Floyd L 17
Patch, Gen Alexander M 2–3
Patton, Gen George S 2–3, 6–7, 13, 18, 21, 41
Payton-Reid, Lt-Col Robert 22, 60, 73, 87–8, 108, 131–2
Perrin-Brown, Maj 103
Pine-Coffin, Lt-Col R J 11
Platlunne Airfield 128
Polish Armed Forces:
    1st Polish Parachute Brigade 18–20, 22, 24, 26, 31, 45, 62, 92, 98, 108–9, 123–4, 132–6, 143, 146, 148–9, 152–3, 155, 160
    1st Battalion Polish Parachute Brigade 22
    2nd Battalion Polish Parachute Brigade 22
    3rd Battalion Polish Parachute Brigade 22
    Parachute Field Ambulance 62
Pont de Faha 11
Ponte di Primosole 12–13, 69
Ponte Grande 12
Pontveen 115
Poppe, Generalleutnant Walther 39, 78
Powell, Maj G 122
Predannack, RAF 10
Provence 2

Queripel, Capt Lionel E, VC 107

Rambouillet 18
Ramsay, Adml 6
Ramsbury, RAF 23, 156
Randall, Lt 157
Randwijk 163

Rastenburg 37
Ratie 50
Red Cross 158
Reichswald Forest 32, 35, 54–6, 80–1, 115
Reijerscamp 73–4, 85, 87
Reims 3, 45
Reinhardt, General der Infanterie Hans 38, 137, 151–2
Renkum Heath 65, 73–4, 85–6, 105
Republic Aircraft:
    P-47 Thunderbolt 48, 50, 53, 77–8, 82, 98, 124, 134–5, 141, 146
Ressen 129
Rethy 51, 100
Rheims 2
Rheine 46
Rhine Pavilion 103–4
Richter, Hauptsturmführer Friedrich 137
Ridgeway, Maj-Gen Matthew B 12–13, 17, 22, 24
Riethorst 54, 80, 117
Roberts, Capt G C 22
Roberts, Lt-Col W G 75
Roermond 41
Rogusti, Marian 158–59
Roosevelt, President F D 10
Roskill, Capt S W, RN 5–6
Rossum 41
Rostel, SS Hauptsturmführer 137
Rotterdam 44
Royal Air Force Units:
    2nd Tactical Air Force (2 TAF) 2, 25, 34–5, 48–9, 74, 88, 146, 150–1, 157, 161
    Army Co-op Command 10
    Bomber Command 34–5, 76
    Coastal Command 35
    Transport Command 15, 110–11
Groups
    No 1 46
    No 2 30, 34, 49
    No 3 46
    No 8 46
    No 38 15–17, 20, 22–3, 25–6, 28–30, 32, 34, 45–6, 51, 56, 62, 74–7, 80, 91–3, 98, 110, 112, 124, 134, 145–7, 149
    No 46 15–17, 20, 22–3, 25–6, 28, 30, 34, 45, 56, 98, 110, 135, 145–7
    No 83 25, 35, 129, 145–6
    No 84 25
Wings
    No 35 (Recce) 25
    No 38 9–10, 12, 14–5
    No 39 (Recce) 25
    No 121 145
    No 124 145
Squadrons
    No 2 25–6
    No 4 25
    No 21 46
    No 48 23
    No 51 9
    No 80 48
    No 107 46
    No 137 145

No 168 25
No 174 145
No 175 145
No 181 145
No 182 145
No 184 145
No 190 23, 124, 135
No 196 23, 124
No 214 (Radio Countermeasures) 46
No 233 23
No 245 145
No 247 145
No 268 25
No 272 23
No 295 23, 91, 124
No 296 (Glider Exercise) 9, 12, 14, 23
No 297 (Parachute Exercise) 9, 12, 23
No 298 23
No 299 23, 124
No 355 62
No 364 62
No 504 48
No 512 23
No 570 23, 124
No. 575 23, 92, 146, 150, 156
No 613 46
No 620 23, 124
No 644 23
No 1665 HCU 124
Royal Canadian Air Force Units:
Wings
    No 143 145
Squadrons
    No 400 25–6
    No 414 25
    No 430 25
    No 437 23
    No 438 145
    No 439 145
    No 440 145
Ruhr River 2–3, 21, 41

Saar River 2–3, 6, 41
St Arnault-en-Yvelines 18
St Elisabeth's Hospital 62, 73, 94, 103–5, 142, 153, 158
St Eval 10
St Lidwinia Maternity Hospital 101
St Lo 18
St Malo 18
St Oedenrode 33, 53, 78–9, 99, 137–40, 150
St Omer 25
Sakkel, Drum Major 73
Salmon, Jim 95
Saltby, RAF 23, 60, 133
Sanders, Spr A C 117–8
SAS (see 'Special Air Service')
Scarpe River 4
Scheldt Estuary 5, 133
Scheltd River 5–6, 25, 27, 39
Schernbening, Generalleutnant 79
Schijndel 77, 80, 101, 137–40

Schliefenbaum, *Major* Ernst 67
Schoonrewoerd 41
Schouwen Island 27, 56, 77–8, 80
Schueler, Horst 70
Schulman, 2nd Lt Herbert E 53
Schwappacher, *Hauptsturmführer* 129
SCR-193 TacAir radio equipment 36, 161
SCR-522 VHF equipment 36, 161
SCR-717 equipment 34
Seine River 1–4, 6, 18–19, 25
SHAEF (see under 'Supreme')
Short Aircraft:
    Stirling 20, 23, 40, 45, 51, 58–9, 76, 91–2, 112, 123–4, 134–5, 146, 148–9
Sicily 12–15, 24, 29, 69, 110
Siegfried Line 2, 7, 21, 38, 41
Sievers, *Generalleutnant* Karl 37–8
Simeto River 12-13
Simpson, Lt D R, MC 83, 120
Sink, Col Robert F 22
Sittard 42
Smith, W/O E A, DFC 92
Smyth, Lt-Col Kenneth B L 22, 107, 122, 130
SOE (see 'Special Operations Executive')
Soesterberg 86
Somme River 1, 4
Sonnenberglaan 122
Sosabowski, Maj-Gen Stanislaw 22, 26, 132–4, 136, 154
Souk el Arba 11
Sousse 12
Southerby, Stan 154
Spaatz, Gen Carl 16
Spanhoe, RAF 23, 133
Special Air Services (SAS) 17, 19
Special Operations Executive (SOE) 17, 26
Spindler, SS *Sturmbannführer* Ludwig 70–1, 93, 108, 141
SS NCO School 41, 74, 86
SS Panzergrenadier Depot 41
Stanmore 34–5
Stearly, Brig-Gen Ralph S 17
Steenwijk-Havelte 46
Stephenson, Lt-Col T C V 22
Steveninck, Col A de Ruyter van 75
Stevenson, Lt John 141
Stoddart, 1st Lt Robert S 53
Student, *Generaloberst* Kurt 37–41, 74, 137
Sunley, Sgt 108
Sunninghill Park 17, 24, 26, 33
Supermarine Aircraft:
    Spitfire 25, 48, 77, 82, 88, 98, 123–4, 134–5, 150, 156
Supreme Headquarters Allied Expeditionary Force (SHAEF) 1–2, 8, 16–9, 44
Swiecicki, Marck 109–110
Swinscow, Capt Douglas 65
Swoboda, *Oberstleutnant* von 110
Syracuse 12
Szczerbo, Col Rawicz 22

Tafaraoni 10
Tafelberg Hotel 67
Talbot, Lt-Col D E B 75

Taranto 14
Tarrant Rushton, RAF 23, 45
Tassigny, Gen de Lattre de 2
Tate, Drum Major 108
Taylor, Capt 94
Taylor, Lt-Col George 75, 143
Taylor, Gen Maxwell 22, 24, 33, 98, 101, 137–9
Tebessa 11
Telecommunications Research Establishment 34
Terraine, John 35
Tettau, *Generalleutnant* Hans von 42, 73–4
Thomas, Maj-Gen Ivor 75, 126, 153, 156
Thompson, Sgt Basil 100–101
Thompson, Sgt Jerry 148
Thompson, Lt-Col W F K 22, 60, 84, 111–2, 131
Thompson Force 130
Thorney Island, RAF 46
Tiel 73
Tilburg 27, 40
Tilley, Lt-Col G 75, 155–6
Tilstock, RAF 124
Timothy, Maj 103
Tournai 4, 19
Townsend, Lt-Col E, MC 62, 142
Tragino Aqueduct 9
Trapp, Rudolf 69
Troyes 1–3
Tucker, Lt-Col Reuben 22, 32
Tunis 11
Tunnel, 1st Lt Robert A 128
Turnhout 26, 38

U-boat 18
Uden 80, 139–40, 145, 147
Ultra 26
United States Army Units:
    Armies
      First Army 2–3, 4, 7, 18, 21
      Third Army 1–3, 6–7, 18–19, 41
      Fifth Army 12
      Seventh Army 2–3, 12–13
    Corps
      VII Corps 4
      VIII Corps 4, 7
      XVIII Corps 12
      XVIII Airborne Corps 17, 22
      XIX Corps 4
    Divisions
      82nd Airborne Division 12–14, 16–17, 22, 24, 30, 32, 33, 45, 50, 53–4, 56, 76, 79–83, 85, 98, 102, 114–5, 123–5, 127, 134–5, 140, 146–8, 150, 160
      101st Airborne Division 12, 16–18, 22, 24, 33, 45, 51–2, 56, 74, 76–8, 82–3, 98–100, 115, 123–25, 134–35, 137, 140, 145–47, 156, 160
      3rd Armoured Division 4
    Regiments
      325th Glider Infantry Regiment 12, 22, 33, 55, 102, 135, 146–7, 160

327th Glider Infantry Regiment 22, 34, 78, 100, 137–40
501st Parachute Infantry Regiment 22, 33, 51–3, 77, 83, 99, 115, 137–40, 147, 150
502nd Parachute Infantry Regiment 22, 33, 52–3, 78–9, 99, 101, 137, 150
503rd Parachute Infantry Regiment 10–11
504th Parachute Infantry Regiment 12–13, 22, 32, 54–5, 79, 117–8
505th Parachute Infantry Regiment 12–13, 22, 32, 54, 80, 114, 117
506th Parachute Infantry Regiment 22, 33, 51–3, 77, 79, 99, 115, 139–40, 150
508th Parachute Infantry Regiment 22, 32, 55–6, 79–80, 117, 139–40
Battalions
    80th Airborne Anti-tank Battalion 22, 56, 80, 146
    81st Airborne Anti-tank Battalion 22, 34, 100–101
    326th Airborne Engineer Battalion 22, 34, 78
    80th Anti-aircraft Battalion 33
    878th Aviation Engineer Battalion 20, 32, 109
    307th Engineer Battalion 56, 80
    319th Glider Field Artillery Battalion 22, 80–1
    320th Glider Field Artillery Battalion 22, 80–1
    321st Glider Field Artillery Battalion 22
    327th Glider Field Artillery Battalion 22, 100, 140
    376th Glider Field Artillery Battalion 22
    377th Glider Field Artillery Battalion 22, 101, 125
    456th Glider Field Artillery Battalion 22, 80
    907th Glider Field Artillery Battalion 22, 100–101, 150
    376th Parachute Field Artillery Battalion 32, 56
    3rd Battalion 327th Glider Infantry Regiment 100, 139
    1st Battalion 501st Parachute Infantry Regiment 51, 115 137–9, 150
    2nd Battalion 501st PIR 99
    3rd Battalion 502nd PIR 51, 137–40
    1st Battalion 502nd PIR 53, 78, 99
    2nd Battalion 502nd PIR 99
    3rd Battalion 502nd PIR 53, 78
    2nd Battalion 503rd PIR 10–11
    1st Battalion 504th PIR 55, 118
    2nd Battalion 504th PIR 55
    3rd Battalion 504th PIR 54, 117–8
    1st Battalion 505th PIR 54, 80
    2nd Battalion 505th PIR 54, 114, 117
    3rd Battalion 505th PIR 54, 80

1st Battalion 506th PIR 51–3
2nd Battalion 506th PIR 52–3, 77, 139
1st Battalion 508th PIR 56, 139
3rd Battalion 508th PIR 56
2nd Quartermaster Battalion 82
Companies
326th Airborne Medical Company 34, 78
United States Army Air Force Units:
Air Forces
Eighth Air Force 34–5, 46–8, 77, 82, 98, 123–4, 134–5, 141, 146
Ninth Air Force 2, 16–17, 35, 48, 77, 99, 123
Tenth Air Force 16
Commands
IX Tactical Air Command 161
IX Troop Carrier Command 12, 17, 22–3, 26, 34, 45–6, 87, 98, 145
Groups
25th Bomb Group (R) 46, 128
4th Fighter Group (FG) 48
56th FG 82, 134–5
78th FG 48, 50, 82, 146
339th FG 146
353rd FG 82, 135, 146
356th FG 82
357th FG 77, 98
359th FG 77
361st FG 48
364th FG 98
474th FG 48
Pathfinder Group (Provisional) 45
10th Tactical Reconnaissance Group 45
60th Troop Carrier Group (TCG) 10–11
61st TCG 20, 23, 60, 81, 102
93rd TCG 83
313th TCG 23, 54, 80
314th TCG 23, 60, 87, 133
315th TCG 23, 55, 87, 133, 148
316th TCG 23, 55, 81
434th TCG 23, 51, 124, 156
435th TCG 23, 51–2, 100, 124, 156
436th TCG 23–4, 51, 124, 147, 156
437th TCG 23, 52, 124, 135
438th TCG 23, 52, 124, 135, 147
439th TCG 23, 45, 56, 102, 125
440th TCG 23, 54, 56
441st TCG 23, 45, 54–5
442nd TCG 20, 23–4, 51, 83, 100, 125
446th Group 83
448th Group 83

489th Group 83
Wings
14th Bombardment Wing 82–3
20th Bombardment Wing 82–3
325th Photographic Wing 46
50th Troop Carrier Wing (TCW) 45, 53, 80, 102, 146
51st TCW 10, 12, 14
52nd TCW 20, 45, 53, 56, 80, 102, 109, 133, 146
53rd TCW 45, 51–2, 54, 78, 80, 100, 124
Squadrons
26th Mobile Repair and Reclamation Squadron 45
29th Troop Carrier Squadron (TCS) 80, 147
47th TCS 80
48th TCS 80
49th TCS 80
654th Heavy Reconnaissance Squadron 128
803rd (Countermeasures) Squadron 46
IX Troop Carrier Command Pathfinder School 23, 45
Urquhart, Maj-Gen Robert E 'Roy' 22, 29–30, 65, 72, 87, 93–5, 105, 107–8, 119, 121, 129, 136, 141, 144, 149, 155–6
Utrecht 34, 73, 76, 87, 94, 108

V-1 missiles 3
V-2 missiles 20–1, 25
Valburg 143
Valenciennes 42
Valkenburglaan 122
Valkenswaard 39–40, 42, 74–5, 96, 149
Van Limburg Stirum School 112
Vandeleur, Lt-Col Giles 75
Vandeleur, Lt-Col J O E 74–5
Vandenberg, Maj-Gen Hoyt S 2
Vandervoort, Lt-Col 22
Veenendaal 73
Veghel 33, 50–1, 53, 74, 81, 99, 102, 115, 137–40, 145, 147, 150–1, 154
Venes, Sgt Henry 63, 154
Venlo 42
Very Light 15
Versailles 17
Vissingen (see 'Flushing')
Vlasto, Lt 69
Voeux, Lt-Col Sir Richard des 22, 93, 107, 122
Volkel 145–6
Vorden 43
Vught 41, 74

Waal Bridge 20, 32, 102, 117, 145
Waal Canal 7
Waal River 20, 32, 40–2, 55–6, 74, 85, 115, 118, 126, 128–9, 140
Waclaw, Maj Ploszewski 22
Waclaw, Capt Sobocinski 22
Waco Aircraft:
CG-4A Hadrian 12, 14, 23, 33–4, 45, 50, 52–3, 56, 74, 78, 80–1, 98, 100–101, 135, 146–7
Wadsworth, Lt 106, 131–3
Wageningen 42, 60, 74, 88, 141
Walch, Brig Gordon 22
Walcheren Island 5, 8, 46
Walker, Lt Pat 128
Walther, *Oberst* 39–40
Walton, Brig B B 75
Warrack, Col Graeme 22
Warsaw 1
Watton, RAF 46, 128
Welford, RAF 23
Wesel 20, 48, 68, 77, 98, 123
West Brabant 41
Westerbouwing 87, 134, 154–6
Westland Aircraft:
Walrus 112
White House 131
Wijbosch 137, 140
Wilhelmina Canal 33, 51, 53, 101, 137
Willems Canal 33, 51, 139
Williams, Maj-Gen Paul L 22–3, 26–7, 29
Wilson, Maj B A 22, 51, 58
Woensdrecht 5–6
Wolfheze 62–5, 70, 72–3, 83, 85, 87, 92–3, 95, 106–110, 122
Wolfheze Hotel 64, 114, 121
Wright, Capt D, MC 120
Wyler 32, 55, 79, 81–2, 115–17

'Y' Service 26
Youks les Bains 11
Yssel River 43

Zangen, Gen von 38
Zeeland 5, 41
Ziebrecht, SS *Obersturmführer* Karl 68
Zilverenberg 94
Zon 33, 51–3, 74, 78, 99–101, 115
Zonsche Forest 33
Zuid Wilhelms Vaart Canal 137
Zuider Zee 48, 77, 163
Zutphen 43, 70
Zwolle 43, 123, 146
Zyfflich 79, 81